*Dress Codes*

# Dress Codes

## Meanings and Messages in American Culture

SECOND EDITION

## Ruth P. Rubinstein

*Fashion Institute of Technology*

Westview
PRESS

A Member of the Perseus Books Group

*To my son Jonathn,*
*with many thanks and my very best wishes*

Copyright © 2001 by Westview Press, A Member of the Perseus Books Group

Published in 2001 in the United States of America by Westview Press, 5500 Central Avenue, Boulder,
Colorado 80301-2877, and in the United Kingdom by Westview Press, 12 Hid's Copse Road, Cumnor
Hill, Oxford OX2 9JJ

Find us on the World Wide Web at www.westviewpress.com

Library of Congress Cataloging-in-Publication Data
Rubinstein, Ruth P.
    Dress codes : meanings and messages in American culture / Ruth P. Rubinstein.—2nd ed.
       p.   cm.
    Includes bibliographical references and index.
    ISBN 0-8133-6795-6
       1. Costume—United States—Social aspects.   2. Costume—United States —History.   3.
Body, Human—United States—Social aspects.   I. Title.
GT605.R835   2000
391'.000973—dc21                                                                                    00-048584

The paper used in this publication meets the requirements of the American National Standard for
Permanence of Paper for Printed Library Materials Z39.48-1984.

10     9     8     7     6

# Contents

# Part 3: Clothing Signs and Social Imperatives

# Part 5: Publicspeak

# Tables and Illustrations

## Tables

## Figures

## Photographs

### Chapter 1

### Chapter 2

## Chapter 13

## Chapter 14

## Chapter 15

## Chapter 16

## Chapter 17

### Chapter 18

### Conclusion

# Acknowledgments

I am grateful to the members of the 1999 Sabbaticals Committee for making it possible for me to complete the revision of this book on time. I would also like to thank the president of the Fashion Institute of Technology (F.I.T.), Dr. Joyce F. Brown, Vice President Dr. Dario A. Cortes, and the Director of Institutional Services, Ellen Conovitze, for their efforts on my behalf.

To past and present students of F.I.T. goes my deepest gratitude for the curiousity and insights expressed in their term papers and other projects.

*Ruth P. Rubinstein*

# Part One: Introduction

# 1

# Dress in Societal Discourse

**M**OST SOCIAL SCIENTISTS take it for granted that an individual's clothing expresses meaning. They accept the old saw that "a picture is worth a thousand words" and will generally concede that dress and ornament are elements in a communication system. They recognize that a person's attire can indicate either conformity or resistance to socially defined expectations for behavior. Yet few scholars have attempted to explain the meaning and relevance of clothing systematically. They often mistake it for *fashion*—the desired appearance of a particular period—whereas *clothing* refers to long-established patterns of dress. As a result, neither clothing images nor the rules that govern their use have been adequately identified or explicated. Writing on the changes that occurred in the early part of the nineteenth century in London and Paris, Richard Sennett (1977) points out that standardized modes of dress offered a protective "cover up" at a time when the distinction between private space and public space first emerged. When one lived and worked among strangers rather than among family members, there was a need to protect one's self and one's inner feelings. Wearing the expected mode of dress enabled individuals to move easily among the various spheres of social life. "Appearance was a cover for the real individual hiding within," observes Sennett. Clothing, as Sennett sees it, provides a buffer between the public and the private self.[1]

For the American economist and social critic Thorstein Veblen (1953), the desire to cover up a lower social origin underlay the consumption patterns in the United States. He claimed that in American society there is a general tendency to buy more expensive clothing than one should. This practice applies, as well, to groups and institutions, with the intent "to cover up the ignoble, selfish motives, and goals."[2]

In his article "Fashion," Georg Simmel (1957) observed that fashion, the latest desired appearance, allows for personal modification, enabling the individual to pursue the competing desires for group identity and individual expression. There is no institution, "no law, no estate of life which can uniformly satisfy the opposing principles of uniformity and individuality better than fashion."[3] The self is also an audience, and clothing allows individuals to view themselves as social objects. By extricating the self from a setting or situation, the individual can scrutinize the image he or she presents in view of the social response that is desired. This separation and objectification, in turn, allows the individual to correct the image if necessary.[4]

In contrast to the social scientist, writers of fiction typically imbue a specific image of clothing with meaning. Nineteenth-century novelists such as Honoré de Balzac, Gustave Flaubert, Marcel Proust, Charles Dickens, and Anthony Trollope wrote detailed descriptions of what their characters wore. For example, when Flaubert describes Madame Bovary's initial appearance in the kitchen of her father's small farm, she wore a blue merino wool dress with three flounces. The clothing carried a message: she is fun-loving, frivolous, fashion-conscious, and out of place. Playwrights also use descriptions of garments as a means of delineating a character. Today, no newspaper reporter would write a profile of someone without describing the person's style of dress. The implication is that a person's style of dress somehow reflects his or her character.

Fashion historians usually discuss clothing in terms of style and the aesthetic tastes of a particular period or a particular group in society.[5] They may identify the textiles and the skills used to create the garment but pay little attention to the clothing iconography, thereby losing sight of the clothing's social significance. Examining fascist propaganda, Laura Malavano in *Fascismo e politica dell'immagine* (1988) demonstrates the relationship between politics and patterns of dress, style and appearance. She analyzes the ways in which Benito Mussolini successfully utilized visual images to encourage consensus among his followers, creating a "new organic whole" comprising people from all levels of society. To promote this ideal, he commissioned artistic representations that combined images from the classical art of the past with those from traditional folk art. In the art that resulted, men assumed various postures of victory as such postures were portrayed in ancient Roman times, yet they held familiar farm implements; they were thus seen as agricultural victors. It was this appeal to a pride in a shared past, made visible through synthetic images, that supported Mussolini's political program.[6]

Political figures, adolescents, and young adults have long recognized the significance of clothing. In his run for the governorship of Tennessee in 1978, Lamar Alexander conducted a grass-roots campaign. He walked across the state wearing a working man's attire—a red and black plaid Levi's shirt. He won the election. In his campaign for the Republican presidential nominations in 1996 and 1999, Alexander wore a similar shirt. Lack of support led him to withdraw from the primaries. His work shirt was seen as using style instead of substance to win the nomination. Self-interest was suspected. Lamar Alexander complained that his shirt acquired more recognition than he did.[7]

Vice president Al Gore, in his campaign for the Democratic presidential nomination, was also accused of using clothes to manipulate the public and to project the desirable image of an aggressive personality type.[8] The vice president explained to reporter Maureen Dowd that his clothes identify who he is. From his father he assimilated his somewhat formal style, the three-piece suit he wore as a congressman and as a senator. As with most married men in the United States, his wife Tipper picked his casual clothes and she chose what he wore on the campaign trail—a blue shirt to bring out his eyes, heathery brown sweater, khakis, and black cowboy boots.[9]

To signal connectedness and to distinguish themselves from others, groups of young people adopt styles of dress to express their particular, distinct identity. In making these choices, they demonstrate their awareness that a style or mode of appearance has meaning.[10]

## The Notion of Public Memory

Visual images from the past and present form what French sociologist Maurice Halbwachs calls the collective memory. They are a part of core culture, like time and space, and give shape to a child's orientation to social realities. Ideas, beliefs, and values—that is, the basic constructs of collective life—are embodied in images. They contain the central system of rules of behavior and thought that controls much of what we do. The growing child is bombarded by these images and their shared public meaning. As Halbwachs explained, learning begins early in life in a most informal way, but full understanding requires both biological maturity and social experience.[11]

An experiment conducted at the Johns Hopkins School of Medicine in 1988 provides further evidence that information builds up in the brain bit by bit but quickly. The experiment consisted of measuring the amount of time it took the brain to name and categorize images of everyday objects.[12] The researchers found that it took about four-tenths of a second to comprehend pictures of familiar objects and up to three-quarters of a second for less familiar ones.[13]

Public memory includes depictions of people in carvings, in sculpture, in paintings, mosaics, stained glass windows, and in prints and drawings in books. These images are concrete, tangible representations of "currents of collective thought" from the various historical periods. The clothing in these visual portrayals has been so closely associated with ideas that the clothing itself is seen as embodying them.[14]

Prior to the nineteenth century, the majority of the people thus represented in Western European art were figures of political power, religious authority, or both. Their dependents—wives, mistresses, children, or servants—might also appear. As might be expected, their clothing and accessories came to be seen as a physical manifestation of the ideas, the institutions, and the power held by these people. In a given society at a given time, therefore, the clothing worn by individuals in authority has automatically provided information about their position and power in society.

Because many of these works of art have survived, they now form a part of the cumulative public memory. For example, the crowning of a new monarch often

*Public memory. Seventeenth-century Protestant Holland was a middle-class society whose* *ideals were harmony and self-restraint. Its population had fought against monarchy and had* *chosen self-government. The people were expected to live a neat, orderly life. "The Linen* *Cupboard," by Pieter de Hooch, 1663, illustrates the ideals of cleanliness, neatness, and* *harmony. (By permission. Collection of the Rijksmuseum, Amsterdam.)*

set off a round of new paintings depicting the new court. These visual images would be added to those of the previous monarchy. In some cases the new ruler continued and elaborated on past traditions. In other instances new leaders attempted to distinguish themselves by espousing new ideas and values, which led to new styles of painting and dress. However, these would not wholly replace the old and would eventually be added to the existing body of images of royalty. The result has been an expanding vocabulary of visual images. A group searching for a visual image to embody its ideas might choose from among the elements represented in the storehouse of images and create a new synthesis. This novel synthesis or pattern of appearance would, in turn, be added to the existing repository. In

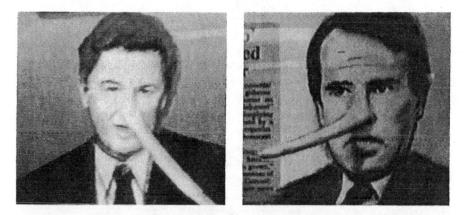

*Public memory. Contemporary use of nineteenth-century image from* Pinocchio: *Jim Florio and Jim Courter portray each other as lying in the New Jersey gubernatorial race.* (New York Times, *Oct. 16, 1989.)*

each instance the clothing, the accessories, and the style would be seen as embodying the ideas represented by those images.

Giacomo Balla's "Futurist Manifesto of Men's Clothing 1913," a proclamation that argued for a totally new approach to dress, attests to the powerful persistence in Western society of a storehouse of images and meanings. Leaders of the avantgarde Futurist movement sought to reject the images existing in public memory: the "pretty-pretty," "tight-fitting," "decadent," "unhygienic," "symmetrical," and "boring," the "gloomy" and "humiliating hypocritical custom of wearing mourning," (i.e., the black three-piece suit celebrated in the early nineteenth century by Thomas Carlyle). The Futurists called for abolishing "sadness in dress," as well as "timidity," "harmony," and "good taste." In a world transformed by science and technology, observes Balla, "we must invent Futurist clothes, clothes that are happy and practical," and "spread good humour." Items of dress must have strong colors and dynamic designs, "triangles, cones, spirals, and circles" and come in a variety of styles to complement each mood. The cut must incorporate dynamic and asymmetrical lines. Above all, clothes must be made to last for a short time in order to encourage industrial activity and "to provide constant and novel enjoyment for our bodies." The "consequent merry dazzle" produced by the clothes in the noisy streets "will mean that everything will sparkle like a glorious prism." Within their noisy cries of rebellion, the Futurists demonstrated a tacit awareness of the necessary connections between appearance, the self, and society.[15]

## Clothing Semiotics

The first step toward a systematic understanding of clothing images and meanings in American society is to define the basic constructs of the discourse system.

This entails identifying the language and vocabulary of images that give shape to contemporary communication. All systems of communication consist of language and speech. A language provides a basic vocabulary and accepted rules of usage. It offers a structural framework within which an individual speaker can operate. As defined by Ferdinand de Saussure, language is a system of signs and symbols that exists prior to and outside its use by a given individual.[16]

When applied to clothing, the term *language* refers to the use of a particular vocabulary derived from the storehouse of images that support the structure of social interaction, the system of statuses and roles. Like words, clothing images become significant only when they are used in a specific social context. Images may function as *signs* that convey a single, relatively clear-cut meaning or as *symbols* having multiple meanings and connotations or associations. Images are signifiers that carry meaning and value.[17] Seen from this perspective, the language of clothing can be analyzed, as sociologists Erving Goffman (1951) and Gregory P. Stone (1956) have suggested, in terms of signs and symbols.

Since our contemporary vocabulary has been culled from the collective memory, the storehouse of images in Western history and supplemented by the "American experience," to define the parameters of the language of clothing requires a study of the historical record (that is, the types of images, their origins, their purposes, and their permutations over time).

## Style of Dress

Style of dress has significance beyond that of conveying information. The early twentieth century psychologist J. C. Flugel suggested that styles of dress and elements of appearance act to summon distinct feelings that enhance role performance. One's sense of importance is increased when "different parts of the whole, body and clothes, fuse into a unity."[18] This style "expands the proper self." Flugel called this visual image confluence.[19]

When a person's appearance is augmented by elements that extend the body's reach, as when one is accompanied by guards carrying arms, the resulting visual image increases a person's physical ability to control the environment. "The consciousness of our personal existence is prolonged," and the sense of power is enhanced when using a walking stick or carrying tools.[20] Conversely, clothing that is too big, too tight-fitting, too small, that "refuses to become a part of an organic whole with the body," can "dwarf the body" and imbue the person with a sense of insignificance. Flugel called this image *contrast*.[21]

Style of dress also tells about other societal categories such as maturity. In 1989 Erik and Lyle Menendez killed their parents, claiming self-defense.[22] They were tried twice. The first trial ended in a deadlock in January 1994. The two juries, one for each of the brothers, couldn't decide whether the act was murder or manslaughter. Legal observers noted that throughout the trial the brothers wore sweaters, which made them look more juvenile. During the retrial, which ended in conviction, they had abandoned the sweaters in favor of adult shirts and ties.

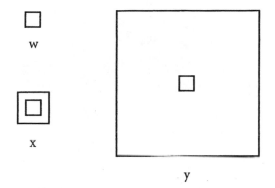

W = The size of the person

X = Confluence: The mind fails to distinguish between the body and the clothes, "expanding the proper self."

Y = Contrast: Clothes that are too big or too small make the person seem smaller, imbuing the person with a sense of insignificance.

FIGURE 1.1   Effects of "Contrast" and "Confluence"
*Source:* J. C. Flugel (1966), *The Psychology of Clothes,* figure 4 (London: Hogarth Press). Originally published in 1930.

By wearing adult-style dress, the brothers presented themselves as adults and placed themselves "at a decided disadvantage," conclude legal observers.[23]

### Clothing Signs

Attire that is a clothing sign is characterized by (1) being task-oriented or instrumental; (2) having one primary meaning; and (3) being generally recognized as a sign by those who wear it. A formal code, promulgated by those in authority, mandates the wearing of the specific elements of dress in a particular pattern to signify the particular social position with its distinct rights and responsibilities (e g , military or fire department uniforms). Those wearing this clothing arouse a set of expectations for behavior in both the wearer and the audience.

Clothing signs make visible the structure and organization of interaction within a specific social context, as Thomas Carlyle pointed out in 1838 with respect to English justice: "You see two individuals, one dressed in fine Red and the other in threadbare Blue; Red says to Blue: Be hanged and anatomized." The man dressed in red has the power to order the death and dismemberment of the other, and this right is signified by the red judicial robes. Such "visible emblems" are points of reference that give members of a society their bearing.[24]

Exercising authority, wielding power, differentiating the sexes, and arousing sexual interest are all facilitated by the employment of categories of clothing

*Contemporary example of confluence. (From 1993
J. Press Brochure.)*

*Contemporary example of contrast. (From* Mademoiselle, *April 1993.)*

*Through the portrayal of royalty in fairy tales, children are introduced to ideas of social hierarchy and power. The illustration depicts a monarch with the power to protect and to punish.*
(Illustration by Françoise, in Margaret E. Martignoni, ed. [1955], The Illustrated Treasury of Children's Literature [New York: Grosset & Dunlap]).

signs. Carlyle's example of a British judge wearing red judicial robes and the prisoner wearing "threadbare blue" is about an interaction in which the judge has authority to exercise force. A judge, moreover, is supported by men carrying implements capable of inflicting harm; they convey the image of power

Manifested in clothing, the social distinction between male and female is the third category of clothing sign. Sex differences, as G. P. Stone noted, are forcefully regulated by the personal evaluation, social judgments and expectations governing "appropriate" dress.[25] Male–female dress distinction is signified by the shapes, colors, and fabrics of clothing and by the two basic forms—skirt and pants. As M. Gottdiener observes, women in American society have traditionally been given a weaker social position than men, and the mere act of wearing women's clothes situates the person in a subordinate role, validating male dominance.[26]

The final category of clothing signs is seductive attire. The church fathers suggested that attire is seductive when it is characterized by an interplay between covering the body and exposing it, by employing "transparencies and half concealments," as well as color and ornament. To feel sensual and to show an inclination toward sexual intercourse requires something more than sex-specific attire, observes Flugel. The décolletage, for example, which first came into being toward the end of the Middle Ages, was expected to arouse sexual desire.[27]

### Clothing Symbols

In "Symbols of Class Status," E. Goffman observes that, unlike clothing signs, which identify positions within a social institution and are governed by rules and regulations, few rules apply to the wearing of clothing symbols—items of dress that reflect the achievement of certain cultural values.[28] The wearing of such attire is not required and does not indicate group membership. The example Goffman gives to demonstrate the notion of clothing symbol is the wearing of clothing associated with a high socioeconomic class. The decision to wear it is personal. It is worn in the hope of acquiring social prestige.

According to Thorstein Veblen, attire that reflects the achievement of cultural values, what the society considers good and desirable, enhances one's sense of social significance.[29] The elements of dress, ornament, and appearance that demonstrate such achievement he called "status symbols."[30] Veblen used the style of dress worn by the European aristocracy to illustrate that leisure or freedom from physical labor was a basic cultural value. Members of the aristocracy used expensive fabrics that were fashioned in the latest style, thus indicating that they could not possibly toil in a field. While demonstrating wealth, the symbolic significance of such attire implies social superiority and entitlement.[31]

Through the centuries visual images emerged as a way of instituting specific cultural values. The desirability of wealth, beauty, aesthetic awareness, freedom from physical labor, youthfulness, and health are all conveyed in images embedded in "public memory." Since clothing symbols reflect ideas about what is valued in a society at a particular time, their meaning is to some extent open to individual interpretation. Unlike clothing signs, the wearing of clothing symbols implies nothing about the particular individual's rights and obligations, nor is it a reliable predictor of behavior. Symbols may have more than one meaning, and values may have more than one manifestation. An accurate interpretation of the choice of a symbol—a style, a color, or an ornament—by a particular individual requires a more intimate understanding of the person and his or her history.

## Individual Speech

Clothing "speech" can be defined as an individual's manipulation of language to produce specific utterances characterized by personal intonation and style. A person's clothing speech reflects intrapsychic dynamics with few implications for society. It is analogous to "talking to oneself." Consciously or unconsciously, clothing with a particular meaning may be chosen by that person. The choice might express a personal vision, mirror an emotional state, be idiosyncratic, or be important to the individual, yet it may contain no real social significance. As G. P. Stone notes, clothing speech reflects an individual interpretation of a situation, attitude, and mood. Some people dress in dark-colored clothes when they are depressed. Others may purposely choose bright and cheerful colors to counteract feelings of depression. The choice and meaning are specific to the individual.[32]

Just as vocabulary choices often reflect a person's cultural background and upbringing, clothing speech reflects the individual's resources and the extent of his or her exposure to the elements of the language of clothing. The color red, for example, may be chosen by an individual because it is easier to see, or because a favorite aunt was known to prefer it, rather than for its association with passion. Analysis of clothing speech may be of interest to persons concerned with an individual's psychic and intrapersonal dynamics.

## "Publicspeak"

When a large number of individuals choose a style or element of dress that lies outside the established vocabulary of images, the choice is no longer individual "speech," but "publicspeak." Publicspeak reflects the sentiments of similar and dissimilar individuals and aggregates.[33]

Such dress may serve as a public announcement that the group has declined to accept the ideas or values of mainstream culture; their clothes indicate heresy. Moreover, such clothing may convey a message about a particular social condition or political or economic event. As such, the styles are a form of societal discourse.

*Fashion,* clothing *tie-signs,* and clothing *tie-symbols* are three categories of dress that reflect a collective response to the structure of interaction, to events, or to the inner necessities that animate social life. Because of the right to free speech and the tradition of individualism, the public memory may be searched for newly appropriate visual expression. In bypassing the established vocabulary and existing definitions, new associations are formed and new categories of behavior may be legitimated. Leather jackets, an element of dress worn by soldiers in the ancient past, for example, had suffered many centuries of neglect before being resurrected by the movies of the 1940s and the 1950s to signify toughness and gang membership. Again today, American youth have come to consider it a very desirable element of dress (except among animal-rights activists).

Each category of appearance has its own set of authors, its own intended audience, and each has the capacity to equip the wearer to feel, think, and act in a different way.

## Fashion

In his "shifting erogenous zones" theory of fashion (1930), Flugel observed that the purpose of fashion is to create sexual interest and that the phenomenon of fashion requires that a designer shift focus from one part of the female anatomy to another.[34] Observing the fashion process in the 1960s, Herbert Blumer argued that a style becomes a fashion through the process of "collective selection." A designer offers a large number of styles on the runway, Blumer explains. Only a few of these, those emotionally most relevant, are chosen by buyers, magazine editors, and boutique owners, to be offered to their clients. When consumers actually buy the clothes, those styles become the fashion. Consumer relevance, not the designers, turns a style into a fashion.[35]

### Fashion Magazines

Fashion magazines fall into three categories. Two are those that merely depict what is shown on fashion runways and those that edit the collections and have the opportunity to influence the production and consumption of fashion. The third category is that of magazines that show the work of photographers who explore new dimensions in art, culture, and society. Animated by their passions, these photographic images could be a source of new ideas and visions for culture and society.[36] The most influential fashion photographers at the end of the twentieth century seem to have been men: Bruce Weber, Craig McDean, David Sims, and Paolo Roversi.[37]

### Clothing Tie-Signs

Tie-signs refer to the attire of social subsets, such as followers of Hare Krishna or the Amish. It is a category of dress adopted by groups that reject the Establishment's ideas, beliefs, and values. Members of social subsets develop a world of meaning separate from institutional social arrangements. Their clothing ensemble is carefully conceived to set their behaviors apart from those of others and to reflect the group's distinct ideas, beliefs, and values.[38] The wearing of group-designated attire is required, distinguishing members from nonmembers. It conveys a single meaning while communicating norms of behavior, rights, and obligations.

### Clothing Tie-Symbols

Just as there are clothing tie-signs, there are also clothing tie-symbols, elements of dress and styles of appearance that reflect an individual's fears, hopes, dreams, or desires. Tie-symbols are worn to inform that person and others of rejection or support for a political idea or a social agenda. For example, a baseball cap in black with the mark "X" reflects Spike Lee's admiration for Malcolm X. The T-shirt with a political message, such as "Save the Earth," is another example of a tie-symbol.[39]

In the 1990s an important category of tie-symbols was so-called trendy attire, the prevailing styles of young adults. Three "looks" were popular: the pierced or tatooed body, a somber black costume called Gothic, and the oversized hip-hop attire. In 1999 there were also down vests and glittery beads.

The wearing of tie-symbols is governed by personal choice. The meaning of the attire and the reason someone elects to wear it are specific to the person. Some wear the attire because it reflects their beliefs. Others wear it to claim an association in order to obtain "social gains," while still others may appropriate such symbols because they like the look or the color. Hence, the meaning of a tie-symbol is often ambiguous.

Tie-symbols are similar to clothing symbols, in that they imply little about the particular individual's rights and obligations and are not reliable indicators of

*Clothing tie-sign. Guardian Angels, an organization founded in 1979 in New York City by Curtis Sliwa (center). A voluntary group with no formal authority, the members patrol city streets and trains. Their uniform consists of a red beret, a T-shirt with "Guardian Angels" insignia, and a red jacket. The insignia "I support the Guardian Angels" identifies those in training.*

behavior. Nevertheless, tie symbols are important because they are an expression of grass-roots sentiments and the first step in the organization of a social movement and social change.

To conclude, in American society clothing is significant primarily in terms of the visual image it conveys. The contemporary vocabulary of clothing is based on those found in the "repository" of images, the collective memory that has accumulated in Western society. These images are the primary constructs of social organization and interaction. They direct and inform social behavior. To quote Carlyle, "For neither tailoring nor legislating does man proceed by mere Accident, but the hand is ever guided by mysterious operations of the mind."[40]

## Notes

1. R. Sennett (1974), *The Fall of Public Man* (New York: Knopf).
2. T. Veblen (1953), *The Theory of the Leisure Class* (New York: Mentor Books). Originally published in 1899.

3. G. Simmel (1957), "Fashion," *American Journal of Sociology* 62: 294–323. Originally published in 1904.

4. Ibid.

5. M. and A. Batterberry (1977), *Fashion: The Mirror of History.* (New York: Greenwich House); A. Hollander (1978), *Seeing Through Clothes* (New York: Viking); E. Wilson (1987), *Adorned in Dreams* (Berkeley: University of California Press).

6. L. Malvano (1988), *Fascismo e politica dell'immagine* (Torino, Italy: Bolatti Boringhieri), pp. 77–140. Translated for the author by J. Cascaito.

7. *New York Times Magazine,* Nov. 14, 1999, p. 116.

8. Maureen Dowd (1999), "The Pals and Palettes of A1," *New York Times,* Nov. 10.

9. Ibid.

10. D. Hebdige (1979), *Subculture: The Meaning of Style.* (New York: Methuen).

11. M. Halbwachs (1980), *The Collective Memory,* trans. F. J. Ditter, Jr., and V. Y. Ditter (New York: Harper and Row).

12. "Clues to Comprehension" (1998), *New York Times,* Aug. 18.

13. Ibid.

14. Ibid., pp. 20–24, 40–41, 152–157.

15. U. Apollonaire, ed. (1973), *Futurist Manifesto: Documents of Twentieth Century Art* (New York: Viking Press), pp. 132–133.

16. E. de Saussure (1974), *A Course in General Linguistics* (Huntington, N.Y.: Fontana).

17. E. Cassirer (1961), "Ideational Content of the Sign," pp. 1004–1008 in *Theories of Society: Foundations of Modern Sociology,* vol. 2, ed. T. Parsons, E. Shills, K.D. Naegele, and J. R. Pitts (New York: Free Press). Also E. Goffman (1951), "Symbols of Class Status," *British Journal of Sociology* A (4): 294–303. Also see G. P. Stone (1962), "Appearance and the Self," in *Human Behavior and Social Processes,* ed. A. M. Rose (Boston: Houghton Mifflin), pp. 86–118.

18. J. C. Flugel (1966), *The Psychology of Clothes* (New York: Hogarth Press), p. 157. Originally published in 1930.

19. Ibid., p. 34.

20. Ibid., pp. 36–37.

21. Ibid., pp. 11, 36, 48.

22. Kenneth B. Noble (1996), "Menendez Brothers Guilty of Killing Their Parents," *New York Times,* Mar. 21, p. A12.

23. Ibid.

24. T. Carlyle (1967), *Sartor Resartus* (New York: Dutton), p. 26. Originally published in 1838.

25. Stone (1962), op. cit., pp. 107–108.

26. M. Gottdiener (1977), "Unisex Fashions and Gender Role Change," *Semiotic Scene* 1 (3): 13–37.

27. Flugel, op. cit., p. 103.

28. Goffman (1951), op. cit., pp. 259–261.

29. Veblen, op. cit., pp. 118–130.

30. See also H. Spencer (1969), *The Principles of Sociology,* ed. S. Andreseki (Hamden, Conn.: Archon Books), pp. 160–161. In contrast to status symbols, attire that exhibits a departure or deviation from cultural values has been termed "stigma symbols." E. Goffman (1963b), *Stigma: Notes on the Management of Spoiled Identity.* (Englewood Cliffs, N.J.: Prentice-Hall), p. 45.

31. Veblen, op. cit. The idea of social superiority and entitlement is discussed in Veblen's chapter "Conspicuous Leisure," pp. 51–60.

32. Stone (1962), op. cit., pp. 226–227.

33. The concept of "publicspeak" has its roots in the work of C. Wright Mills and Herbert Gans. Mills pointed to a distinction between "personal troubles," which are a private matter, and "public issues," where factors outside one's personal control affect daily life. Gans used the term *culture publics* to suggest that a great variety of "taste cultures" exists in the United States. See C. W. Mills (1959), *The Sociological Imagination* (New York: Oxford University Press), and H. J. Gans (1974), *Popular Culture and High Culture* (New York: Basic Books).

34. Flugel, op. cit., p. 160.

35. H. Blumer (1969), "Fashion: From Class Differentiation to Collective Selection," *Sociology Quarterly* 10: 275–291.

36. Those having the reputation for such impact are Stefano Tonchi, the fashion director of *Esquire* magazine, and Franca Sozzani, editor of *Italian* and *L'Uomo Vogue*.

37. Critics Notebook (1998), "The Splash Heard Round the World," *New York Times*, Sept. 13, pp. 1, 4.

38. A. Rockford and E. Burke (1985), *Hare Krishna in America* (New Brunswick, N.J.: Rutgers University Press); H. B. Thompson (1967), *Hell's Angels: The Strange and Terrible Saga of the Outlaw Motorcycle Gangs* (New York: Ballantine Books).

39. *New York Times*, Sept. 17, 1989.

40. Carlyle, op. cit., p. 25.

# 2

# Nineteenth-Century Theories of Clothing

In *The Tewa World: Space, Time, Being and Becoming in a Pueblo Society* (1969), anthropologist Alfonso Ortíz demonstrated how the various aspects of social life are interconnected. For the Tewa-speaking Indians of northern New Mexico, the realms of the sacred, physical, and social are integrated into everyday life.[1] Each pueblo is demarcated by four sacred mountains, each associated with a direction, a color, an animal, a mineral, and a star.

Within the ring of sacred mountains is a ring of sacred mesas, and within that a ring of sacred shrines. The Tewa people divide themselves into three categories, each mirrored by a group of spirits dwelling in the netherworld. An intricate set of forces thus affected the development of customs and traditions in the social life of the Tewa-speaking people. Dr. Ortíz's analysis was informed by his anthropological fieldwork, his experience of Pueblo rituals and religion, and the knowledge he gained as member of the San Juan Pueblo.[2] His study was also informed by the scholarly traditions that developed in the nineteenth century.

Prior to the nineteenth century, learned discussions of clothing behavior focused on persons who dressed in fashionable attire that exceeded their social rank. Critics claimed that wearing the clothing of "one's betters" was an immoral act that would lead to dire consequences for the person, the economy, and even society as a whole.[3]

In the nineteenth century, however, the discourse on clothing acquired a new dimension. The belief that all phenomena should be systematically examined encouraged scholars to ask questions about the very nature and significance of clothing. Such scholars as Thorstein Veblen (1953) and Georg Simmel (1957) distinguished the fashion of the moment from everyday attire and focused on the socioeconomic advantage that accrued to individuals who wore fashionable clothes.[4]

At the same time, a general interest in the origins of things led to scholarly discussions about the origin of clothing. Christian thinkers insisted that the interaction between Adam and Eve in the Garden of Eden made clothing simply basic to human nature. Medical scientists attributed the origin of clothing to the need to

*A "tiger cap" is worn by babies of tribes in the American Pacific Northwest and some Pacific Islands. This hat includes images of the child's guardian spirits—an eagle, a jaguar, a serpent. It is meant to mask the child's identity in the hope of warding off evil. Nineteenth century. (Art from the Pacific Basin. Courtesy George Dorsch.)*

*Fiber headdress designed to protect the individual from malevolent forces. It was worn by tribes in New Guinea, and Pacific Island villages of Sepik, Iatmul, and Tambunum. Nineteenth century. (Art from the Pacific Basin. Courtesy George Dorsch.)*

protect the biological integrity of the body and the need to survive treacherous physical environments. Other scholars observed that while there are many societies in which the people are unclothed, there are no societies in which the people are unadorned; hence, the origin of clothing may lie in adornment.

Three theories regarding the origin of clothing emerged: the modesty theory, the protection theory, and the adornment theory. These theories and their critical reevaluations provide a context for a modern explication of the language of clothing.

## The Modesty Theory

English costume historian James Laver pointed out that "Until quite recently—less than a hundred years ago perhaps—it was almost universally agreed that the primal and fundamental reason for wearing clothes was modesty. . . . For those who accepted the literal truth of the Genesis story, there was no question about it." Adam and Eve, having eaten of the fruit of the Tree of the Knowledge of Good and Evil, "knew that they were naked" and made themselves "aprons of leaves."[5]

*The biblical origin of clothing. Adam and Eve cover their
genitals in shame, having sinned in the Garden of Eden.
(Detail from the* Sarcophagus of Junius Bassus, *ca. AD
355, Vatican Museums.)*

Saint Augustine (AD 354–430) was the clearest of the early Church Fathers on
the subject of covering the body. He explained that prior to the Fall, nakedness
was the natural state and neither sexual organs nor bodily functions were shameful. When Adam and Eve disobeyed God in the Garden of Eden, man became unable to control his lust, and lust became independent of man's will. All mankind
became afflicted with the insubordination of the flesh.[6]

The injunction to cover the body initially applied to men only, according to
Augustine, because only in men is sexual arousal obvious. Soon, however, women
also had to cover their bodies. Their ability to seduce, Church Fathers argued,
would lead men to stray from the spiritual.[7]

James Laver suggested that every society develops its own ideas of what is appropriate and that these ideas are associated with social identity and expected behavior. He observed that the wearing of clothes is a learned behavior and not in-
stinctual, as the Church Fathers had claimed. Missionaries and other observers of
"primitive" or nonliterate societies have told of people who walk around naked
and seem to feel no shame, guilt, or any other ill effects. Australian aborigines, for
example, are indifferent to their nakedness but are deeply embarrassed if seen

eating. An Arab peasant woman caught in the fields without her veil will throw her skirt over her head, thereby exposing what to the Western mind "is a much more embarrassing part of her anatomy."[8]

Moreover, Laver observed that the term *modesty* applies differently to each gender. In societies in which women are expected to cover their bodies to "dampen sexual allure," women offend modesty by wearing sexually alluring attire. Conforming to the expectation of modesty entails concealing the body and denying sexual allure, encouraging sexual inhibition. Expectations for male appearance and behavior dictate that men must restrain the self. They must dress in a manner that fosters conformity with the public definition of maleness. Men offend modesty by "swagger," an attempt at self-aggrandizement.[9]

Christian thinkers and their injunction to modesty instituted two images and their associated meanings in Western society. The first image denies the body and is nonseductive. It signifies a social self directed toward obedience to Church authority. The second, a style of dress that exposes the body or alludes to the body underneath, is seductive. (See chapter 8.)

## The Protection Theory

The need to keep warm in the bone-chilling dampness of Europe, as well as reports of expeditions that perished from exposure in the vast reaches of Canada and Antarctica, gave weight to the commonsense view that the origin of clothing lay in the need to maintain the physiological integrity of the body. Yet observations by Charles Darwin and other travelers to "primitive" societies described people who walked around naked in harsh environments with strong gales, heavy rains, and powerful winds.[10] Reporting on the Yahgans of Tierra del Fuego (at the tip of South America), for example, Darwin noted that in inclement weather they went about wearing nothing. At night they slept naked on the wet ground, "coiled up like animals." When Darwin and some of his crew went ashore, they had to huddle around a fire and wrap themselves in blankets to keep warm. In contrast, a family of Yahgans, all naked, were some distance from the fire and yet perspiration streamed down their bodies.[11] Similarly, B. Spencer and F. J. Gillen described the ability of Australian aborigines to walk about without any body covering despite sharp changes in temperature.[12]

In attempting to discover the secret of how to survive sharp changes in temperature without shelter or clothing, medical researchers looked for, but could not find, any special biological differences between Europeans and Australian aborigines. They thus concluded that people who lived on the continent of Europe in the remote past were probably just as able to endure the cold as the indigenous peoples of Australia and Tierra del Fuego. They observed that the skin—when accustomed to exposure—provides an efficient protection for body organs. When covered, however, it loses this ability. In other words, the unintended consequence of wearing clothes is dependence on them; once worn,

*In the desert and away from camp, Bushmen prefer to sleep in the warmth of the daytime sun. At night, they huddle close to their fire. (Photo by Constance Stuart.)*

clothing becomes a necessity. The origin of clothing, the researchers concluded, could not lie in the need to protect the body, because the wearing of clothing decreased the body's ability to protect itself.[13]

These scientists also described the elaborate mechanism through which the body attempts to keep the brain, heart, lungs, and abdominal cavity at a constant temperature (37°C, or 98°F) despite fluctuations in the surrounding environment. This mechanism calls for the production of heat by the body at the same rate at which it is being lost. Such a balance can be achieved by consuming enough food and engaging in sufficient physical activity to produce the required amount of heat. Another means of preventing heat loss is using clothing as a barrier.[14] Their discussion concludes with the suggestion that a study of clothing developed by various societies and designed to cope with severe climatic conditions may be informative with regard to the impact of clothing on survival.

Although individuals in small groups can survive in a harsh environment, effective clothing makes social life possible, enhancing the comfort and quality of life. The Athabascan Indians, who live in the frigid Arctic environment of Alaska and northern Canada, for example, have neither housing nor weatherproof clothing. They sleep coiled in front of a fire, keeping only half the body warm. When awake, they are restless and in constant motion trying to keep warm. They seem to be irritable and unable to welcome guests. In contrast, the Eskimo who live in the same large region share a culture that better enables them to cope with their treacherous environment. Moreover, they lead an active social life. The clothing of the Eskimos throughout the region is tailored in the same style, they travel by dogsled and kayak, and they heat and cook with shallow open lamps of stone or pottery, in which they burn animal fat. The harpoon is the universal weapon. The myths and legends told in the igloos by central Alaskan and Canadian Eskimos are also told by the Eskimos of both the Pacific and Atlantic coasts. Their religious practices are similar, and when rites vary they do so only in detail. The Eskimo religion is predominantly made up of a number of taboos, mainly concerning food and clothing supply. In order to have the raw materials necessary for survival, the unseen spirits of the invisible world must be properly appeased.

Eskimos go almost completely naked inside their heated winter homes. So effective is the insulation of their housing that outside temperatures can drop as low as −80°F, while inside homes they live at a comfortable +80–90°F. Inside the domed snow house in winter and inside tents made of skins during the summer, the Eskimo sits half naked, wearing only knee breeches that extend from the waist to the knees.[15]

Outdoor clothing for men and women consists of only two layers of caribou furs. The hide closest to the body is worn with the fur facing the skin, trapping beneath it a layer of air and body heat. The outdoor attire encases the body but allows freedom of movement. The looseness of the cut enables the Eskimos, when standing still in the extreme cold, to pull their arms from their sleeves and place them close to the body. When they become warm from working, or when the outside temperature rises, belts can be loosened, mittens taken off, hoods thrown back, and overshirts removed.[16]

Similarly, for people who live in areas with frequent extreme temperature changes—for example, where days are hot and nights are cold—appropriate clothing makes it possible to engage in commercial enterprise. The Rewala Bedouins, cattle-breeding nomadic people who live in the Syrian and Arabian deserts, have to deal with 50-degree temperature changes between day and night, as well as the exigencies of a nomadic and warlike existence. The attire they have adopted is composed of long, loose-fitting layers that can be added or subtracted as the need arises: to combat a sandstorm or a dramatic temperature change, to allow freedom of movement to climb onto a camel, or to jump up quickly to defend themselves.[17]

In ancient civilizations such as Egypt and India, and in many parts of the world today, physical labor was and is performed by individuals who are almost naked. Minimal covering allows heat to evaporate more quickly, making work less taxing and physically more tolerable. It also gives the body access to cool breezes when they arise. The white or light-colored clothing typical of countries close to the Equator reflects the rays of the sun, providing the best protection against solar radiation.[18]

Wandering about almost naked, wearing only a brief layer of leaves or bark, the inhabitants of the rain forests of Africa have survived in a hot and humid climate. Because their body covering is minimal and does not retain water, it does not become cumbersome or inhibit movement. It enables evaporation, the chief means of protection against overheating, and it is, of course, easily replaced.[19]

## Modern Protective Garb

Advances in technology, affluence, and leisure in the second half of the twentieth century facilitated the development of garments that made participation in sports and other outdoor activities more comfortable.[20] Ski wear underwent the most radical change. In the 1940s men slid down the slopes in suits and sports jackets. Warmth was provided by "awkwardly thick thermal underwear and heavy woolen turtleneck sweaters."[21] Synthetic fabrics made possible light, weatherproof and waterproof parkas and padded pants. In this clothing, style derives from function, giving skiers a sense of freedom.[22] Down-filled vests, waterproof fishing ponchos, hiking boots, warm-up jackets, and jogging suits[23] are regarded as "gear" rather than clothes.[24]

Wearing protective attire is an important way of continuing to enjoy riding a motorcycle, according to insurance companies like GEICO; but it is also a must for comfort and safety.[25] The recommended body attire includes leather pants to protect the legs and a leather motorcycle jacket to shelter key parts of the upper body. A full-face helmet provides the most protection to the head, along with motorcycle goggles to shield the eyes from wind and debris. Padded gloves protect the hands without interfering with the operation of the bike.[26]

Even when clothing is not essential for physical survival, appropriate dress allows a more complete enjoyment of the outdoors and enhances the opportunity for sharing ideas and development of group life. In this sense protective clothing further increases the chances of survival.

## The Adornment Theory

In the introduction to *Sartor Resartus* (1967), Thomas Carlyle complained that "considering our present advanced state of culture and how the Torch of Science has now been brandished about, with more or less effect for five thousand years and upwards . . . it might strike the reflective mind with some surprise that hitherto little or nothing of a fundamental character . . . has been written on the subject of clothes."[27]

Carlyle proposed that the origin of clothing lies in adornment; a hypothesis that stems from the evolutionary theory of change, which was prevalent in the nineteenth century. Scientists asserted that there were fixed stages of development through which all societies must pass. Each stage was considered more advanced than the one that preceded it. The theory suggested that, since Western society in the nineteenth century represented the highest stage yet in the evolutionary sequence, nonliterate societies were "lawless" cultures in which individuals were free

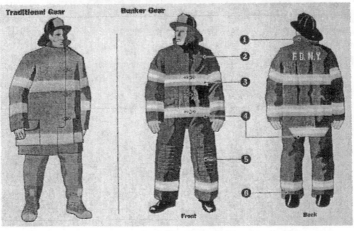

*Firefighter trainees in "bunker gear" at the New York City Fire Training Academy. The garments shield them from flames as hot as 1,500 degrees and include a five-inch-high collar with extra insulation to protect the neck and face; a jacket of a lighter fabric composite with increased thermal protection; reflective bands on the jackets consisting of glass beads with greater heat resistance; shorter jacket hems in front for freedom of movement; and changeable knee pads providing different levels of protection or flexibility. (Angel Franco, New York Times, Feb. 22, 1996.)*

to act as they wished. (Research in the twentieth century has, of course, found this theory wanting.)

"Among wild people we find tattooing and painting even prior to clothes" and the purpose of clothing "was not warmth or decency but ornament," Carlyle proclaimed. In such societies, a person's appearance was determined by individual, idiosyncratic behavior based on whim. Among the "barbarians," Carlyle explained, once the pangs of hunger were satisfied, the next need was for ornament. The desire for adornment emanated from "a man's spiritual realm."[28] Ethnographic reports, however, reveal that, for the most part, people in nonliterate societies still ornament their bodies for two major purposes. The first is to make it easier to organize and maintain group life, and the second is to help them cope with a sinister supernatural world.[29]

Members of nonliterate societies find the practice of modifying the body in characteristic patterns necessary for defining their distinct social identities. To separate group members from nonmembers, the Batonga in Africa scar their bodies, the Ibo scar their faces and cut traditional geometric patterns in their hair, and the Mentawei Islanders in Sumatra file their teeth. To identify group members, the Tchikirin Indians of South America pierce the earlobes of boys and girls and insert cigar-shaped plugs of reddened wood into the holes. The plugs are replaced from time to time with larger ones until the holes in the lobes become very large. And to place a boy into his gender category, they insert a string of beads into his lower lip at birth.[30]

Among the Nuba, a people who live in the southern Sudan, the distinction between the sexes is emphasized as a child approaches puberty. Body adornment focuses on the different responsibilities borne by adult men and women.[31] As soon as a girl's breasts begin to develop, the first of a series of scarifications takes place. At this stage cuts are made at each side of the abdomen; they join at the navel and continue to a point between the breasts. Further incisions are made at the onset of menstruation. Nuba men, in contrast, turn their bodies into a canvas. The young man and the artist who will execute the painting decide together on the individual design that will most complement the wearer. Only those with firm, youthful bodies will present themselves in this way. Men of any age who are sick, injured, or incapacitated cover their bodies with clothing.[32]

The Suya, a Ge-speaking people who live in South America, use lip and ear ornaments to emphasize that hearing and speaking are sex-specific. At puberty, the ears of the adolescents of both sexes are pierced. Ear disks are white, a color the group associates with passivity and coolness. In their late teens, when young men begin to be considered as adults, the lower lip is also pierced. The lip disk is red, a color associated with belligerence and masculine self-assertion. Women wear an ear disk but not a lip disk. They are expected to be the audience and supply the food during ceremonies when the men are busy singing. In other words, among some people adornment places the individual in a gender category.[33]

Adornment also supports desired role behavior. The Kayapo Indians of central Brazil insist that at puberty young men wear a penis sheath to encourage sexual restraint.[34] A vulva mostly closed with scar tissue is considered beautiful among many groups from southern India to northern Africa. To be so ornamented, the women undergo a clitoridectomy, a surgical procedure in which part of the labia majora, the labia minora, and the clitoris are excised and the vulva completely closed except for a small orifice kept open by a match or a reed tube.[35]

Among many groups in Africa, Melanesia, and Indonesia, new erogenous zones are created in order to make women more desirous of sex. After menstruation begins, or when plans for marriage have been confirmed, a young woman's abdomen may be scarified or tattooed. The Tiv in Africa, for example, incise a shape called "catfish" on a woman's belly. In the language of the Tiv, this word is similar to the expression used to describe lust. The Tiv report that the scars remain tender for some years, thus heightening sexual arousal. They believe that the scars make the women more desirous of sex and therefore more likely to bear children.[36]

To succeed in an economic exchange, the Trobriand Islanders believe one should be attractive to the trading partner. The Trobrianders will not attempt a transaction, Bronislaw Malinowski (1948) reported, until they have perfumed themselves and rubbed their bodies with coconut oil, medicated leaves, and paint. When going to a faraway island, they will not get on the boat without their cosmetic kits. They adorn themselves again before disembarking, for they believe that their use of cosmetics will soften the hearts of their trading partners and lead to a more valuable exchange.[37]

The Hageners of New Guinea, too, share an elaborate network of exchange relationships with neighboring groups to achieve socioeconomic goals. These relationships are marked by ceremonial get-togethers for which the men decorate themselves lavishly with feathers, shells, and animal ornaments.[38]

Some hunting peoples decorate their bodies to resemble the animal they are after. This decoration provides camouflage and enables them to be more successful in the hunt. When stalking game, the Australian aborigines evade detection by coloring their bodies with red ocher and earth or clay; when stalking kangaroos, they disguise themselves with blue earth. Bushmen in Africa use paint, posture, sound, and movement to aid them when hunting. They paint themselves in red and yellow stripes to look like zebras, they may sway like the animal or remain perfectly still, and they imitate the animal's noises.[39]

Reshaping the infant's head by elongating its bone structure made it impossible for the individual to carry heavy burdens on his head. The practice was popular in Africa and among the Thompson Indians in the Pacific Northwest. This reshaping of an infant's head may have been a means of demonstrating affluence, i.e., having animals to carry heavy loads. It could also have been a means of escaping slavery, since it made the person useless as a beast of labor.[40]

*Film actress Sharon Stone in a fringed shawl photographed in fall 1999. A shawl shields the person from wind. The fringes are evocative of shamans, who often wear garments with fringes for healing rituals. The dances they perform around sick people are believed to create energy and scare evil spirits away. (Photo: Diane Cohen.)*

In times of war, the Hageners use body painting, facial designs, and accessories to transmit the message of fierceness and aggressive power. Their bodies are charcoaled to a deep black hue. The Hageners believe that ghosts dwell in men's hair, and a good growth is evidence of their favor and support. Baldness, on the other hand, is a sign that the ghosts have abandoned the man. They wear wigs made out of human hair, mounted on a bamboo frame, and shaped to look like a bird that had spread its wings.[41] Gathered together and identically adorned, the Hageners appear to be an overwhelming force. Fulani warriors paint themselves in bright, gaudy colors before going to war because they believe their appearance will intimidate the enemy.[42] Ethnographic reports thus reveal that groups vary greatly in their use of visual adornment as a means of creating a social identity and of performing social tasks.

Some objects that we consider adornment today were originally amulets believed to help the wearer master fears and anxieties relating to the supernatural world as well as those relating to the natural world, such as natural disasters, darkness, illness, and death. Observers of nonliterate societies—including Ruth Benedict, Sir James George Frazer, and Bronislaw Malinowski—have noted that items of dress and adornment are often endowed with supernatural qualities and are used to cope with fear of sterility, hunger, and failure. The supposed supernatural powers of these items were believed to bolster a person's courage and enable him or her to proceed with the task at hand. Since it was felt that no single amulet

*At the end of 1999, shimmering fabrics were considered good-luck charms and were popular among celebrities. The prevailing mood was described earlier by A. M. Schiro of the* New York Times *in this way: "As the Millennium rapidly approaches fashion . . . is not about mundane matters, hemlines, and silhouettes. There are intimations of a world wide recession looming, and fears that the Y2K computer glitch will disrupt communication and transportation." Oct. 27, 1998. (Photo: Diane Cohen.)*

could imbue the individual with sufficient power and protection from all nefarious forces, it was usually desirable to wear as many as possible.[43]

To increase personal power, individuals and groups wear distinctive objects, which they believe contain special strength that can be transferred to the wearer. The sparkle of rock crystal, for example, suggests that a stone possesses energy that can be called on as needed. Claws of birds of prey and other ferocious creatures and horns and tusks of wild animals are thought to have magical attributes that empower the person who wears them.[44] The Eskimo believe that an owl claw helps the wearer have strong fists, caribou ears makes the wearer quick of hearing on the hunt, and the skin of a loon carried in a kayak gives it speed.[45]

For protection against evil and malevolent forces, individuals in nonliterate societies wear amulets threaded with grass or thongs made from animal skin around the neck. Leaves, seeds, berries, nuts, and roots with unusual colors or shapes, and animals and insects such as the leopard and scarab—believed to be invested with magical powers—are copied and made into protective images. Earrings fashioned from stones in the color of the sea and sky are attached to newborn babies' ears; black soot from the burning of coconut oil at a religious shrine is put on the soles of the left feet of babies in India. To protect them from evil spirits, Eskimos have foxtails and caribou teeth sewn across their backs at shoulder height and carry bone buttons and weasel tails.[46] For the Navajo, blankets

*Bead bracelets were popular at the end of 1999. Called "power bracelets," they were believed to bring the wearer wealth, love, health, and good luck. The more strands, the greater the results. Their popularity reflected public apprehension over the prospect of Y2K computer crashes and societal disruptions predicted to begin on January 1, 2000. (Photo: Diane Cohen.)*

possess a force beyond that possessed by any single piece of apparel. They are worn for warmth, for aesthetic expression, and most important, for protection from evil.[47]

In southeast Asia handwoven cloth is often imbued with spiritual qualities that provide protection. Threads, colors, and design motifs have been credited with supernatural powers.[48] The T'boli of the southern Philippines believe that the t'nak cloth has special spiritual powers and that, apart from making clothes, the cloth should not be cut, since cutting it could result in sickness and even death. If the cloth is to be sold, a brass ring is attached to the cloth to appease the spirits. At a time of birth a woman will be covered with a T'nalack blanket to ensure safe delivery.[49] To protect themselves from harm, Mormons wear sacred undergarments called G's.[50]

Men in hazardous occupations often wear pendants as charms against seen and unseen dangers. The three most popular pendants among Catholics at this turn of the millennium are those of Saint Christopher, Saint Michael, and Saint Jude.[51] A Saint Christopher medal symbolizes safe return from a journey. Among the Romans, the palm frond was traditionally the symbol of victory. This meaning was carried into Christian symbolism. A palm-tree staff refers to the legend that Saint Christopher uprooted a palm tree to help him bear the weight of the infant Jesus whom he carried across the river. The mission complete, he thrust the staff into the ground, where it took root and bore fruit.[52] Saint Christopher is considered the patron saint of travelers.[53] When their sons are bound for war or a arduous journey, mothers give them a Saint Christopher medal.

Policemen are partial to a symbol pictured on Saint Michael's medal.[54] Saint Michael is often shown with a dragon underfoot, which represents his victory

*Ethnic fusion. A T-shirt with Chinese
letters was considered a means of
obfuscating one's identity and bringing
good luck. December 1999. (Photo:
Diane Cohen.)*

over the powers of darkness.[55] When people are in trouble, however, they ask for
Saint Jude, observed Phyllis Kunich of the Holy Land Art Company.[56] Saint Jude
is the saint for lost causes. He wrote the last epistle in the New Testament and after the death of Christ he preached the gospels in Syria and in Persia. He was
killed in Persia, either pierced by a lance or beheaded by a halberd.[57] Saint Jude's
symbol is a lance or a halberd.

To obtain a desired result, that result has to be communicated to the appropriate powers. Toward the end of 1999, as if to deflect the anxieties associated with
the end of the millennium, peddlers on city streets, department stores, and international airports offered low-cost ornaments of magical significance.[58] They
were designed to inform superhuman entities of the individual's need for protection. These included Louis Vuitton's "Good Luck" leather bracelets with sterling
silver, clover-shaped clasps, and cowhide necklaces with pendants, which were
sold in expensive airport shops.[59] Design enterprises like Anne Klein advertised
good-luck pieces such as multistrand beaded stretch bracelets in shades of light
purple, crystal, and sterling silver at affordable price levels of $12.99 and $32.00.

Buddha praying beads and Tibetan love pellets were turned into bracelets.
Their tags promised "Perfect health and happiness, good fortune, freedom from
obstacles, support of nature for success, and spiritual progress toward enlightenment."[60]

Clothing worn during an interaction that resulted in success, like attaining a
desired role or winning a game or a contract, is often worn again when a similar
outcome is desired. As reported by Philip Shenon of the *New York Times*, Energy
Secretary Bill Richardson first wore a Brooks Brothers navy blue blazer when he
was a diplomatic troubleshooter while a member of Congress. He was assigned

*Horseshoes, four-leaf clovers, and rabbit's feet are popular good-luck charms worn with the hope that they will assist the owner in achieving certain goals. Here, Dawn Bunting-Berry holds a horseshoe ornament she was given after a church wedding ceremony, Oct. 2, 1993. (Photo by Jon Rubinstein.)*

the task of freeing American hostages from Iraq, North Korea, and the Sudan. In Congress it was to become his sartorial trademark and good-luck jacket.[61]

Fifteen years later, facing the oil crisis in 2000, he resurrected the (by now) shabby suit and wore it again when he needed to convince Saudi Arabia that the dramatic jump in oil prices was threatening the world economy.[62]

Items of apparel worn in successful interactions for which the outcome could not have been predicted are thus more likely than other apparel to become a "lucky outfit." Be it a bracelet, a ring, a baseball cap, a sweater, or even a pair of socks, it may constitute good-luck clothing.

As Laver noted, however, it is often difficult to distinguish protection magic from the impulse of vanity. A necklace made from the teeth of tigers or another strong beast is both an amulet and an ornament. In both cases it has "a life-enhancing value."[63] The wearing of amulets enables a person to contend with an existing reality. It may also have an indirect effect on role behavior.

## Notes

1. A. Ortíz (1969), *The Tewa World Book: Space, Time, Being, and Becoming in a Pueblo Society.* (Chicago: University of Chicago Press.)

2. Dr. Ortíz earned his bachelor's degree in sociology from the University of New Mexico in 1961 and his master's and doctoral degrees in anthropology at the University of Chicago in 1967—G. Johnson (1997), "Alfonso Ortíz, 57, Anthropologist of the Pueblo, Dies," *New York Times,* Friday, Jan. 31.

3. P. Stubbs (1583), *Anatomy of Abuses.* Quoted in J. Laver (1969), *Modesty in Dress* (Boston: Houghton Mifflin), p. 22.

4. T. Veblen (1953), *The Theory of the Leisure Class* (New York: Mentor Books) (originally published in 1899). Also G. Simmel (1957), "Fashion," *American Journal of Sociology* 62: 294–295 (originally published in 1905). Both authors examined social-class distinctions, clothing, and their impact on the self and society.

5. J. Laver (1969), *Modesty in Dress* (Boston: Houghton Mifflin), pp. 9–11.

6. In S. Lyman (1978), *The Seven Deadly Sins: Society and Evil* (New York: St. Martin's Press), pp. 54–57. Also Laver, op. cit., p. 17.

7. Lyman, op. cit., p. 56.

8. Laver, op. cit., p. 9.

9. Ibid., pp. 20–25.

10. L. H. Newburgh, ed. (1968), *The Physiology of Heat Regulation and the Science of Clothing* (New York: Stretchet Haffner).

11. F. R. Wulsin (1968), "Adaptation to Climate Among Non-European peoples," pp. 26–30 in Newburgh, op. cit.

12. Quoted in Wulsin, op. cit., p. 31.

13. D. Hardy (1968), "Heat Transfer," pp. 65–93 in Newburgh, op. cit.; also H. C. Bazett (1968), "The Regulation of Body Temperature," pp. 109–117 in Newburgh, op. cit.

14. Wulsin, op. cit., pp. 4–25.

15. W. H. Forbes (1968), "Laboratory Field Studies: General Principles," in Newburgh, op. cit., pp. 320–329.

16. Wulsin, op. cit., pp. 4–11; also Forbes, op. cit., pp. 323–324.

17. Wulsin, op. cit., pp. 57–53.

18. Ibid., pp. 38–47.

19. Forbes, op. cit.

20. G. B. Boyer (1995), *Elegance: A Guide to Quality in Menswear* (New York: W. W. Norton), p. 218–231.

21. Boyer, op. cit., p. 231.

22. Ibid., p. 221.

23. Ibid., pp. 219, 223.

24. An advertisement in the *New York Times,* Dec. 12, 1999, p. 12.

25. *GEICO Direct,* Spring 1999, p. 6.

26. Ibid.

27. T. Carlyle (1967), *Sartor Resartus* (New York: Dutton), p. 2. Originally published in 1838.

28. Ibid., pp. 1–47.

29. R. P. Rubinstein (1985), "Color, Circumcision, Tattoos and Scars," in *The Psychology of Fashion,* ed. M. R. Solomon (Lexington, Mass.: D.C. Heath), pp. 243–254.

30. R. Brain (1979), *The Decorated Body* (New York: Harper and Row), p. 86; V. Ebin (1979), *The Body Decorated* (London: Thames and Hudson), pp. 42–44; J. C. Faris (1972), *Nuba Personal Art* (London: Duckworth).

31. Brain, op. cit., p. 70.

32. Faris, op. cit., p. 8.

33. A. Seeger (1975), "The Meaning of Body Ornament," *Ethnology* 14: 218.

34. T. S. Turner (1979) "Social Structure and Political Organization of Northern Kayapop," Ph.D. diss., Harvard University.

35. Brain, op. cit., p. 86.

36. Ibid., pp. 50, 78.

37. B. Malinowski (1948), *Magic, Science and Religion and Other Essays* (Garden City, N.Y.: Doubleday Anchor). Originally published in 1925.

38. A. M. Strathern (1971), *Self Decoration in Mount Hagen* (Toronto: University of Toronto Press).

39. Brain, op. cit., p. 86.

40. D. Hemenway (1993), *Prices and Choices: Microeconomic Vignettes,* 2d ed. (Cambridge, Mass.: Ballinger), p. 36.

41. Brain, op. cit., pp. 40–41.

42. Ibid., p. 42; J. G. Frazer (1959), *The New Golden Bough,* ed. T. H. Gaster (New York: Criterion Books), p. 17.

43. W.E.A. Budge and W. Thompson (1961), *Amulets and Talismans* (New Hyde Park, N.Y.: University Books), pp. 14, 19, 27.

44. Frazer, op. cit., pp. 401–446; R. Benedict (1933), "Magic," in *Encyclopedia of Social Sciences,* vol. 10 (New York: Macmillan), pp. 39–44.

45. L. M. Gurel (1979), "Eskimos' Clothing and Culture," in *Dimensions of Dress and Adornment: A Book of Readings,* ed. L. M. Gurel and M. S. Beeson (Dubuque, Iowa: Kendall/Hunt ), p. 41.

46. S. Fraser-Lu (1989) *Handwoven Textiles of South-East Asia.* (Oxford, Eng.: Oxford University Press), pp. 9–11; also Gurel, op. cit., p. 42.

47. M. H. Kahlenberg and A. Berlant (1972), *The Navajo Blanket* (New York: Praeger); also G. Witherspoon (1977), *Language and Art in the Navajo Universe* (Ann Arbor: University of Michigan Press).

48. Frazer, op. cit., pp. 73–74.

49. Frazer-Lu, op. cit., p. 165.

50. "Glossary," *New York Times,* May 31, 1998.

51. S. Talty (1998) "Something to Watch over Me," *New York Times,* May 3.

52. G. Ferguson (1977), *Signs and Symbols in Christian Art* (New York: Oxford University Press), pp. 36, 45.

53. Talty, op. cit.

54. Ibid.

55. Ferguson, op. cit., p. 12.

56. Talty, op. cit.

57. Ferguson, op. cit., p. 227.

58. H. Paul (1979), *Magic and Superstition.* (New York: Hill and Wang.)

59. E. Hayt (1999), "What I'm Wearing Now, The Fashion Model Agent," *New York Times,* Dec. 5.

60. Advertisement in the *New York Times.* Dec. 12, 1999.

61. P. Shenon (2000), "The Magic Blue Blazer vs. an Oily Patch of Bad Luck," *New York Times,* Mar. 13.

62. Ibid.

63. Laver, op. cit., p. 3.

# Part Two:

# Characteristics of Modern Social Discourse

# 3

# New Institutional
# Patterns of Discourse

INSTITUTIONAL PATTERNS of discourse are the organized, formally established procedures for pursuing a given objective. Such patterns consist of the usual and expected methods by which people acquire goods and services, engage in commerce and industry, and obtain official appointments. They form the standard against which the conduct of decision makers and other individuals is measured. Clothing is an essential part of the entire process.

What a political authority considers good or desirable is a reflection of the ideas and values underlying institutional patterns of discourse. It is significant that the values of a political authority are portrayed in the basic style of *male* dress. (Female style is another matter.) When impatience with established political authority develops to the extent that a new group with different values gains power, the pattern of discourse is altered, as is the basic style of male dress.

The early Church Fathers instituted the human body as the principal expressive vehicle for individual and social values.[1] The monarchs of the royal courts, as well as the Protestant reformers, continued this tradition. The aristocracy, for whom wealth was essential and physical labor contemptible, adored pomp and splendor. In contrast, the Puritans and the bourgeoisie found security and comfort in work. They abhorred ostentatious displays of wealth and power and dressed in attire characterized by simplicity, order, and durability.

The Commercial Revolution of the fourteenth century brought new cultural values: individualism and economic success. With these new values came a basic change in the style of male dress. Loose-fitting monochromatic robes that hid the body were replaced by body-hugging, multicolored attire. The subsequent Industrial Revolution of the nineteenth century introduced rationality as the principal value underlying economic discourse. The basic style of male dress changed again; it became somber in color and was tailored essentially to hide the body. In Western society, therefore, changes in the political power structure and in the mode of economic discourse usually go hand in hand with changes in the basic style of male dress.

## Spirituality and the Denial of the Body

Until the fourteenth century, spirituality was society's core value, and religious piety, humility, and modesty governed most social discourse. Spiritual authorities thought it appropriate to distinguish between themselves and laypersons. Further distinctions were made within the ranks of the clergy, such as between cardinals and bishops. Thus the church created a hierarchy of social significance emulating that of the military.[2]

Unlike the Romans, who had conceived of the body as a neutral thing placed between nature and society, Christian leaders saw the body as a clearly visible locus of spiritual order, subject to certain limits with regard to religious teachings. In the first century AD, the apostle Paul explained that the body is merely an "earthly vessel" to be infused by the Holy Spirit.[3] Early Christian writers insisted that what separates Christians from non-Christians is spirituality. Sexual desire, the consumption of food, and the longing for sensuous garments must be curtailed, not only to maintain personal spirituality, but to protect the Christian community as a whole. In the second century AD, for example, the church father Tertullian warned: "With their alluring hairstyles and disturbingly unveiled faces," the women of Carthage could breach the defenses of the Church and gain an entry into the "somber assemblies of the male saints."[4]

In the fourth century, Ambrose likened the body to a perilous mud slick on which the individual might slip and tumble at any moment. However, the heaving powers of the flesh could be "reformed." The flesh could be made perfect by having been taken up, in Christ, by God himself. Conversion and baptism were a means of sharing in the tranquillity that flowed from the spotless flesh of Christ. Christian leaders agreed that sexual continence or long periods of abstinence— that is, suppressing bodily needs—made it possible for a Christian to achieve communion with God. The laity and the married priesthood were advised to live with their wives "as if they were not wives," to bear children yet live the rest of their lives abstaining from sexual intercourse. An orientation toward the spiritual was the expected public and private demeanor.[5]

The connection between religious piety and the asexual body was encouraged by pilgrimages to the shrines of the martyrs, which contained the bones of "men and women on whom the Holy Spirit has come to rest." In the fifth and sixth centuries, and again during the later Middle Ages, these shrines were visited with increasing fervor. They were portrayed as places where new life and healing bubbled up for the faithful from the cold graves of the dead.[6]

Monochromatic, body-concealing attire that denied the very existence of the physical body was worn from the beginning of the Christian Era until the mid-fourteenth century.[7] It consisted of a tunic with a cloak or a robe of varying length. It was essentially the same for men and women. When minor modifications of style did occur, they were visible only in details, such as changes in the manner of fastening the tunic or variations in the length of the robe. The basic

*Robed attire from the Middle Ages. (Illustration from W. Bruhn and M. Tilke,* A Pictorial History of Costume. *Copyright 1955 [New York: Praeger], an imprint of Greenwood Publishing Group, Inc., Westport, Conn. Reprinted with permission.)*

loose-fitting style remained unquestioned and unaltered for more than a thousand years.

Nonetheless, the type of cloth and ornament served to differentiate the social classes. Evidence of superior rank was "carried" on the backs of the nobility. Bedecked with all the jewels and gold they could muster, members of the upper classes competed with one another through their sumptuous garments. By law, damask, velvet, and satin could be used only by nobles; broadcloth was reserved for burghers; and the poor wore whatever they could come by.[8] Thus, a fabric hierarchy paralleled the social hierarchy.

## Renaissance Individualism and Economic Success

In the fourteenth century a politically independent, urban, and affluent commercial class rejected much of the medieval ideology of fixed social positions and strict standards for behavior. Its leaders also objected to the Church's attempt to curtail commerce by the usury laws, which served to prevent economic growth, and other obstacles. Rejecting the Church's ideal of modesty, the rising commercial classes wore attire that celebrated individual initiative, announced pride in personal economic success, and demonstrated some degree of freedom from sexual constraints.[9]

Beginning most likely in Italy in the middle of the fourteenth century, young men in the towns abandoned the traditional loose-fitting gown in favor of attire that hugged the body and celebrated its physical attributes. A short, fitted jacket,

*Body-hugging attire of the Renaissance, shown in an illustration portraying a reception and banquet at the court of the Duke of Burgundy. (Miniature from the* Geschichte des Karl Martell *[History of Charles Martell]. Painted by Loyset Liédet, 1470. Illustration from W. Bruhn and M. Tilke,* A Pictorial History of Costume. *Copyright 1955 [New York: Praeger], an imprint of Greenwood Publishing Group, Inc., Westport, Conn. Reprinted with permission.)*

drawstring shirt, and long, tight hose clung to and exposed the forms of the body. The codpiece, a visible covering for the male genitals, was padded and protruding, suggesting aggressive virility. The tight hose, in combination with the codpiece, dramatized male genitalia in a manner and to a degree that was unprecedented.[10] Male clothing became form-fitting, colorful, playful, and personal. Men could adopt any variation in color and ornament they desired.

In a sixteenth-century Renaissance guidebook to manners for aspiring gentlemen, *The Courtier,* Balthasar Castiglione defended young men against "aging reactionaries" who attacked the new style. He argued that it was appropriate for the young "to strut and swagger in bright colors and snug contours appropriate to [their] natural energy, beauty and sexual drive."[11] In addition, the new clothing articulated for the first time "the biological distinctions" between the sexes.

Whereas the loose-fitting unisex clothing of the medieval period was replaced by short, tight costumes for men, women's dresses now had snug busts, daring décolletages, and long skirts, the latter hampering physical mobility.[12]

The new Renaissance style symbolized a shift from preoccupation with the spiritual to interest in worldly matters, the here and now. Upper-class and middle-class urban dwellers had found a way to display their new power and manifest their pride in the world they were building.

## Modern Rationality

The rediscovery of the classics during the Renaissance, the religious skepticism initiated by the Reformation, and the academic rationalism that had advanced into both the Protestant and Catholic traditions provided groundwork for the belief that objective analysis is the most direct and valid approach to understanding the physical and social universe.

Printing facilitated the spread of new ideas. The Reformation is typically portrayed as a movement that replaced a priestly religion with a *religion of the book*. In a sense, Protestantism was created by people reading and raising questions about religious beliefs and practices. Printing facilitated the dissemination of information and made it possible to evaluate and compare texts. Further, people could respond to written texts with further observations and analyses.[13] Since authors, unlike speakers, could not see their public to gauge their response, they were forced to make more elaborate and extensive arguments so that a more complete idea would be available. Moreover, texts were arranged in chapters and paragraphs and were indexed by page. As Chandra Mukerji (1983) argued, this internal orderliness furthered the impression of a text as a complete system.[14]

Increasingly, European academicians perceived nature as a single system of finite materials and forces accessible to human comprehension. By the beginning of the nineteenth century the scientific method—observation, measurement, and comparisons—had become widely accepted and rationality had become essential to the study of social and physical phenomena. From this worldview emerged a style of dress and adornment that favored self-restraint.

Until the French Revolution, the image of the proper appearance for a gentleman emanated from France. The attire was elaborate: a waistcoat of rich velvet, damask, or satin embroidered with petit point and emblazoned with gold, silver, or enameled buttons; a shirt with a frilled ruffle; close-fitting breeches buttoned just below knee, where they met silk stockings; and a coat that fitted the body down to the waist and then flared away in soft folds. Vented in the back and elaborately braided, the coat was always left unbuttoned so that the ornate waistcoat could be seen. Gold and silver buckles were worn on belts, garters, and shoes; a heavy gold and silver chain hung from the neck and from waistcoat pockets. The tricorn, or three-cornered hat, weighed down with braid and other ornaments, completed the sumptuous outfit.[15] However, as members of the business and

*Costumes Parisiens.*

"A Stroll," 1815. *Male dress saw a transition from traditional style—where male dress was sumptuous and body-hugging, signifying sexuality and economic success—to the modern expectation for male behavior—long pants and tall hat, representing self-restraint and the male as the person of authority. (M. Braun-Ronsdorf [1964],* Mirror of Fashion: A History of European Costume 1789–1929. *[New York: McGraw-Hill].)*

*"Gentleman's Wear," 1882. By the end of the nineteenth century, color, ornament, and body-revealing styles were rejected. The newly established style was the prototype of the contemporary business suit, signifying rationality and self-restraint.(M. Braun-Ronsdorf [1964],* Mirror of Fashion: A History of European Costume 1789–1929. *[New York: McGraw-Hill].)*

professional classes acquired economic and political power in the late eighteenth century, they rejected the rich color, gay ornament, and embroidered frills of the aristocracy. They discarded the pomp and expense of the traditional style in favor of clothes that proclaimed a more *rational* use of resources. The new style was based on the attire chosen by professional men in England in the second half of the seventeenth century, after the Puritan Revolution. The attire was somber, austere, and nondistracting—so that people could better focus on the task at hand. The clothing was designed to represent mastery over one's feelings and to demonstrate rationality, the state of making decisions on the basis of calculation, organization, abstract rules, and procedures.

Charles-Pierre Baudelaire saw the modern man's outfit that had emerged a generation or two later—the gray or black suit—as a symbol of a suffering age and of perpetual mourning.[16] In Baudelaire's view, modern life was loathsome and empty of even the potential for beauty, and the dark suit was the appropriate garb.[17] Described by Flugel as "the great masculine renunciation," this change in the basic style of male dress was profound, essentially involving a rejection of sensuality and individuality. Breeches, the style of pants favored by the aristocracy because they revealed the shape of the leg, were rejected in favor of long trousers such as those worn by sailors and farmers. The long pants provided a measure of protection and symbolized activity and utility. Instead of the customary form-fitting style that displayed each individual's physical attributes, a form-following style that hid nearly all personal features, desirable and undesirable alike, was now preferred.[18]

This change in attire involved all social classes, from the king and members of Parliament to the fruit and vegetable vendors in the marketplace. Only the quality of fabric and fit differentiated the social classes. Men were now concerned with being dressed in "correct" and useful attire.[19] Renouncing color, ornament, frills, embroidery, velvet, and rich colors in favor of plain dark suits composed of a jacket, vest, and trousers, men left the brighter, more elaborate, and varied forms of ornamentation entirely to women.

Fashion historian René König (1973) describes the change in this manner: The 1789 revolution in France set the stage for the Puritans to "steer the course of new developments," and their values came to characterize modern dress. König asserted that "the man's suit of today, is fundamentally a direct descendant of the puritan dress, a political demonstration against the ostentation of the courts."[20] Male attire became desexualized and austere. There was another factor that helped establish this style, however: after the Revolution the nobility in France hid behind long trousers, ragged or dirty clothes, beards, and a generally seedy look in order to avoid losing their lives.[21]

German sociologist Norbert Elias described the change in attire in a similar manner: "In the industrializing countries the ideals, hopes and long-term goals of the rising industrial classes gradually gained advantage over those seeking to preserve the existing social order in the interests of the established courtly dynastic, aristocratic or patrician power elites."[22] Education and talent largely overshadowed birthright as the important conditions for employment. Hence, the style of dress that proclaimed the aristocracy's values was no longer viable. By the mid-nineteenth century, rationality had displaced feudal loyalty as the principal basis for social discourse and institutional arrangements.

## Notes

1. In "The Body versus the Social Body in the Works of Thomas Malthus and Henry Mayhew," Catherine Gallagher observed that a two-millennia tradition sees the individual body as a sign of health or infirmity of the larger social body. In C. Gallagher and T. Lacquer, eds. (1987), *The Making of the Modern Body: Sexuality and Society in the Nineteenth Century* (Berkeley: University of California Press), p. 83.

2. P. Hughes (1948) *A History of the Church* (London: Sheed & Ward).

3. P. Brown (1988), *The Body and Society: Men, Women and Sexual Renunciation in Early Christianity* (New York: Columbia University Press) p. 51.

4. Ibid., p. 149.

5. Ibid., p. 443.

6. Ibid., pp. 272–273; also M. Chambers et al. (1974), *The Western Experience* (New York: Knopf) p. 406; C. F. Lawrence (1981), "The German 'Bauernkrieg' of 1525: Organization and Action in Peasant Revolt," Ph.D. diss., New School for Social Research, New York City. (Available through University of Michigan Microfilm International.)

7. M. and A. Batterberry (1977), *Fashion: The Mirror of History* (New York: Greenwich House), p. 73; F. Boucher (1965), *20,000 Years of Fashion* (New York: Harry N. Abrams), p. 164.

8. Boucher, op. cit., pp. 162–163; A. Hollander (1978), *Seeing Through Clothes* (New York: Viking) p. 363.

9. L. G. Deruisseau (1939), "Dress Fashions of the Italian Renaissance," *CIBA Review* (Jan.): 589–594; also Batterberry, op. cit., pp. 94–95.

10. A. Ribiero (1986), *Dress and Morality* (London: Batsford). In "Visual Art As Social Data: The Renaissance Codpiece," G. Q. Vicay argued that the hardened construction of the codpiece served as a container for medicine. Syphilis had struck Europe. She suggested that the codpiece may have been used for protection, but it was probably also used as a container for mercury salts and unrefined animal grease used to treat the infected penis. See G. Q. Vicary (1989), "Visual Art As Social Data: The Renaissance Codpiece," *Cultural Anthropology* 4(1): 3–25.

11. Cited in Batterberry, op. cit., p. 101.

12. Hollander, op. cit., pp. 214–216.

13. E. Eisenstein (1979), *The Printing Press As an Agent of Change* (New York: Cambridge University Press).

14. C. Mukerji (1983), *From Graven Images: Patterns of Modern Materialism* (New York: Columbia University Press), pp. 98, 142–164.

15. J. Laver (1963), *Costume* (New York: Hawthorne Books), pp. 67–81; also R. König (1973), *A la Mode* (New York: Seabury Press), pp. 84–85; J. C. Flugel (1966), *The Psychology of Clothes* (London: Hogarth Press), p. 111 (originally published in 1930).

16. M. Berman (1982), *All That Is Solid Melts into Air: The Experience of Modernity* (New York: Simon and Schuster), p. 143.

17. Berman, op. cit., p. 140.

18. Flugel, op. cit., pp. 110–111.

19. König, op. cit., p. 157.

20. Ibid.

21. Hollander, op. cit., p. 385.

22. N. Elias (1978), *The Civilizing Process: The Development of Manners* (New York: Urizon Books), p. 235.

# 4

# Dressing the Public Self

## Sociocultural Background

The centralization of production in the nineteenth century took place in the cities, and cities became magnets for people from rural areas searching for work opportunities and upward mobility. Their new social environment became a place where they could construct new identities. Life in the city necessarily involved meeting a variety of people and mingling with strangers. It was perceived as full of complexities.[1]

Behavior that was personal and unique was expected to be relegated to the private realm and not expressed in the workplace. Men had to become actors. Just as actors on the stage touched people's feelings without revealing their own offstage characters, people in the public sphere concealed private imagery and individual feelings. The desire to suppress and shield the personal self led to common codes of belief, the terms of which were familiar to others. In public, people had to be sociable on impersonal grounds. Their attire acquired new formality. It was contrived with regard to the requirements of a social situation, to the specific status held, and to the officially specified goals of the organizations for which they worked.

In the United States toward the end of the nineteenth century, there was a gradual shift from manufacturing to a service economy rooted in commercial, professional, and technical relationships, as C. Wright Mills observed. This shift further encouraged self-restraint. More individuals became involved in the public workplace. The division of labor in modern American society involved a "hitherto unknown specialization of skill: the ability to deal with paper, money and symbols." The new class at first consisted mostly of men, "who are expert at dealing with people transiently and impersonally," Mills pointed out. He called this new occupational category "white-collar workers" because they wore clothing to work that was generally suitable for street wear—white shirts, gray wool pants, and jackets.[2]

The distinction between clothing worn in the industrial production sector and that worn in the emerging service sector was confirmed in a 1955 study of occupational clothing by W. H. Form and G. P. Stone.[3] They found that overalls, aprons, or other protective garb identified manual workers, whereas suits and sport jackets identified professional, commercial, and technical service workers.

Clothing discourse in the United States in the twentieth century was shaped by the political and economic changes that had taken place in the nineteenth century. With industrialization, centralization of production, and the movement of the workplace out of the home, two distinct realms of interaction emerged—the public and the private.[4] *Goal-directed* behavior and *self-restraint* became the preferred modes of deportment in the public place. In contrast to the body-hugging style worn by the aristocracy, the new desired appearance consisted of a loose-fitting three-piece suit in a somber color, a white shirt, and a tie—familiar and often required attire in the United States until the last decade of the twentieth century—which conveyed in a visual form the desired modes of conduct.

## The Demise of Male Fashion

After the French Revolution, scions of aristocratic families in France and England were ridiculed for constructing highly elaborate sartorial expressions.[5] Literary, academic, and social critics denigrated their attempts. In France they were called "les incroyables et les merveilleuses" (the incredible and the marvelous ones). In England, Carlyle labeled them dandies and "dandiacals"—"social parasites who glorified themselves, not God."[6] These young men followed Count D'Orsay (b. 1801), a good-looking man who rejected somber colors and loose-fitting suits in favor of tight-fitting suits in shimmering pastels and soft velvet and silks, and who wore perfumes and jewels. He sought to create an artistic expression that enhanced his physical presence.[7]

In the 1880s, Oscar Wilde and Max Beerbohm attempted to challenge the negative image associated with men attractively attired in exquisitely tailored costumes. They claimed that beauty and art were an essential dimension of a well-lived life. The reaction was strong. Men who looked beautiful continued to be denigrated as not being men.[8]

In France in the second half of the nineteenth century, where men were expected to be involved in commerce, business, and the professions, Napoleon III decreed that the only clothes appropriate for men were the military uniform, the riding habit, and the English gentleman's business suit. The task of expressing French taste and the opulent spirit of the period fell to women and was carried out through female dress and a feminine fashion ideal. The French fashion industry today continues to receive government support, and it remains the world's most important laboratory for style and fashion.[9]

## Goal-Directed Behavior

In the United States, at least since the beginning of the twentieth century, goal-directed behavior has been the standard in industrial production. The goal of sci-

*Time came to be perceived differently in the nine-*
*teenth century. Precision timing characterized the*
*reality of urbanization and industrialization. The*
*importance of punctuality is conveyed by the fig-*
*ure of the White Rabbit in* Alice in Wonderland.
*(Illustration by Sir John Tenniel [1896].)*

entific management studies has been to eliminate wasted motion. The worker
had to perform the job exactly as described by managers, who knew the fastest
way to perform necessary tasks. The studies conducted by Frederic Taylor (1911)
were designed to create humans who performed with machinelike precision and
speed. Comedians from Charles Chaplin to Lucille Ball have, of course, ridiculed
this concept by dramatizing its inhuman quality.[10]

Goal-directed behavior has also come to characterize business relations. In a
recent report on the problems Americans face in conducting business in Eastern
Europe, business consultant Fred Martin observed that directness and clearly
stated goals hampered the ability of his client, an American businessman, to accomplish his purpose. The client sought to rent space for a copy shop in Hungary
after its conversion to a market economy. Hungarians observe formalities, are
careful to preserve the dignity of the situation, and are therefore circumspect,
Martin explained. The American businessman tried to convince the officials that
they would benefit by granting him the appropriate space. He kept repeating that
this was a mutual partnership, and he told them of the large sums of money he
was prepared to invest. The Hungarians, however, viewed his direct approach as
an attempt to hide the real purpose of his request and considered him dishonest.
His lack of proper attire further provoked their suspicion. They believed that any
legitimate businessman would wear a suit and a tie. (In general, informal attire is
associated with self-expression and personal goals, rather than a more enduring,
formalized economic transaction.)[11] In this situation, the businessman did not
support his goal-directed behavior by wearing the self-restrained business attire
of the public place.

*International suit. The shoulders and lapels are wider than in other Brooks Brothers suits offered in 1993. It is designed to imbue the person with a greater degree of authority. Brooks Brothers advertised the suit as right for any business environment.*

## The Norm of Self-Restraint

The norm of self-restraint, reinforced by dress, makes possible the success of goal-directed behavior. Attire that denies the body leads to self-restraint. This idea, which is basic to Christian beliefs, includes the injunction to modesty and codes of dress devised for priests and monastic orders, requiring that the body be covered from head to toe. Not until the Renaissance, when the notion of individual self-expression assumed importance, were parts of the body exposed.

An essential element of male dress that is symbolic of holding in one's feelings is the neckcloth or tie. Historically, in England and the United States some men wore neckpieces that were starched to preserve the proper folds. Others favored wearing two cravats at the same time—a white one wound twice around the neck and a black silk one tied over it. Stiff collars and cuffs also became important accessories.[12]

It was not until the growth of bureaucracies in the 1940s that the tie emerged in the United States as a required accessory for white-collar workers. A *New York Times* op-ed article entitled "A Diploma, a Tie and a Lie," by a graduate journalism student, described the personal impact of wearing a tie. The author, Greg Spring, complained that when he wore a tie to job interviews, he said things that did not reflect his individual concerns and interests. His behavior at the interviews was "tailored" to meet the social expectations that he get a job regardless of where it was and what he was expected to do. The attire structured his responses and prevented him from stating his personal preferences.[13]

Responding to the story, working journalist Scott R. Schmedel affirmed the observation that a jacket, shirt, and tie represent a public self that has incorporated the societal expectation of self-restraint. He wrote that although he does not allow himself the time to put on a tie, he nevertheless mistrusts the "spongy opinions of people committed to jeans, people who let it all hang out—hair, shirttail, shoe laces, moral superiority." To strangers, the manner in which the individual is dressed, the author suggested, seems to reflect the hidden self. "When I do put on my pressed suit instead of my baggy blazer, and my polished shoes, and I carefully knot a four-in-hand or a half Windsor, I find I stand a little taller. I am reminded of my professional commitment, my responsibility to society—to be upstanding, perceptive, accurate." The suit, polished shoes, and tie deny personal preferences and feelings; they emphasize the social role. Schmedel continued, "When you feel you are losing your grip the act of tying a necktie may pull everything together."[14] The tie helps to integrate the public self.

On the other hand, the act of removing one's shirt is associated with the expression of angry personal feelings. Examining the origins of the expression "keep your shirt on" in a *New York Times Magazine* article, lexicographer William Safire explained that it implied strong displeasure. The picture it brings to mind is that of a person tearing his shirt off to fight with someone. "The unshirted one is angry and ready to give hell to the clothed recipient." In keeping calm, you keep your shirt on.[15] The earliest reference to the phrase "keep your shirt on" appears in Hotten's slang dictionary published in England in 1859.

The institution of a dress code for taxi drivers confirms the idea that wearing a proper shirt is generally recognized as encouraging self-restraint. In a news story entitled "A Dress Code for Cabbies: No T-shirts," Richard Levin reported that New York City regulations prohibit cabbies from wearing T-shirts, tank tops, tube tops, and body shirts. They must wear shirts with a collar and sleeves. The purpose of the code, according to the authorities, is "to professionalize the drivers."[16]

## Presentation of the Public Self

### Spheres of Interaction

Encouraging the trust of those one does not know is difficult in a world full of strangers and in modern impersonal work relationships. The clothing one wears may demonstrate that one is aware of the behavior expected of those with the status one holds.[17] Individuals take great pains to have others consider them rational, noted Erving Goffman. They attempt to project the desired image, knowing that people read significance into such cues as manner of dress, body position,

*President Clinton dressed for front-stage performance. The president is shown walking to the East Room of the White House on November 10, 1993, for a news conference.*

gestures, and facial expressions. They may make use of "props," elements *not* necessary to the performance of a task, such as a beard, a pipe, or an expensive attaché case. The clothing and props reflect the extended reach of the modern workplace. The meaning and importance of appearance in the public place, however, depend on its relevance to social rewards. Goffman identified three interactional spaces: *front stage, backstage,* and *outside region.* In identifying these three regions of interaction, Goffman inadvertently explained the diversity of appearance on city streets, where the public is left with the impression that "anything goes."[18]

### Front Stage

Drawing a parallel between performing in the theater and appearing in public, Goffman divided everyday situations into his three categories of significance. A park setting may be a front-stage situation for members of a sports team who are required to wear appropriate attire to play. Yet a man relaxing in the park may loosen his tie and take off his jacket. He is unfettered by interactional constraints, and his chances of receiving social criticism or rewards for this behavior are minimal.

Teachers in the classroom, physicians in the office or operating room, and guests at a dinner party announce, through appropriate attire and demeanor, that they will perform their roles in the socially expected manner. Personal feelings will be withheld and the norms of politeness and decorum will prevail. Before entering the space where front-stage performance is to take place, Goffman pointed out, men usually make sure that they are clean-shaven and neatly dressed, with hair in place and face and hands immaculate. They check their appearance to ascertain, for example, that their trouser zippers are closed. Women are expected to exercise "limb discipline." Many take care that their undergarments and upper thighs are concealed when they walk and sit.[19]

According to Goffman, the dropping of one's "personal front" (a standard persona regularly employed by the individual, such as gender identity) or the failure to present oneself in a "situational harness" is likely to be taken as a sign of disregard for the other participants and as an act of distancing oneself from the social world of those present on the front stage. As Goffman commented, people who are unkempt in formal situations, women who wear dresses or skirts but sit with legs wide apart, and men who forget to zip their trousers all exhibit deviant behavior (though to different degrees) that disrupts the flow of orderly communication and interaction. The most obvious means by which individuals show their acceptance of social roles and their awareness of the demands of social situations is through their appearance.

### Backstage

Backstage, according to Goffman, is the interactional space in which individuals prepare their "personal front" for front-stage performance. It is the place where a person can assume that no member of the "audience" will intrude. A beauty parlor, a department store dressing room, and a locker room are all front-stage areas for the beautician, the store salesperson, and the coach. However, for users of such services they are backstage areas. Here, an individual is free to dress informally, behave emotionally, and manipulate his or her appearance to create a desired identity. The attire worn may represent the person's feelings, attitude, or mood. In American society, a bathroom is normally a backstage space. People expect to clean and clothe themselves in private. Observing someone prepare for a front-stage performance may detract from the desired effect. A young man is usually shielded from seeing his date in hair rollers, just as the groom often does not see his bride before the ceremony.

In certain settings a backstage can be turned into a front stage. A gym was once a place where people went to keep their bodies in shape for their performance in front-stage situations. How they looked in the gym was of little concern. Today's "singles," however, use gyms and health clubs as meeting places. They carefully plan their work-out and warm-up outfits to appear attractive to the opposite sex.

### Outside Region

While the front stage is a place where performances take place and the backstage is a place where people prepare for front-stage performances, the outside region is the place where appearance is the least socially significant. Attire may be incomplete, Goffman suggested, because the situation is not formally connected to a role performance, and one's appearance is left to the immediate circumstances and the individual's momentary needs. Here, the individual is "outside" prescribed role relationships. There are no social expectations, and he or she need not demonstrate any particular expertise. Models hurrying to their assignments carry the clothing and accessories needed to complete their appearance for the photo shoot. Individuals often do not bother to dress well to run a neighborhood errand. In cities, women commonly rush to work wearing sneakers, with their business suits and work shoes in their briefcases.

Dress for the backstage or the outside region may acquire an unexpected significance and may tip the balance. Salespersons and airline personnel, it has been reported, are likely to be more helpful if a man wears a suit and if a woman wears a dress or a fitted suit.[20] In the 1990s the airline industry's standards of service and comfort for passengers flying coach declined. Passengers were being packed into "cattle cars," and flying became a grind. Many passengers found that wearing comfortable clothes such as T-shirts, sweatsuits, and sneakers made travel easier.

Airline staff, however, along with staff at most hotels and aboard cruise ships, report that they are often influenced by customers' appearance. Shoppers and travelers are more likely to receive a service they request if they are respectably dressed. Airline managers, moreover, require that those being upgraded to first-class be properly attired. Reporter Aline Sullivan suggests that the decision to "dress down" should be reconsidered.[21]

Attending the theater used to be front-stage performance requiring formal attire, but the theater seems to have become an outside region in which many who attend have no concern for negative sanctions. In "Notes on Fashion," *New York Times* fashion reporter Michael Gross complained that jogging suits, sneakers, and T-shirts were worn by audience members at the New York premiere of *Pygmalion* in 1987.[22] He commented that Broadway openings once epitomized cosmopolitan glamour, but in this setting the well-dressed have become a distinct minority.

## Stability of Appearance

Nursery-school teachers, judges, ushers, health-care personnel, ward attendants, and supervisors, among others, are guardians of tradition who formally or informally identify the boundaries of acceptable appearance. They are gatekeepers, in that they prevent those inappropriately dressed from entering or ask them to leave. In Goffman's view these guardians of tradition help to create stability in appearance.[23]

The media often consider such cases news, as seen in the following examples. The *New York Times* reported that the school board in Pharr, Texas, refused to waive the dress code for a four-year-old boy whose parents maintained that they had promised God that they would not cut his shoulder-length hair until they were certain that he was free from cancer. The board ruled that the school had the right to bar the boy from classes.[24] One of the most publicized examples of trying to maintain a standard of appearance involved Don Mattingly, first baseman for the Yankees. In addition to its being a news story in the sports pages, it was used in the "Quotations of the Day" section of the *New York Times*. The baseball team's manager was quoted as saying "If someone from management says you need a haircut, then you get a haircut." Mattingly's response was "Maybe I don't belong in the organization anymore." His answer reveals his awareness that standards of appearance affect employment. However, the *New York Times* reported that by the next day Mattingly had gotten his hair cut.[25]

A business suit devoid of ornament has been adjudged by the courts as the proper attire for lawyers appearing before them. On March 19, 1980, a New York appeals court ruled that priests who are lawyers may not wear clerical attire to court. In June 1992 a judge in Washington, D.C., banned an African-American lawyer from wearing an ethnic neckpiece of African Kente cloth, which partially covered his suit.[26] A suit is also the required attire for lawyers in public employment. And on May 2, 1991, a headline on the editorial page of the *New York Times* announced, "Legal Code: Goodbye Jeans." The editorial related that a memo had been sent to the 143 assistant prosecutors at the U.S. district courthouse in Brooklyn, informing them that during business hours they were to wear "dress appropriate for a law office." Coming to work at the office (when not scheduled to appear in court) in jeans and open-collar polo shirts was described in the memo as "a little too laid back" and unprofessional.[27]

## Stigma Symbols

Looking unkempt and wearing torn clothing violate cultural emphasis on neatness and cleanliness. Such appearance may have an effect on the *face* a person claims.[28] It may also have an impact on how the person feels about himself or herself. In situations where the appearance connects individuals to a valued social identity, they see themselves as being in their proper "face," and are likely to feel good about themselves. For example, Gene Sperling, an aide to President William Clinton since the beginning of his presidency, is now director of the National Economic Council and an assistant to the president for Economic Policy. He was portrayed by reporter Robin Toner as dressing in a manner that conveys "the air of a graduate student after an all-nighter."[29] He is a "legendary workaholic," working late into the night and alternating "between Diet Coke and coffee even at 10 P.M. on Thursday."[30]

The reporter thus associated Sperling's sloppy appearance with a youthful identity, individual achievement, and hard work—the most desirable attributes in American society—"causing" him to stay within his "face" and feel good about himself.[31]

An appearance that stigmatizes people is often displayed in contexts in which they have no choice. A person's appearance may have characteristics that are negatively evaluated in American society. Someone whose style of dress demonstrates lack of knowledge or lack of financial resources may project a sense of worthlessness. Such an individual, if vulnerable to the judgment of others, is likely to acquire "a shamed face."[32] In the United States the homeless may be the best example.

Because of real or imagined group pressure, people conform to social expectation and may put on a dress or a necktie though they dislike doing so.[33] Teachers, judges, newspaper reporters, and television comedians, each in their own way, offer social feedback and are ready to employ negative sanctions, again each in their own way, to secure compliance.

## Clothing Signs in the Public Place

Established by those in authority, clothing signs are required attire that have only one meaning and indicate expected behavior. A study conducted at the University of Nevada over a four-year period found that the more clearly certain clothing was associated with a social identity, the greater the sharing of meaning. Pictures of a nun, a policeman, a bride, and a rodeo rider were easily recognized. However, the study subjects could not place the picture of a woman wearing stretch pants and a ruffled blouse in an occupational category. Clothing signs endow strangers with known characteristics, making them less threatening.[34]

Many companies have dress codes. Some are formal and written into the company handbook. In some companies the code is informal and people dress according to unwritten rules. Most employees know what is acceptable and what is unacceptable.

Because clothing signs identify expected role behavior, their significance is not limited to the specific context. The attributes of a clothing sign are relevant and carry weight beyond the boundaries of front-stage performance. They also enable individuals to *fabricate* an identity. By wearing the appropriate attire a person can convince others that he or she has the special qualities and skills the clothing signifies. It is illegal to impersonate a physician, a police officer, or a member of the clergy, but it is not difficult.[35]

Recent examples of fabricating an identity include persons engaged in undercover operations, such as journalists and the police. Sophie Rhys-Jones was a reporter who married Prince Edward of England in June 1999. Reporters who had worked with her on assignment reveal that Rhys-Jones had often worked undercover to get her story. She had dressed and posed as a nurse and a nun and also as a prostitute in a leather miniskirt and thigh-high boots.[36] (The Palace was upset by the revelation.)

*Bang* is a documentary film shot in Los Angeles in 1997. It examines the impact of the motorcycle police uniform when worn by a minority woman—in this case, an Asian.[37] Since Asian women are considered to be submissive, the filmmakers wanted to know: Would wearing the uniform change the behavior of the

*Fabricating an identity: Asian actress Darling Narita impersonated a Los Angeles motorcycle policewoman for the video* Bang. *Despite her ethnicity, long hair, and wobbling on the motorcycle she "passed." Photo: Greg Kitchen. (New York Times, Nov. 13, 1998).*

subject in the film? Would it influence people's impression of her? Would she get caught for impersonating a police officer?

She was not caught. Police were startled when they saw the young woman, actress Darling Narita, in full police regalia on her motorcycle. She simply waved the police on, and they thought that she was assigned to the movie set. She had impersonated a Los Angeles motorcycle policewoman by wearing the uniform, dark glasses, bristling gun belt, and high black boots and climbing onto the motorcycle. She had wobbled, fallen, and blundered throughout. Yet, because of her uniform, no one had questioned her identity, not even the police officers who joined her for breakfast in a coffee shop. She reclaimed her own identity when she retrieved her clothing.[38]

In an article on burglars, reporter Susan Black pointed out that successful burglars affect an appearance that will get them into their target buildings. On countless occasions, clerks in the best hotels have allowed access to thieves dressed in well-fitting, high-quality suits because they did not look like thieves.[39]

The believability of any identity depends on coherence between the impression one gives (a conscious effort to communicate a certain image) and the information one "gives off" (the not-so-conscious nuances that may cut away at the desired impression). Goffman cited examples from conversations as sources of dis-

*Fabricating an identity: A quack surgeon in fashionable clothes, ca. 1696. Here the costume and full wig of a physician cover up for an absence of medical qualifications.*

crepancy, but the manner in which one is dressed may also discredit a claim to a social identity. To protect themselves from being duped, people usually look for corroborative evidence. An authentic cowboy, unlike a dude, wears his pants long to protect himself from the brush. He has no need for well-polished boots, and his Stetson will have accumulated fingerprints, for it is used as a water bucket, waved in the air to steer cattle, and tipped to keep off bugs and to supply shade. The extent to which a performer can imitate an authentic appearance and demeanor determines his or her credibility and the successful fabrication of an identity.[40]

To summarize, as contractual relations became central to interaction in the economic and political spheres in the nineteenth century, the structure of daily life changed. A person's social realm became differentiated into the public self and the private self. There was a decrease in the role of informal social control mechanisms, such as community and home, and the public realm consisted of two spaces, formal and informal. Two types of rhetoric came to characterize the public self: one *contractual and formal*, the other *noncontractual and informal*. A dress code governs dress in the formal realm, where clear lines are drawn between acceptable and unacceptable attire. Gatekeepers and other social-control mechanisms offer feedback and are ready to apply negative and positive sanctions. Social roles, power, authority, gender, and seductiveness are governed by this rhetoric. In the informal realm, rewards and punishments are less exact and less certain.

## Challenges to Nineteenth- and Twentieth-Century Work Orientation

### The "Workaholic"

By the 1970s, an awareness emerged that advancements in technology and labor-saving devices designed to increase leisure time had had the opposite effect. More work time was being added to the day, the week, the month, and the year. Mental health professionals noted that, in the drive toward peak performance, the amount of leisure time and the ability to enjoy leisure has declined.[41]

In his book *Confessions of a Workaholic: The Facts about Work Addiction* (1971), pastoral counselor Wayne E Oates observed that work in U.S. society has many functions. It indicates religious virtue; it is a form of patriotism; it is a way to win friends and influence people; and it is also the way to be healthy, wealthy, and wise.[42] The culture thus breeds the compulsion to work, Oates claimed.[43] He suggested that for many professionals, work has become an addiction and that there are more and more "workaholics" (a term he is credited with inventing).[44]

Like the word *alcoholic, workaholic* suggests the futility of excess.[45] As with drink and alcoholics, work can be an obsession, a sickness in which the addict forgets how to play. Preoccupation with work steers marriage and family life into serious trouble,[46] encouraging workaholics to produce tangible signs of their labor.[47] They take on more speaking engagements, more chairmanships, more patients, and more clients, conveying the illusion of omnipotence.[48]

Oates's second book, *Workaholics: Make Laziness Work for You* (1978) is addressed to work-addicted individuals who have earned the right to be "lazy" and to enjoy leisure.[49] He suggests that a "successful business or professional person may need two full days of leisure a week."[50] It can be seen as adding some ingredient, as dressing on a salad, to give it flavor, character, and strength, Oates argues.[51] Moreover, in the Judeo-Christian civilization, he commented, God created the heavens and the earth in six days and rested on the seventh day.[52] Rest is thus a part of creation rather than an interruption of it. Even from the religious perspective, leisure is necessary for the maintenance and renewal of a balanced life.[53]

### "Runners Who Don't Care About Speed"[54]

An assault on achievement and goal-directed behavior is reflected in the emergence of an organization to support slow runners. This new category of runners ran in the 1999 marathons organized by the U.S. Marine Corps in Washington, D.C., and by the Portland, Oregon, and New York City marathon organizations. As the message on one "running" T-shirt asserted, "I'm slow. I know. Get over it."[55]

These runners reject "the traditional asceticism of road racing for a more relaxed, noncompetitive ethos."[56] They do not care about speed. Rejecting the universal symbol of running, the winged foot, they have adopted the penguin for its girth and waddling gait to emphasize that their interest is in fun rather than

*Steve Jobs, Apple Computer's interim CEO in this photograph,*
*credited the turnaround of Apple to (from left) Fred Anderson, Mitch*
*Mandich, Jon Rubinstein, Nancy Heinen, Jobs, and Avie Tevanian—*
Fortune Magazine *identified the team as having brought Apple back*
*from the dead. The men wear their shirts with collars unbuttoned and*
*wide open.* (Fortune Magazine, *Nov. 9, 1998.)*

speed. They amble their way through marathons, dancing, cheering, and enjoy-
ing the flowers.[57]

## Challenging the Norm of Self-Restraint

A challenge to attire that conveyed self-restraint—the suit, shirt, and tie—
emerged in the mid-1990s. Several forces made this possible. New technology enables people to work at home, where they have little use for expensive and confining suits. The computer industry continues to draw upon the talents, energy, and
abilities of recent college graduates and other young adults and demands total
absorption.

Employees in the computer industry dress in a manner that ignores details and
allows maximum freedom from physical constraints. News stories show them
dressed in T-shirts, shorts, and "flip-flops" or sandals. In a 1997 photograph of
Paul G. Allen, a 45-year-old "guitar-playing hacker geek" and a billionaire, wears a
rumpled shirt and a beard.[58] Similarly, one of the most important figures on the
business scene today, William H. Gates, is seen in a tie only on formal occasions.[59]

To adopt an egalitarian and more friendly image, companies such as Charles Schwab & Company and the Hewlett Packard Company relaxed their dress codes in the early 1990s, allowing their employees to come to work without jackets and ties.[60]

The world's largest casual dress manufacturer, Levi Strauss and Company, initiated the casual dress movement in the United States. It sought to acquire new consumers by influencing their employers. Levi Strauss advised more than 22,000 corporations in the United States, including IBM, Nynex, and Aetna Life & Casualty. It mailed 65,000 human-resource managers a newsletter and a videotape "trying to create a dress code for dress-down wear," reported Peter W. Harding of retail consultants Kurt Salmon Associates.[61] In 1992, 37 percent of businesses allowed their workers to dress casually at least once a week. By 1996 the practice grew to 75 percent.[62] According to *Business Week*, to kick off a campaign against the suit and tie, Levi Strauss hired one hundred actors dressed in suits and staged mock demonstrations outside stock exchanges and in financial districts around the world.[63] To demonstrate that they can look professional without the suit and tie, they removed their ties and changed into khaki trousers.[64]

Those working on Wall Street and in the advertising agencies in New York have traditionally eased the transition from work time to leisure time by coming to work on Fridays casually dressed. To attract younger members, the Yale Club in New York City in the summer of 1999 eliminated the requirement for a jacket and tie on weekends during the summer months.

## Casual Wear

"Casual wear is here to stay, as firmly entrenched as traditional dress," concludes Fred Villegas in the December 1999 *Management Review*.[65] Companies seeking to maintain a dynamic market profile must have their key personnel project an image that communicates their objectives, Villegas explains. Until they achieved business success, computer giants Bill Gates and George Allan (Microsoft) and Steven M. Case (America Online) wore informal attire, usually jeans and T-shirts. Reporter Amy Harmon observed that Case was known for "clinging to his casual costume of denim shirts and khakis on even the most formal occasions."[66] To announce the merger of American Online with Time Warner, however, Case wore the uniform of a business suit and a tie, just as Gates and Allan had done before him. They had become businessmen.

The decision by the law firm Cadwalader Wickersham and Taft to encourage casual dress may be an acknowledgment that most lawyers have no reason to dress up at all, observed Cameron Stracher, author of *Double Billing: A Young Lawyer's Tale of Greed, Sex, Lies and the Pursuit of the Swivel Chair*.[67] He noted that most lawyers in big law firms are never in court, rarely meet clients, and never leave their offices. They spend the bulk of their time in the library or in

*Chief executives can usually choose how to present themselves in public. When announcing the merger between America Online and Time Warner, Gerald M. Levin, chief executive of Time Warner, wore his customary open-necked shirt and no tie. On the other hand, Steve M. Case, chief executive of America Online, gave up his usual denim shirt and khakis for a business shirt and tie. He had officially assumed the responsibility for running a company not completely his own. (Photo: Ruby Washington/New York Times, Jan. 11, 2000.)*

front of the computer with the door closed, and they could work just as well in their pajamas.[68]

To introduce lawyers from Cadwalader Wickersham and Taft to its line of casual office wear, Polo Ralph Lauren on Madison Avenue staged a fashion show with lawyers from the law firm as models.

The company, moreover, is urging that its attorneys donate their "gently worn" suits to groups that provide business attire to lower-income people looking for jobs. By being appropriately dressed in clothing that suggests impersonality and self-restraint, the job applicants gain confidence and are helped to conform to the requirements of the workplace.[69]

The movement toward casual clothing allowed men to become more aware of color and style. Reporter Jennifer Steinhauer quoted a Well's Fargo executive in Phoenix: "Before I had all dark suits and all white shirts. Now I get pants with patterns in them and wear them with a sport coat. I guess I could say I've become a little more fashion-oriented."[70]

To help employees avoid "fashion mistakes" that convey the wrong message, several companies in addition to Levi Strauss offer guidance. Philips Van Heusen,

Inc., for example, prepared a manual identifying degrees of casualness,[71] and Brooks Brothers set up mannequins in a conference room to illustrate different casual looks. New distinctions and codes are emerging. Casual traditional, for example, refers to the wearing of Izod shirts and khakis; dress casual traditional to oxford shirts and khakis; casual contemporary to jeans and a black shirt; dress casual contemporary to black slacks and black shirts.[72] Introduction of these styles led to an increase of over 30 percent in sales of men's casual wear in 1997.[73]

Has the business suit come to symbolize a work uniform that hinders creativity and imagination? Has the informal attire characterizing the computer industry come to symbolize the encouragement of creativity and innovation and, therefore, future affluence?

## Notes

1. R. Sennett (1974), *The Fall of the Public Man* (New York: Knopf), pp. 17–20, 165.

2. C. W. Mills (1951), *White Collar* (New York: Oxford University Press), p. 65.

3. W. H. Form and G. P. Stone (1955), "The Social Significance of Clothing in Occupational Life," Michigan State University Agricultural Experiment Technical Bulletin, no. 247.

4. R. Sennet(1974), *The Fall of Public Man* (New York: Knopf), pp. 3–27; W. H. Form and G. P. Stone (1957), "Urbanism, Anonymity and Status Symbolism," *American Journal of Sociology* 62 (5): 504–514.

5. M. and A. Batterberry (1977), *Fashion: The Mirror of History* (New York: Greenwich House) p. 139; A. Hollander (1978), *Seeing Through Clothes* (New York: Viking), p. 385.

6. T. Carlyle (1967), *Sartor Resartus* (New York: Dutton) pp. 139–147. Originally published in 1838.

7. E. Moers (1960), *The Dandy: Brummel to Beerbohm* (New York: Viking), pp. 147–163; also see L. H. Lofland (1973), *A World of Strangers—Order and Action in Urban Public Space* (New York: Basic Books). Lofland argued that the appearance of the preindustrial city did not survive the chaos and confusion of early industrialization. The economic and social revolution made it virtually impossible to retain the traditional expressions of identities. The spatial ordering of the modern city makes it a place for living among strangers. City living requires learning the skill for moving in a world of strangers.

8. Moers, op. cit., pp. 287–230; V. Steele (1985), *Fashion and Eroticism* (New York: Oxford University Press), pp. 151–152.

9. V. Steele (1988), *Paris Fashion* (New York: Oxford University Press), pp. 143–144.

10. F. W. Taylor (1911), *The Principles of Scientific Management* (New York: Harper Brothers).

11. *New York Times Magazine*, Dec. 16, 1990.

12. Batterberry, op. cit., p. 216; also Steele (1988), op. cit.

13. *New York Times*, Sept. 19, 1989.

14. *New York Times*, Sept. 29, 1989.

15. *New York Times*, May 13, 1990.

16. *New York Times*, June 13, 1987.

17. Form and Stone (1957), op. cit.; also J. Thompson, ed. (1983), *Image Impact for Men* (New York: A&W Publishers).

18. E. Goffman (1959), *The Presentation of Self in Everyday Life* (Garden City, N.Y.: Doubleday), pp. 1–30; E. Goffman (1963a), *Behavior in Public Places* (New York: Free Press); E. Goffman (1967), *Interaction Ritual* (Garden City, N.Y.: Doubleday Anchor Books), pp. 16, 55; also M. Wood (1990), "Consumer Behavior Impression Management by Professional Servers," paper delivered at the 85th Annual Meeting of the American Sociological Association, Washington D.C., Aug. 11–15.

19. E. Goffman (1961a), *Asylums: Essays on the Social Situation of Mental Patients and Other Inmates* (Chicago: Aldine), p. 27; also E. Goffman (1961b) *Encounters* (Indianapolis, Ind.: Bobbs Merrill), pp. 99–115. See also R. M. Barker (1968), *Ecological Psychology: Concepts and Methods for Studying the Environment of Human Behavior* (Stanford, Calif.: Stanford University Press); R. E. Turner and C. Edgley (1976), "Death As Theater: A Dramaturgical Analysis of the American Funeral," *Sociology and Social Research* 60 (4): 377–392.

20. A. Sullivan (2000) "Dressing Down for Travel? Best to Think Again, " *International Herald Tribune*, Apr. 7.

21. Ibid.

22. *New York Times*, Apr. 28, 1987.

23. Goffman (1961a), op. cit., pp. 20–21.

24. "Schooling of Boy, 4, Snarled by Long Hair," *New York Times*, Mar. 9, 1991.

25. J. Curry (1991), "Mattingly Chooses Seat on Yank Bench over Barber's Chair," *New York Times*, Mar. 9.

26. "At the Bar," *New York Times*, Law Page, June 5, 1992.

27. *New York Times*, May 2, 1991.

28. "Face" is an image of self delineated in terms of approved social attributes. E. Goffman (1967), *Interaction Ritual* (Garden City, N.Y.: Anchor Books), pp. 5–9.

29. Ibid.

30. Ibid.

31. Goffman (1967), op. cit., pp. 5–9.

32. Ibid.

33. C. Kiesler and S. Kiesler (1969), *Conformity* (Reading, Mass.: Addison-Wesley).

34. M. J. Horn and L. M. Gurel (1981), *The Second Skin: An Interdisciplinary Study of Clothing*, 3d. ed. (Boston: Houghton Mifflin), pp. 181–182, 187–188.

35. E. Goffman (1963b), *Stigma: Notes on the Management of Spoiled Identity* (Englewood Cliffs, N.J.: Prentice-Hall).

36. W. Hoge (1999), "Royal Fiancee Is Unveiled. 'Cruelty,' Says the Palace," *New York Times*, May 27.

37. P. M. Nichols (1998), "Home Video," *New York Times*, Nov. 13.

38. Ibid.

39. "Where the Hat Is the Man," *New York Times*, May 27, 1973.

40. Goffman (1963b), op. cit., pp. 3–5.

41. W. E. Oates (1971), *Confessions of a Workaholic: The Facts About Work Addiction* (New York: World Publishing) pp. 24, 37.

42. Oates (1971), op. cit., p. 12.

43. Ibid., p. 1.

44. *Oxford English Dictionary*, 1989, 2d ed., vol. 20. Oxford, Eng.: Clarendon Press, p. 547.

45. W. E. Oates (1978), *Workaholics: Make Laziness Work for You* (Garden City, N.Y.: Doubleday), pp. 4–6.

46. Ibid., p. 9.

47. Ibid., p. 8.

48. Oates (1971), op. cit., pp. 45–49, 89.

49. Oates (1978), op. cit., pp. 4, 8.

50. Ibid., p. 9.

51. Ibid.

52. Oates (1971), op. cit., p. 24.

53. Ibid.

54. M. Bloom (1999), "The Fast Growth of a Very Slow Movement," *New York Times,* June 4.

55. Ibid.

56. Ibid.

57. Ibid.

58. L. J. Flynn (1999), "He's Got the Team and a Whole New Look," *New York Times,* May 17.

59. M. Weber and the Van Heusen Creative Design Group (1997), *Dress Casually for Success for Men.* (New York: McGraw-Hill), p. 4.

60. N. Himelstein and N. Walser (1996), "Levi's vs. the Dress Code. Its Stealth Campaign Is Redefining Business Wear," *Business Week,* Apr. 1, p. 57.

61. Ibid.

62. *Business Week,* Apr. 1, 1996, p. 58.

63. In New York City the event took place on Mar. 22, 1992.

64. Himelstein and Walser (1996), op. cit.

65. F. Villegas (1999), "Millennium Fashion," *Management Review,* Dec., p. 62.

66. A. Harmon (2000), "AOL Chief Relaxes a Dress Code but Not His Vision of Internet," *New York Times,* Jan. 11.

67. C. Stracher (2000), "The Law Firm's New Clothes," *New York Times,* Mar. 24.

68. Ibid.

69. Ibid.

70. J. Steinhauer (1997), "What Vanity and Casual Friday Have Wrought," *New York Times,* Apr. 9.

71. Weber, op. cit., p. 67.

72. Ibid.

73. Steinhauer, op. cit.

# Part Three:
# Clothing Signs and Social Imperatives

# 5

# The Image of Power

$\mathbf{P}$OWER, observed German sociologist Max Weber, is the ability to realize one's own will even against the resistance of others.[1] The image of power stems from the desire for obedience and personal loyalty. The ability to reward and the ability to impose the threat of physical harm are the animating forces behind the image of power. The details of the image are dependent on the source of its legitimacy and the right to exercise physical force.

Power relations are asymmetrical: the power holder exercises greater control than the power subject over the subject's behavior. Legitimacy, however, must be demonstrated for one to achieve and maintain a position of power, according to Weber.[2] The validity of the legitimacy claim may be based on (1) charismatic grounds—resting on the devotion to heroism, exceptional sanctity, or exemplary character of an individual; (2) traditional grounds—resting on an established belief in the sanctity of long-held traditions and the legitimacy of those exercising authority under them; or (3) rational grounds—resting on a belief in the enacted rules and the rights of those elevated to authority by those rules. These three types of authority are pure types, two of which, charismatic authority and traditional authority, are dependent on personal loyalty. In their desire to remain unchallenged, dictators and monarchs dominate the image of power. In their appearance, they make their ability to reward or inflict harm obvious to increase the probability that their commands will be obeyed. Their dress contains elements that extend the body's reach; and when they appear in public they (and their appearance) are supported by attendants.

In a democracy, obedience is owed to the established rules. The exercise of power is impersonal; the ability to inflict harm is displayed only by those charged with that responsibility, usually the military and the police. A plurality of power centers exists, each strong enough to compete with the others but not strong enough to undermine the entire political system. The responsibility of wearing or carrying elements that extend the body's reach and increase one's physical ability to control the environment is confined to attendants.

## Charismatic Dictatorship

A dictatorship may have its roots in charismatic leadership. A charismatic leader, with the intent of transforming society, preaches, creates, or demands new obligations to which the populace must accede. Members of his party or group who are familiar with his ideas consider obedience to them and to him their duty. Those who do not recognize or who reject the leader's superior or extraordinary qualities are forced into submission. The threat of physical force or death encourages such obedience.

The dictator usually adopts a military uniform, the elements of which reflect his ideology. The choice of a uniform is designed to impress both his followers and his antagonists. To his followers the uniform represents the "cause." It signifies single-mindedness, discipline, and self-restraint. To his detractors the uniform is intended to denote a superior commitment to the collectivity, to the society.

Twentieth-century dictators such as Joseph Stalin, Adolf Hitler, Benito Mussolini, Mao Tse-tung, and Fidel Castro began their careers as charismatic leaders. Their followers considered them to have exceptional powers and extraordinary qualities. Each claimed legitimacy and was acclaimed in turn by a community of "believers." Others, however, had to be "convinced" to comply. The uniforms with their implements capable of inflicting physical harm encouraged pride among supporters and fear among dissenters.

## Monarchy

Traditionally, the royal court was the residence of quasi-divine monarchs at the center of political and administrative power, national and international in range. No group was more acutely aware of the way in which images had to be deployed and manipulated for political effect than these ruling aristocracies.[3] Artistic spectacle, the dress and ornament of the monarchs, performed at least three major tasks: It protected and sustained the sacred character of kingship; it served to demonstrate political and administrative power; and it constituted an exemplary appearance for foreigners and nationals alike.[4]

The sacred character of kingship and its legitimacy were signified by a crown, a scepter, and a chain worn around the neck. These emblems served to display and justify the exercise of power. Both in formal ceremonies and in the organization of the household, the monarch was presented as God's representative on earth, the center of a universe carefully designed to duplicate the harmonious ordering of the heavens.[5]

The relationship between the monarch and his subjects was characterized by the threat of force, according to French historian Michel Foucault. The sword in royal regalia was designed to encourage voluntary obedience. It exhibited the right of seizure—of a person's belongings, body, time, and ultimately life.[6] In Western society, however, from the fourth century AD, when Roman Emperor

LEFT: *A boy under six years of age wears a skeleton suit and carries a whip. The whip extends the boy's reach, enabling him to inflict harm. From a book of children's clothing styles worn in England between 1775 and 1825. (Photo: Greg Kitchen.)*

BELOW: *Mayor Rudolph W. Giuliani in a 1999 press conference. Observers note that "those who displease the mayor suffer negative consequences." Be it a parent, a teacher, or the mayor of New York City, wagging an index finger informs the audience about who is in charge. (Photo: Frances M. Roberts, New York Times, Oct. 10, 1999.)*

Constantine crowned himself as the first Christian ruler of the empire, the crown came to be the main symbol of royal power. Whenever a pope or an emperor awarded a kingship, the appointment was accompanied by the gift of a crown. The crown established the king as the legitimate ruler and upheld his authority to reward as well as to punish. The details of crowns differed from one kingship to

*Codex Manesse, illuminated between
1298 and 1304, Heidelberg Library.
King Wenzel II sits on the throne,
dominating the picture because of his
size and ample clothing. Like the
Egyptian pharaoh, he wears a crown
and carries a mace.*

another, but the elements from which they were constructed and their basic
structure remained the same. Made of gold, the radiance of which is associated
with the heavens, and encrusted with jewels, which were thought to contain the
creative powers of the universe, the crown indicated access to both divine powers
and superhuman force.[7] The crown invested the monarch with authority to grant
individuals and groups the right to engage in commercial or industrial enterprise, and economic exchange occurred mainly between persons so designated.
The monarch thus had the power to enrich and give life, as well as to destroy it.[8]

The scepter, another integral part of royal regalia, was a staff, or batonlike implement, that signified the king's right to exercise authority. It was used to dele-
gate permission. When a king invested an organization, such as the British Parliament, with royal approval, he often accompanied this announcement by the
award of a scepter.[9]

Court etiquette, with its fine hierarchical gradations and its exact delimitation
of functions, proved—whether in London, Paris, or Madrid—to be an important
device for inculcating social discipline. It provided education in politeness, taste,
and service. Court behavior thus became an example for others to follow. Supported by monarchical power, the court played a vital role in the "civilizing
process," as Norbert Elias pointed out.[10]

*President Lyndon B. Johnson signing the Medicare and Medicaid programs into law on July 30, 1965. (Photo: Greg Kitchen.)*

## Power in the American Presidency

By contrast, visual images of power are deliberately limited or absent in the context of the office of president of the United States. Whereas monarchs had personal ability to punish those who violated the law or threatened the integrity of the state, presidents are limited in their ability to exercise physical force to secure a course of action. Regardless of whether a monarch acquired the crown through inheritance or conquest, his power was unrivaled. The will of the people was subject to his desire or whim. Equating monarchy with tyranny and subjugation, the Founding Fathers insisted that rationality and democracy were necessary to ensure liberty. The signers of the Declaration of Independence rejected the notion of a divine right to rule. The U.S. Constitution and the Bill of Rights specify protection for individuals and minorities. Under the Judiciary Act of 1789, the first Congress emphasized the rule of law. It created the federal court system and established the form and structure of the Supreme Court, with a chief justice and five associates, and the office of attorney general. The chief justice, John Jay, adopted the black robe and cap as the appropriate judiciary attire.

The framers of the Constitution rejected the traditional nature of the monarchy and thus, too, the attire of power.[11] They insisted that power be shared in an effort to guard against its concentration in the hands of one man. Policy, they decided, should be the sum of the visible and formal decisions of the three branches of government: the executive, the legislative, and the judicial. The Constitutional Convention of 1787 created a government of limited and separate powers, thus limiting the president's power to command. Influence, rather than coercion, and leadership through persuasion and bargaining became the principal means to power for the president.[12]

In organizing the proceedings of the Constitutional Convention, however, the delegates employed some elements connected with monarchical power. They placed sentries—armed guards—at the State House doors so that only official delegates would be allowed in, the proceedings would be kept secret, and "some headway could be achieved." But to encourage the free exchange of ideas, the sign of royal authority, the mace, was removed from its place in front of the speaker.[13]

On ceremonial occasions, the president's three leadership roles are each signified to some degree in images: As commander in chief of the army and navy of the United States, the leader of the forces of peace and war, for example, the president is attended by uniformed members of the armed forces. As chief of state, the symbol of the sovereignty, continuity, and grandeur of the American people, he is accompanied by an honor guard holding swords. As chief executive, the leader of the executive branch, who shapes policy, takes care of the government's administrative tasks, and signs legislation into law, he wields a special pen that is often sought as a symbol of presidential favor and power.

People in power exercise it by virtue of the offices they hold; their commands are exercised only within the legal scope of those positions.[14] Accordingly, the attire of modern power holders, the somber suit, has its roots in the values that underlie the institutional context and guide organizational behavior. It denotes holding back personal feelings, or self-restraint, and focusing energy on achieving organizational goals, or goal-directed behavior.

Looking the part is important, as was suggested by a Defense Department publication, *The Armed Forces Officer 1965,* which was distributed to all branches of the military. It advised that as far as being a leader is concerned, "It is good . . . to look the part, not only because of the effect on others, but because from out of the effort made to look it, one may in time come to be it."[15]

### Origins of the Image of Power

The word *origins* means both beginnings and causes, and there is frequent cross-contamination of the two meanings. With regard to the origins of the image of power, historical evidence suggests that both meanings apply. Perhaps the first instance of an image of power is seen in the Palette of Narmer, a pictorial record commemorating the consolidation of Egypt under the rule of a pharaoh in 3300–3100 BC. On one side of the palette, Narmer wears a tall double crown, the conical white crown of upper Egypt and the superimposed red one of lower

*Palette of Narmer, ca. 3000 BC, Egyptian Museum, Cairo. Wearing the tall crown, the pharaoh dominates the palette. He holds a mace aloft with his right hand, about to smite a captive held in his left. At the back of his kilt, he wears a bull's tail, a symbol of power and strength. Holding the pharaoh's sandals is his attendant. He is diminutive in size and wears little clothing. The captives at the bottom of the palette are nearly naked. (Reprinted by permission of Giraudon/Art Resource.)*

*Codex Manesse, illuminated between 1298 and 1304, Heidelberg Library. The image of power applies to the classroom. Magister Henricus (the teacher), holding a birch branch in his left hand, lectures from a high chair. The birch is an emblem of Grammatica, one of the Seven Liberal Arts. Some students wear ragged clothes and appear to have suffered under his hand.*

Egypt. Together they signify that the nation has been unified under his rule. At the center of the palette, occupying his own distinct space, the pharaoh is bigger and taller than all the other figures. His raised arm wields a club and he threatens a captive. His posture signifies his ability to inflict harm. At a distance stands an aide, smaller and with his body turned toward the pharaoh, as if ready to serve him. The vanquished warriors, naked and small, have been hurled to the bottom of the palette. The pharaoh and the men he defeated provide the interrelated images of power and victimhood.[16]

According to Henri Frankfort, the crown has its origins in the semisacred occupation of the boatmen on the Nile. This river and its canals were the sole roads in ancient Egypt. When people died, their bodies, accompanied by statues of the gods, were carried to the place of interment by boat in religious processions. To prevent the strong north wind from blowing hair in their eyes, the boatmen plucked weeds from the river's edge and wove them into circlets, which they tied over their brows with a bow in back, the ends dangling. Lotus flowers, tucked into the headband, were often used as amulets to provide protection. This headdress was transformed into a crown by the pharaoh, who sought to demonstrate that power is sacred in origin. Access to nonhuman powers was demonstrated in the royal headdress. Seeming to rear itself up on his brow, a jeweled image of a brightly colored poisonous snake often adorned the pharaoh's headdress as a warning to potential enemies. The pharaoh's wife wore a crown in which the vulture, a sacred bird that shielded the pharaoh in battle, appeared to spread its wings over her head, suggesting that she too was similarly protected.[17]

Outside the palace the pharaoh was carried on a gilded chair held aloft by eight pole-bearers. Wearing his golden skirt, a sword, a crown, and a gold ring, he shone like the sun. Because gold embodies all the fire and glory of the sun, the attire indicated access to superhuman powers and signified his divinity and sovereignty. Like the sun, the pharaoh had power over life and death. Worn by the pharaohs for two thousand years, the short, royal skirt, called Shend'ot (Shenti), was made of gold cloth and decorated with gold embroidery. This type of garment predates the development of agricultural communities and the pharaohs' rise to power; it is based on a skirt worn by chieftains that consisted of two pieces of matting that hung from a string around the waist. The chieftains' skirt had a lion's tail on the back panel, signifying a strong and successful hunter.

When appearing in public, the pharaoh induced in those around him a sense of their own insignificance. His crown, his body raised high on a throne, and his demand that people kneel before him made him appear bigger, extending his space and his reach. The other royal insignia—a scepter, a crook, and a flail—symbolized his loyalty to his subjects and his intent to defend and protect them as a shepherd protects his flock.

The personal nature of royal administration was seen in the pharaoh's granting of the right to wear elements of royal attire. When individuals outside the royal family were given the task of administering the land, the pharaoh bestowed upon them the right to wear a skirt in the style of the Shend'ot or to wear his signet ring, which indicated that the individual's decision-making powers had been expanded.[18] The warrior's sword, which made possible the centralization of power, and the other signs and symbols of royalty were based on existing notions of sacredness and emanated from the wishes of the monarch to indicate a monopoly of force. In the ancient civilizations, those at the top of the social hierarchy were the first to adopt clothing signs, initially used only for ritual and ceremony.[19]

## Images of Power in Christian Art

The sword, crown, and scepter, signs of royal power and authority, were popularized through Christian art.[20] They were used to portray the attributes of saints and martyrs and to indicate the role they played in Church history as well as for eternity. A jeweled crown, or a diadem, denoted divine powers and spiritual force. When the Madonna is evoked as Queen of Heaven, she is portrayed wearing a crown. When the heavenly messenger Saint Michael is depicted as the defender of the Church against Satan, he is shown wearing a crown and dressed in the clothing of a warrior or a knight.[21]

Prior to the Renaissance, paintings of the Annunciation nearly always showed Gabriel, the chief messenger of God, richly robed, wearing a crown and carrying

*Painting of Saint Michael,
with a sword, armor,
and scales, by Domenico
Ghirlandaio, 1490.
(Portland Art Museum,
Gift of Samuel H. Kress.
Reprinted by permission.)*

*The "suffering Christ" and the "victorious Christ." Details from* The Crucifixion and Last Judgement *by Jan van Eyck, ca. 1420–1425. (The Metropolitan Museum of Art, Fletcher Fund, 1933. All rights reserved, The Metropolitan Museum of Art. Reprinted by permission.)*

a scepter. His majestic appearance is intended to signify that he had been invested with divine and royal authority.[22] Other depictions of the archangels also demonstrate this point. When the archangel Raphael is portrayed as the protector of the young, innocent, pilgrims, and wayfarers, ready to come to their aid, he is dressed in the attire of a pilgrim or traveler and wears sandals. His hair, however, is bound with a diadem. He carries a staff, indicating formal authority, and there is a gourd of water or a wallet slung on his belt, indicating access to a necessary scarce resource. When Raphael is portrayed as a guardian spirit, he is often shown richly dressed with a sword in one hand and the other raised in a warning gesture, as if he is saying, "Take heed." The sword is interpreted as an instrument appropriate to a knight or warrior, defender of the forces of light against the forces of darkness.[23]

## Power and Victimhood

There are two basic images of Christ: the victorious Christ and the suffering Christ. The image that prevailed during the first thousand years of Christianity and celebrated in Coptic and Byzantine churches is that of the victorious Christ. He is depicted sitting or standing, tall, often splendidly dressed, holding a cross. Prior to the eleventh century, even when nailed to the cross, he is portrayed alive and upright. His eyes are open, his arms straight. A halo encircles his head like a

*Nicolas Poussin's* Rape of the Sabine Women, *1636–1637. (The Metropolitan Museum of Art. Harris Brisbane Dick Fund, 1946. All rights reserved, The Metropolitan Museum of Art. Reprinted by permission.)*

crown, and sometimes it seems as if it emanates from within him. His image is that of a triumphant sovereign.[24]

When shown in the second image, that of a victim, Christ is portrayed as dead on the cross with his head slumped on his right shoulder, his eyes closed, and his face twisted. Often he wears a crown, but this one is of thorns. Tears and blood are often visible. Except for a loose-fitting loincloth that looks like it can be easily unraveled, he is naked. He is the object of attention in these paintings, and the demeanor of all those who are gathered around him is one of sorrow.[25]

In Western secular art, too, the image of power has been supported by its counterpart, victimhood. Rape is often used to convey violence. Paintings of rape by Rubens, Poussin, and David, for example, portray male warriors on horseback wearing military helmets and shields, swinging swords and spears, while unarmed women on foot gesture distress. Their clothes are torn and their breasts are often revealed. Similarly, Madonna's 1989 video "Like a Prayer" (Sire Records) depicts rape and contrasts modern images of power and victimhood. Policemen with guns, clubs, whistles, and screeching police cars are juxtaposed with images of people with clothing torn off their shoulders, Christlike stigmata, and tears of blood. In both realms, religious and secular, in the past and today, the image of power is more commanding and its impact stronger when accompanied by the image of the victim. When the image of power is divorced from that of victimhood, brutality and violence are less discernible. The threat of harm that underlies all explicit images of force becomes less overtly fearful, less likely to be a source of terror.

## Notes

1. M. Weber (1947), *The Theory of Social and Economic Organization,* trans. A. M. Henderson and T. Parsons (New York: Free Press), p. 152; C. W. Mills (1959), *The Sociological Imagination* (New York: Oxford University Press). In his May 29, 1993, essay in the *New York Times,* Russell Baker observed: "The British Empire was almost surely destroyed by the swagger stick. It made imperial Britain's military men look so hatefully arrogant to the rest of the world that the empire was doomed." It is important to note that a swagger stick extends the person's reach; and when employed, it inflicts pain.

2. M. Weber (1993), "Power, Domination and Legitimacy," in *Power in Modern Societies,* ed. M. E. Olsen and M. N. Martin (Boulder: Westview Press), pp. 37–47; M. Weber (1978), *Economy and Society: An Outline of Interpretive Sociology,* ed. G. Roth and C. Wittich (Berkeley: University of California Press), chap. 3.

3. M. Chambers et al. (1974), *The Western Experience* (New York: Knopf), pp. 435–454, 581; F. L. Ganshof (1964), *Feudalism* (New York: Harper and Row); M. and A. Batterberry (1977), *Fashion: The Mirror of History* (New York: Greenwich House), p. 110.

4. A. Hollander (1978), *Seeing Through Clothes* (New York: Viking), p. 371.

5. J. G. Frazer, *The New Golden Bough: A New Abridgement of Sir James George Frazer's Classic Work,* ed. T. H. Gaster (New York: Criterion Books), pp. 3–142.

6. M. Foucault (1978), *The History of Sexuality, vol. 1: An Introduction* (New York: Random House), pp. 135–143.

7. The 1804 coronation of Napoléon I, for example, which was commemorated by Jacques Louis David in *Le Sacre,* was a spectacle that consisted of traditional signs of power—ecclesiastical and secular. In *Le Sacre,* the pope, seated high, is wearing a gold-edged miter and an elaborately decorated crimson and gold embroidered orphrey and is holding a cross staff. Invoking Imperial Rome, Napoléon is wearing the laurel wreath of the Roman emperor and his vestments, including the ankle-length gold embroidered satin gown and crimson velvet mantle. He holds high the customary gold crown. Velvet and silk, crimson and gold—fabrics and colors restricted in Europe to holders of power—are also used for the attire of his wife Josephine. The women in Josephine's court are clad in Grecian-style dresses and hairdos, women's latest fashion, which contributes to the grandeur.

8. M. Mann (1986), *The Sources of Social Power,* vol. 1 (Cambridge: Cambridge University Press), pp. 456–457.

9. G. Ferguson (1977), *Signs and Symbols in Christian Art* (New York: Oxford University Press). Also J. Mayo (1984), *A History of Ecclesiastical Dress* (New York: Holmes and Meier), p. 171.

10. N. Elias (1978), *The Civilizing Process: The Development of Manners* (New York: Urizon Books).

11. C. D. Bowen (1966), *Miracle at Philadelphia* (Boston: Little, Brown).

12. Ibid., pp. 54–67.

13. Ibid., pp. 47–51.

14. M. Weber called the exercise of power within such a structure "legal-rational authority." M. Weber (1968), *Economy and Society* (New York: Bedminster Press). Originally published in 1922.

15. B. Schlenker (1980), *Impression Management: The Self-Concept, Social Identity, and Interpersonal Relations* (Monterey, Calif.: Brooks-Cole), p. 243.

16. H. Frankfort (1951), *The Birth of Civilization in the Near East* (Garden City, N.Y.: Doubleday Anchor Books), pp. 111–113; also H. Frankfort (1961), *Ancient Egyptian Religion* (New York: Harper and Row), pp. 33–43.

17. M. Lurker (1980), *The Gods and Symbols of Ancient Egypt* (London: Thames and Hudson), pp. 44, 124, 127; W.E.A. Budge and W. Thompson (1961), *Amulets and Talismans* (New Hyde Park, N.Y.: University Books), p. 150; Frankfort (1961), op. cit.

18. A. Erman (1971), *Life in Ancient Egypt* (New York: Dover Publications), pp. 228–229. Originally published 1894.

19. Ibid., pp. 200–280.

20. Ferguson, op. cit.

21. Ibid., pp. 166, 182.

22. Ibid., p. 180.

23. Ibid., pp. 99–100.

24. Ibid., p. 38; also Budge and Thompson, op. cit., pp. 350–352.

25. C. Morris (1972), *The Discovery of the Individual: 1050–1200* (New York: Harper Torchbooks), pp. 23–24.

# 6

# The Image of Authority

THE TERM *authority* has three distinct root meanings, as sociologist Richard Sennett observed.[1] In one sense, the word is related to the Latin word *auctor*, which means beginner, creator, author of something; in this sense the word implies productivity. Another set of meanings derives from the Latin *auctoritas* (the actual source of the English word), which means coming from an author. An authority has legal powers and is in a position to grant permission, that is, an "authority gives guarantees to others." In this sense, the term connotes something permanent, stable, solid, and, hence, of lasting value. Finally, the term is used to describe a person who has power over other people. In this situation, the individuals on the two sides are perceived as unequal. All three meanings are encapsulated in the role behavior expected of those holding positions of authority. Authority holders represent a social entity: They are required to be concerned with production—the achievement of an organization's goals—and as members of a hierarchy they are expected to relate differently to those below and those above.

In Western society the image of authority is characterized by form-following rather than form-fitting attire, observed Flugel. The image consists of vertical continuity of fabric, a generalized unity from head to toe. The style increases the size and volume of the person, effecting a commanding presence and making it easier for the officeholder to perform his or her expected task.[2]

The image of authority has two distinct manifestations in attire. One is the uniform. Here each person's attire is identical in style and detail, and expectations for role performance are explicit—for example, the clothing worn by police officers. The attire indicates the person's right to represent a group. With the second manifestation, a "nonuniform uniform," dress and behavior are less specified, but in style and sentiment the image demands respect, as in a businessman with three-piece suit.[3]

## Uniforms

The category of uniforms encompasses required attire. Formal, negative sanctions follow acts of omission or commission, that is, not wearing an element of

*A representation of Adam and Cain in the attire of workers of the land, ca. 1330. Adam, the father, is more completely covered. Over a tunic, stirrup, and hose he is wearing a sheepskin cloak, which offers protection while the side vents enable him to move freely. He is thus portrayed in the image of authority. Cain wears only a tunic hitched up by a belt.*

the attire, adding to the specified dress, or modifying it in any shape or form. Emblems, implements, and other visual elements identify the extent, sphere, and boundaries of social control. The extent of deference accorded to the status holder may thus vary.[4]

The attire required by sanitation departments, hospitals, airlines, and hotel and restaurant employees, for example, identifies *the right to enforce policy*. Company badges, logos, and special insignia on ties, blazers, and coveralls mark those with such privilege. Uniforms can also identify *the right to interfere with an ongoing action*. Here the uniform includes implements such as batons, whistles, timers, whips, and axes. These instruments enable orchestra conductors, umpires and referees, and firefighters perform to their roles. Similarly, the display of keys in areas where admission is legally limited—in mental hospitals, prisons, and stockrooms, for example—proclaims *the right to control access. The right to exercise force* is demonstrated by uniforms that include coercive instruments, tools capable of inflicting harm. Armed guards, police, and uniformed military personnel support the operations of justice, peace, and public order.

### The Social Meaning of Uniforms

In his study of uniforms, Nathan Joseph (1986) pointed out that uniforms are a device used by organizations to distinguish members from nonmembers and inform the actor and the audience of what behavior to expect.[5] A uniform exerts a degree of control over those who must carry out the organization's tasks, encour-

*Attire showing the right to enforce policy worn by St. Patrick's Day Parade marshals. ("Irish March Up the Avenue, Gay Protesters at Bay" [New York Times, Mar. 18, 1993].)*

aging members to express the ideas and interests of the group rather than their own and thus enhance the group's ability to perform its tasks.

The conferring of a uniform or the salient parts of it, such as a police officer's shield or a nurse's cap or pin, signifies that legal rights have been transferred from the institution to the individual who represents it. The attire authorizes individuals to act on the organization's behalf. Because they represent the organization, those in uniform are not permitted to wear buttons and other insignia that announce a political or some other competing loyalty.

When an organization authorizes an individual to wear its uniform, it certifies that the person has acquired relevant values and skills and that the group will assume responsibility for the person's conduct. In turn, by wearing a uniform, a person outwardly displays acceptance of and allegiance to the organization's goals. The individual signals his or her intention to abide by and adhere to standardized expectations for role behavior and to be guided by the group's ideas, beliefs, and values. Suppressing personal choice of dress, the organization binds the individual to his or her peers, underscores common membership, and encourages a sense of loyalty among members and faithfulness to the same rules. The uniform serves to integrate wearers into a cohesive unit that will act to ensure that organizational goals are attained. The withdrawal of the right to represent the group is accompanied by a ritual that involves removing parts of the uniform. Police officers lose the authority to arrest when they are asked to turn in their guns and shields.

To summarize, a uniform designates membership in a group and is a certificate of legitimacy. It shows that the individual has mastered certain essential skills and values. By wearing a uniform, an individual displays adherence to group norms and standards. The uniform embodies the attributes of the group and affects the wearer's behavior. Through the uniform, the individual signifies that all other allegiances will be suppressed.[6]

### Displaying Rank and Power

In work that involves emergency conditions and in situations that require quick response, such as military and police work and fire and marine services, the display of rank is necessary and made clearly visible. Through insignia, the line of command in the heat of the situation is always in evidence, ensuring that there will be uncritical obedience.[7]

Where uniforms are required, only those with the highest rank can avoid wearing the attire. Julius Roth, in his study of a tuberculosis hospital, discovered that physicians were the least likely of all individuals to put on the protective gown and mask required by hospital rules, because not wearing the attire indicated their freedom from gatekeepers and other social-control mechanisms. In their behavior they laid a claim to their true status, power—the right to exercise force. Similarly, the New York City police commissioner and other security chiefs appear in public in white-collar attire, that is, civilian clothes.[8]

## Nonuniform Uniforms in the Corporate World

The image of authority, because it denies the personal, was chosen as the preferred mode of dress by the business class of nineteenth-century England. The male suit in its form-following style denied the body; in its somber color it repudiated public expression of feelings. It indicated that, so attired, the individual will suppress personal desires and sentiments and conduct himself or herself in the expected "professional" manner. A somber-colored suit with all elements coordinated to create a unified whole emerged as *respectable* attire in the white-collar workplace.[9]

In pairing men with types of neckties, fashion reporter Ruth La Ferla identified four general categories of tie wearers: the collegian, the corporate worker, the cosmopolite, and the iconoclast. The collegian's tie is diagonally striped ribbed silk (rep) and ties embroidered with shields or heraldic insignia (club ties). It communicates that the student wearing it is ready to meet the scrutiny of a vigilant parent or headmaster. Invariably the tie is worn with a neat, button-down collar, and the wearers often prefer ties in school colors. Brooks Brothers and other college stores carry such ties. The corporate worker's tie suggests "power, authority and unflappable decorum." Its message is conveyed by a suitably weighty pattern on a background of blue or claret-colored silk. The cosmopolite, more dashing than the corporate worker, wears solid-color satins or crisp knit ties. The rich lus-

ter of the fabric betrays a love of finery, observed La Ferla. Finally, the conven-
tion-flouting iconoclast prizes wit and inventiveness above stiff propriety. He
uses the tie to set the tone for the rest of his ensemble.[10]

Although personal preference can determine the tie's color and pattern, as well
as the style of shirt, collar, and cuffs, one's occupational group seems to have a
major impact on these choices. A 1989 study of American male attitudes, purchasing patterns, and behavior patterns with respect to ties, commissioned by the
Tie Rack, found that American men believe that the type of tie a man wears often
reveals his occupation and title. The more elevated they are, the more likely he is
to wear an expensive tie.[11] The study found that a civil servant, on the average,
spent no more than $13.00 on a tie, whereas chief executive officers (CEOs) spent
$31.00. Conservative colors, such as blue, were associated with investment
bankers (53 percent), lawyers (59 percent), and corporate executives (62 percent),
whereas the study participants believed that advertising executives were almost as
likely to wear red ties as blue ties. The participants believed accountants and advertising executives, of all the occupational groups, were most likely to prefer bow
ties.

American men also felt that different occupational groups typically wear particular styles, with the civil servant maintaining the most downscale, unimagina-
tive profile. Over 90 percent thought that his tie would be a standard type, and
just about half (49 percent) indicated that it would be made of polyester. Only 10
percent felt that a civil servant would wear a silk tie. By contrast, CEOs were
thought most likely to wear silk (71 percent). Blue was the most dominant color
selected for them (71 percent).

In his well-attended seminars and workshops, John Molloy (1978), the author
of *Dress for Success*, has insisted that his research shows that the appropriate
mode of dress for those who wish to command respect continues to be the
somber business suit. The attire conveys authority because in the public mind it
is associated with knowledge.[12] Banker J. P. Morgan insisted that his employees
dress in a solid-patterned, dark, three-piece suit because it conveys stability and
reliability. Lawyers, on the other hand, have adopted a pin-striped pattern, perhaps a symbolic reference to "straight as an arrow," or honest. Those working in
the entertainment and cosmetics industries often choose a more stylish appearance—body-hugging attire with a more visible fabric motif or texture.

The general assumption is that, as in the theater, many roles cannot be believ-
ably performed without the aid of a costume. It enhances credible performance.
Similarly, the quality of fabric and fit makes rank visible in the corporate hierarchy.

Members of the corporate world generally recognize that the better the quality
of cloth and the better the tailoring work, the more likely the attire is to cover
body imperfections, a paunch, or sagging muscles. Usually it is the older, more
established executive who recognizes the need to conceal the ravages of time;
moreover, he usually has the resources to purchase the more costly attire.
Whereas most junior executives buy their clothes ready-made, their immediate

superiors often have theirs made by custom tailors. The superiors' superiors may secure theirs from even more exclusive tailors who provide even better quality and fit. Through their more imposing appearance, the higher-level executives limit the threat of competition from the younger, more energetic men.

## The Executive Role

"An orderly and handsome" appearance seems to have been imperative for men in authority before and after the American Revolution, as historian Alice Morse Earle observed.[13] With new wealth from bountiful crops and growing industry, these men replaced the durable leather doublets and breeches with suits of plush velvet and silk damask, their brocade coats trimmed in lace and embroidery. Massachusetts governor John Winthrop (1588–1649), a leading Puritan, had several dozen scarlet coats sent from England. In the colonial towns of the North, shops offered imported fabrics, a rich assortment of ornaments, and the latest fashions. In the South, planters had to wait for their crops to be sold before they could have the means to buy luxury clothing from London merchants. Because of this time lag, their clothing was more often sumptuous than fashionable.[14] In sharp contrast to the plain attire of persons lacking an official position or wealth, the attire of the signers of the Declaration of Independence "showed no Republican simplicity," observed Earle. John Hancock's attire was of the richest material available and displayed striking colors. The scarlet velvet suit he wore when he became governor (October 26, 1780) was designed to "make an impression, and yet not to appear over-carefully dressed."[15]

The importance attributed to "executive" attire may be appreciated from the following story: On the eve of Revolutionary War, George Washington wrote a letter to his nephew (George Steptoe Washington) in which he told him that to be considered for a leadership position he must abstain from pursuing the latest fashion. His choice of dress must conform to the prevailing fashion to "stand well in the eyes of other people," and to "impress the simpler of their own folk"; he must be aware that distinct situations each require their own distinct attires.

> A conformity to the prevailing fashion in a certain degree is necessary—but it does not follow from thence that a man should always get a new coat, or other clothes, upon every trifling change in the mode, when perhaps, he has two or three very good ones by him.—A person who is anxious to be a leader of the fashion, or one of the first to follow it, will certainly appear, in the eyes of judicious men, to have nothing better than a frequent change in dress to recommend him to notice.—I would always wish you to appear sufficiently decent to entitle you to admission into any company where you may be:—but I cannot too strongly enjoin it upon you—and your own knowledge must convince you of the truth of it—that you should be as little expensive in this respect as you properly can;—you should always keep some clothes to wear to Church, or on particular occasions, which should not be worn every day.[16]

Knowingly or unknowingly, George Bush took heed. In a report on the then-president's style of dress, Ruth La Ferla observed that when William Thourlby, a New York image consultant and a former actor, said that George Bush had "taken an adjustment," he was not talking tailors' talk. He was using a fancy thespian term for slipping into character—one that aptly described the president's shift of gears sartorially to match each occasion. He wore a hard hat when touring a Kentucky steel plant, a ten-gallon hat in Texas, and a lab coat when warranted, and he changed into camouflage when going hunting. Moreover, he followed a deliberate sartorial strategy during his campaign. Mr. Bush wore a nondescript tan jacket, button-down collars, and bright-red regimental ties. His style said, "We are second in command," Mr. Thourlby explained. After the election, the public saw a one-hundred-day metamorphosis from a modestly outfitted Everyman to an icon of power in pinstripes, straight collars, and subtle ties. His switch to blue was significant. It ascribed to the president a stronger look, Thourlby suggested.[17]

## Origins of the Image of Authority

In artwork from ancient Mesopotamia and Imperial Rome, those with social responsibilities that entailed a public role are presented in erect postures and in torso-concealing attire. In reliefs, monuments, statues, and commemorative plaques of the Sumerian and Assyrian civilizations, the military uniforms and the battle formation of warriors convey an image of solidity. In identical-looking garments—tunic-gowns to the midcalf and nail-studded leather stoles—the warriors are shown marching in columns; moreover, the king's voluminous presence appears in sharp contrast to the scantily dressed captives.[18]

In the *Stele of Hammurabi*, ca. 1792–1750 BC, Hammurabi, the king of Babylon, is shown representing his people before an enthroned sun god and receiving the code of laws. He stands erect. His attire is long, form-following, and body-concealing. The priests and rulers of Mesopotamia (the land between the Euphrates and Tigris rivers) saw themselves as leaders by virtue of greater knowledge. Their authority came out of their ability to provide for the economic and spiritual needs of the population and their desire to protect the people from natural disasters.

Swollen rivers and mud brought down from the mountains often threatened crops in Mesopotamia.[19] The desire of the priests and rulers to overcome the precariousness of the physical environment is mirrored in the strong, emphatic images they created in sacred and secular realms. The most dramatic example is the raised temple known as a ziggurat. Built on stepped levels, as if to unite the world below and heavens above, the ziggurat resembled the solid structure of a mountain, as Joseph Campbell suggested.[20]

In the Roman Republic and during the early empire, the toga was a sign of citizenship. It consisted of a large piece of off-white cloth worn over a tunic. It en-

Stele of Hammurabi, *ca. 1780* BC, *Louvre, Paris. This, the earliest written body
of laws, is engraved on a diorite slab. At the top is an engraving of Hammurabi
standing in front of the sun god, Shamash, who is seated on a mountain. The
god's hand holds a staff and is outstretched toward Hammurabi.*

veloped both shoulders, wrapping the left hand against the chest. Only the right
hand was left free. All male citizens were required to wear the toga for public ceremony. It was the "standard uniform of all classes from a senator to the lowest
plebeian." A man banished from Rome would first be stripped of his toga.[21]

Togas distinguished Roman citizens from the many visitors and the barbarian
slaves that thronged Rome. To receive respect, Roman men had to present a dignified appearance, and wearing a toga helped. The toga limited the number of
tasks a citizen could perform. Also, because the toga was held together only by
draping, movement and gesture had to be refined and poise maintained, lest the
dress come apart. The toga style of dress could be adopted only because Roman
citizens did not have to engage in physical labor; they could leave that to slaves.[22]

The Christian sects that hid in the catacombs in Rome took on the humble tunics of the servant class. These "servants of the Lord" replaced the toga with a
symbol of asceticism. The early Christians also adopted a rectangular pallium

wrap, rejecting the Romans' new emphasis on status symbols, such as blond wigs, makeup, jewels, and silk. They also rejected Persian regalia, barbarian wool cloaks, and the bright plaids and trousers that were worn during this period.[23]

During the first centuries of the Christian era, Roman costume in the countries conquered by the empire as well as in Rome was of two types: long for the wealthy and cultivated classes, short for workers and soldiers. By the sixth century, liturgical costume consisted of several layers of garments worn one on top of the other concealing all personal characteristics. The style, embroidery, and other details of these garments signified *the right to represent the Church.*

Throughout time authority has been carried by the garment: More complete covering and uniformity conveys more authority. The individual must measure up to the garment, or rather must *appear to become* the garment. If it is worn constantly, clothing of authority will ultimately be dehumanizing, subsuming the person it contains.

## The Sociocultural Background of Uniforms

In the early twentieth century, members of the medical profession wore white uniforms to promote the image of a scientific approach to illness and of themselves as professionals whose ministrations in hospitals would result in healing.[24] Similarly, as social life began to acquire a new complexity after AD 1050 and pilgrim traffic, changes in industry, agriculture, and trade began to encourage the development of distinct occupational groups, each group sought to make its authority visible.[25] Uniforms emerged as a means of centralizing authority, identifying hierarchy, and claiming expertise over a specific body of knowledge. The belief prevalent at the time, that God's universe is orderly and each person has a place within it, made possible the institution of a mode of dress that categorized people by occupation and rank.[26]

### The Spiritual Realm: Monastic and Priestly Attire

Within the spiritual realm, between 1000 and 1350 AD, two basic uniforms were confirmed, monastic attire and priestly dress. They represented the two different paths to religious training and life in the Church. From reading the Gospels, the founders of monasteries concluded that a life that was contemplative in nature and lived alone in austere and ascetic fashion was the only true path to God, who alone can fill "inner emptiness." Monks acquired their religious education individually, under the guidance of a spiritual father and through the reading of the Bible within the liturgical framework of monastic life. Within the monastery walls they copied manuscripts and set up libraries, keeping alive an intellectual tradition.[27]

Later clerics acquired their education in theological schools near the cathedrals in cities. Already versed in the liberal arts, they were prepared for an active life in the secular world. The Christian bishops decided the clerics should make visible the ideas and power of the Church to enlighten the population and increase its involvement with religion.[28]

In the medieval period, almost as soon as children were weaned, they were regarded as small adults. They dressed in adult styles and as they got older mingled, competed, worked, and learned expected adult behavior in interaction with adults. Through close supervision of the offsprings' attire, the family guided a child's orientation to adult roles. One of the earliest examples of the use of dress to encourage a very young child to pursue a clerical vocation can be found in the memoirs of Abbot Guibert of Nogent. Written in 1115, when he was in his forties (b.1053?), the memoirs tell of Guibert's childhood experience. His mother's difficulty in giving birth led his father to pledge the unborn child to the service of God. Before Guibert was a year old his father died and thus the pledge could not be revoked. When he was only a young child, his mother dressed him in rich clerical garb to promote the kind of self-control he would need as a priest—the anticipated adult role. So attired, the boy remained on the sidelines, but he watched the other children in their "games and merrymaking." Talking to God through his memoirs, he wrote, "O God, Thou knowest what warnings, what prayers she daily poured into my ears not to listen to corrupting words from anybody. She taught me how and for what I ought to pray to Thee."[29]

*Monastic Attire.*   Monastic life required detachment from the world. It demanded vows of poverty, chastity, and obedience and a life of prayer rather than the act of prayer. The principles of monastic attire were set down in the Rule of Saint Benedict (AD 480–543) and were followed by all the orders created in the eleventh and twelfth centuries. Monks were to be clothed in long, loose-fitting, wide-sleeved habits made of plain wool. The habits were to be simply belted with leather or with a knotted rope. The cuts of the monks' hair, the shapes of their hoods, and the colors and weaves of their habits distinguished the various orders. Saint Benedict believed that the vice of private ownership would be avoided if the abbot supplied all necessary clothing: two cowls, two tunics, stockings, shoes, and a belt. When monks received new clothes, they had to return the old ones to the clothes room for donation to the poor. Saint Benedict was concerned about the image monks presented to the outside world; he did not want them to be considered negligent in their appearance. Monks traveling abroad or receiving important visitors to the monastery were allotted better quality clothing, but it had to be returned after use.[30]

Three of the major monastic orders had female counterparts, and the nuns wore plain, inexpensive dress that enveloped the body from head to toe. In the case of Benedictine and Cluniac nuns, it consisted of a white undertunic, a black gown, and a black veil with a white wimple (headcloth) that covered the head completely except for the face. Cistercians dressed entirely in white and were called the "white ladies."[31]

*Franciscan monk's habit. The clothing reflects the monks' vows of poverty, chastity, and obedience.*

*Priestly Attire.*   In addition to negating sexuality, as monastic attire did, the clothing of the priesthood emphasized the *act* of prayer and connectedness to spiritual and supernatural powers in the liturgy. Hierarchy and access to wealth were also visible.

Ecclesiastical authorities viewed Roman attire as dignified and carrying the image of authority, which was in contrast to that of the invading barbarians, who wore pants. They adopted the Roman style and created the priestly uniform. In AD 573 the Council of Braga ordered that the cassock, an ankle-length, long-sleeved tunic, be worn underneath liturgical vestments. By AD 600 the ecclesiastical authorities had designated the chasuble to be the garment required for celebrating mass. From the Latin word *casula*, meaning "little house," the chasuble projected a sense of solidity. It was worn over the cassock, which was lined in fur to suit the colder climates of northern Europe. The surplice and the alb, overtunics with wider sleeves, white and ornamented, were also worn over the bulky cassock though under the chasuble. The amice and the dalmatic, too, added to the size and volume of the priestly appearance.[32]

Emulating military hierarchy, the Church mandated that those at the top— such as the pope, for whom the white cassock is still reserved, and cardinals and

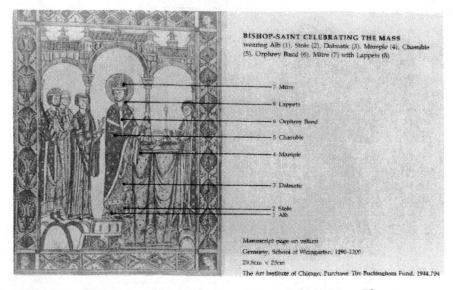

*Priestly attire. Bishop-Saint celebrating the mass, 1190–1200. (C. C. Mayer-Thurman [1975], Raiment for the Lord's Service: A Thousand Years of Western Vestments. [Chicago: The Art Institute of Chicago].)*

bishops—should dress differently from those farther down the ecclesiastical order. With the strengthening of Church authority in the late Middle Ages, the color and the sumptuousness of the clothing began to be used to create distinctions between occasions and ranks. Silk, elaborately embroidered with threads of gold, was reserved for the most solemn affairs. All colors were worn by everyone who said mass, but when they were in street dress, white was reserved for the cassock of the supreme pontiff. Cardinals wore scarlet, bishops purple, and abbots green.[33]

Pope Leo IX (1048–1054) introduced the miter, a tall gilded hat, as part of the distinctive liturgical dress of bishops. In 1049 he placed a miter on the head of the archbishop of Treves, saying: "We adorn your head with a Roman Mitre which you and your successors will always use in the ecclesiastical office after the Roman manner in order to remind you that you are a disciple of the Roman See."[34] The cope, the most opulent outer garment, together with the miter, pectoral cross, pastoral staff, and jeweled rings bishops wear on gloved fingers are all indicators of rank and bear witness to the bishops' spiritual marriage with the Church. As vestments have gradually become more elaborate and costly, they have acquired more mystical associations and sacred connotations.[35]

For many years, during mass, priests presented their backs to the congregation. Consequently, the backs of their vestments were elaborately embroidered with Christian images. In 1963, when the Church moved toward more direct communication, the priests were expected to face the congregation. Since then the front and back of their vestments have been decorated more or less the same, and the vestments have been less richly ornamented.

Ecclesiastical attire increased the body's dimensions and thus its visual significance. It also served to distinguish laity from the clergy, creating a clear line of demarcation between the secular and the sacred and between personal attire and attire that represents the group. By identifying the particular rank of each member of the priestly hierarchy, it specified degrees of authority, which, in turn identified the extent of deference due an individual wearing some type of priestly attire. The specialized dress for priests of different ranks thus came to control their interaction with one another and with the public.

The symbolic significance of priestly attire can be gathered from the following historical evidence: In the past, when a priest was punished, he was required to remove his garb so he could be whipped without demeaning the office or damaging the vestments. When an individual wore the priestly garb, he ceased to be seen or to function as an individual. Instead he became the embodiment of the Church, speaking for it and *vested* with its power.

### The Economic Realm and Guild Attire

The term *guild* is usually taken to mean an organization of those engaged in a particular craft. In the Middle Ages there were many guilds, among them those of carpenters, weavers, shoemakers, goldsmiths, and ironmongers.[36]

The guild had two principal aims, both of which were reflected in the members' attire. First, the guild acted to maintain the guild's economic position in society by regulating who could produce a specific object and how it would be produced. Second, it tried to preserve equality among the masters of the craft. Each guild developed an insignia or a dress that identified the product and the task and allowed for little distinction in rank. This uniform was worn to guild meetings, which were held outside the workplace. For example, the shoemakers guild, organized in 1272, had the motto: "Leather and Skill." Its insignia was a golden chevron and three goats' heads. It was different from the insignia of the cobblers, whose task it was to repair shoes rather than make them.[37] So important was the guild's uniform that "to be clothed" meant that one had attained membership in the guild. As a social observer in 1347 remarked, a uniform was a means of "cherishing the unity and good love among guild members and the common profit of the mastery craft or group of craftsmen."[38]

Because of the advantages that guild membership conferred, the right to wear the uniform was restricted. Although some women developed the skills necessary to excel at a craft, men disregarded their proficiency and discouraged their admission to the guilds.

The few women who did belong were not allowed to wear the group's attire because it would have given them a valued social identity.[39] For the most part women's economic activity was expected to take place in the home. The word *spinster* indicates that spinning was the habitual means of support for many un-married women.[40] But such women could not use their skills for entrepreneurial enterprise. A statute of the Siena guild of wool merchants that covered the period from 1297 to 1309 read: "No one subject to the guild of wool merchants can or should lend any money to a spinster (woman who spins), nor pay for any wool or carded wool until she has done the work. Whoever violates this rule must pay 5 soldi in deniers to the Guild."[41]

The decline of the guild system led to the demise of guild uniforms. Guilds be-gan to diminish in importance in the sixteenth century, when widening horizons and increasing trade led to a demand for new products. The manufacture of these products often necessitated importing expensive raw materials, which entailed increased costs that the guilds could not bear. Guild members became employees of merchant entrepreneurs—men with capital who could carry the costs of the productive process and wait for the return on their investments. The ultimate dissolution of the guilds, however, did not occur until long after the triumph of industrialism.

### The Governmental Realm: Judicial and Military Attire

In the early Middle Ages, law was the province of the kings' courts, clerics, and wise old men. Justice was administered by feudal lords, noblemen, and others en-joying the kings' confidence. As cities, states, and nations developed, the informa-tion necessary for the performance of judicial, military, and police tasks became specialized, requiring special learning. Specialized clothing naturally followed.

*Judicial Attire.*   By the twelfth century, law became a matter to be treated with scientific accuracy, and justice was administered by judges trained in the law and legal thinking. From the twelfth century on, judges were juristic professionals who were expected to know by heart all the pertinent laws. As the number of years of required study and the numbers of doctors of law increased, the jurists demanded to be called lords, rather than doctors or masters, although that title was usually reserved for noblemen and prelates. The attire they adopted was like that of the nobility they succeeded. It resembled court dress.[42]

In all the countries of Western Europe, a new status was created—professional judges. They replaced the feudal lords as administrators of justice. During the fourteenth and fifteenth centuries, judges were understood to be the legal repre-sentatives of the monarch. Elements of dress were part of the drama used to show transfer of the monarch's power to the judge. By wearing robes of the royal er-mine, judges showed that they had the right to decide the fate of many. The king continued to be present vicariously in the law courts, through a state portrait, coat of arms, or the color of judicial robes. Moreover, when judicial decrees were promulgated, armed guards stood by ready to enforce the court's decision.[43]

For the most part, sovereigns clothed their judges. By the sixteenth century, ju-dicial robes in England were no longer bound to the fashion popular among the

*Britain's chief legal officer, Lord Mackay, shown in April 1989. Wigs and robes are mandatory dress in all British courts above the lowest level.*

*U.S. Supreme Court Justice Byron White, June 24, 1993. John Jay, the first chief justice of the United States, designated a simple black gown as appropriate judicial attire. (Photo: Jose Lopez.)*

nobility. The robes assumed the general shape they possess today, with the color, shoulder piece, hood, and wigs marking levels of authority. In England, scarlet silk was and still is reserved for those of the highest judicial rank.[44]

After the French Revolution, with the rejection of the aristocracy in France, traditional judicial attire was abolished. It was later reconstituted, in altered form, because government leaders considered it vital to preserve the dignity of the law. The black robe that judges now wore was free from the implications of court dress and military uniform, yet it conveyed solemnity.[45]

In the New World, the colonies of the South continued the pomp and ceremony established in the English court. Scarlet robes identified judges; lawyers who argued cases wore black.[46] In Massachusetts, where the monarchy was rejected as a source of law, traditional judicial attire shared the same fate. Since the Bible was regarded as the appropriate source of law, the clergy assumed judicial positions. Judges appeared in public wearing black robes, which had earlier identified the clergy of the Church of England. In 1789 John Jay, the first chief justice of the United States, instituted the black academic gown as the appropriate judicial attire in the new nation. The voluminous black robe hides the physical characteristics of the body, denies the personal being, and offers the image of solidity.[47]

*Military Attire.*    Military service grew out of loyalty to the feudal lords. As knights became involved in the Crusades, they were also considered soldiers of the Church. After the Crusades, knights were replaced by retainers, who fought as soldiers when needed. Their attire proclaimed their relationship to a particular lord because they wore his colors or his coat of arms. In fifteenth-century England, many lords had private armies to protect their economic and political interests, and the retainers wore distinctive uniforms. In 1458 the earl of Warwick insisted that his six hundred retainers wear red jackets with an embroidered badge; the marquess of Winchester had his gentlemen and yeomen wear uniforms of "Reading Tawny"; and the earl of Oxford had his entourage wear embroidered suits with the image of a blue boar on the left shoulder and chains of gold around the neck.[48]

Henry VII of England clothed his retinue in white satin. When he visited the French king, the uniforms of the kings and their armies were so lavish that historians called the meeting "the field of the cloth of gold."[49] As the power of monarchs increased, so did the splendor of their armies' uniforms. By the end of the fifteenth century, the king of England and the king of France each had developed a standing army with uniforms so dazzling that the uniforms themselves were expected to intimidate the enemy. Military uniforms were patterned after the sumptuous attire of the aristocracy with weapons added.[50]

English and French soldiers on the American continent wore the colorful, fashionable attire prevalent in their countries at the time, observed Alice Morse Earle. The first inkling the English had that their army uniforms were not conducive to winning a war came during the American War of Independence. Redcoats became easy targets for the nonuniformed, volunteer American soldiers.[51]

The extension of royal power to the seas and the founding of the Royal Navy led to the adoption of seamen's informal garb as the new naval uniform. The officers, as holders of a higher rank, demanded a distinct appearance; they were dissatisfied with the "Quaker plainness" of the blue uniforms assigned to them. In 1775 they petitioned for gold epaulets, which to this day characterize naval attire both in Europe and the United States.[52]

In response to the rise in crime in England in the early part of the nineteenth century, a formalized police force was developed in 1840. A special uniform was designed that was intended to provide an image of discipline and strength: a dark suit with a tall hat, special insignia, a club, and a whistle. The police officer replaced the earlier informal status of watchman or parish constable, who made nightly rounds wearing a simple cloak and carrying a rattle. Through the organization of the new police force and the use of uniforms, the government extended its power.[53]

*Occupational attire acquired new precision and importance in the nineteenth century, as seen in the shift from the watchman's uniform to that of the policeman.*

### The Sports Realm

In its January 25, 1999, issue, *U.S. News & World Report* noted that the International Volleyball Federation is introducing a new dress code for women beach volleyball contestants. They must wear two-piece uniforms with bikini-style bottoms no wider than 2.3 inches at the hips. The rule is designed to ensure a professional standard and uniformity for commercial sponsors' logo. Gabrielle Reece, the most famous woman professional volleyball player, protested because she prefers playing in tights.[54]

A uniform is one means of subordinating the individual to the group effort. Visible uniformity reminds the individual performer that individual excellence should be subsumed in the group endeavor. In choirs, choruses, orchestras, dance lines, and marching bands, uniformity of dress supports and enhances audience appreciation of the performance, leaving them gratified and grateful.[55]

### Notes

1. R. Sennett (1980), *Authority* (New York: Random House), pp. 18–20, 126.

2. J. C. Flugel (1966), *The Psychology of Clothes* (London: Hogarth Press), p. 36. Originally published in 1930.

3. N. Joseph (1986), *Uniforms and Nonuniforms: Communication Through Clothing* (Westport, Conn.: Greenwood Press), pp. 21–27.

4. N. Joseph and N. Alex (1972), "The Uniform: A Sociological Perspective," *American Journal of Sociology* 77 (4): 719–730.

5. Joseph, op. cit., pp. 37–38.

6. In a study that reviews the literature on the wearing of uniforms, Michael Wood pointed out that in a novice the quality of one's appearance affects judgments of competence and technical efficiency. M. Wood (1990), "Consumer Behavior: Impression Management by Professional Servers" (Paper delivered at the 85th Annual Meeting of the American Sociological Association, Washington, D.C., Aug. 11–15).

7. N. Elias (1950), "Studies in the Genesis of the Naval Profession," *British Journal of Sociology* 1 (4): 291–309.

8. J. Roth (1957), "Ritual and Magic in the Control of Contagion" *American Sociological Review* 22: 310–314; also E. Goffman (1963b), *Stigma: Notes on the Management of Spoiled Identity* (Englewood Cliffs, N.J.: Prentice-Hall), p. 141.

9. J. Laver (1969), *Modesty in Dress* (Boston: Houghton Mifflin), pp. 56–58.

10. R. La Ferla (1986), "Tales That Ties Tell," *New York Times Magazine,* June 8, p. 66.

11. Tie Rack U.S. (1989), *The Book of Ties* (New York: Ruder and Fin). The Tie Rack U.S. is Britain's specialty designer and retailer of ties.

12. J. T. Molloy (1978), *Dress for Success* (New York: Warner Books).

13. A. M. Earle (1971), *Two Centuries of Costume in America, 1620–1820* (Rutland, Vt.: Charles E. Tuttle), pp. 725–728. Originally published in 1903.

14. E. Warwick, H. C. Pitz, and A. Wycoff (1965), *Early American Dress* (New York: Benjamin Bloom), pp. 105–109.

15. Earle, op. cit., p. 726.

16. Ibid., pp. 729–730.

17. R. La Ferla, *New York Times,* April 30, 1989. In a similar vein, rather than conforming to traditional executive style, President Ronald Reagan, and earlier President John F. Kennedy, availed himself of custom tailoring for the purpose of projecting an image. In "Live Men Do Wear Plaid" (*Time,* June 28, 1982, p. 39), journalist Hugh Sidey, reporting on the attire President Reagan wore to Europe, observed "Not since John Kennedy posed boldly in a two button coat, defying decades of three button tradition, has a suit of clothes gained so much attention as the blue-and-grey glen plaid outfit that Ronald Reagan wore to Europe." The others in attendance, all swathed in blue and gray, were pained when they saw "Reagan's cheery plaid." "Reagan's glen plaid" has good lineage, the reporter continued. The fabric was manufactured by the British firm of Illingworth, Morris & Co. A bolt was sent to Beverly Hills tailor Frank Mariani, who made all Reagan's suits. Sidey noted that "men in the executive suite rejected President Reagan's choice."

Jack Haber of *GQ* insisted that President Kennedy, by refusing to wear the traditional headgear to his inauguration, put the last nail in the coffin of the men's hat industry, as reported in H. Sidey, "Live Men Do Wear Plaid." Kennedy was proud of his bushy hair and refused to wear a hat, despite the pleading of the industry. In contrast to those before him, President Jimmy Carter sought to project an image of a "less imperial presidency." He abandoned the limousine for the mile and a half walk from the Capitol to the White House for his inauguration and was photographed wearing jeans in the White House and to Cabinet meetings. See G. M. Boyd (1989), "Bush Inaugural Will Signal Open, Accessible President," *New York Times,* Jan. 13, 1989.

18. H. Frankfort (1951), *The Birth of Civilization in the Near East* (Garden City, N.Y.: Doubleday Anchor Books), pp. 56, 63.

19. Ibid.

20. J. Campbell (1974), *The Mythic Image* (Princeton: Princeton University Press), pp. 71–87.

21. F. Boucher (1965), *20,000 Years of Tradition* (New York: Harry N. Abrams), pp. 119–120.

22. Because the toga was held together by draping, Tertullian, one of the Church Fathers, called it "a burden, not a garment." M. and A. Batterberry (1977), *Fashion: The Mirror of History* (New York: Greenwich House), pp. 57–69.

23. M. Johnson (1972), "What Will Happen to the Gray Flannel Suit," *Journal of Home Economics* 64 (8): 5–12.

24. D. W. Blumhagen (1979), "The Doctor's White Coat," *Annals of Internal Medicine* 91 (1): 111–116.

25. C. H. Krueger (1966), "Economic Aspects of Expanding Europe," in *Twelfth-Century Europe and the Foundations of Modern Society*, ed. M. Clagett, G. Post, and R. Reynolds (Westport, Conn.: Greenwood Press), pp. 59–75.

26. M. Mann (1986), *The Sources of Social Power* (Cambridge: Cambridge University Press), pp. 376–377; also C. Mukerji (1983), *From Graven Images: Patterns of Modern Materialism* (New York: Columbia University Press), pp. 39–46; J. M. Vincent (1935), *Costume and Conduct in the Laws of Basel, Bern and Zurich 1370–1800* (Baltimore, Md.: Johns Hopkins University Press), pp. 44–45.

27. R. H. Bainton (1962), *Early and Medieval Christianity* (Boston: Beacon Hill); D. Knowles (1969), *Christian Monasticism* (New York: McGraw-Hill).

28. A. B. Cobban (1975), *The Medieval Universities: Their Development and Organization* (London: Methuen); D. Knowles, *The Evolution of Medieval Thought* (London: Methuen).

29. Guibert of Nogent (1970), *Self and Society in Medieval France*, ed. J. F. Benton (New York: Harper Torchbooks), pp. 40–41. Originally published 1064?–1125.

30. C. Brooke (1947), *The Monastic World* (New York: Random House: Random House); J. Mayo (1984), *A History of Ecclesiastical Dress* (New York: Holmes and Meier), pp. 11–37; I. V. Duchenne (1976), "The Development of Religious Habit of the Faithful Companions of Jesus," *Costume* 6: 00–00.

31. Mayo, op. cit., p. 36.

32. G. Ferguson (1977), *Signs and Symbols in Christian Art* (New York: Oxford University Press), pp. 151–153; Mayo, op. cit., pp. 38–61.

33. M. S. Enslin (1956), *Christian Beginnings* (New York: Harper Torchbooks); Ferguson, op. cit., p. 157; Mayo, op. cit., pp. 123, 167.

34. Mayo, op. cit., p. 40.

35. Ferguson, op. cit., pp. 155–159; Mayo, op. cit., p. 110.

36. P. Cunnington, C. Lucas, and A. Mansfield (1967), *Occupational Costume in England from the Eleventh Century to 1914* (London: Adam and Charles Black), pp. 371–377.

37. E. Wilson (1974), *History of Shoe Fashions* (London: Pitman), pp. 68, 70, 91, 142.

38. T. Wright (1922), *Romance of the Shoe* (London: C. J. Forncomb), pp. 163, 170, 181.

39. J. O'Faolain and J. Martines, eds. (1973), *Not in God's Image* (New York: Harper Colophon Books), pp. 155, 157, 163; M. Richmond-Abbott (1979), *The American Woman: Her Past, Her Present, Her Future* (New York: Holt, Rinehart and Winston), p. 637.

40. M. Chaytor and J. Lewis (1982), "Introduction," in *Working Life of Women in the Seventeenth Century*, ed. A. Clark (London: Routledge and Kegan Paul).

41. O'Faolain and Martines, op. cit., p. 154.

42. M. Bloch (1961), *Feudal Society,* trans. L. A. Manyon (Chicago: University of Chicago Press), pp. 359–374; E. H. Kantrowicz (1966), "Kingship Under the Impact of Scientific Jurisprudence," in *Twelfth-Century Europe and the Foundations of Modern Society,* ed. M. Clagett, G. Post, and R. Reynolds (Westport, Conn.: Greenwood Press), pp. 89–105.

43. W. N. Hargreaves-Mawdsley (1963b), *A History of Legal Dress in Europe* (Oxford: Clarendon Press).

44. Ibid., pp. 31–58.

45. E. McClellan (1904), *Historic Dress in America* (Philadelphia: George W. Jacobs), pp. 148, 335.

46. Ibid., pp. 114–115.

47. Ibid., p. 340.

48. Bloch, op. cit., pp. 312–319; P. Cunningham (1974), *Costume of Household Servants from the Middle Ages to 1900* (New York: Barnes and Noble), pp. 156–160.

49. L. Twining (1967), *European Regalia* (London: B. T. Batsford), pp. 4–19.

50. W. Y. Carman (1957), *British Military Uniforms from Contemporary Pictures: Henry VII to the Present Day* (London: Leonard Hill).

51. Earle, op. cit., pp. 697–698.

52. Elias, op. cit., pp. 291–309.

53. Cunnington, Lucas, and Mansfield, op. cit. pp. 254–260.

54. *U.S. News and World Report,* Jan. 25, 1999, p. 16.

55. J. B. Eicher, S. L. Evenson, and H. A. Lutz (2000), *The Visible Self,* 2d ed. (New York: Fairchild), p. 364.

# 7

# Gender Images

## Theories of Gender Distinction

Gender distinctions have been central to the construction of Western culture and to the organization of American society. Basic to a discussion of the relationship between clothing and gender is the understanding that sexual characteristics at birth are the basis for the "script" identifying social expectations for sex-appropriate behavior.[1] Recent research has shown that very early in life, before children are aware of physical sexual differences, they are alerted to differences in dress; and that as early as age two they classify people according to gender.[2]

Gender scripts help to create two social categories, the members of which deal with their bodies differently, as Goffman observed. Men are socialized to use their bodies in a straightforward manner; they learn to manipulate, grasp, and hold. Women learn to convey the feeling that their bodies are delicate and precious, and that they are expected to caress objects and people.[3]

Gender distinctions arise from gender stratification, feminist theorists suggest. Sally Hacker, for example, observed that the armies of 5,000 years ago provided the model for the subordination of women and for all other forms of social hierarchy.[4] In modern military institutions with male-only student bodies, the curricula stress technical education and a cultural socialization that focuses on hierarchy, discipline, loyalty, and self-control. By excluding women through training in technology, military institutions construct the kind of masculinity that is useful for them. As the graduates of these military schools become leaders in civilian society, they shape organizations and institutions along military lines, reaffirming patriarchy and gender stratification.[5] Military training and competency in mathematics and science have served to keep men in the public sphere, relegating women to the private, unpaid world of warmth and feelings.[6]

Psychologist J. C. Flugel (1930) suggested that the basis for sex-specific attire is sexual *interdependence*. He noted that visual distinction between the sexes has been seen throughout history in most places and in most parts of the world. The fact that people wear sex-specific attire is seen to be "the natural order of things." Sex-specific attire was, and is, intended to alert an approaching individual about *suitability for sexual intercourse*. Even articles of clothing associated with a specific sex have the power to arouse passion in members of the other sex. The tie, jacket,

trousers, and shoes of the male, for example, and the high heels, garters, and girdles associated with the female have been found to elicit sexual responses. Hence,
the purpose of sex-specific attire is to spur interaction between the sexes. Survival
of the species depends on such a distinction.[7]

Sex-specific attire identifies the social spheres in which men and women function, British costume historian James Laver suggested. The "hierarchy principle"
underlies male dress: Men wear class-conscious attire that reflects their standing
in the wider social sphere. Female attire is governed by the "seductive principle":
It is designed to make women attractive to men and hence less significant.[8] The
meaning of appearance, thus, is closely tied to gender expectations for behavior.
To escape such distinction, perhaps, the "cultural elite" in Los Angeles and New
York who shop in high-end stores choose to dress their infants and young children in black.

## Socialization to Gender

Commenting on the use of clothing to reinforce a gender distinction, Gregory P.
Stone observed that dressing a newborn in blue begins a sequence of interaction
that is different from those experienced by a baby dressed in pink.[9] The infant's
appearance in clothing of a sex-specific color sets up expectations about how the
child should act, think, and feel. Among other things, it has traditionally been
anticipated that a baby dressed in blue will be handsome, strong, and agile,
whereas the pink-clad infant will be beautiful, sweet, and graceful. The color
acts as a cue or stimulus that influences how people behave toward the child and
how that child is expected to conduct himself or herself. It is the response of
others to gender-specific attire that encourages gender-appropriate behavior,
Stone concluded.

Norms governing gender-appropriate attire are very powerful, Stone pointed
out. He recalled the revulsion of male participants in a study he conducted from
times  in their childhood when their mothers dressed them in "fussy" attire. They
had wanted to wear what they had learned was "manly" attire. Sex-specific attire,
Stone maintained, enhances the internalization of expectations for gender-
specific behavior. Through subtle rewards and punishments such as those given
through tone of voice, parents encourage or discourage specific behavior, which
leads to the development of a gender identity.[10]

### Gender-Specific Toys

In early childhood, toys and the clothing worn in play may be an important
means of encouraging gender orientation. Girls are more likely than boys to play
dress-up. Many girls also have fun creating ensembles for their dolls, coordinating the color and style of the doll clothes. Playing with Barbie, an extremely popular doll (more than 600 million Barbies have been sold worldwide since 1959),
encouraged awareness of textiles and styles.

*The 1959 Barbie doll displayed the tradi-*
*tional emphasis on female characterist-*
*ics—breasts and hips. Wearing a playsuit*
*and carrying sunglasses, she is outside of*
*the "rough and tumble" work world.*
*(Barbie doll photo used with permission*
*of Mattel, Inc.)*

*Barbie's clothes in the year 2000*
*represent a new ideal: active, modern,*
*and American. This Barbie is wearing*
*the required attire of a "goalie" together*
*with soccer jersey and shorts.*

With the 1970s women's movement and the demand for equal rights, Barbie acquired a variety of costumes: that of an astronaut, a business executive, and a pilot, among others. Her wardrobe, in appropriate colors and fabrics, covered everything from space travel to summit meetings. Playing with Barbie, however, required staying close to home, limiting the opportunity to explore the outside world.[11]

Barbie's body was designed principally to look good in clothes. She is tall and the dimensions of her body, 36-18-33, are unrealistic. She offers a standard that is almost impossible to achieve and thus encourages a sense of inadequacy in young girls.[12]

A decline in sales in 1998 and 1999 may have underlain the "updating" of Barbie and competing dolls, turning them into more realistic role models.[13] In 2000, Mattel and manufacturers of competing dolls introduced dolls with an expanded

*In children's books aprons often identify housewives, whereas self-restraint characterizes the appearance of the male figure. (Illustration by T. Hutchings in* Chippy Goes to the Dentist, *1985.)*

educational purpose to prepare girls for futures based on contemporary opportunities. A presidential candidate, a physician in family practice, and a soccer player were presented as role models. Along with the play value, the dolls were provided with literature or CD-ROMs that emphasize education and other requirements for employability.[14]

The physical characteristics of the toy figures for boys are often menacing. Batman, Superman, G.I. Joe, the Masters of the Universe, and the recent Killer Tomatoes convey power and action.[15] Boys' toys are thus characterized by activity and toughness, even those used indoors, like Nintendo. Functionality and goal-directed appearance inform boys' orientation to clothing.

### Children's Picture Books

Children's storybooks also offer two distinct orientations to appearance. *Confluence* characterizes the portrayal of men, and *contrast* typifies that of women. In these books, the father is portrayed wearing form-following, or loose-fitting, body-concealing attire coordinated to create a unified whole. Dressed in a housedress or a skirt and blouse in contrasting colors, the mother is often depicted wearing an apron. Visually, these outfits cut the body in half, dwarfing the person and suggesting a figure of less significance.

*Girls at work. They are wearing adult-style skirt and blouses—traditional female dress. "Little Suzie, Gotham Court." Circa 1890. (By permission. Museum of the City of New York, the Jacob A. Riis Collection, #130.)*

The apron, moreover, has always been associated in European society with manual tasks and the person who wore it was deemed to have less authority and social standing than someone who did "head work."[16] The aproned person continued as a social category in the new land. In the *New England Courant* of April 2, 1722, Benjamin Franklin wrote that people were unwilling to express their opinions of what they read until they knew who its author was, "whether he is poor or rich, old or young, a Scholar or a Leather Apron Man . . . and give Opinion on the Performance according to the knowledge they have of the author's circumstances."[17]

From aprons to business suits, gender-specific attire varies along with the dimension of authority. Even when animals are used in place of humans, their identity is made visible through gender-stereotypical attire.

Comic books are a popular medium of cultural expression. They offer mythical images of desired behavior. Most comic book characters portray the male in heroic postures. The costumed heroine "Wonder Woman" was invented just before America's entry into World War II. She was the creation of psychologist William Morton Marston and artist Harry J. Peters, and she made her debut in the November 1941 issue of *All-Star Comics*.[18] Wonder Woman thwarted the plans of Master De Stroyer, who had stolen an "atomic engine" from the United

States in order to manufacture bombs to bring the world to its knees.[19] After the war, Wonder Woman was ascribed a more submissive role, and she mostly vanished from public awareness.

As they get older, children increasingly associate dress with stereotypical behavior patterns.[20] They feel that "femininity" requires a docile demeanor, and that negative sanctions follow women who behave in gender-inappropriate ways. When young girls aged seven through thirteen were asked to select one of four clothing styles for a girl who is "bossy"—a characteristic expected of a male—77 percent chose one of the two most extreme styles: either jeans and a T-shirt (the most androgynous outfit) or a frilly dress (the most feminine). From the girls' comments, it became clear to the investigator that they viewed only two kinds of "scripts" leading to bossiness: a prissy, spoiled girl who is likely to wear frilly dresses and a tough person, tomboy, or bully who is not afraid to get on the ground and get dirty. The respondents viewed "bossiness" as an attempt to exercise control, a negative female attribute.[21]

The findings of this study bring to mind the fact that the word *tomboy* was coined in sixteenth-century England. It was used to describe a bold and immodest girl, one who violated society's expectations for meek behavior. That the phenomenon was recognized and given a name suggests that there were many young women at the time who engaged in such behavior. The word was coined during the reign of Elizabeth I, who inherited the throne and successfully ruled for more than fifty years. When badgered by Parliament to marry in order to assure succession, she publicly prayed to God "to continue me still in this mind to live out of the state of marriage."[22]

### Religious Injunctions

The Church Fathers always insisted upon a visual distinction between the sexes and have specified guidelines for sex-appropriate appearance and behavior. Three beliefs underlay their use of dress to establish gender distinction: that real differences exist between the sexes; that the male is the more superior being; and that women's social participation should be limited to reproduction. During the first century, for example, St. Paul criticized the prevailing practice of men and women wearing each other's clothing. He claimed that this habit violated the order of nature because each sex had its own place in the universe. He implored men and women to dress in a manner that demonstrated the superiority of men. Men, he said, must keep their heads uncovered when praying, whereas women must cover their heads as a sign of subservience to men:

> Any man who prays or prophesies with his head covered dishonors his head, but any woman who prays or prophesies with her head unveiled dishonors her head—it is the same as if her head were shaven. For if a woman will not veil herself, then she should cut off her hair: but if it is disgraceful for a woman to be shorn or shaven, let

*Bess Truman, Eleanor Roosevelt, and Edith Wilson, all in hats (1954). (Bettman/Corbis)*

her wear a veil. For a man ought not cover his head, forasmuch as he is the image and glory of God; but woman is the glory of man. For man was not made from woman, but woman from man. Neither was man created for woman, but woman for man.[23]

Later he said:

As in all the churches of the saints, the women should keep silence in the churches. For they are not permitted to speak, but should be subordinate, even as the law says. If there is anything they desire to know, let them ask their husbands at home. For it is shameful for a woman to speak in church.[24]

And in Paul's Epistle to Timothy, he explicitly demanded women's submissiveness:

Let a woman learn in silence with all submissiveness. I permit no woman to teach or to have authority over men; she is to keep silent. For Adam was formed first, then Eve; and Adam was not deceived, but the woman was deceived and became the transgressor. Yet woman will be saved through bearing children, if she continues in faith and love and holiness, with modesty.[25]

Clement of Alexandria, a Church Father of the first century AD, reiterated that passivity is the behavior expected of women.[26]

Prior to the sixteenth century (before the Protestant Reformation and printing), a period when most of the world's population was illiterate, paintings of religious themes warned men and women against the pursuit of sexual and other personal interests. One popular account portrayed in paintings was the story of Salome, which alerts men to female trickery and seduction and informs women of their power and their ability to get what they want despite disapproval and objection. For example, in the *Altarpiece of St. John the Baptist and St. John the Evangelist* (1479) by Hans Memling, King Herod and the soldiers are depicted in the attire of power. Salome is demure and tentative in manner, with eyes cast down, as she stands with a platter to accept the head of John the Baptist.[27]

The cautionary tale of Saint Ursula directs young women to obey their fathers. The Saint Ursula Shrine, now in the Memlingmuseum in Bruges, Belgium, is a glittering miniature house of the late Gothic period (before 1489). The shrine consists of small-scale sculpture and paintings that depict how Ursula went to Rome with ten thousand virgins to appeal to the pope to override her father's decision that she marry. Pope Cyriac is shown blessing Ursula, who is kneeling before him dressed in feminine attire and submissive in posture. He is giving her the Sacrament and bidding her to return home and obey her father's wishes. She complies, but on the way home the travelers are attacked by the Huns and Ursula is killed by an arrow. By disobeying her father she opened herself and her followers to misfortune.[28]

## Female Gender

### Chivalry and Courtly Love

Between the tenth and fifteenth centuries, in the feudal courts of medieval Europe, gender expectations gradually changed. Female submission, male modesty, and self-effacement evolved into a new form: chivalry. Members of the nobility who acquired the title of knight also acquired a new set of expectations for gender-appropriate behavior and appearance. These warriors on horseback viewed women as an inspiration to heroism. The code of chivalry, their rules of conduct, included a pledge to *protect* women.[29] The initial phase of training entailed service in the house of the lord, where the aspiring young knight acquired more polished manners and an appreciation of the important part women played in his culture.

A different kind of relationship between the genders is seen in the courtly love ideal that existed alongside chivalry. It consisted of the idea that love between a man and a woman is of supreme value to life on earth and that love uplifts and ennobles the lover. The courtly love ideal led to the elevation of women as objects of devotion. Today, the customary signs of deference toward women—holding the door for a woman, moving her chair, and so on, are reflections of the code of chivalry and courtly love. Etiquette books continue to espouse these practices but in a somewhat diminished form.

Beauty was the desired characteristic for woman. She was beautiful if she was small, well-rounded, slender, and graceful, "with a small willowy waist."[30] Delicacy and refinement were the desired qualities of female attire in the feudal courts. Long hair was often braided with ribbons or enclosed in long tubes of silk or leather. Women adorned themselves with splendid necklaces. Dresses were made of wool, linen, and sometimes leather and were completed with embroidery, precious jewels, and fur.[31] The floor-length jumperlike garment was the style of the time. It had a long, fitted bodice, low neckline, and very deep armholes. It was figure-revealing, and the generous open expanses around the neck suggested vulnerability.[32]

### Female Appearance and Behavior

The belief on the part of Church Fathers that men were unable to control sexual passion underlay their demand that women cover their bodies. The specific evil evoked by lust was its mastery over the whole man. Saint Augustine wrote

> This lust assumes power not only over the whole body and not only from the outside, but also internally; it disturbs the whole man, when the mental emotion combines and mingles with the physical craving resulting in pleasure surpassing all physical delights. So intense is the pleasure that when it reaches its climax there is an almost total extinction of mental alertness: the intellectual sentries, as it were, are overwhelmed.[33]

Christian thinkers argued that a man's affections should be expressed in the love of God. Shame was expected to accompany even the lawful practice of procreation. To help men remain pure and reach spirituality, this philosophy required women's attire to obscure the body and to be drab and colorless.

In the medieval period many admonitions were prescribed for women.[34] "Thirty-Four Rules" for female deportment held that women's "eyes must be cast down, they must not glance left or right, . . . they must neither look at nor address a man, and must not swing their arms when walking, or cross their legs when sitting; and their hands must be hidden in their cloaks." These expectations for female behavior limited women's involvement with society, according to M. von Boehn.[35]

The rules for female deportment were reinforced in religious art, especially art depicting the Holy Family and Nativity scenes. In the *Book of Hours*, an illuminated prayerbook that first appeared in the second half of the thirteenth century, women are shown in domestic settings, praying and reading the Scriptures or working in the fields. The message conveyed is that women are pure, pious, and submissive. Often women are pictured holding babies. Spirituality, motherhood, and submission to those in higher authority were the characteristics of the ideal woman.[36]

The Church's definition of modest attire that hides the female body was integrated into secular life. Even today, it continues to guide female role behavior.[37]

### The Secular Sphere

Female labor was essential in medieval times. In most social classes, men depended on their wives to do household chores. Tasks assigned to wives varied from manor to manor, from region to region, and from countryside to city. Within a manor women controlled the production of dairy, poultry, and vegetables. In the cities they were involved in the home brewing of beer and the making of cloth.[38] W. Boulting (1910) reported that single women worked at occupations that included water carriers, house painters, and governesses.[39]

Wives were dependent on a husband's protection and support. Men monopolized the more lucrative and rewarding trades and professions, leaving unattached women economically vulnerable. According to French historian Philip Aries, they were also physically vulnerable. Impoverished and with no family protection, they were subject to rape. The community saw itself as a vast gathering of householders, in which living within a family context was the ideal. Departure from this ideal was unacceptable. For an unmarried woman living alone, a house of prostitution became a "safe harbor."[40]

Clothing regulations recognized that to attract a husband women had to wear more frivolous attire than at other times. Women in the courting stage were allowed to make use of color and ornament different from what a wife could use. A woman remained under the jurisdiction of her father and was entitled to wear the attire of his rank until she married. Once married, she was under the control and protection of her husband and wore the clothing of *his* rank.[41]

Although most women could not be party to business contracts, buy or sell land, or control significant amounts of money, some women achieved this end through inherited positions. In the "Wife of Bath," Chaucer (1342–1400) wrote about a merchant's widow who took part in the pilgrimage to Canterbury. She carried on her husband's business after his death, "making cloth that bettered that of Ypres and of Ghent." In company she loved to chat and laugh. She was skilled in love, having had five husbands, and knew how to take care of "love's mischances." Chaucer described her attire in this manner: Her kerchiefs were finely woven, her hose of the finest scarlet red, and her shoes soft and new. He concluded that her attire testified to her income. Contrasting herself to women who decided that they would live in virginity, "as clean in body as in soul, and never mate," she acknowledged, "I'll make no boast about my own estate."[42] The Wife of Bath clearly viewed the body as a source of sensual pleasure. This pleasure carried over to her joy of dressing and ornamenting herself in a manner that would attract male interest. Her resources, of course, made that possible.

Jan Arnolfini and His Wife *by Jan van Eyck, 1435 (London, National Gallery). It was fashionable to stress the woman's abdomen in art during this period.*

### The Procreative Role

Throughout time women have been expected to marry and assume their biological role of procreation. In Indian art from prehistoric times, an emphasis on the hips, breasts, and belly alluded to women's biological ability to bear and nurture children. Over a two-hundred-year period in the late Middle Ages, the black plague decimated a large portion of Europe's population and the iconography of death became a popular subject in art. Women's power to nourish through breast feeding also acquired religious meaning, and breasts as "containers of

*The "trapeze line" by Yves St. Laurent,*
*1953 (Jardin des Modes). The focus is*
*again on the abdomen.*

nurturing" were frequently portrayed in art. The prevailing style of dress focused on women's abdomens, simulating a pregnant look. It was as if to remind
women that bearing and nurturing children was their unique privilege and responsibility.[43]

After World War II, in the late 1940s and through the 1950s, fashion styles
again alluded to pregnancy. Yves Saint Laurent's 1953 "Trapeze line" consisted of
clothes that emphasized wide hips and called attention to the abdomen, glamorizing maternity and womanhood. The breasts assumed new importance. It was
during this period that the large bosoms of Marilyn Monroe and Jayne Mansfield
were celebrated.[44] The exhortation by those in authority in the workplace, that
women return to the traditional female role and leave the jobs to men returning
from the war, led to the so-called baby boom (1946–1960).

### The Wife's Role

With the advent of commerce and the growth of monarchies, it was no longer
sufficient for a man to dress himself in attire that supported his claim for rank. To
demonstrate his power and wealth, a husband had to dress his wife and other
members of the household. The family members' appearance signified the consciousness of a "we." In style, texture, and color the attire was similar to that of
the head of the household. To create dynasties, monarchs established the authority to rule through birthright. The royal wife wore sumptuous garments and dazzling jewelry, supporting the king's claim to the monarchy and helping to create
an image of stability, power, and wealth.[45]

*Eleonora of Toledo, wife of Cosimo I de Medici, and her son, Giovanni de Medici, c. 1550. (Galleria degli Uffizi, Florence.) Her lavishly ornate costume represents her high social rank, freezing her into immobility.*

## Women in Male Roles

In the sixteenth century three women ascended the throne: Isabella of Aragon/Castile, Catherine de Médicis in France, and Elizabeth I in England. They wore female attire—dresses, in a style that extended the body but deemphasized the maternal and nurturing role. A high-necked masculine bodice flattened the chest, and its V-shaped padded front resembled the armor of noblemen. The bodice extended over a voluminous skirt that was supported by a farthingale, a structure of stiff hoops. Like the high neck and skirt, puffed sleeves drew attention away from the body, thus enforcing distance and creating a sense of amplification. The many gemstones the women wore provided the brilliance characteristic of male monarchs. Unlike male monarchs, queens carried no arms, but they were surrounded by attendants who did.[46]

Women of the nobility in other European courts also dressed within this new paradigm. The image they adopted was that of confluence: the breasts flattened, the waistline repudiated, their dress form-following rather than form-fitting, coming straight down and just touching the floor. A stiff white ruff effectively denied access to the expression of feelings.

Similarly, in the 1970s, women in managerial positions observed that a key to being considered professional was dressing in a manner that minimized the maternal, nurturing, and sexual dimensions of their appearance. A form-following jacket over a blouse concealed the contours of the female body and, like a shield, created distance. They felt that this distance strengthened their ability to give orders and the probability that they would be carried out.[47]

Women holding male roles adopt occupational attire similar to that of the male. The practice seems to go back to at least ancient Egypt where in the "Seated Statue of Hatshepsut," the queen is dressed in the royal attire of a male pharaoh.

Queen Elizabeth I *by Cornelius Ketel, n.d. The queen's breasts are deemphasized by the dress, but her ability to extend her reach is emphasized by both the dress and the attendants seen in the background. Pinacoteca, Siena.*

Women who hold authority positions in contemporary society are expected, like men, to project self-restraint. In her chambers at federal court in Washington, D.C., Judge Ruth Bader Ginsburg wears a form-following jacket that hides the waistline and obscures the breasts. (Photo: Paul Hosefros/ NYT Pictures.)

Canon Anne Richards of the Episcopal Diocese of New York, Mar. 28, 1999. (Photo: Nancy Siesel/New York Times.)

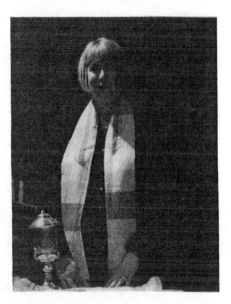

Rabbi Jill Kreitman of Central Synagogue, Mar. 28, 1999. (Photo: Nancy Siesel/New York Times.)

*Up to the sixteenth century, women artists remained mostly anonymous. The first woman to emerge as an artist and become widely recognized in her own lifetime was Sofonisba Angussola (1535–1625). She was called to Madrid as a court painter and worked there for twenty years. Before leaving for Spain, she painted her sister Minerva's portrait. The painting projects openness and a sense of intimacy. (Sofonisba Angussola [1559], "Portrait of the Artist's Sister Minerva." Milwaukee Art Museum, Layton Art Collection. Gift of the Family of Mrs. Fred Vogel, Jr.)*

In the last three decades of the twentieth century, more and more women have become ministers, rabbis, and new age spiritual leaders. By March 1999 there were about 500 women rabbis nationwide, and the Episcopal Church had about 1,500 active female priests.[48] These women feel comfortable in the flowing liturgical robes that allow clergywomen to blend easily with men.

For a dramatic effect, clergywomen drape stoles around their shoulders like the men, but they personalize the shade. For example, purple is the customary color for Lent. Women may choose the shade of purple they prefer, be it lavender, gradations of pink, or stoles with fuchsia highlights, observed reporter Elizabeth Hayt.[49] Beauty for women entering the ministry is acceptable.

Dressing for the pulpit requires that women appear neither too feminine nor too mannish. Clothing that hints at sexuality is threatening. Even something as small as a belt may be a problem. A female Episcopal priest being interviewed as a candidate for bishop wore a black dress with a slight V-neck, allowing her to wear a clerical shirt and collar underneath. The dress was cinched at the waist with a narrow belt. The outfit was hardly suggestive, but it revealed the contours of her figure. She lost the election and was later told that one of the reasons might have been her dress.[50]

Women clergy live in the real world, and if they wish to be promoted, the length of their skirts, the height of their heels, and the color and style of their hair must be appropriate, observed Rabbi Sherre Zwelling, of Sinai Temple in West Los Angeles.[51]

In Connecticut, female priests usually wear clerical shirts with prim dirndl skirts and Shetland sweaters. The collar is the sign of the priesthood; the skirt affirms their femaleness, and the sweater hides the breasts, denying their sexuality.[52]

A carefully chosen outfit will not serve as a lightning rod for criticisms. People who have problems with female clergy will then focus on some other issue to voice their complaints. "A woman's dress is the most socially acceptable way to do this," said Rabbi Merdechai Liebling, senior consultant to the Jewish Reconstructionist Federation in Philadelphia. The challenge is to look modern, yet modest.[53]

Rejecting the traditional female role has usually been accompanied by a change in dress. For example, prior to the Renaissance, the Church allowed women who renounced their sexuality and publicly announced their virginity to wear *male attire* and to preach. The Acts of the Apostles, a text thought to have been written about AD 160, tells the story of Thecla, a beautiful young woman engaged to be married. One day, she hears Paul preach chastity. Enthralled, she rejected her suitor. When an attempt to burn Thecla at the stake failed, she appealed to Paul and was accepted as his student. After she completed her training, she went out to teach dressed in male attire.[54]

Historian Marina Warner observed that there is ample evidence to suggest that many women who wanted to escape arranged marriages cropped their hair in male fashion, donned male attire, and arrived at monastery gates disguised as men. Often their identity as women was not discovered until their death. In the third century, Margaret of Antioch, bearing the name Brother Pelagius, lived quietly as a monk until she was accused by a young woman of fathering her child. Margaret suffered the accusation in silence and was condemned to solitary confinement for the rest of her life. With death at hand, she wrote a letter revealing her innocence. She was then recognized as a woman and honored as a saint for her suffering.[55]

The most celebrated example of a woman who rejected female passivity is Joan of Arc. After proclaiming her virginity, and thus asserting her right to wear male attire, she donned a knight's armor and led men into battle on a white horse. Because a woman bearing arms was not acceptable in the Church's view, she was accused of immodesty. For political reasons Joan was burned at the stake as a heretic, and, to the end, she refused to change into women's clothes.[56] It was not until World War I that women could formally wear military attire.[57]

## *Decline of Passivity: The Gibson Girl*

The image of the Gibson girl was distinctly American.[58] Her hair was long, her bust was big (thirty-six-inches), she displayed a narrow, anatomically precise waist and broad hips, and her legs were well concealed. She was maternal and wifely, and her clothes appeared decorous and reputable. She conveyed stability.[59]

At the beginning of the twentieth century, the expanding economy and increasing military needs in the United States encouraged women to move out of the home and into factories, offices, schools, hospitals, and shops. The Gibson girl dress—the shirtwaist—signified the change. The shirtwaist was worn with a tailored skirt. This practical style was chosen by working women and by women who were serious about sports. Artist Charles Dana Gibson popularized the style by portraying beautiful young women.

Feminists at the time saw the Gibson girl as the prototype of the new woman—"braver, stronger, more beautiful, and more skillful and able and free, more human in all ways" than the traditional woman. According to the November 1911 issue of the *American Businesswoman,* there were five million self-supporting women in the United States employed in 295 occupations. Mass production made shirtwaists available for as little as $1.50 and suits for $10.00.[60] Even the poorest woman could dress comfortably and attractively for an active life at a minimal cost.[61]

The movement of middle-class women into the full-time labor force has been increasing throughout the twentieth century. The 1970s women's movement and the civil-rights acts made it possible for women to wear police and firemen's uniforms. This clothing indicated that they had the right (in the past held only by men) to interfere in public incidents and assert their authority.

Modern working women can also afford to make extensive use of jewelry. In addition to identifying married or engaged status, they ornament themselves, their outfits, or both by wearing earrings, brooches, necklaces, beads, pearls, and precious and semiprecious stones.[62] An outfit, mood, or occasion determines the choice. Secretary of State Madeleine Albright, for example, wears a different brooch with each outfit as a way of "completing" the look, i.e., creating a unified whole.

On the basis that national security was undermined by considering sex ahead of talent, the U.S. Senate voted on July 31, 1991, to remove the ban on women combat pilots.[63] The capacity of women to think rationally and to make effective decisions was thus recognized. The movement of women to positions of authority was legitimated by the Puritan rejection of waste, with its emphasis on self-determination, together with higher education and an expressed need for the abilities of the entire population. Nearly five hundred years have passed since Joan of Arc was burned at the stake for donning a knight's armor and leading men into battle.

### The Demise of Subservience: The Flapper

The flapper of the 1920s was the antithesis of the Gibson girl. The aesthetic that characterized the flapper was that of youthfulness, suggested Flugel.[64] Visually, the flapper conveyed intensity, energy, and volatility.[65] Social critics described its impact as leading to "a revolution in morals and manners."[66] She bobbed her hair, her dresses were tight, straight, and short, with a low waist, usually placed about the hips. Her chest was flattened, her waist was hidden, and her legs were kept in plain view.[67] Bones, stays, and long skirts were gone. Flappers' clothing was not stiff, or rigid, and fewer garments were required.[68] In the workplace the flapper joined the Gibson girl as a new category of womanhood.[69]

Articles published in the *Literary Digest* of the 1920s complained that the flapper style of dress supported an assault on male prerogatives. Men had always been the initiators of sexual encounters, and the saloon had been a male preserve. Now women were drinking with men, swearing, smoking, and using contraceptives.[70] The flapper's style of dress supported female assertiveness, breaching traditional ideals of femininity and masculinity.

### Rise of the Active Ideal

Women had been required to cover their heads in public as a sign of submission and obedience to men since early Christian times. In the United States, hats, which some women had interpreted as symbols of middle-class respectability, were repudiated in the 1950s.[71] As the wife of President John F. Kennedy, Jacqueline Kennedy did popularize the pillbox hat, which sat on her well-groomed hair like a crown. But by the end of the 1960s, women in general stopped wearing hats except in church. By the late 1960s women also rejected other upper-class refinements, such as the look consisting of a basic black dress, white gloves, and a strand of cultured pearls. That attire was generally replaced by pantsuits and slacks.

In 1982 actress Jane Fonda brought out her first aerobics videotape, helping to bring exercise to a whole new segment of the population—those who never venture out to an exercise class. Youthfulness and health were emphasized by women's magazines and the cosmetics industry, which encouraged more women to join exercise classes. The popularity of working out resulted in what reporters called "the fitness craze."[72]

As aerobics and working out became popular, the dancer's black leotard and tights and the sweat suit were gradually replaced. With the development of spandex-like fabrics that allowed greater freedom of movement, the unisex capri-length "wrestler" unitard came into use, which was worn over a cropped top. The unitard and similar two-piece sets made of stretch fabrics were skintight, hugged the body, and allowed no place for bulges to hide. In addition to allowing for a wide range of motion, these exercise outfits encourage *restraint* in the consumption of food. The newest exercise attire, a thong-style brief or leotard with high-cut legs, gives high visibility to the upper thigh muscles, and long well-toned legs are the current fitness ideal.

## Conclusions

Throughout many centuries, the Church's injunction to sex-specific attire has remained essentially unchanged. As Church Fathers decreed long ago, the body continues to function as a blackboard upon which values and expectations for behavior are displayed. Within the secular realm, styles of dress have at times differed from Church prescriptions, depending on expectations for participation in the public sphere. As the male role became differentiated from that of the female, men's style of dress became visually separated from that of women, and contrasting images of masculinity and femininity evolved to support the expectation that men and women would function in separate spheres. Visual interdependence existed in the monarchical courts, where men depended on women to support their claim to the right to rule. Female attire developed around the same principles of power and authority as did male attire.

Economic and political conditions in the United States in the twentieth century gradually made it possible for women to reject clothing that suggested submission; and public education enabled them to reject relegation to the domestic sphere. Women exercise, thereby reducing stress and acquiring new energy. In the public sphere, women have the option of dressing in clothes that hide the breasts and deny the hips, giving them greater opportunity to participate in the decision-making process.

## Male Gender

### Rational Piety and Worldly Engagement

As noted earlier, Church Fathers continued the biblical tradition of establishing visual distinction between the sexes and set up guidelines for sex-appropriate appearance and behavior. In the first century AD, Clement of Alexandria declared that beards were the badge of masculinity and that it was sacrilegious to trifle with them because they were a symbol of man's stronger nature. He claimed that "by God's decree hairiness is one of man's conspicuous qualities. Whatever smoothness or softness there was in him God took from him when he fashioned the delicate Eve from his side . . . his characteristic is action; hers, passivity."[73]

The prohibition against sloth, one of the seven deadly sins, was directed to men in particular. It supported the idea that males should play an active role in social life and encouraged males to take part in the socioeconomic process.[74] Medieval literature depicted idleness, or sloth, as the "feet of the devil that halt man in his tracks" and declared that it demonstrated a lack of feeling for the world, the people in it, and oneself.[75] Church authorities in medieval times interpreted Saint

Paul's dictum, "He who shall not work will not eat," as a universal injunction against withdrawal from society. Monks were enjoined to remain in touch with secular matters in order to gain better control over "satanic forces."[76]

In the medieval period, teachings about the sin of pride advocated humility and modesty in dress. Thomas Aquinas preached that work was essential for the survival of the individual and the community. Protestantism subsequently viewed labor as glorifying God and proclaimed it the moral duty of every man. Resistance to one's calling was considered blasphemy.[77] *Rational piety* and *worldly engagement*, the expectations for male behavior, were supported by attire that complied with the injunction to modesty and self-effacement.

Desired appearance and behavior for each of the genders was radically different in the feudal courts.[78] To be a knight was a male privilege that had to be earned by the individual and bestowed by his king or lord. Horsemanship and swordsmanship were part of the training. From early childhood on, male members of the nobility jousted, wrestled, and exercised to develop coordination and strength. Medieval jousts and tournaments pitted one man against another. Combative games were played during solemn occasions and social events, such as coronations and royal marriages, and physical prowess was regarded as a virtue. In his erect posture, with armor, shield, and sword, the knight conveyed an image of invulnerability.[79]

### Male Physical Ideal of the Nobility

The posture, agility, and physical strength that men of the nobility enjoyed became an ideal for the mercantile middle class during the Renaissance. Pope Pius II (1458–1464) recommended that schools adopt games and exercises to develop "the general carriage" of children. They were to be trained to hold their heads high and to look straight ahead, unafraid. Whether walking, standing, or sitting, children were to bear themselves with dignity.[80]

Male members of the royal courts exercised and played sports. The kings of England saw tennis as essential for developing agility, speed, and the kind of strategic thinking they believed would help them run the country. Henry VIII even had thin-soled shoes designed to help him improve his chances of winning at tennis.[81]

### Aggressive Masculine Personae

An aggressive physical persona began to emerge as an ideal in the United States at the beginning of the nineteenth century. Among men who made their way west a strong physique symbolized the victory of man over nature.[82] The election of President Andrew Jackson (1829–1837) represented the ascendancy of the brawny man, whose rough-and-tumble image diverged dramatically from the refined sensibility of the European aristocracy.

To define themselves, identify their status, and attract female interest the American landed aristocracy of the colonial period wore European fashions.[83]

*P.S. 105 Manhattan: Vacation Playgrounds, Bronx Park, Aug. 19, 1902. The counselors' muscles are well-developed and put into evidence. The students are somewhat suspicious of the whole exercise. (Museum of the City of New York, the Jacob A. Riis Collection, #UN76.)*

Well to-do American men continued to wear sumptuous attire well into the nineteenth century.

In the mid–nineteenth century, however, merchants and industrialists in the United States who acquired wealth began rejecting European fashion. They were, in part, influenced by middle-class moralists who had decreed that it was decadent for men to wear powder, wigs, and richly ornamented and patterned clothing in the cavalier style.[84]

Even the older, venerated patriarchs such as Thomas Jefferson were chided as "dandified" and accused of having what were identified as female characteristics—"timidity and whimsicalness." He was criticized as being a man who took counsel in "feelings and imagination." Jeffersonians were accused of a "womanish attachment to France."[85] The new industrialists decided to wear plain and simple clothing so as "to impart trust and confidence in business affairs."[86]

New immigrants from Germany and Ireland, who competed physically among themselves or against others, brought an interest in muscle power to the United States. Youths seeking to distance themselves from an older immigrant generation, which they considered sedentary, seized the opportunity to engage in sports. They believed that to be successful in life they needed to develop physically strong bodies.

Encouraging the development of an aggressive masculine persona after the mid–nineteenth century were two additional forces. The first was a growing concern among men that they were being enfeebled by the doctrines of "feminized Christianity"—a version of Christianity that emphasized God's love rather than wrath.[87] Writers in the popular press rejected the eastern establishment as effete, and encouraged men "to take their manhood back from Christian women." They proclaimed the new man as a "natural nobleman," whose values sanctioned self-discipline and a capacity to continue in the face of exhaustion.[88]

### Gay Male Culture

The appearance of a gay male culture was the second force. On city streets gay men imitated women's dress, manner, and voice. Heterosexual men sought to avoid being perceived as feminized males and began defining themselves in opposition to all that was soft and womanlike.[89]

### Nineteenth- and Twentieth-Century Male Physical Ideals

Overcoming a sense of physical inadequacy became a goal for many young men on the eastern seaboard. Masculinity required proof, and proof required serious physical effort. Changing one's physique to appear tough and strong was one important way to affirm one's manhood.[90]

In the past, reaching manhood had entailed holding a job, getting married, and demonstrating the capacity for autonomy and responsibility. By the turn of the century these qualities were no longer sufficient to differentiate heterosexual men from effeminate men.[91] Characteristics of the "sissy" such as weakness, dependency, helplessness, and outward feminine appearance were contrasted with a sturdy, muscular frame that suggested strength and courage.[92]

The desirability of fitness, agility, and strength was also reflected on college campuses. A German professor at Harvard University, Charles Follen, introduced the students who studied German to fitness. He met with them twice a week, on his own time, and introduced them to gymnastics. A formal program in physical education was instituted at Harvard in 1861. All students were required to appear at the newly constructed gym for half an hour four times a week. Erect posture, agility, physical strength, and competition were incorporated into Ivy League education.

In the 1870s athletic clubs and baseball leagues were established in many American cities. In the 1880s football gained importance at American colleges, and the Young Men's Christian Association (YMCA) made working out with weights a key part of its program. Famous weightlifter Eugene Sandow made bodybuilding popular among men. Those who relentlessly pursued muscle power and achieved their goal were admired for their "iron will."[93]

In 1895 the *Wesleyan University Bulletin* observed that the end of the century had become an era of "rampant athleticism" in which athletic activity was thought to make men healthier and instill moral virtue.[94] A massive nationwide

*Promoter of the mythical cowboy,*
*William F. Cody, 1846–1917.*
*(Photo: Marceau, New York 1908.*
*Chester County Historical Society;*
*West Chester, Pa.)*

health and athletic craze emerged as men sought to acquire manly physiques. Many men, working and middle-class, heterosexual and homosexual, did whatever they could to appear manly. Thousands of men worked out in gyms and on athletic fields. There was a dramatic increase in bicycle riding, tennis playing, golfing, weight lifting, and boxing. It was as if men were determined to confirm the sentiments of G. Stanley Hall that "you can't have a firm will without firm muscles."[95]

In the 1860s and 1870s cowboys were called herders and presented in public print and writing as rough, uncouth, shaggy, and dirty. Their behavior was violent, barbarous, and rowdy and unlikely to appeal to women. Laura Winthrop Johnson, writing in 1875, reported that there was no glamour in these "rough men with shaggy hair and wild staring eyes, in butternut trousers stuffed into great rough boots."[96]

The mythic cowboy was born around 1882 in the fictional biography of a cowhand named Buck Taylor. Taylor was part of a traveling circus organized by Buffalo Bill Cody to portray the taming of the Wild West.[97] This book and the Wild West show presented the cowboy as a man of action, daring, bravery, and skill. His compassion was generalized—not directed toward a particular person. The mythic cowboy wore dramatic outfits. He was a man women dreamt about but did not marry. In Owen Wister's 1902 novel *The Virginian*, and in Harold Wright's *When a Man Is a Man* (1916), the cowboy moved in the world of men but formed no lasting emotional bonds.[98] He lived alone, a "hermitted horse-

*Going West. Last party sent out by Mrs. John Jacob Astor before her death. Children's Aid Society, ca. 1890. (Museum of the City of New York, the Jacob A. Riis Collection, #23.)*

man" out on the range. Taylor's fictional character caught the attention of novelists and movie producers. In the literary and film genres that emerged, the glamorized cowboy represented rugged, outdoor masculinity.[99]

Stories about the "wild west," where men had the freedom to ride and guns to shoot, instilled a sense of inadequacy among many young American men, and they strove to "reform" their bodies. In his autobiography, Theodore Roosevelt recalled that he had been a sickly child, a delicate boy who suffered from asthma. His father had constantly exhorted him to "make your body."[100] Like other young men, Theodore Roosevelt journeyed west in 1885 seeking to exorcise his disability and attain manliness. He went to what had been the frontier, the Dakota territory, to try his hand at ranching. There he transformed himself from a "a pale, slim young man with a thin piping voice"[101] to the embodiment of strength, self reliance, and determination by practicing riding and shooting.[102]

Charles Atlas was another example of a young man who "reformed" his body to acquire a sense of physical adequacy. Born Angelo Siciliano in Italy in 1893, Charles Atlas came to the United States in 1910. He was scrawny, pale, nervous, and weak, a "97-pound runt." One day he went to Coney Island with a very pretty girl. They were sitting on the sand when a big, husky lifeguard kicked sand in his face. He felt he could do nothing about it and told the girl that someday if he met this man again he would beat him. The girl moved elsewhere on the beach. Walk-

*In the film* Commando, *Arnold
Schwarzenegger is Colonel John
Matrix, a retired commando who
is forced back into action. (1985
Twentieth Century Film Corp.)*

ing home and feeling dejected, he passed a large poster of the mythic Atlas lifting
the weight of the world. At that moment he resolved to alter his body into one capable of heroic feats. With weights he transformed his body into "the world's
most perfectly developed" and changed his name to Charles Atlas.[103]

Charles Atlas promoted his body-building technique, promising to turn other
"97-pound weaklings into real he-men." He began by advertising his technique,
Dynamic Tension, in boys' magazines, in comic books, and in the pages of *Super-
man*. The advertising continued in virtually every issue of *Superman* thereafter.[104]
His ads asked, "Are you a redblooded man?" and "Do you want to be a tiger?"[105]
He thus linked a masculine identity to animal-like blood-thirstiness.

### Boxing

At the turn of the century, boxing was seen as an effective means of countering
the "womanishness" of modern "overcivilized" society. A boxing fan in 1888
wrote, "This vaunting age needs a saving touch of honest, old-fashioned bar-
barism, so when we come to die, we shall die leaving men behind us, and not a
race of eminently respectable female saints."[106]

Boxing began on city streets among working-class men to compensate for the
undermining of their masculinity by the regimentation of factory work.[107] The
goal of the boxers was to win.[108] Male anger was rechanneled through physical
aggression, and boxing matches enabled spectators to become vicarious consumers of success. The game depended on violence but required craftsmanlike
deftness and skill.

*The Internet economy has made it possible for some newly wealthy men to
spend more time with their children, play with them, and feed them lunch.
Pictured is computer millionaire Jeff Treuhaft, formerly of Netscape
Communications. (Photo: Peter DaSilva, New York Times, Oct. 27, 1999.)*

Boxers were celebrated as embodying the qualities of toughness, physical
prowess, and ferocity, negating all that was soft, feminine, or sentimental. Being
manly now meant not being womanly. The "manly art" defined a man's masculinity by his sensitivity to insult, his coolness in the face of danger, and his ability to give and take punishment.[109]

Bodybuilders, on the other hand, attempted to evoke the aesthetic ideal of classic statuary. It was their appearance that mattered, not action. To achieve "the
look," they had to remove their body hair. The shaved body gave the bodybuilder
a more childlike appearance and feel.[110] The shaved body of the American body
builder Steve Reeves, for example, canceled out the image of a super-normal
adult male body.[111] The denuded body informed the observer that this is not a
body to fear on account of its size but a body to admire.[112]

Hollywood movies that exposed the male body usually focused on the chest.
The powerfully polished muscular physique spoke of male power. To display their
virility, male film actors huffed and puffed and expanded their chests.

Throughout much of the twentieth century, modern men have given little
thought to jewelry. The jewelry they do wear is designed to support a particular
identity. The most common types of jewelry men buy are religious pendants, depictions of the American flag, and insignia that denote connectedness, such as a

school ring, a wedding band, or an identity bracelet.[113] Once men put on such jewelry, it usually becomes a permanent part of their social personae.[114]

*     *     *

In American society, film and television actors depicting the masculine fighting ideal often imbue the character with a moral strand. The medieval knightly tradition of righting wrongs continues in Hollywood films featuring actors like Clint Eastwood, Charles Bronson, Sylvester Stallone, and Arnold Schwarzenegger, and television programs popular at the end of the twentieth century such as "The X-Files" and "Walker, Texas Ranger." They portray the idea that the male role entails a battle to protect the innocent and helpless and invest fighting and winning with a higher ideal.

## Notes

1. G. P. Stone (1962), "Appearance and the Self," in *Human Behavior and Social Processes*, ed. A. M. Rose (Boston: Houghton Mifflin). Also T. de Lauretis (1987), *Technologies of Gender: Essays on Theory, Film and Fiction* (Bloomington: Indiana University Press), pp. 1–26.

2. S. M. Levin, J. Balistieri, and M. Schukit (1972) "The Development of Sexual Discrimination in Children," *Journal of Social Psychology and Psychiatry* 13: 47–53.

3. E. Goffman (1979), *Gender Advertisements* (New York: Harper and Row).

4. S. Hacker (1989), *Pleasure, Power & Technology* (Boston: Unwin Hyman), p. 59.

5. Ibid., pp. 60–61.

6. Ibid., p. 61.

7. J. C. Flugel (1966), *The Psychology of Clothes*. (London: Hogarth Press), pp. 25–30. Originally published in 1930.

8. J. Laver (1969), *Modesty in Dress*. (Boston: Houghton Mifflin), pp. 1–44.

9. Stone, op. cit., pp. 107–110.

10. E. Gross and G. P. Stone (1964), "Embarrassment and the Analysis of Role Requirements," *American Journal of Sociology* 57: 1–15.

11. R. L. Coser (1986), "Cognitive Structure and the Use of Social Space," *Sociological Forum* 1: 1–26.

12. "She Is No Barbie, Nor Does She Care to Be," *New York Times*, Aug. 15, 1991. In this article Santa's list included a "Happy to Be Me" doll, an alternative to Barbie. Her measurements, 36–27–28, were more realistic than those of Barbie's 36–18–33.

13. Sales had declined from a high of $1.5 billion in 1997 to about $750,000 per year. C. L. Hays (2000), "A Role Model's New Clothes," *New York Times*, Apr. 1.

14. Ibid.

15. "Seeking a Place on Santa's List," *New York Times*, Feb. 11, 1991.

16. T. Carlyle (1967), *Sartor Resartus* (New York: Dutton), p. 23. Originally published in 1838.

17. C. M. Picket (1977), *Voices of the Past: Key Documents in the History of American Journalism* (New York: John Wiley and Sons), p. 26.

18. *Comics, Comix and Graphic Novels* (London: Phaidon Press, 1996), pp. 86–88; M. Benton (1992), *The Illustrated History of Superhero Comics* (Dallas: Taylor Publishing), pp. 110–111.

19. Ibid.

20. A. A. Albert and J. R. Porter (1988), "Children's Gender Role Stereotypes," *Sociological Forum* 3: 184–210.

21. S. B. Kaiser, M. Ruddy, and P. Byfield (1985), "The Role of Clothing in Sex-Role Socialization: Persons' Perceptions vs. Overt Behavior," in *The Social Psychology of Clothing*, ed. S. B. Kaiser (New York: Macmillan), p. 101.

22. A. L. Rowse (1971), *The Elizabethan Renaissance: The Life of the Society* (New York: Charles Scribner's Sons), p. 161.

23. I Cor. 11: 4–10.

24. I Cor. 14: 34–35.

25. I Tim. 2: 11–15.

26. B. P. Prusak (1974), "Women Seductive Sirens and Source of Sin," in *Religion and Sexism: Images of Women in Jewish and Christian Traditions*, ed. R. R. Reuther (New York: Simon and Schuster), p. 101.

27. The *Altarpiece of St. John the Baptist and St. John the Evangelist* (1479) is in St. John's Hospital, the Memlingmuseum, in Bruges, Belgium.

28. H. Lobelle-Caluwe (n.d.), *The Memlingmuseum in St. John's Hospital* (Bruges, Belg.: Die Keure), pp. 66–82.

29. Metropolitan Museum of Art (1982), *The Art of Chivalry* (New York: American Federation of Arts).

30. A. Marwick (1988), *Beauty in History* (London: Thames and Hudson), p. 68.

31. R. Pistolese and R. Horsting (1970), *History of Fashions* (New York: John Wiley and Sons), pp. 118–121.

32. B. Payne, G. Weinakor, and J. Farrell-Beck (1992), *The History of Costume* (New York: Harper Collins), pp. 190–203.

33. Augustine (1972), *Concerning the City of God Against the Pagans*, book 14, trans. H. Bettenson, ed. D. Knowles (Harmondsworth: Penguin), p. 577.

34. L. White, Jr. (1970), *Medieval Technology and Social Change* (Oxford: Oxford University Press).

35. M. von Boehn (1932), *Modes and Manners*, vol. 1, *From the Decline of the Ancient World to the Renaissance*, trans. J. Joshua (New York: Benjamin Blom), p. 280.

36. R. S. Weick (1988), *Time Sanctified: The Book of Hours in Medieval Art and Life* (New York: Braziller).

37. B. Castiglione (1959), *The Book of the Courtier*, trans. C. H. Singleton (Garden City, N.Y.: Doubleday Anchor Books). Originally published in 1510.

38. S. Thurp (1948), *The Merchant Class of Medieval London* (Ann Harbor: University of Michigan Press), pp. 169–174. Similarly, W. Boulting (1910) reported that women in the fourteenth, fifteenth, and sixteenth centuries worked in occupations that included water carriers, house painters, and governesses. See W. Boulting (1910), *Women in Italy* (London: Methune), pp. 336–339. See also A. Abrams (1916), "Women Traders in Medieval London," *Economic Journal* 26: 276–285.

39. Boulting, op. cit., pp. 336–339. See also Abrams, op. cit.

40. J. Roussiaud (1985), "Prostitution, Sex and Society in French Towns in the Fifteenth Century," in *Western Sexuality: Practice and Precept in Past and Present Times*, ed. P. Aries and A. Bejin (New York: Basil Blackwell), pp. 76–113.

41. J. M. Vincent (1935), *Costume and Conduct in the Laws of Basel, Bern and Zurich 1370–1800* (Baltimore: Johns Hopkins University Press), pp. 44–45. Also Q. Bell (1976), *On Human Finery* (New York: Schocken Books), pp. 139–141.

42. G. Chaucer (1952), *Canterbury Tales*, trans. N. Coghill (Baltimore: Penguin), pp. 29–30, 274–296.

43. See M. R. Miles (1985), "Virgin's One Bare Breast: Female Nudity and Religious Meaning in Tuscan Early Renaissance Art," in *The Female Body in Western Culture*, ed. S. R. Suleiman (Cambridge, Mass.: Harvard University Press), p. 110.

44. C. B. Milbank (1989), *New York Fashion: The Evolution of the American Style* (New York: Harry N. Abrams), pp. 170–199.

45. M. and A. Batterberry (1977), *Fashion: The Mirror of History* (New York: Greenwich House), pp. 100–108; A. Hollander (1978), *Seeing Through Clothes* (New York: Viking), pp. 365–367, 383.

46. F. Boucher (1965), *20,000 Years of Fashion* (New York: Henry N. Abrams), pp. 223–225; Batterberry, op. cit., pp. 124–127.

47. J. T. Molloy (1977), *The Women's Dress for Success Book* (Chicago: Follett).

48. E. Hayt (1999), "Women of Which Cloth? Tweed? Cashmere?" *New York Times*, Mar. 28.

49. Ibid.

50. Ibid.

51. Ibid.

52. Ibid.

53. Ibid.

54. M. Warner (1982), *Joan of Arc: The Image of Female Heroism* (New York: Vintage), p. 149; P. Brown (1988), *The Body and Society* (New York: Columbia University Press), pp. 1–2, 156–159.

55. Warner, op. cit., p. 135.

56. Ibid., pp. 154–155, 169.

57. L. M. Guthrie (1984), "I Was a Yeomanette," in *Proceedings, U. S. Naval Institute* (Annapolis, Md.: U.S. Naval Institute); S. H. Godson (1984), "Women Power in World War I," in *Proceedings, U. S. Naval Institute* (Annapolis, Md.: U.S. Naval Institute).

58. K. A. Yellis (1969), "Prosperity's Child: Some Thoughts on the Flapper," *American Quarterly* 21 (1): 44–64.

59. Ibid., p. 44.

60. U.S. Bureau of Census, Fifteenth Census of the United States: 1930, "Population," vol. 5, Occupations (Washington, D.C.: Government Printing Office, 1933), Tables 1–4, pp. 272–73. Roughly the prices would be equivalent to $40.00 and $250.00, respectively, in the year 2001. The reports say that there is a marked increase in the proportion of all women and particularly of married women gainfully occupied.

61. K. and G. Lang (1965), "Fashion: Identification and Differentiation in the Mass Society," , pp. 322–346 in *Dress, Adornment and the Social Order*, ed. M. E. Roach and J. B. Eicher (New York: John Wiley and Sons).

62. S. Talty (1998), "Something to Watch over Me," *New York Times*, May 3.

63. *New York Times*, Aug. 1, 1991.

64. Flugel, op. cit., pp. 161–162.

65. The term *flapper* emerged in England to describe the awkwardness of girls in their mid-teens who had not yet reached mature, dignified womanhood. The flapper was suppose to need clothing with long, straight lines to cover her awkwardness. E. Sage (1926), *A Study of Costume* (New York: Charles Scribner's Sons),p. 216.

66. Yellis, op. cit., p. 45.

67. Ibid.

68. Ibid., pp. 48–49.

69. R. S. and H. M. Lynd (1929), *Middletown* (New York: Harcourt Brace), pp. 159–160.

70. Yellis, op. cit., pp. 46–47.

71. R. Borker (1978), "To Honor Her Head: Hats As a Symbol of Women's Position in Three Evangelical Churches in Edinburgh, Scotland," in J. Hoch Smith (1978), *Women in Ritual and Symbolic Roles* (New York: Plenum), pp. 55–72.

72. See D. Hofman (1989), "The Fashion of Getting Fit," *New York Times*, Nov. 5.

73. Prusak, op. cit., p. 101.

74. S. M. Lyman (1978), *The Seven Deadly Sins: Society and Evil* (New York: St. Martin's Press), pp. 23, 110–117.

75. Ibid., p. 23.

76. Ibid., p. 22.

77. Ibid., pp. 110–111.

78. Metropolitan Museum of Art (1982), *The Art of Chivalry* (New York: American Federation of the Arts).

79. Ibid.

80. D. B. Van Dalen, E. D. Mitchell, and B. L. Bennett (1953), *A World History of Physical Education* (Englewood Cliffs, N.J.: Prentice-Hall), pp. 104–155.

81. J. Strutt (1876), *The Sports and Pastimes of the Peoples of England* (London: Chatto and Windus); P. Cunnington and A. Mansfield (1969), *English Costume for Sport and Recreation* (New York: Barnes and Noble), p. 134.

82. M. Kraus (1959), *The United States Through 1865* (Ann Arbor: University of Michigan Press), p. 327; F. R. Dulles (1965), *America Learns to Play: A History of Recreation* (New York: Appleton-Century), p. 137; L. W. Banner (1983), *American Beauty: A Social History Through Two Centuries of the American Idea, Ideal, and Image of the Beautiful Woman* (New York: Knopf), pp. 229–231; C. W. Griffin (1982), "Physical Fitness," in *Concise Histories of American Popular Culture*, ed. M. T. Inge (Westport, Conn.: Greenwood Press), pp. 262–269; Van Dalen, Mitchell, and Bennett, op. cit., pp. 366–369.

83. A. M. Earle (1903), *Two Centuries of Costume in America 1620–1820* (Rutland, Vt.: Charles E. Tuttle), vols. 1 and 2.

84. Ibid.

85. M. Kimmel (1996), *Manhood in America: A Cultural History* (New York: Free Press), p. 27.

86. Ibid.

87. Ibid., pp. 150–151.

88. Ibid.

89. Ibid., p. 100.

90. Ibid., p. 123.

91. Ibid., pp. 138–139.

92. Ibid., p. 122.

93. Ibid., pp. 136–137.

94. Ibid., p. 132.

95. Ibid., p. 127.

96. Ibid., p. 148.

97. Ibid., p. 148.

98. Ibid., pp. 150–151.

99. Ibid., p. 150.

100. Ibid., p. 181.

101. Ibid., p. 182.

102. Ibid.

103. Ibid., pp. 210–211.

104. Studies of the impact such advertisements may have had on boys growing up with these comics remain to be done.

105. Kimmel, op. cit., p. 211.

106. Ibid., p. 138.

107. S. Cohan (1997), *Masked Men* (Bloomington: Indiana University Press), pp. 102–103.

108. R. Barthes (1972), *Mythologies* (New York: Hill and Wang), p. 16.

109. Cohan, op. cit., p. 103.

110. K. R. Dutton (1995), *The Perfectible Body: The Western Ideal* (New York: Continuum), p. 306.

111. J. F. Lane (1960), "The Money in Muscles," *Films and Filming,* July 9, p. 33.

112. Dutton, op. cit., pp. 300–301.

113. Ibid.

114. Talty, op. cit.

# 8

# Seductive Images

## Female Seductive Images

Male sexual interest is concentrated on and directed toward the genitals, which press forward with irresistible urgency and are therefore nearer to men's consciousness.[1] Men, moreover, respond to what they think, imagine, or see. Their desire is as easily satisfied as it is aroused.[2] The story of King David and Bathsheba in the Old Testament is an example. King David had spied on Bathsheba, who was bathing on the roof of her house. Aroused, the king dispatched one of his attendants to invite her into the royal bedchamber, and she accepted.[3] (2 Sam. 11:2–4).

Men seem to respond to a beautiful female body in a similar manner. Marilyn Monroe, for example, appealed to almost all men, *Life* magazine reported in 1954.[4] There was no male movie star whose appeal to women was so widespread. Throughout much of Western history it was women's bodies that were gazed at, and a glimpse of a woman's naked body encouraged men to visualize sexual possibilities.

For most people, defining seductive attire appears to be extremely easy; clothing that arouses sexual desire is, of course, seductive.[5] However, people from different countries or different time periods might disagree about which styles of clothing are seductive. Each culture develops its own concepts of attire that provokes sexual interest. Those who wear such attire within that cultural milieu will be seen as inviting onlookers to engage them sexually. Alluding to the body beneath it, seductive clothing is part of sexual foreplay.

Seductive images are different from pornographic ones. Seductive images are designed to elicit interest in further communication and interaction, are "home-made," and can be found in family gatherings and snapshots. Pornographic images, on the other hand, address an audience with immediate interest in sexual acts. They are commodities constructed by professionals within distinct sets of social and economic circumstances and are designed to furnish sexual pleasure.[6]

In the Holy Land at the time of the Hebrew patriarchs, it was believed that certain styles of dress and ornament could make the wearer feel, think, and act differently. Widows, for example, wore a sacklike black dress with no makeup or ornament, which encouraged depression, sadness, and withdrawal from festivities.

Harlots, on the other hand, wore special makeup, dress that partly exposed the body, and ornaments that dangled around the neck toward the breasts. This attire, together with perfume, was designed to arouse sexual passions and announce one's availability as a paid sexual partner. As today, a harlot was a figure of disrepute and shame, but there was nothing unusual in encountering her and buying her services. These could often be bought for as little as a loaf of bread (Prov. 6:26).[7]

The prophet Hosea identifies what a seductive image is when he calls on his adulterous wife to "put away her harlotries from her face, and adulteries from between the breasts, lest I strip her naked" (Hos. 2:4).

The biblical story of Tamar tells how seductive dress was used to seduce Judah, one of the patriarchs. In biblical society a woman was defined by her ability to bear children, and having a child was a matter of life and death. A childless woman was seen as someone cursed by God, without a male figure to protect and provide for her. If her husband died before impregnating her, a "levirate marriage," a form of stud service, was rendered by a brother-in-law to his widowed sister-in-law. A child conceived in a levirate marriage was named after the dead brother and inherited the property of the dead brother.[8]

Tamar went back to her tribe to await the maturity of her dead husband's youngest brother. As years went by, Tamar became increasingly desperate. She decided to seduce her father-in-law Judah into giving her a child by dressing as a harlot (Gen. 38:14). She knew that Judah, now a widower, had just completed a long period of mourning for his wife and needed a sexual companion. The woman whom Judah saw on the road to Timnah was sexually desirable and available. She was dressed as a harlot and wore a bag of myrrh between her breasts but hid her identity with a veil over her face. Having seduced him, Tamar went back to her family. When her pregnancy became apparent, she was brought to trial for adultery and was sentenced to death. When she revealed that Judah was the father, she was absolved, and she later gave birth to twins. Judah "knew her no more, but recognized her children as his rightful heirs" (Gen. 38:26).Feminist scholarship suggests that in Western society the role of seductive tempter has been assigned almost exclusively to woman.[9] This designation stems from the fact that early Church theologians placed Eve in this category. She not only succumbed to temptation and disobeyed God, but, even worse, she tempted Adam to do the same. As St. Augustine (AD 345–450) explains,[10] prior to the Fall, nakedness was the natural state of affairs and neither the sexual organs nor bodily functions were shameful. But when Adam and Eve disobeyed God in the Garden of Eden, both attained "knowledge of good and evil"; that is, they saw that they were naked and were ashamed. Simultaneously, man became unable to control his lust, and lust became independent of man's will. As a result of lustful sexual unions, all mankind was afflicted with the insubordination of the flesh. Thus, the knowledge of evil is associated with the body, specifically, the sexual parts of the body. In this context, the word *beguile* is appropriately used to describe Eve's temptation of Adam because it connotes sexual allurement and deceit. And although Adam and Eve were actually condemned for disobeying God, it was through their sexual union that their original sin was transmitted to all mankind.[11]

From this Augustinian perspective, every sexual act can be viewed as a repetition of original sin. Every human being who must, of necessity, be conceived by such an act, is born in sin and subject to death. The hostility to sex that results from Augustine's thinking has become, in turn, a justification for disdain of the body, as well as an antipathy to pleasure of any kind.

The basic and most important category of seductive attire consists of *alluring images designated by Christian thinkers*. Informed by biblical prohibitions and pagan practices, church authorities sought to prevent women from serving as a source of carnal temptation. They condemned as seductive the use of color, of ornament, and of any style of dress that exposes the body or emphasizes its curves.[12]

These prohibitions placed women in a difficult position. Because they were dependent on men both socially and economically, they had to attract male attention, and to do that, a woman needed to stand out. Over the centuries, Western European women developed styles of attire that remained within the bounds of modesty while simultaneously enhancing their physical appeal. Such styles might become popular and then disappear, only to be rediscovered later. These styles belong to a second category—*alluring images developed by women*.

In the twentieth century, with the development of the mass media, the outbreak of wars, and long periods when American men were away from home, *Esquire* magazine,[13] comic books,[14] and *Playboy* magazine[15] introduced images that men found alluring. These images have become part of the vocabulary of seductive images. They form a third category, *alluring images developed by men*. All three categories of images have become part of "public memory" and provide sources for today's designers. Each will be discussed in turn in this chapter.

### Alluring Images Designated by the Church

Between AD 100 and 500, the Church Fathers defined the fundamental characteristics of seductive attire as ornamentation, varied colors of clothing, and a style of dress that exposed body parts. Clement of Alexandria (ca. AD 150–220) argued that to prevent male transgression, women should cover their bodies from head to toe. However, "their dresses should not be overly soft and clinging and should be hemmed below the ankles rather than above the knees. . . . For that style of dress is grave, and protects her from being gazed at." "And," he added, "she will not fall who puts before her eyes modesty and her shawl; nor will she invite another to fall into sin by uncovering her face."

Clement required that women wear veils but forbade them to circumvent the purpose by wearing purple ones, since colors attract attention and "inflame lusts." Tertullian wrote that if "God wanted dresses made of purple and scarlet wool, he would have created purple and scarlet sheep." In a diatribe against jewelry, Clement complained that certain ornaments used by women served as symbols of adultery; Tertullian also observed that women learned about cosmetics from the fallen angels.[16]

The objection to ornament and the injunction against adornment were clearly expressed by Cyprian in his work *The Clothing of a Virgin*:

> Let your countenance remain in you incorrupt, your neck unadorned. . . . Let not rings be made in your ears, nor precious chains of bracelets and necklaces encircle your arms or your neck; let your feet be free from golden bands, your hair stained from no dye, your eyes worthy of beholding God.

Similarly, the first *Epistle to Timothy* advises

> women should adorn themselves modestly and sensibly in seemly apparel, not with braided hair or gold or pearls or costly attire but with good deeds, as befits women who profess religion.[17]

According to the scriptures, clothing that exposes the body or a style of dress that reveals the body's shape or color is sexually enticing and must, therefore, be avoided. Taking these prohibitions a step further, and recognizing possible complicity on the part of men, St. Augustine demanded that men also cover their bodies so that their "shame" will not be visible. These injunctions against seductive attire have been so powerful that, as English costume historian James Laver points out, "Until quite recently—less than a hundred years ago perhaps—it was almost universally agreed that the primary and fundamental reason for wearing clothes in general, was modesty." "For those who accepted the literal truth of the Genesis story, there was no question about it." Adam and Eve, having eaten of the fruit of the Tree of Knowledge, "knew that they were naked and made themselves aprons of fig leaves." Thus, for centuries, it was accepted that the primary function of clothing was to hide the shame of nakedness and prevent insubordination of the will.[18]

### Unintended Consequences

The requirement that women keep their heads and bodies covered to signal their modesty had several unintended consequences. The first was that the body became like a chalkboard upon which sexual intentions could be written or from which they could be erased. This was the state of affairs until after World War I. Wearing high heels and a tight-fitting dress with a lowered neckline showing the bosom or side slits showing the thighs, as well as letting one's hair down when it is normally held up or back, were interpreted as announcements of sexual desire.

The second unintended consequence was that by covering and uncovering, all parts of the female body have been sexualized, so that a hemline shortened to expose the ankle or the removal of a glove to allow a glimpse of hand and wrist could arouse sexual interest. Likewise in contemporary America, a person who is partially clad usually provokes sexual interest. In contrast, costume historian Lawrence Langner (1959) found that in cultures whose members do not usually wear clothing the covered or clothed body arouses sexual desire in others. Therefore he suggests that, ironically, the Church's insistence on covering the body provided women with a means of contravening the Church's original intentions.[19]

The third consequence is that the attire the Christian thinkers proscribed as arousing became the category of dress that was catalogued, recognized, and used deliberately for that purpose. This consequence was logical and was not necessarily unforeseen, since those who chose to wear such clothing provided a warning as well as an invitation. People knew which women to "shun" and men knew which women to avoid or to seek out after dark.

A law in England dating from 1352, for example, acknowledged that prostitutes needed special clothing to elicit sexual response. It states

> No known whore should wear thenceforth, any hood except red or striped of divers colors, nor furs, but garments reversed or turned the wrong side outward upon pain to forfeit the same.[20]

The regulation thus recognized that both color and a style of dress that alludes to the body underneath are seductive.

In the nineteenth century a prostitute's attire demonstrated the same characteristics. It was made of cheap, flashy material (it was brightly colored and, sometimes, turned wrong side out to suggest closeness to the body), and—"nothing besides in the way of undergarments." Bonnetless, without shawls, they presented themselves "in their figure" to male passersby.[21] Any of the early Church Fathers would have recognized from the lack of head covering that such women represented the temptation of the devil.

### Alluring Images Developed by Women

*Respectable Allure.* The medieval whore in her gaudy headdress and the unbonneted nineteenth-century prostitute readily attracted male attention. Each stood out in stark contrast to the norm.[22] But attracting the attention of a desired male was also a goal of ordinary, "modest" women who sought access to wealth, power, and prestige. In a crowd of women covered from head to toe in dark clothing, how was one to stand out? Her appearance had to be interesting, it had to differentiate her from the others, and yet it had to avoid evoking disapproval or censure that would result from being considered "immodest and shameless." To achieve this latter goal, her clothing had to remain within the confines established as "respectable."

The women best known for achieving such goals are those who were "certified seductive," the royal courtesans. They were women who succeeded in attracting the attention and interest of the monarch. Their success in attracting a king and receiving legal recognition of their status legitimized their clothing style. Consequently, they became what are today called trend setters, and other women sought to copy their style. Courtesans were responsible for initiating and popularizing three distinct tactics (images), which were then adopted by modest women. These tactics, rediscovered in the twentieth century, continue to influence styles today.

*Adapting Elements of Male Dress.*   The first tactic appeared during a period of social and political change. The fourteenth century was a time of increasing prosperity in Europe. With the growth of commercial centers such as Venice, Genoa, Barcelona, and Marseilles, and with the establishment of the great northern ports of Bruges and Antwerp, the old feudal system began to disappear. In its stead came the establishment of royal and princely courts in which political power was increasingly centralized. These courts were supported by a prosperous mercantile class and an ambitious bourgeoisie.

The resulting concentration of powerful and wealthy families made it necessary for members of the nobility to distinguish themselves from the rich merchants. Distinctions in clothing provided a ready method for the court nobility to assert its higher social rank. These distinctions became the means by which the rich merchant class, in turn, identified itself with the nobility and its privileges.[23] Almost inevitably the clothing worn by these groups displayed their wealth and power. As it spread across Europe, the new look of luxury in courtly attire became known as the International Gothic style of dress. For men, the wearing of precious gems such as diamonds and pearls became a mark of status.

In some paintings from the fifteenth, sixteenth, and seventeenth centuries, certain women are depicted wearing elements of male dress. The credit for making such daring behavior acceptable goes, perhaps, to the first officially recognized courtesan in the French court, Agnès Sorel (1440s?). To set herself apart, she borrowed diamonds from the men in her family and had them mounted into a feminine-style necklace. By wearing the unexpected (diamonds, which had hitherto been worn exclusively by men), she succeeded in catching the eye of the French king, Charles VII. As Baerwald and Mahoney (1960) have noted, the charm of the unexpected is at work when women adopt elements of male dress.[24]

Because Sorel succeeded in becoming the king's mistress, she quickly became a fashion leader among women. In addition, she popularized the high-domed forehead, a hairstyle that requires that the forehead be immaculately plucked. It is the style she wears in the painting "Virgin and Child" by French painter Jean Fouquet (ca. 1480). In this painting Agnès Sorel was elevated by the painter to the highest status available to a woman—placed "on a pedestal," and depicted as the Virgin Mary. Though the dress she wears in the painting is simple, its curved seams outline her figure smoothly; one breast is exposed. Round and seemingly full of

Hunting with Falcons at the Court of Philip the Good *(also known as* The Marriage of Philip the Good to Isabella of Portugal*), French school, 1430. (Versailles Museum.)*

milk, it is directed toward the baby on her lap. As befits the Queen of Heaven, a crown studded with gems and pearls sits firmly on her head.[25]

Male gloves, hats, and hoods are the other elements of male dress adopted by women in this period.[26] In a painting called *Hunting with Falcons at the Court of Philip the Good* (ca. 1442), all the guests are dressed in white as part of the theme of the festivities. The focal point in the painting is Duke Phillip the Good, himself lounging elegantly against a banquette table in the center of a magnificent ensemble of courtiers. In different parts of the painting are clusters of guests, all in elegant costumes that seem more appropriate for display than for hunting.

In one cluster, among a group of couples participating in a stately dance, is a woman wearing scarlet gloves. Traditionally only cardinals wore scarlet gloves. But by the fifteenth century so many women had adopted this element of male dress that the cardinals refused to wear theirs. Despite the protest, the Pope ordered them to continue wearing scarlet gloves.[27]

Masculine headdress, specifically the bourrelet (a round padded roll placed over the hair), is also worn by a few of the women in the painting. This style of headdress also appears quite frequently in other northern European paintings.

Hoods worn by men were also adopted by women of the nobility.[28] In the background of a drawing of Saint Barbara by Jan van Eyck (ca. 1437), several ladies out for a walk are depicted with hoods. The trousseau of Agnes of Cleves included several hoods, at least two of which also had bourrelets attached to them.[29]

In a chronicle describing the customs and habits of Venice, Cesare Vecellio reports that by 1590 the prostitutes had adopted elements of male dress as part of their seductive attire. Made of silk or other cloth, depending on their social class, the prostitutes' "vests were padded and fringed in the style of young men, particularly Frenchmen." Next to their bodies they wore a man's shirt "more or less delicate according to what they can spend." Instead of wearing a skirt, many of them appeared in men's breeches, which made them instantly recognizable.[30]

In a portrait of Peter Paul Rubens and his wife Isabella Brandt (1610), she wears a man's hat. It rests precariously on one side of her head over a traditional female bonnet. It would seem that by the seventeenth century women of the bourgeoisie had also discovered the charm of wearing elements of male dress.

Men's apparel does not appear to figure in the art and fashion of women's wear in the eighteenth or nineteenth century. But at the beginning of the twentieth century, Gabrielle Chanel rediscovered its allure. Attending the races at Deauville one chilly day, so the story goes, she was cold. She borrowed a polo player's sweater, belted it, and pushed the sleeves up. Chanel was so entranced with the image that she soon produced similar sweaters for other women and they sold immediately.[31] At the races she wore a Shetland sweater and pearls, while other women wore silk and lace. A leather belt, sailor pants, and a twin sweater set were the elements of male dress that she introduced into female fashion. Chanel was also one of the first women to cut her hair short in the 1920s.

Elements of male dress worn by women call attention to the wearer because they are unexpected. The novelty is disarming and sexually alluring. Actress Marlene Dietrich discovered this in 1933 when she made international headlines by appearing in mannish attire offscreen. Warned by the Paris chief of police that she would be asked to leave town if she continued to wear pants, she changed into a skirt but still used a man's hat, collar, and tie. The tight-fitting jacket that emphasized her female curves came from a boy's clothing store.[32] Perhaps male clothes make femininity all the more obvious.

*Peter Paul Rubens and his wife Isabella Brandt (1609). The hat sits precariously on one side of her head over a traditional female bonnet (Pinakotek, Munich. Photo: Greg Kitchen.)*

*Designers Joan and David adapt male attire to the female body. (George Chinsee/* Women's Wear Daily, *Aug. 23, 1993.)*

The oversize male shirt or pajama top, fedora hat, baseball or sailors' cap, a tie worn loose, and a male-style leather jacket were adopted by women in the 1970s. Giorgio Armani's use of haberdashery fabrics and Ralph Lauren's form-fitting tuxedo suit are 1980s examples. Designers thus came to realize the seductive charm of the unexpected when women wear elements of male dress.

*Creating an Image of Harmony.*    Creating an image of harmony was a tactic adopted by one of the best-known French courtesans, Jeanne Antoinette Poisson, known as Madame de Pompadour (1721–1764). Two concepts seem to underlie her style. According to M. and A. Batterberry, the first is that "the sensual and lighthearted" are "delightful"; the second is that "the elements of appearance should be fused to create a whole greater than the sum of its parts."[33] These two principles characterize the clothing she wore when she set out to establish herself as Louis XV's mistress.

The story goes that the king, long estranged from his Polish wife, Marie Leczinska, and brooding over the death of his most recent mistress, was restless and devoted much of his time to hunting in the Forest of Senart. Jeanne Antoinette Poisson followed the hunt in a brightly colored carriage. One day she would be dressed in light blue and ride in a rose-colored carriage; the next, she would be wearing a rose-colored dress while the carriage would be light blue. She followed a similar procedure in Paris, where she ensconced herself at the theater in full view of the king. She succeeded in catching his eye. Then, under cover of the festivities and masked balls celebrating the marriage of the dauphin, she lured him into her bed. Shortly thereafter she was publicly acknowledged, and in 1745 the king awarded her the title marquise de Pompadour. For nearly twenty years, until her death in 1764, she was considered *de facto* queen of France.[34]

In her time many court observers paid tribute to what was considered her extraordinary beauty. Despite all their praise, however, her facial characteristics as depicted in portraits and sculpture are less than beautiful, scholars have insisted. They note that the accuracy of the depiction is not in question. A number of artists portrayed her at different times (including Jean Marc Nattier, François Boucher, Carle Van Loo, Charles Nicholas Cochin, François Hubert Drouais, François Lemoyne, and Jean-Baptiste Pigalle). They depict her with the same facial characteristics—a round face with even features and a dazzling complexion; eyes not very large but "brilliant, witty and sparkling."[35]

Costume historians note that court observers reported that it was her style of dress that attracted the king's attention and led, in turn, to the many tributes to her beauty. In keeping with the times, she followed her belief that the elements of appearance should be fused to create a whole greater than the sum of its parts and that the individual should be in harmony with nature. Accordingly, she chose fabrics of pale and delicate shades that complemented her dazzling pink and white complexion and her sparkling eyes. To provide a sense of flirtatiousness, her richly decorated, low-cut gowns were adorned with many ribbons, flowers,

Madame de Pompadour, *by François Boucher, n.d. (Louvre, Paris.) The color, material, and trimmings of the decorations on her head and around her neck correspond to those of the dress, leading to unity and harmony.*

ruffles, and lacy flounces and pagoda-shaped sleeves, also of lace. This profusion of exquisite tiny details, like those in the world of nature, were placed to convey the impression of a unified whole, and the style of her gowns was known as the *robe à la française*. People who knew her almost never mentioned her beauty without also mentioning the "consummate elegance with which she dressed."[36]

Although the *robe à la française* had come into fashion before her time, Madame de Pompadour's preference for it had an impact on other women. Throughout Europe, for the remainder of the eighteenth century, women's fashions were inspired by Madame de Pompadour's clothing.

The preference for harmony grew out of the rise of new ideas and disturbing questions about freedom, responsibility, and ethics in eighteenth-century France and England. Enlightenment thinkers argued that the development of science obviated the need for supernatural guidance. Instead, humans were urged to rely on the power of right reason. These thinkers pointed out that the study of nature, unaided by divine guidance, had revealed itself to be both knowable and regular—and hence predictable. For many of them, the study of nature, to be undertaken through the use of reason and logic, replaced the study of the mysteries of God.[37]

In keeping with this change, writers began to emphasize that individuals were in and of themselves increasingly capable of good and that when they at last reached harmony with nature, they would be judged perfect. This desire for harmony of the parts within a whole also reflects a desire for political and social accord, the roots of which lie in classical Athens. With the establishment of itself as a democracy, Athens in the fifth century BC viewed balance and order as essential for social life. Athenian artists of the time strove to balance strength with grace and gentleness in their statues of the gods. Symmetry and just proportions (in which the parts are subordinate to the whole) became the classical period's criteria of beauty.[38] Eighteenth-century philosophers readily adopted the classical Greek principles of beauty. In 1757 Edmund Burke suggested that beauty comprises a "smoothness" such that parts melt into each other.[39]

The definition of beauty by James Barry in 1784, cited in the *Oxford English Dictionary,* similarly focuses on the unity that emerges when variety exists. The result, in art, is resolution—a static, balanced artifact.[40]

In the 1960s, the "youth revolution" and the call for an "authentic self" encouraged women in middle America to reject fashion that they considered "conspicuous consumption." Women in small towns and suburban communities were listening to Suzanne Caygill, who toured the country lecturing on natural color harmonies, a phenomenon reported by Johannes Itten, an art teacher at the Bauhaus.[41] The Enlightenment idea that harmony with nature is basic to happiness was taken by Caygill as her underlying principle.

The most effective way to place a person in harmony with the environment is for him or her to dress and live in the appropriate color and style. In the natural world, Caygill notes, the palette of each season consists of harmonious colors. Each individual's skin and eye coloring, hair, body contours, and personality can be complemented by a palette that exists in nature. The effect engenders in both wearer and onlooker a feeling of being at peace—with oneself and with nature. Wearing compatible colors conveys a sense of unity and harmony.[42] Caygill evolved and eventually codified for the public the principles that Madame de Pompadour had utilized so successfully. In *Color Me Beautiful* (1973), Carol Jackson popularized Caygill's ideas about color and personal appearance.[43]

*The Glamorous Look.*   A third tactic developed by women to make themselves stand out in the eyes of men can best be described as the creation of a glamorous look. Glamour is particularly difficult to define because it is "An elusive mysteriously exciting and often illusory attractiveness that stirs the imagination and appeals to a taste for the unconventional, the unexpected, the colorful, or the exotic." The term may also connote personal charm and poise, and may imply unusual physical and sexual attributes.[44]

The nineteenth century witnessed a turning away from the profusion and richness of the Pompadour style. Decent, modest women were expected to wear structured dresses in dark, somber colors. Such colors and styles were in harmony with society's conception of the proper place and role for women. Women's styles in this period were not expected to create the impression of an individual as a harmonious whole but rather to indicate conformity among individual women with society's expectations for them. The dark-colored, enveloping garb

*Marguérite Bellanger (1840–1886), mistress
of Napoleon III, was known for her playful
use of daisies. She wore them in the form of
pins and hats. A sense of enchantment is
conveyed by the shimmering satin and light
colors and the playful delicacy of her clothes.
(The Hulton Deutsch Collection.)*

appealed to middle-class women precisely because it was both practical, useful,
and economical. During long cold winters in small, drafty, sometimes smoky
houses, the warmth of the relatively coarse, heavy fabric in such garments was
useful. Equally important, most of the fabric was produced locally, as was the
clothing itself; in addition, the preferred dark colors did not require costly dyes or
dying processes; hence, such garments were practical, useful, and inexpensive.[45]

Wearing such somber garments, however, forced women to confront once
again the problem of how to stand out among a group of women wearing the
same "practical" clothing. In contrast to the dark and gloomy colors of the voluminous, heavy-looking dresses, broad brimmed-bonnets, and enveloping capes
of the times, courtesans set out to look sensual. They wore satins in white, light
yellow, light green, or orange. They decorated their clothing with dainty bows,
ribbons, and frills, and their bosoms were emphasized and trimmed with lace.
Frivolity and lightheartedness characterized their appearance. Their attire glis-
tened, it was soft and encouraged touch.[46]

In earlier centuries, a woman who attracted the king's attention could be officially recognized as a courtesan—she moved in court circles and became the mistress of the reigning monarch. Nineteenth-century courtesans, however, were
women who could have formerly been respectable but of humble birth, or could
have been cast down by an unhappy affair. The only hope for fortune for these
women was their physical attractiveness. Men who recognized their attributes
helped them to become independent and self-supporting.[47]

*The glamorous look. Cora Pearl, one of the most desirable Parisian courtesans in the 1870s. Although respectable women dressed in dark colors and wore hats, courtesans wore satin dresses in light colors and flowers in their hair. (Collection Sirot.)*

A courtesan is less than a mistress and more than a prostitute, Richardson (1966) reports. "She is less than a mistress because she sells her love for material benefits; she is more than a prostitute because she chooses her lovers. The courtesan is a woman whose profession is love, and whose clients may be more or less distinguished."[48]

The women who became courtesans sought to escape traditional constraints of poverty and marriage. Those born between 1814 and 1830 grew up in a time of economic and political change. The monarchy had fallen; the old aristocracy was discredited; and Napoleon's meteoric rise and fall served as a warning to any who might attempt to reach the heights of the pre-1779 nobility. Instead, industrialization, trade, and the burgeoning cities were the new sources of opportunity and wealth.[49]

The courtesans sexualized sensuality. Because female sexuality is diffused and consists of skin-muscle eroticism, female sexual response is less overt than that of men and can easily escape recognition.[50] To simulate (and stimulate) sexual passion, the courtesans reddened their cheeks and nails and widened the pupils of their eyes with atropin. Dubbed "les grandes horizontales," and "les grandes coquettes," they were renowned for being beautiful, talented, imaginative, and fun to be with. They were reputed to have raised to an art interaction with men in general and sexual discourse in particular; had an impact on the poetry, literature, and visual arts of the period; and became members of the fashionable set.[51] International in origins, each had her own distinct features and style. What they had in common was that they were flirtatious, witty, and entertaining.[52] As Richardson describes a typical scene:

> All of Paris turned out to see the glorious sight of the courtesans in their handsome carriages. . . . [Their exclusion]from formal ceremonies by those who set the standards for respectability, was most evident when they were not allowed to enter the grandstand at the Longchamps races. They had to park their carriages on the other side of the track. To offset this humiliation, the courtesans saw to it that their return from races would be like a triumphant procession. Reclining languidly against the plump cushions of their satin upholstered carriages, attended by footmen in elaborate and colorful uniforms and powdered wigs, they competed and often outshone the more respected wife. They drove from Longchamps to the Place de la Concorde, to the Bois de Boulogne and back again until nightfall imparting radiance as they and their carriages reflected the last rays of the sun.
>
> Esteem accorded to a man from other men often depended on how well he had provided for his courtesan. For her services she would often receive financial support in the form of a well-appointed home, liveried servants, art objects, magnificent clothes and jewels.[53]

To some women the courtesan's ability to attract a man, to receive his gifts of support, and to maintain his interest became proof of the desirability of their style. Many women, among them members of the court, tried to adopt a glamorous look.

In the United States in the last half of the nineteenth century, the radiance of satin, the zest of champagne, the plushness of costly furs, and the attentions of wealthy admirers characterized the image of chorus girls and movie stars.[54] The media conveyed the message that any woman with beauty and talent could dance or sing her way to affluence. It encouraged the notion that this was indeed a land of opportunity. Newspapers presented movie stars and chorus girls as modern Cinderellas, and the clerks and secretaries who swelled the ranks of women workers from 1900 to 1920 read with envy about their exciting lives, freedom, romance, and adventure.[55] Female movie stars were presented as radiant and larger than life, and movies were capable of transforming viewers across barriers of time, space, and class. The luminosity of the stars' image replaced the drab confinement of everyday life with a magical world of fantasy.[56]

Women regarded movie stars as experts on appearance. Everything Gloria Swanson (1899–1983) did was news. She became the epitome of elegance and feminine enchantment. When she bobbed her hair in the early 1920s, millions of women rushed to have their hair bobbed. Until then, throughout the centuries women kept their hair long and their heads covered. Short hair had been consid-

*Mae West in a glamorous and revealing negligée,
1932. (Still from the movie* Night After Night.)

ered an affront, a violation of the norm of modesty. Suddenly it was seen as romantic, chic, and classy. The lacy black negligée worn by Mae West in *Night After
Night* was celebrated and copied by many women.

Two distinct seductive images were made popular by the show-business industry: the one that was condemned as immodest by the Church consisted of sequins, color, plunging necklines, and dresses draped to swathe the body snugly.
The other was praised as glamorous by the media. Constructed with much less
emphasis on the female attributes, it merely alluded to the body underneath.
Satin and makeup conveyed radiance and sensuality.

### Alluring Images Initiated by Men

In the twentieth century, with the development of mass media, the female body
emerged as the central focus of female desirability. With outbreak of war, and
long periods when American men were away from home, *Esquire* magazine,[57]
comic books,[58] and *Playboy* introduced images that men considered alluring.

*Jungle Queens.*   Jungle queens were fictional characters in comic books. They
were designed to entertain adolescent male readers and an older audience of servicemen. The jungle queen image consisted of long hair, long legs, large breasts,

physical agility, and an inclination to respond in an emotional rather than an intellectual way.[59]

*"Pinup" Girls.*   Female sexuality was viewed as an inspiration to American fighting men, and popular media were an important source of seductive images of women. *Esquire* magazine began publication in 1933. The magazine was aimed at affluent men with a taste for stylish clothes and beautiful women. The famous air-brushed pinups drawn by George Petty and Alberto Vargas, among others, were given greater prominence during World War II, so that the magazine could qualify for a bigger paper allocation by claiming that it boosted GI morale and contributed to the war effort.[60] The artists commissioned depicted images of ideal females, which came to be known as pinup girls.[61] Famous actresses such as Marilyn Monroe, Betty Grable, and Rita Hayworth also became pinup girls.[62] They accompanied men through the depths of the Depression, to the battlefronts of World War II, and during the war in Korea.[63]

Military men used pinups to adorn their vehicles and anything else they could. One of the most popular images adorning the noses of many bombers was "The Memphis Belle," drawn by George Petty.[64]

Pinup girls designed by Vargas became a major source of inspiration for tattoo artists and those who wore tattoos. The first pinup Vargas did for *Esquire* in 1940 depicted a woman stretched out in bed, wearing a short black nightgown and talking on the telephone. The *Esquire* collection consists of curvaceous young women in skin-tight short shorts in a variety of military uniforms, and one pictures a cowgirl in bright blue shorts brandishing two six-shooters.[65]

*The Playmate.*   From its initial issue, November 1953, the central feature of *Playboy* magazine was a color photograph of a naked, white, young, blond, wholesome American woman designated "the Playmate." Every month a different woman was chosen as the Playmate of the Month, and her picture would be the magazine's centerfold.[66] The Playmate was part of the magazine's vision of sexuality free of guilt. The Playmate was someone most men could partake of, mostly in fantasy. By the end of the 1950s, Playmates had become a part of America. Pictures of blond, big-breasted, and red-lipped young women artfully draped in chiffon and white fur could be found pinned up in college rooms across the nation and in factories, offices, and filling stations.[67]

Protestant churches were the first to realize that a new cultural landscape was emerging. In the fall of 1960, Reverend Michael Bloy, Episcopal chaplain at MIT, found *Playboy* magazine in dormitories, common rooms, and classrooms. Students stuffed copies of the magazine in raincoat pockets and into bookbags.[68] Carefully folded Playmates provided off-duty solace to paratroopers sent to Little Rock, Arkansas, by President Dwight D. Eisenhower to assist in enrolling nine black students in school. They were read "Under the sheets in bed or in the privacy of a lavatory, where the doors could be locked without suspicion."[69]

Second Lieutenant John Price wrote a letter to *Playboy* in November 1965, telling why Playmate photos were popular among the GIs stationed in Vietnam. He wrote: "Everything critics at home put down about the pictures—the milk and honey, the rosy glow, the absence of warts and blemishes, the glossy perfection, the bursting health of all those corn-fed blonds, their undemanding prettiness and those sweet, safe, innocent and empty smiles, the Gouda cheese of vaulting breasts, dazzling whiteness of their skins—was magic to the soldiers. They turned Playmates into talismans, symbols of hope."[70]

*The "Bombshell."*   The "bombshell" first emerged in the 1930s during the Depression. The name referred to big-bosomed women who worked outside the home and were economically and socially emancipated.[71] The Civil Preparedness Agency resurrected the image in 1972 in a pamphlet educating the public to protect itself against atomic attack. It portrayed the three deadly rays of radiation, alpha, beta, and gamma, as bombshells—large-breasted bathing beauties in seductive poses.[72]

Female sexuality, like the rays, was powerful and dangerous. Rita Hayworth's sexy character in the 1947 film *The Lady from Shanghai*, for example, destroyed her man.[73] A photograph of Rita Hayworth was actually attached to the hydrogen bomb dropped in a test on the Bikini Islands.[74]

*The Vulnerable Look.*   In the last two centuries a sexual liaison between an older male and a young female was satirized and usually discouraged. The term a "dirty old man" reflects such sentiments. In the advertisement for the *Caprichos*, published in *Diario de Madrid* on February 6, 1799, Francisco Goya describes the satirical prints as deriding "vice and error." Goya was a keen observer of society, confronting directly the darkest and most basic human impulses, notes art historian Reva Wolf, who in 1991 served as curator for an exhibit of prints at Boston University. Many of the prints mock older men who attempt to seduce young women.[75]

In the art and literature of the 1950s, however, a liaison between the older sophisticated male and young teenager was legitimized. It began with ballet, which had acquired a new importance after World War II. Designer Clair McCardle offered the "ballerina" look for everyday attire, making it popular. The style emphasized long limbs, flat-chestedness, ballet slippers, and hair swept back to reveal a long delicate neck.[76]

Embodying the essence of youthful innocence and the vulnerability of a new bloom, Audrey Hepburn, a former ballet student, was picked by the writer Colette in 1951 to play the character of Gigi on Broadway. It is a story of an older sophisticated male captivated by the innocent, childlike charm of a teenager.

The heart of all twelve romantic comedies that Audrey Hepburn later starred in is the same fantasy: a coy and playful relationship between a young teenager and a mature, sophisticated male. Her attire in each of the movies denies the at-

*Audrey Hepburn shown personifying the vulnerable image. Ballerina slippers with droopy leggings nullify the elegance of the dress, an A-line designed by Givenchy. The delicate long neck and bare shoulders suggest access and youthful delicacy, hence vulnerability. (Corbis/Bettman.)*

tributes that anchor a woman in society, breasts and hips.[77] In the film *Funny Face*, for example, Hepburn is wearing a ballerina-style tunic, a black turtleneck, and tights. Whether running with balloons in the rain, looking pensive in a railroad station, or floating down the steps at the Paris Opera, Audrey Hepburn gives the film an aura of "enchanting innocence," reviewers noted. She is described as waiflike with her long arms, neck, and legs.

Her popularity and success surprised Hepburn. She repeatedly insisted: "I have no illusions about my looks" and described herself as a "skinny broad." To her amazement, she was chosen to represent a new seductive ideal. The vulnerable look inspires the older adult male to view her as a child and perhaps as "Daddy's little girl," an immature being in need of care and instruction.

Cultural fascination with adolescent sexuality is reflected in the success of *Lolita*, the novel by Vladimir Nabokov (1954) which was initially banned, as well as the "baby-doll" fashion that was popular by the mid-1960s. The style literally featured little girls' attire. It consisted of a very short skirt, high waistline, puffed sleeves, jumper or apron effects, lots of lace and ruffles, and sometimes even bloomers. Legs were clad in lacy, pale stockings and feet in Mary Jane shoes. Geoffrey Beene, Chester Weinberger, and Bill Blass designed for the baby-doll look. The clothing was accessorized by elaborate doe-eye makeup and spiky eyelashes, sometimes painted on in a doll-like fashion. Cheeks were rosy and lips pale and frosted, with hair worn in ringlets around the face.[78]

Without really knowing it, high school and college women offered a different version of the vulnerable

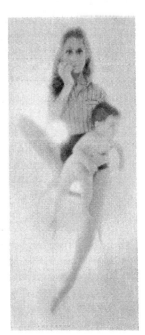

*Lauren Hutton portraying the "babysitter" image in* Esquire, *Dec. 1968. (Photo by Carl Fischer.)*

*In 1999 the best representation of the vulnerable look was the role played by Calista Flockhart in the television series "Ally McBeal." (The Everett Collection.)*

look. Rebelling against fashion magazines with its emphasis on gender differences, they rummaged in thrift stores and family closets for the oversized shirt, sweater, and coat. Their image was seductive for two reasons. First, it is familiar yet unfamiliar because we are used the seeing women in women's clothing and men in men's clothing. Second, a teenager's body inside unstructured, oversized shirts or coats and jackets seems small and vulnerable, waifish. The softness of the look makes her seem to be wearing her father's or big brother's hand-me-downs. She is lost and in need of male protection; some men want to hold and comfort her.

Several cultural forces offered legitimacy to the teenager's image of vulnerability so that it could now be included in the gallery of seductive images. Chosen by a panel of analysts and sociologists consulted by *Esquire*, the vulnerable look was featured in its December 1968 issue. The headline reads "Season's Greetings! 4 naughty dreams to last you till March." Lauren Hutton, a model and actress using makeup and costume, represents four different seductive images, including the "babysitter."

The teenager is portrayed in short shorts with bare feet, and her innocent-looking blouse is partially unbuttoned. She is sitting precariously on a stool holding a naked baby, and she and the baby are in danger of tipping over. She shows a transfixed fascination that is not at all without fear. Since at least the eighteenth century, a woman's extended pale leg, exposed to the thigh, and an undone bodice alluded to sexual availability.[79]

To summarize, the art and literature of the 1950s initiated a cultural dialogue that rejected old definitions and sexualized the childlike look. Adopted by teenagers, the vulnerable look represents the incorporation of a deviant male desire into the realm of public fantasy. This amalgam helped to widen the boundaries of the acceptable.

*Media Images.* By the end of the twentieth century, with increasing affluence and a media emphasis on beauty and youth, two desirable marriage stereotypes emerged. "Barbie," a good-looking, long-legged model type, was preferred by men who had focused on work and had not married. The "trophy wife" is a young woman married to a previously married mature man who is twice her age. Both marriages are generally considered "status symbols," reflecting a male's achievement.

### Impact of Alluring Images

There is a difference between seductive images designated or initiated by men and those developed by women. Their authorship seems to affect male-female interaction.

Alluring images that emanate from men call attention to the body and define the relationship more fully in terms of sex. Nourished by the view that sexuality is a biological drive pressing for release or orgasm, the focus of the interaction is sexual satisfaction. Fulfillment entails mastery over the other, or the use of women as sexual objects.

This category of images can be seen as transporting men from "triumph to trauma." The male, in comparison to a female, proceeds from a position of greater access to wealth, prestige, and power—or triumph. Sexual intercourse that reaffirms such superiority may preclude female sensuality, warmth, and caring. Interaction with an "object" is likely to result in paltry long-term rewards. The rejection of an opportunity to take advantage of the nourishing qualities of women limits the experience, ultimately leaving a sense of unfulfillment and insufficient mastery over the situation. Such feelings may do violence to the male's sense of personhood, hence a "trauma."

Alluring images that women developed, on the other hand, entail attire that encourages sensual pleasure. It can be described as enabling a woman to shift her lot from "trauma to triumph." The trauma stems from recognition that she is shut out of the significant social realms, the challenge for wealth and power. The clothing that women adopted alluded to play, encouraging eroticism, fun, and gentler sex. The courtesan's interactions with the king and the other suitors enabled her to overcome the humiliation of her condition of birth. These women were given the opportunity to influence policy, to develop their talents and abilities, and to achieve economic independence. Relationships with men made it possible for them to resolve the initial trauma and secure a personal triumph.

## Male Seductive Images

For most of the 4000 years of Western history it was the degree of power and authority a man held that was signified in his dress. Among the upper and middle

*Lorenzo the Magnificent is portrayed
in body-hugging attire to reveal the
ideal Renaissance male physique.
A detail from* Archers,
*by Benozzo Gozzoli,
c. 1460.*

classes a man's attire was designed to enhance his public image.[80] It informed a woman of his ability to protect and support her and their children, observed J. C. Flugel. His rank identified the quality of social life that they were likely to enjoy.[81] Male sexuality and eroticism for the most part were obscured by clothing representing masculine power. There were instances, however, where male dress alluded to sexuality and was deemed seductive.

### Renaissance Style

Until about 1350 it was women's attire that delineated the body and identified its sex. Men, young and old, wore robes in somber colors. The robe fell from the shoulders to below the knees, or to the ground depending on the person's age and choice. The robe formed a full, vertical silhouette,[82] keeping the male body and its sexuality out of sight.

In the city-states of Renaissance Italy, where increase in trade had led to affluence, young men rejected the body-concealing robes and adopted tight-fitting attire that defined the shape of the body and made its sexuality visible. The hose, in the form of separate stockings, reached farther and farther up the legs. They finally became tights, with a seam that joined them in the back, and a codpiece in the front accentuated male genitalia. "The doublet was short and it ceased to cover either buttocks or genitals," Anne Hollander observed. "The male rear was always on view."[83]

An undergarment slyly peeking out from under the shirt neckline alluded to the body underneath. Broad padded shoulders gave the shoulders a horizontal line that suggested physical strength.[84] Raiment that was slashed or incomplete also exposed the undergarments.[85]

### Cavalier Fashion

The cavalier style also became possible with economic affluence. It was fashionable from the end of the sixteenth century through the first half of the seventeenth century. The image was seductive because it was designed to make the wearer appear to be adventurous and pleasure-loving. Even men who wore traditional attire adopted elements of the cavalier style such as a mustache and a hat worn on the side of the head to convey the desired image.[86]

The man who embodied the style was Henry IV (1589–1610), first Bourbon king of France. He was described as relentlessly amorous, "aglitter with precious stones and pearls, and a suit of utmost richness, dressed so people say, as a lover."[87]

Henry IV spent his childhood among the peasants of Gascony. His mother Jeanne, queen of Navarre, sought to protect her son from the corrupt practices at court and had him raised by the peasants. He was dressed in rough, shapeless peasant clothes, ate peasant food, and was allowed to run wild with peasants.[88] His reign was characterized as an interlude before absolutist reigns of Europe.[89]

Henry IV was betrothed to Marguerite de Valois. When Henry's mother went to Paris to make the wedding arrangements, she wrote to him, "Here the men do not solicit the women," it is the women who solicit the men.[90] After their wedding, Henry and Marguerite decided on an extramarital lifestyle. Their separate liaisons became public knowledge, predating the scandalous novel of extramarital sex by mutual consent *Les Liaisons Dangéreuses*.[91]

In 1601 Henry IV married his second wife, Marie de Médicis, in Lyon, and they then went their separate ways. She set off for Paris to furnish her quarters, and he dashed off in a different direction to his mistress Henriette d'Entraigues at the Château de Verneuil.[92]

The cavalier style began to take shape during the reign of Henry IV. It entailed flirtatiousness and constant readiness for an amorous encounter. The clothes were distinguished by lavish trims of lace, ribbons, and pearls, with or without colored gemstones. Heels, roses, or bows decorated men's shoes. The many tiny buttons designed to close the front of the doublet or jerkin were usually only partly buttoned,[93] adding to the impression that the man had not finished dressing. A cloak slung over one shoulder and the spur straps on the boots indicated that the wearer was a man of action. The feather in the hat, the dangling sword, the falling hose, and the broad boot tops conveyed dash and swagger. A pointed beard and a mustache proclaimed virility.

Cavalier fashion portrayed "studied dishevelment," observed art historian Anne Hollander. A man's appearance seemed to be in disarray, suggesting sexual

The Ball, *by Abraham Bosse, 1635, conveys the essence of the cavalier fashion.*

provocation. Barriers to interaction were eliminated. The ruff became smaller, then softer, and later flat. The shirt was soft. The wire and padding that traditionally gave male attire its structure and stiffness were eliminated.[94] The suggestion of nudity was created by the clothes themselves, not by their absence, Hollander concluded.[95]

Costume historian M. A. Racinet observed that the hallmarks of cavalier fashion—swagger, bravura, and voluptuous curves—made it easy to breech the barriers posed by clothing. The image suggested that access to the body was easy.[96]

### Military Uniforms

The impact of military uniforms on women is reflected in the disappointment women express when they see a man in civilian clothes after first seeing him in uniform, observed C. J. Flugel.[97] Military uniforms have traditionally been structured to make men look impressive. During World War II scores of women "swooned" at the sight of khaki-clad GIs only to be let down when the battle was over and heroes turned into ordinary men in ordinary clothes. "With sickening clarity these women realized they were victims of the irresistible allure of uniform."[98] Imperfect physical features were hidden by the uniform, which was padded and provided with stiffness, Flugel observed.[99] Then and now a uniform elevates the wearer to a higher plane. Part of the appeal of uniformed men is that they are usually dedicated to a greater good. The uniform suggests that the person is a solid, honest, and dependable individual.[100]

Accessories were designed to impress. Epaulets increased the apparent width of the man across the shoulders, suggesting strength. Embellishments of gold buttons and other decorations dazzled the observer. Even the spurs had an ornamental function.[101] The resplendent appearance suggested that the wearer had greater access to superhuman power.[102]

The sword and the helmet strongly projected male sexuality and their removal constituted "a painfully clear symbol of castration."[103]

### Fashion in the United States

To define themselves, identify their status, and attract female interest, the American landed aristocracy of the Colonial period wore European fashions.[104] Well-to-do men of this class continued to wear sumptuous attire well into the nineteenth century.

Merchants and industrialists, on the other hand, began rejecting European fashion. They were in part influenced by middle-class moralists who criticized the "decadence" of men who wore powder, wigs, and richly ornamented and patterned clothing in the cavalier manner.[105] The new industrialists adopted plain and subdued clothing so as "to impart trust and confidence in business affairs."[106]

In the presidential campaign of 1840 the sober style of male dress was pitted against cavalier fashion. William Henry Harrison ran against Martin Van Buren, who was described as a man who wore a "ruffled shirt and silken hose" and corsets and who splashed cologne on his whiskers. In the campaign literature it was claimed that Van Buren had no taste for fighting and preferred "scheming" and "intrigue" like women. Van Buren was short, and songwriters called him "little Van" and suggested that he was all "used up."[107]

William Henry Harrison, on the other hand, was a man who wore "homespun hodden grey." Harrison was described as a log cabin dweller, a drinker of homemade hard cider, a strong man who was ready to fight. Hardiness, physical strength, and a readiness to do battle were identified in the campaign literature as the American version of desirable manhood.[108]

Harrison won the election, but on the day William Henry Harrison took the oath of office it was bitter cold. Lest he appear weak and unmanly, he refused to wear a topcoat and caught pneumonia and died one month after taking office.[109]

### Maleness, Acts of Seduction, and Manhood[110]

After the mid–nineteenth century, many well-to-do men rejected the sumptuous, body-hugging style, the velvet coat, breeches, perfume, and lace, and adopted a matched suit consisting of a coat, waistcoat, and trousers. The coat was quilted, the trousers were cut full and long, reaching the heels of the shoes. Together they helped to create a blocky silhouette,[111] a substantial image proclaiming authority.[112]

Only the waistcoat (the vest), which was usually worn under the coat (later a jacket), could be ornamented to reflect a man's personal taste. The vest could be a variety of fabrics, including brocades, striped satins, and fabrics with floral motifs. The principal piece of masculine jewelry was a watch chain to announce modernity.[113] Time had become the dimension upon which social life was organized. The standing collar and the bow tie men wore suggested impersonality and self-restraint.

The doctrine of self-restraint was espoused from the pulpit, in the medical press, and on the lecture circuit.[114] Writers of advice manuals suggested that, in controlling sexual desires, a man's energy would be harnessed to productive activity.[115]

The transition to adulthood began as soon as boys developed an interest in girls. Starting usually in the middle or late teens, boys willingly accepted the clothes they had once resisted as confining, wiped off the grime of outdoor activity, and began appearing in public with clean hands and faces and with their hair neatly combed.[116]

*Clothes that American boys considered too confining. Charlie W. Hanna, from a carte de visite by T. M. Mackey, Cambridge, Ohio (1875–1881). (Chester County Historical Society, West Chester, Pa.)*

Illustrator and founder of the American Boy Scouts Daniel Carter Beard described it in this way: "When girl consciousness entered my young life it swept through it like a tornado."[117] He fought vigorously against the change, but threw up his hands and succumbed. Yet he felt ashamed of himself for abandoning things he had once found reassuring, such as rough games, dirty fingernails, and raucous teasing.[118]

Unlike the tradition in European countries, where the path to love, work, and adult identity was determined by custom and class, confusion and anxiety marked the route to adulthood of adolescents in the United States in the second half of the nineteenth century.[119] Patriarchal lineage and political, economic, and social rank were no longer clear-cut. Industrialization and urbanization made it impossible for a young man to take his family's identity for granted. Some men could rise as high as they aspired, but democracy made competition fierce. Young men practiced competition and self-assertion skills, the qualities they would need for survival in the adult world, and they used their skills on young women of the lower classes.[120]

Young middle-class men considered marriage a personal, sexual, and social union that could take place only within one's social class. In their search for marriage partners, young men and women took part in sleigh rides, skating parties, church socials, balls, and cotillions "to measure and be measured" for romance, observed historian Anthony Rotundo.[121] For a man to be able to marry, however, he first had to establish his breadwinning ability. Wealth was the key to manhood, and wedded life completed his transition to adulthood.[122]

Young middle-class women were less anxious to get married early. They realized that they could expect little recreation after marriage, since domestic duties were likely to constrain their social lives. They often postponed marriage, and engagements could last for several years.[123]

Many young men tried to manage their lives through the exercise of self-control. In trying to comply with the injunction to self-restraint, some young men revered the ethereal concept of romance and practiced sexual self-restraint, but many failed in their resolve. Between 1761 and 1800, among "nice women"—middle-class women the men expected to marry—one bride out of three went to the altar pregnant.[124]

Other young middle-class men engaged in "sexual aggression." They sought erotic pleasures by trapping women of the lower classes into having sex. The young men needed no seductive attire. They invaded amusement parks and "evening streets" looking for young, lower-class women called "chippies." Through a ritualized program of games, raids, hunts, and other diversions they had enjoyed within the boy culture, the so-called chippies were seduced. Also bearing the imprint of the boy culture, each seducer used his own strategy and style, continuing the competition that had begun in boyhood.[125] The game of seduction, moreover, was used to reassure other young men that the player was in fact a real man.[126]

Being of a higher social class, the men's attire paved the way to interaction. Female sexual libido helped. Luce Irigaray observed that women are more vulnerable to seduction, both anatomically and biologically, because of their numerous pleasure zones and their responsiveness to male touching and kissing.[127]

But for men the liaisons were impersonal and exploitative, Henry Seidel Canby reported. The interaction entailed no romance, no personal or social union. "Her pretty face, her shapely limbs was all there was to her."[128]

### Homosexual Allure

A gay subculture in which gay men used effeminate appearance to identify themselves to other men emerged in American cities sometime around 1850.[129] Homosexuals continued to display an effeminate appearance until the end of the nineteenth century. To exaggerate the differences between themselves and straight, they walked with hands on hips, swaying like women. They used powder and paint, and some paid finicky attention to their appearance and clothing, noted a police investigator in 1899.[130]

The term *sissy,* coined in the 1840s, was first used as an affectionate term for "sister." By the 1880s, however, in the heterosexual culture the term had become associated with boys and men who were dependent, helpless, spineless, and weak. By 1900 the term *sissy* came to be applied to male effeminacy, cowardice, and lack of aggression.[131] In "Gay New York," historian George Chauncey reports that the gay subculture became organized, multilayered, and self-conscious. It had its own meeting places, language, folklore, and moral codes.[132]

### Masculine Representations

In the early decades of the twentieth century, expressions of male sexuality were overridden by the need to maintain a public image. Clark Kent, the other persona of Superman, was a bespectacled mild-mannered newspaper reporter. The costumed Superman was the nemesis of criminals but was unable to connect to his beloved Lois Lane.[133] When called upon, Clark Kent would change into his Superman costume and destroy the criminals, displaying speed and strength. Invulnerable to man-made weaponry, he seemed the most courageous manly man.[134]

### Film Noir

Another fantasy hero was the cynical, dangerous, hard-boiled detective. He was sexually alluring but unavailable for marriage. The character's origins lie in Dashiell Hammett's novels of the late 1920s. The detective was portrayed as an urban pioneer who made the world safe for women and children. He was "A man going forward . . . through mud and blood and death and deceit—as callous and brutal as necessary."[135]

In film, the hard-boiled detective genre developed before the mid–twentieth century and was called film noir. It was different from traditional Hollywood films characterized by happy endings in which the hero "got the girl." In film noir the hero was often thwarted and sometimes killed. A film might have no conclusive ending or resolution and evil could be "smashingly and leeringly triumphant."[136] In story after story the film insisted that a masculine man was one who acted—and killed—without a moment's hesitation.[137] The caption on a lobby card for *Dead Reckoning,* for example, summarized the threat to the woman in his life: "To kiss her . . . or to kill her—he's never quite sure."[138]

The detective was usually a returning soldier who had been alienated from life before he left for the war. He was masculine and tough; his sexuality was often irresistible.[139] The films offered gloomy scenarios of family disintegration and tales of personal anxiety, vacuous heroism, danger, sexuality, and alienation. For the women in these films his persona was most alluring.[140] It was as if his leeriness of women presented them with a challenge to get him involved.

A press release from June 1945 announced that Humphrey Bogart was no Romeo and the star claimed, "I'm tough and intend to stay that way."[141]

A scientific study of sexuality was made public after World War II.[142] Alfred C.

Kinsey and his associates reported that male sexual desire peaked in the late teens and declined progressively thereafter. Females, on the other hand, were reported to be most sexually responsive in their twenties and thirties, with a capacity for sexual activity remaining constant late into their fifties and sixties. Women were also characterized as being capable of multiple orgasms.[143]

### Erotic Sexuality

Until 1951 representations of male eroticism in mainstream culture were rare. According to the media, women were also attracted to the masculinity of male actors in epic movies starring Charleston Heston and Yul Brynner. The ornaments and sumptuous garments they wore projected the power of the characters they personified. The virility was indicated by the physical strength they projected and by the pomp and circumstance surrounding them. Reporters also noted that Yul Brynner's shaved head made baldness sexy.[144]

The characters portrayed by Marlon Brando and James Dean were unabashed about their candid desire for women. They turned the torn T-shirt and the semi-naked, tightly muscled male body into a spectacle of male eroticism. In 1951, as Stanley Kowalski in *A Street Car Named Desire*, Marlon Brando wore a wet, torn T-shirt that clung to his body, revealing the expanse of his muscular back. Fan mail revealed that Brando made the torn T-shirt a symbol of male virility.[145]

In *Picnic* (1955), the shirt Hal (William Holden) wore was torn open by a woman who had sensed his sexuality. With his body and feelings exposed, he felt naked. His sexuality absorbed the other women on the scene and he became an object of erotic interest.[146] A photo of William Holden was used on the cover of an issue of *Life* promoting its "Hollywood Album of Male Appeal,"[147] and the text conceded that overt eroticism may be an important dimension in male-female interaction.

In 1955 the film *Rebel Without a Cause* moved beyond open eroticism and sexuality to suggest that honesty and sensitivity are the real basis for relationships between men and women. In the film, Jim (James Dean) and Judy (Natalie Wood) are attracted to each other. Pressured into taking part in a gang fight, or "rumble," Jim changes from a suit to a white T-shirt. A T-shirt at the time was considered underwear, and it signified his desire for an open and honest interaction. Judy helped Jim sort out the conflict between his struggle to express his feelings openly and honestly, and the pressure to act in the impersonal style of the male gender role. Judy told him that his gentleness and sweetness were the qualities she liked in a man, thus reaffirming his gender identity. She also praised his loyalty in standing by Plato (Sal Mineo), an unpopular character in the film.[148]

It would have been impossible for an actor wearing a laundered and properly fitted oxford shirt, a suit, and a tie to convey the tension, eroticism, honesty, and passion that James Dean depicted. John Wayne characterized such actors and films as "trembling, torn T-shirt types."[149]

*"T-shirt exposed." James Dean in*
Rebel Without a Cause, *1955.*
*(The Everett Collection.)*

### Sexuality Within the Marriage

Marriage in the 1950s represented the renewal of the national character, and the title "family man" indicated patriotism and virility.[150] Keeping sexuality within the home, it was believed, would support the nation's moral fiber at a time when American ideals were perceived as being under attack by communism. Virility, at the time, was still considered to be a unilateral expression of male sexuality.[151] Holding the power in the home was the male's role, as were the breadwinning function and participation in the political arena.

The cold war encouraged marriage. Official ideology maintained that by living in sexually fulfilling marriages men would be less tempted by pornography, prostitution, "loose women," or homosexuals.[152] The term *togetherness* was applied to the newly emerging model. Togetherness meant that the married couple shared equally in familial duties, and the wife was her husband's primary companion.[153]

The gray flannel business suit of the 1950s represented hegemonic masculinity. This was the middle-class sexual ideal, in which the male performed as the family's breadwinner and performed vigorously in bed with his wife. Any deviation from this norm was equated with emasculation.[154] To escape stigma and persecution, gay men and lesbian women rushed into marriage for a cover.[155]

### Playboy

On the pages of *Playboy* eroticism and sexuality were integrated.[156] Launched in December 1953, a time characterized by a suburban lifestyle and a high birth rate, *Playboy* offered men fun and freedom from mortgages, life insurance, and

*Richard Chamberlain's clothes in the 1965 movie* Joy in the Morning *depict the "preppie" look. (The Everett Collection.)*

the charge of homosexuality. The playboy was a bachelor, a sophisticated man about town, a masterful lover, and irresistible to women. The attraction of the Playmate was the absence of threatening qualities, suggests Russell Miller.[157] Playmates were nice, clean girls and there was nothing to fear from seducing them. The magazine took to heart Alfred C. Kinsey's findings[158] that "nice girls did" have sex.[159]

*Playboy* was accused of encouraging men to avoid commitment. A playboy didn't need to be a husband to be a man.[160] Sex, for him, was a healthy, enjoyable recreational activity free of guilt. "Like the little bee, he flits from flower to flower, sipping the sweet nectars where he finds them, but never tarries too long at any one blossom."[161]

In the pages of the magazine, a playboy lived in a bachelor pad to which he would invite a female acquaintance for talks, discussion, cocktails, and mood music.[162] Seduction was as much a matter of the mind as of the body. The playboy was portrayed as immersed in romantic social life, in glamorous weekend house parties in the country, and in relaxing getaways on private yachts.[163]

*Playboy* claimed that it enabled its readers to feel sexually self-assured and to conduct themselves in a suave manner. Readers were told what to wear, what wines to drink with what meals, and what records to listen to. At the beach, for example, they were advised to dress in India madras swim trunks with fly fronts and never in those terrible "balloon-bottomed boxer shorts."[164] For the evening they were to wear black, "not midnight blue, maroon, or burnt ochre. Just black. Black looks and feels right so leave rainbow-hued jackets to the funny-type enter-

*Television and film actor Antonio Sabato, Jr. (born in Rome, Italy, in 1972) is widely photographed and is considered by the entertainment industry to exemplify the sexually alluring male. (The Everett Collection.)*

tainers on TV."[165] During business hours, a playboy dressed conservatively in a dark suit, striped tie, button-down shirt, and loafers.[166] On less formal occasions he could wear a silk shirt and a gold medallion on a chain around his neck.[167]

Cuff links were to be seasonably stylish with semiprecious gems in cool colors, particularly onyx, jade, jasper, and topaz;[168] and jewelry was to be set in gold or silver. *Playboy*, moreover, never accepted advertising for hair restorers, acne cures, or further education, implying that its readers needed no betterment.[169]

The attraction of a playboy was that he was single, well-to-do, and experienced in sex, and thus ideal for marriage. Romance literature often presented a playboy's bachelorhood as a challenge that women sought to conquer.

### Eroticizing Masculinity

Before the twentieth century rodeo promoters tried unsuccessfully to attract audiences with free admissions.[170] Then they began to emphasize the sensual element of rodeo. The wild west show, *Cheyenne's Frontier Days*, distributed handbills saying that the rodeo was a "celebration of the unique and daring sports indulged by the *virile* characters of the western frontier."[171] By 1890 there was an audience that paid admission.

In the 1970s technological developments in the fabric industry produced stretch, double-knit fabric that hugged the body.[172] To attract a larger audience, managers decided that ballgames should appeal to women, and that the sport should have some of the entertainment attributes of movies. Uniforms were introduced that were body-hugging, colorful, and sexually attractive.[173] Players were putting their bodies on display as well as their talent, and they referred to the uniforms as the "Double Knit Revolution."[174]

The pants clung to the contours of the lower part of the body, revealing the players' taut muscles.[175] Audiences began talking about Hank Aaron's "cute tush"

*The Mets' Todd Pratt in a uniform, Oct. 26, 1999. (Photo: Chang W. Lee/
New York Times.)*

as much as they did about his quick wrists.[176] "Players like looking sexy when
they play," Ron Blumberg of the New York Yankees said; it helps them run
faster.[177]

The new uniform featured flyless fronts, striped waistbands, tapered calves,
and buttonless sweater tops.[178] This design forced ballplayers to keep in shape
and was a far cry from the traditional flannel bloomer pants.

Danny Whelan, a team trainer for 34 years, observed that in the baggy pants
even Robert Taylor (a handsome 1940s movie star) "looked bad, that the new
uniforms are so well tailored that Mickey Rooney [a popular but unglamorous
character actor] would look good in 'em."[179]

### "Cool" Pose

The "cool" pose consists of a variety of behaviors, several of which entail the seduction of women. Sociolinguistic research suggests that blacks are very sensitive
to the power of words to sexually arouse, to insult, to comfort, and to enhance social status.[180]

In the lower socioeconomic levels of black culture, the passage to manhood often takes place under the tutelage of the streets and peer influences, and manhood
is often defined in terms of toughness, sexual conquest, and thrill-seeking.[181]
Daily encounters with unemployment, racism, and overt discrimination encour-

*John-Eric Hexum (1957–1984), an actor whose appearance in the film* The Making of a Male Model *(1983) won him much acclaim. (The Everett Collection.)*

age an overemphasis on obsessive masculinity. The "cool" pose entails acting suave and charming and wearing stylish, colorful attire and theatrical details like tassels on boxing shoes.[182] To many black males, clothing, hairstyles, and stance and walking styles are ways of achieving visibility and demonstrating pride. These behaviors have been characterized as a response to the inability of low-income black men to provide for and protect their families.

### Male Trophy or Boy Toy

In the 1985 movie *Desperately Seeking Susan,* Madonna Ciccone carried a statuette, a trophy she called "Boy Toy," and it may have been Madonna who coined the term. The example she used was that of a beautiful young man who was proud of his good looks. His body was toned, tanned, and well-oiled, giving him the look of a trophy. His white, lightweight tank top contrasted strikingly with his tan, toned arms.[182]

### Notes

1. J. C. Flugel (1966), *The Psychology of Clothes* (London: Hogarth Press), pp. 108–109 (originally published in 1930); J. S. Hyde (1994), *Understanding Human Sexuality* (New York: McGraw Hill), p. 93.

2. Ibid.

3. Engaging in carnal union outside the marriage was considered a sin. S. M. Lyman (1989), *The Seven Deadly Sins: Society and Evil,* rev. (Dix Hills, New York: General Hall), pp. 66–67.

*John Bartlett's male fashionable attire for spring 2000. The attire meets the criteria for seductiveness established by the Church; they hug and expose the body, employing color and ornament. (Photo: Dan Lecca. Courtesy Paul Wilmot Communications.)*

4. "The Stronger Sex Makes Strong Box Office," *Life*, May 1954, pp. 93–96.

5. *Webster's Third New International Dictionary* (Springfield, Mass.: G & C Merriam, 1967).

6. K. Myers (1988), "Fashion 'n' Passion: A Working Paper," in *Zoot Suits and Second-Hand Dresses: An Anthology of Fashion and Music*, ed. A. McRobbie (Boston: Unwin Hyman), pp. 189–197.

7. P. Bird (1974), "Images of Women in the Old Testament," pp. 41–87 in *Religion and Sexism: Images of Women in Jewish and Christian Traditions*, ed. R. R. Reuther (New York: Simon and Schuster).

8. J. Kirsch (1997), *The Harlot by the Side of the Road: Forbidden Tales from the Bible* (New York: Ballantine), pp. 134–140.

9. B. P. Prusak (1974), "Women: Seductive Siren and Source of Sin," in *Religion and Sexism: Images of Women in Jewish and Christian Traditions*, ed. R. R. Reuther (New York: Simon and Schuster), pp. 85–142.

10. Augustine (1972), *Concerning the City of God Against the Pagans*, trans. H. Bettenson, ed. D. Knowles (Harmondsworth, Eng.: Penguin).

11. Lyman, op. cit., pp. 54–56.

12. Prusak, op. cit., pp. 101, 105.

13. *New York Times*, Nov. 25, 1998.

14. W. W. Savage, Jr. (1998), *Comics, Cowboys, and Jungle Queens* (Hanover, N.H.: Wesleyan University Press), p. 78.

15. The concept underlying *Playboy* is a man who approaches life with immense gusto and relish. H. M. Hefner (1963), *The Playboy Philosophy,* part 1 (Chicago : HMH Publishing), p. 1.

16. Prusak, op. cit.

17. 1 Tim. 2: 9–10.

18. Prusak, op. cit., pp. 100–101.

19. L. Langner (1959), *The Importance of Wearing Clothes* (New York: Hastings House), pp. 46–47.

20. D. Pickering, ed. (1962), *The Statutes at Large from the Magna Carta to the End of the Eleventh Parliament of Great Britain,* vol. 1 (Cambridge, Eng.: Cambridge University Press), p. 383. Originally published in 1701.

21. J. R. Walkowitz (1980), *Prostitution and Victorian Society: Women, Class and the State* (Cambridge, Eng.: Cambridge University Press), p. 26.

22. L. Mahood (1990), *The Magdalenes: Prostitution in the Nineteenth Century* (New York: Routledge, Chapman and Hall), p. 42.

23. G. Simmel (1957), "Fashion," *American Journal of Sociology* 62: 294–323. Originally published in 1904.

24. M. Baerwald and T. Mahoney (1960), *The Story of Jewelry* (New York: Abelard-Schuman); also M. Wilson (1967), *Gems* (New York: Viking), p. 98.

25. M. and A. Batterberry (1977), *Fashion: The Mirror of History* (New York: Greenwich House), p. 107; Also A. Hollander (1978), *Seeing Through Clothes* (New York: Viking), pp. 187–189.

26. M. Scott (1980), *The History of Dress Series, Late Gothic Europe, 1400–1500* (London: Mills and Boon).

27. J. Mayo (1984), *A History of Ecclesiatical Dress* (New York: Holmes and Meier), pp. 40, 61.

28. F. Boucher (1965), *20,000 Years of Fashion* (New York: Harry N. Abrams), p. 184.

29. Scott, op. cit., pp. 57, 63, 112, ill. 63; also M. Davenport (1972), *The Book of Costume* (New York: Crown), pp. 307–308.

30. L. Lawner (1987), *Lives of the Courtesans* (New York: Rizzoli).

31. Batterberry, op. cit., p. 283.

32. Ibid.

33. Ibid. pp. 326, 327.

34. The custom of kings' acquiring mistresses as feminine companions was common. The term *courtesan* surfaced in French in 1549. It was spelled "courtisan" and had no attached definition. By 1587 it designated "one attached to a prince." In court language of 1601 in Italy, a courtesan was described as follows: "A whore is for every rascal, a courtizan is for the cortizen, individuals attached to the court." See *Oxford English Dictionary on Historical Principles* (1955), ed. C. T. Onions (Oxford: Clarendon Press), p. 1061. With Henry IV (1589–1610), courtesans became "status symbols" displayed in public to demonstrate and compare with those of other monarchs. See V. and B. Bullough (1978), *Prostitution: An Illustrated Social History* (New York: Crown Publishers), p. 147. A liaison with the king was "profitable." Many women gathered around the palace hoping to catch the king's eye.

35. Batterberry, op. cit., p. 165.

36. A. Marwick (1988), *Beauty in History* (London: Thames and Hudson), p. 112.

37. G. L. Mosse (1978), *The Final Solution: A History of European Racism* (New York: Howard Fertig), pp. 8-9.

38. Batterberry, op. cit., p, 165.

39. Mosse, op. cit., pp. 8–9.

40. According to art historian Kenneth Clark (1956), in *The Nude: A Study of Ideal Art Form* (London: John Murray), the depiction of the nude in Greek art underwent changes that mirrored changes in desired social conduct. It went "from the physical to the moral sphere." In the fifth century, when democracy became a political and social goal, a new ideal of beauty was evident. Harmonious proportions emphasized a balanced whole, communicating strength, grace, and gentleness and reflected the search for an orderly society.

41. S. Caygill (1980), *Color the Essence of You* (Millbrae, Calif.: Celestial Arts).

42. Ibid.

43. C. Jackson (1973), *Color Me Beautiful: Discover Your Natural Beauty Through Color That Makes You Look Great and Feel Fabulous* (New York: Ballantine Books).

44. Webster's Third New International Dictionary, p. 962.

45. J. Laver (1963), *Costume* (New York: Hawthorne Books) pp. 88–95; B. Payne, G. Weinakor, and J. Farrell-Beck (1992), *The History of Costume: From Ancient Mesopotamia Through the Twentieth Century* (New York: Harper Collins), pp. 486–488, 502–504. In the latter part of the nineteenth century, however, an elitist pattern of consumption emerged. Although courtly life was dead, Rosalind H. Williams observed, the external forms of courtly taste assumed new importance, outlasting the social order in which they originated. See R. H. Williams (1982), *Dream Worlds: Mass Consumption in Late Nineteenth-Century France* (Berkeley: University of California Press), pp. 56, 107–153.

46. J. Richardson (1966), *The Courtesan* (Cleveland: World Publishing), p. 1.

47. Marwick, op. cit., pp 272–282.

48. Richardson, op. cit., 209–210.

49. Marwick, op cit., pp. 272-282.

50. J. W. Petras (1975), *Sex Male Gender Masculine* (Port Washington, N. Y.: Alfred Publishing House), p. 136. See also Flugel, op. cit, pp. 108-109; S. Kitzinger (1983), *Woman's Experience with Sex* (New York: G. P. Putnam's Sons), p. 9.

51. Richardson, op cit.

52. Marwick, op. cit., pp. 272-282.

53. Ibid., pp. 227–230.

54. Models also became objects of envy, as the Ziegfeld girl had before. So esteemed the model had become by the mid-1920s that John Robert Powers, an out-of-work actor who organized the first modeling agency, was able to employ New York debutantes—women who normally considered work degrading. See L. W. Banner (1983), *American Beauty: A Social History Through Two Centuries of the American Idea, Ideal, and the Image of the Beautiful Woman* (New York: Knopf), p. 263.

55. L. A. Erensberg (1981), *Steppin' Out: New York Nightlife and the Transformation of American Culture, 1890–1930* (Westport, Conn.: Greenwood Press).

56. C. F. Funnell (1983), *By the Beautiful Sea* (New Brunswick, N.J.: Rutgers University Press), pp. 148–149.

57. *Esquire* published the originals of the airbrush watercolors of pinup girls popular among the troops fighting in World War II. Comedian Bob Hope was once quoted as saying, "Our American troops are ready to fight at the drop of an *Esquire*." *New York Times*, Nov. 25, 1998.

58. Savage, op. cit., p. 78.

59. Ibid., p 78.

60. R. Miller (1984), *Bunny: The Real Story of Playboy* (New York: New American Library), p. 53.

61. S. Christain (1998), "University's Trove of Pinups Is Admired by All Sorts, Even Some Feminists," *New York Times*, Nov. 25, p. B3.

62. E. T. May (1988), *Homeward Bound: American Families in the Cold War Era* (New York: Basic Books), pp. 62–63.

63. Christain, op. cit.

64. Ibid.

65. Ibid.

66. Miller, op. cit., p. 47.

67. Miller, op. cit., p. 48.

68. T. Weyr (1978), *Reaching for Paradise: The Playboy Vision of America* (New York: New York Times Books), p. 95.

69. Miller, op. cit., p. 48.

70. Weyr, op. cit., p. 164.

71. May, op. cit., pp. 109–110.

72. May, op. cit., p. 109.

73. From *Your Chance to Live* (Defense Civil Preparedness Agency), in May, op. cit., pp. 109–111.

74. May, op. cit., p. 111.

75. R. Wolf (1991), *Goya and the Satirical Print in England and on the Continent* (Boston: Boston College Museum of Art), pp. 1–4.

76. V. Steele (1991), *Women of Fashion: Twentieth-Century Designers* (New York: Rizzoli), p. 108; also M. Turim (1990), "Designing Women," in *Fabrications: Costume and the Female Body*, ed. J. Gains and C. Herzog (New York: Routledge), p. 223.

77. B. Willoughby and R. Schickel (1974), *The Platinum Years* (New York: Random House), pp. 8–11, 245–258.

78. E. Kazan's 1956 movie *Baby Doll* portrays a thumb-sucking child bride who sleeps in a crib.

79. Wolf, op. cit., pp. 70, 84, 85; also see Bullough, op. cit., p. 152.

80. T. Veblen (1953), *The Theory of the Leisure Class* (New York: Mentor Books). Originally published in 1899.

81. Flugel, op. cit., pp. 106, 108–109; Laver, op. cit.

82. F. Boucher (1965), op. cit. Women's dresses were more shapely.

83. Hollander, op. cit., p. 234.

84. Flugel, op. cit., p. 48.

85. R. Pistolese and R. Horsting (1970), *History of Fashion* (New York: John Wiley & Sons), pp. 154, 163.

86. Payne et al., op. cit., p. 252.

87. Batterberry, op. cit., p. 133.

88. Ibid.

89. F. A. Parsons (1923), *The Psychology of Dress* (Garden City, N.Y.: Doubleday, Page), pp. 157–158.

90. Batterberry, op. cit., p. 132.

91. Ibid., pp. 135.

92. Parsons, op. cit., p. 152.

93. Batterberry, op. cit., p. 138–139.

94. Payne et al., op. cit., p. 341.

95. Hollander, op. cit., pp. 235–236.

96. Parsons, op. cit., p. 158.

97. Flugel, op. cit., p. 214.

98. V. Feltz (1995), "Cops, Docs & UPS Men," *Redbook*, June, pp. 47–48.

99. Flugel, op. cit., p. 211.

100. Feltz, op. cit., p. 27.

101. Ibid. p. 107.

102. Flugel, op. cit., p. 33.

103. Ibid., pp. 104–105.

104. A. M. Earle (1903), *Two Centuries of Costume in America 1620–1820* (Rutland, Vt.: Charles E. Tuttle), vols. 1 & 2.

105. Ibid.

106. Ibid.

107. M. Kimmel (1996), *Manhood in America* (New York: Free Press), p. 38.

108. Ibid. Older, venerated patriarchs such as Thomas Jefferson were chided as "dandified" and accused of having female characteristics of "timidity and whimsicalness." Kimmel, op. cit., p. 27.

109. Kimmel, op. cit., p. 39.

110. Maleness refers to the biological characteristics of the male. Seduction refers to attempts to "bed" them. Manhood here refers to males' exercise of authority over women.

111. Payne et al., op. cit., pp. 504–506.

112. See J. Harvey (1995), *Men in Black* (Chicago: University of Chicago Press).

113. Ibid.

114. Ibid.

115. Kimmel, op. cit., pp. 44–45.

116. Rotundo, op. cit., p. 54.

117. Ibid., p. 99.

118. Ibid.

119. Ibid., p. 54.

120. Kimmel, op. cit., p. 2.

121. Rotundo, op. cit., p. 100.

122. Ibid., p. 114.

123. Ibid., pp. 118–119.

124. Ibid., p. 121.

125. Ibid., p. 124.

126. Kimmel, op. cit., p. 101. Kimmel suggests that the young middle-class males used sexual desire to subdue their own feelings of frustration and anxiety.

127. L. Irigaray (1990), quoted in *Seduction,* ed. J. Baudrillard, trans. B. Singer (New York: St. Martin's Press), p. 9.

128. Rotundo, op. cit., pp. 124–125.

129. Kimmel, op. cit., p. 98.

130. Ibid., p. 99.

131. Ibid., p. 99.

132. Ibid., p. 98.

133. Ibid., pp. 211–212.

134. Savage, op. cit., p. 5.

135. Kimmel, op. cit., pp. 212–213.

136. P. Shapiro (1995), "Somewhere over the Rainbow Dorothy Got Totaled: Postmodernity and Modern Film," pp. 197–215 in *Postmodern Representations*, ed. R. H. Brown (Champaign: University of Illinois Press).

137. J. Mellen (1977), *Big Bad Wolves: Masculinity in American Films* (New York: Pantheon), p. 9.

138. S. Cohan (1997), *Masked Men* (Bloomington, Ind.: Indiana University Press), p. 90.

139. Kimmel, op. cit., p. 232.

140. May, op. cit., p. 62.

141. Cohan, op. cit., p. 79.

142. Ibid. p. 56.

143. A. C. Kinsey, W. B. Pomeroy, and C. E. Martin (1948), *Sexual Behavior in the Human Animal* (Philadelphia: W. B. Saunders). Also Cohan, op. cit., p. 58.

144. D. Elley (1984), *The Epic Film Myth and History* (London: Routledge & Kegan Paul).

145. Cohan, op. cit., p. 244.

146. Ibid., pp. 167–178.

147. Ibid., p. 167.

148. Judy omitted the more "militaristic" example in which Jim stood his ground and didn't back down when his peers called him "chicken." The story involves Buzz, a jock, who believed he was entitled to the best-looking girl in high school, Judy. The challenge to a fight occurred when Buzz caught Jim scrutinizing Judy's legs. Judy had joined her friends and pulled herself up to sit on the bumper of Jim's car, exposing her beautiful long legs. Pulling out a knife, Buzz made cuts into Jim's tires and invited Jim to fight. Jim met the challenge head on, and later, Buzz was killed playing "chicken." He was unable to open the door of the car from which he needed to jump, and the car went over the cliff.

149. 1960 interview with John Wayne. Cohan, op. cit., p. 203.

150. May, op. cit., p. 97.

151. H. M. Hacker (1957), "The New Burdens of Masculinity," *Marriage and Family Living* 19: 227–233.

152. May, op. cit., p. 261.

153. It appeared in the 1954 Easter issue of *McCall's*. R. J. Oakley (1990), *God's Country: America in the Fifties* (New York: Barricade Books). Also Cohan, op. cit., p. 9.

154. Hegemonic masculinity refers to the conversion of the 1950s culture to middle-class sexual ideology according to which a man was supposed to perform as the family's breadwinner and perform vigorously in bed with a woman. Hacker, op. cit.

155. See Chauncey, "The National Panic over Sex Crimes," p. 38, in which he cited testimonies of many gay men and lesbians who married because "the pressure to marry had to be comprehended." May, op. cit., p. 261.

156. R. Miller (1984), *Bunny: The Real Story of Playboy* (New York: New American Library), pp. 46–47.

157. Ibid. pp. 46–47.

158. A. C. Kinsey, W. B. Pomeroy, and C. E. Martin (1948), *Sexual Behavior in the Human Male* (Philadelphia: Saunders); A. Kinsey and P. H. Gebhard (1953), *Sexual Behavior in the Human Female* (Philadelphia: Saunders).

159. Miller, op. cit., p. 52.

160. B. Ehrenreich (1983), *The Hearts of Man and the Flights from Commitment* (Garden City, N.Y.: Doubleday) p. 51.

161. P. Zollo(1999), *Wise Up to Teens* (Ithaca, N.Y.: New Strategist Publications), p. 38.

162. Weyr, op. cit., p. 11.

163. Miller, op. cit., p. 47.

164. Ibid., p. 62.

165. Ibid.

166. Weyr, op. cit., p. 56.

167. Miller, op. cit., pp. 156–157.

168. Ibid., p. 46.

169. Ibid., p. 47.

170. Danny Whelan, a team trainer who spent thirty-four years training baseball and basketball teams, observed that the sex appeal of pro athletes has increased geometrically. Prior to the new uniforms, even Robert Taylor looked bad. The new uniforms are so well tailored that, "Mickey Rooney would look good in 'em." Quoted in G. Lichtenstein (1974), "There's Something About a Man in Uniform," *Esquire,* Oct., p. 382.

171. Kimmel, op. cit., p. 148.

172. Lichtenstein, op. cit., pp. 232–234, 382. Before 1970, sports uniforms were made of nonstretch cotton flannel. "The guys wore everything loose," reported Wayne Garrett of the Mets (p. 234). Since players' uniforms allow no easy access to the male body, they are alluring rather than sexy.

173. W. Hedding, clothing product manager for Rawlings, a St. Louis manufacturer of professional athletes' uniforms. Quoted in Lichtenstein, op. cit., p. 382.

174 Lichtenstein, op. cit., p. 232.

175. Ibid., pp. 232–233.

176. Ibid., p. 233.

177. Ibid. p. 232.

178. Ibid., p. 234.

179. Ibid., p. 382.

180. W. Oliver (1994), "The Symbolic Display of Compulsive Masculinity in the Lower Class Black Bar," in *The American Black Male,* ed. R. G. Majors and J. U. Gordon (1994). (Chicago: Nelson-Hall), p. 252.

181. M. R. Langley (1994), "The Cool Pose: An Afrocentric Analysis," in Majors and Gordon, eds., op. cit., pp. 231–245.

182. R. G. Majors, R. Tyler, B. Peden, and R. Hall (1994), "Cool Pose: A Symbolic Mechanism for Masculine Role Enactment and Coping by Black Males," in Majors and Gordon, eds., op. cit., p. 248.

# Part Four:

# Clothing Symbols and Cultural Values

# 9

# Wealth and Beauty in the Middle Ages

CLOTHING SYMBOLS reflect cultural values that one has achieved, and their use is largely a matter of personal choice. Unlike clothing signs, the use of which is governed by norms specifying what people ought or ought not wear, no rules govern the wearing of clothing symbols in contemporary society. In small tribal societies ritual and ceremony reaffirm meaning; the visual representation of a value through appearance tends to be constant. In societies with limited ritual and ceremony, and where change is constant, as in the United States, the meaning of cultural representations of values, as through clothing symbols, is likely to vary; it is specific to the individual, the group, and the period.

Dressing in the attire of a class higher than one's own has been recognized as wearing a clothing symbol. According to Erving Goffman, "Symbols play a role that is less clearly controlled by authority." Rather than having a direct impact on behavior, "class symbols . . . serve to influence . . . in a desired direction." The wearing of clothing symbols, according to Goffman, evokes feelings rather than behavior.[1] Thorstein Veblen also suggested that the impact of symbols lies in the feelings they arouse rather than in behavior elicited. In *The Theory of the Leisure Class* (1953) he argued: "In order to gain and hold the esteem of men it is not sufficient merely to possess wealth or power. The wealth or power must be put into evidence for esteem is awarded only on evidence."[2] The wearing of attire that suggests the achievement of cultural values, what a society considers good and desirable, leads to a positive social evaluation and response. Because physical labor was defined as unworthy by the warrior class, the wearing of attire that signifies leisure demonstrates worthiness. In Veblen's words, "No apparel can be considered worthy or even decent if it shows the effect of manual labor."[3]

Veblen used the term *status symbol* to designate elements and styles of dress that reflect the achievement of cultural values. To identify the meaning of a symbol, one must consider a person's primary group; its resources, information, and experience; and the political, economic, and cultural forces of the period. The social situation in which the symbol is worn must also be taken into account. A particular visual construct may, however, reflect more than one cultural value and thus have more than one meaning. In contemporary society, for example, the wearing of "Michael Jordan" or "Bo Jackson" sneakers may reflect racial pride; a desired alliance with a sport, a person, or male success; a desire to feel "with it"; or simply access to wealth. The wearing of Porsche sun goggles, similarly, may suggest a desired association with male success or the lifestyle that ownership of the car suggests, or it may reflect an association with sports cars in general. The wearing of a "Chris Evert" $1,000 diamond tennis bracelet, marketed to women, may simply reflect that one is in love.

In addition, a different type of evidence is typically required of each social class to convey the same message. To demonstrate the realization of economic success, for example, a member of the Du Pont family and the owner of a small hardware store would be required to present different "proofs." A Du Pont would likely wear understated attire, whereas a hardware store owner may wear heavy makeup and jewelry.[4] The purpose of wearing a clothing symbol may be personal, but its larger meaning and significance depend on its connotation for an audience.

Values are central and distinguishing characteristics of a culture. In the form of ideas and images, they represent societal goals and encourage individuals to act on their behalf. From early childhood on, children are exposed to these ideals and are consciously and unconsciously encouraged to pursue them. Continuity in value orientation enables a society to re-create itself.[5]

As new "aristocracies"—religious, political, or economic—acquired power in Western society, they gave voice to their own values and goals. For example, the accumulation of wealth and the desirability of beauty, along with coordinated, understated attire, emerged in the Middle Ages; hierarchy and leisure, that is, freedom from physical labor, arose in the monarchical courts; artful display and fashion developed in the newly prosperous commercial centers; beauty as the perfection of the physical form, as well as youthfulness and health, emerged with the rise of the middle class and modernity.[6] Each of these elements is a subject of a chapter in Part 4. The cultural values of wealth and beauty are discussed here.

*       *       *

A central feature of the economic and political life in medieval society, according to Michael Mann, was that neither economic power nor political power was centralized.[7] In AD 1000 European society was characterized by a number of small interaction networks. The organization forms of the barbarian invaders (Visigoths, Vandals, Franks, and so on) were confined within the local relationships of the village or tribe, with only loose and unstable confederations beyond. No single group had a monopoly or control over social life.[8] Because no one possessed monopoly powers, almost everyone could have private economic resources hidden from the control of some authority. The lord, vassal, town, church, and even the peasant village were all power actors with autonomous spheres and resources to contribute to a delicate balance of power, explained Mann.[9]

Christianity provided a broad framework for the emergence of cultural values. The economic development that the Church facilitated made it possible to accumulate wealth and the refined symbols of wealth that demonstrate an awareness of beauty. Three factors contributed to the emergence of market relations, according to Mann. The first was literacy; ecclesiastical Latin was a stable means of communication beyond face-to-face relations. The second was the Church's emphasis on moral conduct: its concern for "just" behavior; its preaching for consideration, decency, and charity toward all Christians. Together with the threat of excommunication, this emphasis on moral conduct facilitated long-distance control and regulation of behavior. The third factor encouraging markets and trade was the existence of a monastic-episcopal economy underpinned by Christian norms.[10]

In its retreat from the Roman world, the Church had created networks of monasteries; each monastery had its own economy, yet none was fully self-sufficient. Trade developed among monasteries, the estates of bishops, secular estates, and manors. By 1155, individual families, local villages, and manor communities were participating in a wider network of economic interaction that was governed by institutionalized norms concerning property possession, production relations, and market exchange.[11] Towns emerged between 1050 and 1250, as did merchant and artisan institutions. Economic success and awareness of beauty, and in the religious realm spirituality and asceticism, were the first cultural values to which individuals aspired. By making spirituality a goal that one must strive to achieve, the Church leaders supported the emergence of achievement as a basic value of Christian culture. Achievement can be understood as a "master value" in the sense that it is important to accomplish one's goals no matter what the particular goals are.[12]

## Wealth

Five lines of evidence suggest that the accumulation of personal wealth emerged as a value by the eleventh or twelfth century: (1) the sin of pride, (2) ascetic and heretical movements, (3) legal property rights, (4) luxury dress, and (5) the regulation of dress.[13]

### The Sin of Pride

Christian theologians have always associated luxurious dress with the sin of pride. The increased vigilance against pride in the twelfth century suggests that, indeed, the demonstration of wealth was becoming socially important. One of the earliest Christian thinkers to employ a hierarchy of sins, Evagrius Pontus (died ca. AD 400), distinguished between vainglory, which included luxurious dress, and pride, an attitude of arrogance; he listed them, respectively, in sixth and seventh place in the hierarchy of sins. Gregory the Great (590–604) rearranged the order of significance. He combined vainglory with pride and elevated this cardinal sin to first place. He argued that pride, the attitude of arrogance, and luxurious dress were "at the root of all evil."[14]

A twelfth-century theologian, Alanus de Insulis, who wrote extensively on the sin of pride, identified the elements of this most cardinal of sins: a haughty mode of speech; a manner of silence; and the wearing of fashionable dress, ornament, and cosmetic beautification. "An inner demeanor of pride" could be signified by the outer personal demeanor: "looking up to the things of heaven, lifting of eyebrows, turning up of chin and holding arms as stiff as a bow." According to Alanus, the body was "pressed into service on behalf of arrogance."[15] Humility in deportment and modesty in dress signified the absence of the sin of pride. This sin thus came to include wearing elements of dress that enhance self-importance at the expense of religious authority.

### Ascetic and Heretical Movements

The years between 1050 and 1200 marked a turning point in the history of religious devotion, as English historian Collin Morris (1972) suggested. The focus turned to the suffering of Christ. The individual strove imaginatively to share in the pain of the Lord.[16] A new pattern of interior piety developed that was characterized by a growing sensitivity, marked by personal love, for the crucified Lord. Regular use of the confessional, the position of homage as a posture for prayer, and the increasing popularity of the "dying Christ" style of crucifix were aspects of this new piety. Devotion was compassionate but directed inward. Instead of depicting a living Christ, victorious over the forces of evil and radiant with vitality, works of art portrayed Christ as dead on the cross. An early surviving example is a wooden crucifix made for Archbishop Gero of Cologne (969–1076). Christ's head is slumped on his right shoulder, his eyes are closed, his face is twisted, and his jaw is hanging open. Morris suggested that this style of crucifix was designed to encourage personal grief and a personal bond to Christ.[17]

The new style of devotion was also a result of the growth of education, trade, and industry, the rise of towns, and the incorporation of new territories, all of which led to social dislocation, tension, and reorganization of group life.[18] Angered by the wealth and the moral laxity of the clergy, heretics rejected the claimed privileges of the official priesthood. In part, heretical movements were an attack upon the abuses by the system. Heresy offered a social protest for the poor, the rich, and the nobles. Merchants joined the protests, angered that they were denied respectability because the Church claimed that wealth earned in the marketplace did not assure them a place in heaven. To members of the nobility who envied the property and power acquired by the Church, heresy offered a justification for seizing the wealth of the corrupt Church for themselves. For many of the laity, moreover, the mystical and emotional rewards of religion were lacking; the Church gave them "no opportunity to study the Bible, to hear it read in the vernacular, or to be moved by sermons."[19]

The rise of religious sects, such as the Waldensians and the Albigensians, led to an association of asceticism with spirituality in the popular mind. The Waldensians, or "the poor men of Lyons," emerged around 1170, when a rich merchant

*The Gero Crucifix, ca. AD 975–1000, carved from*
*wood, Cologne Cathedral. (Photo courtesy of*
*Bildarchiv Foto Marburg/Art Resource.)*

from Lyon, Peter Waldo, not only denounced the Church, which had been done
by many others, but offered a solution to its problems: a life of absolute poverty.
He attacked the moral laxity of the clergy and denounced the sacraments it administered. His preaching attracted followers, and the group was declared heretical by the Lateran Council of 1215. The Church of Rome, however, never succeeded in suppressing the Waldensian church. Its theology was later absorbed
and transformed by Protestant reformers.

The Albigensians, like the Waldensians, denied the value of the sacraments and
priesthood of the established church. True Albigensians led a life of rigorous asceticism. They sought to help the god of light vanquish the evil god of darkness,
who had created and ruled the material world. Sexual intercourse was discouraged, even within marriage, because it served only to propagate matter and
thereby extend the dominion of darkness. Considered tainted because animals
reproduce, all animal flesh was also forbidden.

Angered by the luxurious dress, wealth, and moral laxity of the clergy, some
monastic orders also rejected the privileges claimed by the official priesthood. A
leading proponent of "drabness in dress," Bernard of Clairvaux (1090–1153), was

concerned not with people's external actions but with their inner motives.[20] A member of the Order of Templars, he argued that the proper role of clothing is to demonstrate obedience to higher authority. To that end, Templars wore only the clothes their commanders gave them and sought "neither other garments nor other food." "They cropped their hair close because their Gospels tell them that it is a shame for a man to tend to his hair. They are never seen combed or rarely washed, their beards are matted, they reek of dust and bear the stains of heat and harness," noted Michael and Ariene Batterberry.[21] Saint Bernard criticized the immodest size of churches, their enormous height and their immoderate length, their vacant immensity, their paintings, and their sumptuous finish. The purpose of showing these riches, he argued, was to draw more riches, to gorge the eyes so as to open the purse strings. He saw monetary profit rather than veneration of what is sacred as the goal of such ornamentation.[22]

In addition, a Cistercian statute denounced the use of silk, gold, silver, stained glass, sculpture, paintings, and carpets in churches. Similar denunciations were made by others, who argued that these superfluities merely distracted the faithful from their prayers. The basic concern of the ascetics, Umberto Eco (1986) pointed out, was whether the churches should be decorated sumptuously when the children of God were living in poverty.[23]

Despite criticism, Church authorities were proud of their ownership of scarce resources. One of the best known Church authorities, Suger, the abbot of Saint-Denis (1133–1144), argued that the House of God should be a repository of all matter that would show our affection "for the church our mother." He proceeded to identify each of the gemstones and precious metals used in the ornament of "that wonderful cross of St. Elloy."[24] Since the Church's focus in this area was on accumulation, church treasuries contained functional objects, beautiful objects, and some that were merely curious. According to Eco, in acquiring objects medieval people found it extremely difficult to distinguish between those of utility or goodness and those of beauty. They mingled the two because of "a unitary vision of the transcendental aspects of being" and took joy in enumerating these riches. They viewed the act of collecting these objects as a "reflection of, and participation in, the being and the power of God."[25]

### Legal Property Rights

Medieval Europeans were primarily concerned with utilizing the land in their own locality. Their agriculture focused on the penetration of nature, on bringing more land into cultivation.[26] They learned to cultivate heavier, wetter soils and harness more effectively the energy of their animals, skills that enabled some lords and peasants to acquire additional property and wealth. They possessed sufficient autonomy and privacy to be able to keep the fruits of their own enterprise. By AD 1200, property owners, lords, and wealthy peasants revived Roman law on private property as a means of regulating their relationship with the state; the law based ownership claim on custom and tradition. The legalization of private ownership suggests that the acquisition of personal wealth was emerging as a desirable social attribute.

### Luxury Dress

Until the twelfth century, dress was socially stratified. Cost, custom, and law controlled consumption. The wealthy among the Romans wore their dress ankle-length; workers and soldiers wore theirs to the knee. Monks' and peasants' attire was made of a coarse grade of cloth, whereas the attire of the wealthy was made of a finer grade of wool or linen.[27] The luxury of sable, ermine, miniver, and vail was limited by law to the elite in rank and riches. The easy availability of pelts, such as sheepskins, made it possible for the poorer classes to keep warm and at the same time to be recognized and defined as a class.

Social rank determined the quality of cloth one received even as a gift. Charlemagne, for example, chose the highest grade of fabric for himself and to send off as gifts. He gave fabric of a coarser grade to the officers who lived with him at the palace, and he gave an even coarser grade to his servants on feast days, when gifts of cloth were customary.[28]

When the manufacture of cloth was established in Flanders (in the area that is Belgium today) in the tenth century, awareness of social class and differing degrees of access to wealth governed production. Wool was woven into various grades of cloth, enabling the wealthy to acquire a "finer" image.[29] Two levels of clothing consumption affected production: that by the manor and that by the village. Whereas local weavers met the clothing needs of the near-subsistence peasant, the consumption of more expensive attire by the manors encouraged formal production and organized trade.

By the twelfth century, increased exposure to novel artifacts brought in through trade created an interest in luxury dress and ornament. Barbarian chiefs, while maintaining their traditional style of dress—breeches and tunic—had their attire reproduced in fine, luxury-grade silk that came from Byzantine workshops. It was "outstanding for its bright and varied colors."[30] They also ornamented themselves in gold and precious stones acquired at market fairs, where foreign merchants exhibited spices, perfumes, strands of pearls, and fantastic clothes made of powdered ermine, ethereal silks, and the lustrous feathered skins of flayed birds.[31] As Michael and Ariene Batterberry stated in *Fashion: The Mirror of History*, "The rich wore all the jewels, pearl necklaces, and heavy gold bracelets they could lay their hands on."[32]

### The Regulation of Dress

Clothing regulations in the Middle Ages either prescribed what one could or should wear or proscribed what one could not wear. They were used by ruling authorities to control competition for scarce resources, to support differences between classes, and to maintain a superior position at the top of the social hierarchy.[33]

The clothing regulations were based on two ideas: The first was the belief that each person had a predetermined place in God's orderly universe and that each must uphold this order by leading an exemplary life, which involved dressing in rank-appropriate clothing; the second involved mercantilism, the economic ideology of the time. The basic premise of mercantilism was that the world contained only a given amount of wealth and that each nation could enrich itself only at the expense of others. This belief led people to hoard gold and silver rather than spend it on imported cloth, attire, and jewelry. Sumptuous attire, since it was imported from the East, was expensive and required an "excessive" expenditure of bullion.[34]

The emergence of wealth as a cultural value encouraged individuation in two paradoxical ways. Ownership of material objects, on the one hand, invited personal experimentation, comfort, and pleasure. Asceticism, the denial of material objects and normal pleasures of life, on the other hand, emerged as a means of achieving what some felt was a deeper and more significant kind of satisfaction than that derived from consumption. It spoke of a state of spirituality and of a moral good.

## Beauty

Between the fifth and eleventh centuries, Church theologians feared that a keen interest in earthly and physical things might endanger the soul. They urged their followers to resist the lure of beauty and to attend to spiritual matters. They associated beauty and art with the pagan cultures of Greece and Rome; replacement of those cultures with Christianity required that pagan ideas and artifacts be obliterated. However, the Synod of 1075 recognized that art offered the illiterate peasant population a legitimate aid to piety. Sculpture, pictures, color, and light were increasingly seen as facilitating religious endeavor, and art began to acquire status. Theologians sought to help by providing a theory that explained the beauty of art, as described in the section that follows.[35]

### Saint Thomas Aquinas on Beauty

Saint Thomas Aquinas (1225–1275) taught that beauty and art are within the realm of the transcendental, that the beautiful is "good" because it is capable of affecting the human soul. He claimed that in creating works of beauty the artist is dedicated to the humble service of faith; the artist is an associate of God and is, in fact, continuing his work.[36] When creating an art object, the artist achieves "a mean," controlling the extremes of excess and defect, which is a moral virtue.[37]

"Beauty is the splendour of form shining on the proportioned parts of matter," wrote Saint Thomas. He quoted Saint Augustine as saying that "unity is the form of all beauty. . . . If beauty delights the mind, it is because beauty is essentially a certain excellence or perfection in the proportion of things."[38] The mind likes the beautiful because it likes unity, order, and brightness or clarity of color, explained Saint Thomas. Defining the nature of the beautiful, he identified four qualities: (1) excellence in the perfection of proportion; (2) integrity of design, order, and unity of form; (3) brightness, clarity in color; and (4) a degree of splendor, something luminous in itself.

The bearer of beauty, according to Aquinas, is the concrete organism in all the complexity of its relations. Deciding that an image is beautiful requires judgment, not intuition, and involves "a dialogue" with the object. Beauty is what pleases when it is seen, "not because it is intuited without effort, but because it is through effort that it is won." He warned that however beautiful a created thing may be, it may appear beautiful to some but not to others "because it is beautiful only under certain aspects which some discover and others do not."[39]

To touch beauty is to ascend to the realm of God. The presence in the organic whole of all its parts is essential to beauty. The human body, for instance, is considered deformed if a limb is missing. Eco supported this contention with his comment, "We call mutilated people ugly, for they lack the required proportion of parts to the whole."[40]

### *The Acceptance of the Ideal of Beauty*

In the thirteenth century, the ideal in art and attire changed from merely showing off one's wealth to creating a harmonious unity. The term *elegance* was incorporated into the French language to describe this ideal, according to Michael and Ariene Batterberry (1977).[41] It referred to gracefully refined and luxurious attire. Such attire can be seen in a medieval miniature of Tristan and Isolde in conversation. Isolde is wearing a crown and a dress of simple line with a high waistline and wide sleeves lined in fur. In the fourteenth century, gowns were less elaborate than before but made of soft golden cloth called panno d'oro. With simple dresses women wore a demi ceint, a chain with hanging pendants of precious metals that draped loosely on the hips.

The Renaissance inspired further explorations of style by artists. Jewels continued to be used sparingly. The emphasis was on creating a harmonious appearance by the careful use of details. Depictions of dress and ornament considered the interplay of texture, color, and pattern. Sandro Botticelli (1445–1510), a painter of line and grace in movement, sought a perfect harmony between the person, costume, and environment. Antonio Pisano, known as Pisanello (1395–1455), focused on precise contour and balance in his designs for male costumes. The asymmetrical hosiery-shoes worn by the men were remarkable in their highly contrasting designs. In the painting Lady in Green by Raphael (1483–1520), a woman's bare white neck and shoulders are framed with a contrasting rich but dusky dress. In contrasting her dark eyes and her white face, the artist repeats the theme. Taken together, the image conveys a sense of unity.[42]

### The *Book of Hours* and the Diffusion of the Beauty Ideal

The *Book of Hours* encouraged awareness of art and taste within an upper social class that had spread across large geographical areas. This illustrated prayer book for the laity first appeared in the second half of the thirteenth century and was reissued regularly. It enabled individuals to commune with God directly, without benefit of clergy. It was the most popular book read for nearly 250 years, and its popularity was due largely to the illustrations. The text was supported by richly elaborate, brightly colored paintings, which helped to tell a complete story. The goal was to create a unified visual whole.[43]

In addition to prayers to the Virgin Mary, arranged by the time of day, and other prayers such as litanies and the Office of the Dead, the *Book of Hours* included a calendar of the cycle of the seasons to remind the individual of farming tasks, feasts, and holidays. Commissioned by the nobility, the book also contained stories and paintings commemorating events enjoyed by the patron's family, such as weddings, births, and travel. The cost of the book was such that for the first 150 years of its life only the nobility of rank and wealth could afford it. The inclusion of prayers created especially for the patron and the depiction of the patron in the paintings suggest that the book was the product of a consultative effort between consumer and artist.

During the fifteenth century, changes in the method of manuscript production enabled the book to be produced in larger numbers and more locations, making it possible for those of lesser social rank to also acquire it. Merchants, shop owners, and lesser rural landowners could now order the prayer book from French and Flemish centers and request that their own portraits or events that they wanted to commemorate be added to the book's existing illuminations. Urban dwellers could acquire the book from scribal shops. Produced from standard exemplars, their copies were more mundane.[44] The cost, however, made it impossible for an ordinary peasant or urban worker to own a *Book of Hours*.[45]

Art historian Lawrence R. Poos (1988) pointed out that the *Book of Hours* was a possession prized for far more than its spiritual function. Its ownership, he suggested, is the earliest example of conspicuous consumption. People carried it around to show off. It became what Veblen called a status symbol. The fact that medieval piety incorporated a substantial emphasis on public display prepared the ground for people to "show off" ownership of the book, Poos pointed out. He observed, "More than one satirical broadside aimed at the social pretensions of the urban middle class singled out the vogue for carrying about richly adorned Books of Hours."[46]

In a 1989 exhibit at the Walters Art Gallery in Baltimore, Maryland, entitled "The Medieval Clothes Horse," the curator called attention to what we call today "nostalgia dressing"—the phenomenon of reaching back and "resurrecting" a fashion popular in an earlier period. The pages of the *Books of Hours* portrayed customary dress as well as fashionable attire and current trends. They became

*Detail from* The Trials of Moses *by Botticelli, n.d., Vatican Museums, Rome. Two young shepherdesses display elegant hairdos that were inspired by the embroidery on their clothing. (Reprinted by permission of Alinari/Art Resource.)*

sources of style and an important example of what Maurice Halbwachs called public memory.

## Notes

1. E. Goffman (1951), "Symbols of Class Status," *British Journal of Sociology* A (4): 294–303.
2. T. Veblen (1953), *The Theory of the Leisure Class* (New York: Mentor Books), p. 42. Originally published 1899.
3. Ibid., p. 199.
4. S. A. Ostrander (1984), *Women of the Upper Class* (Philadelphia: Temple University Press), p. 3.
5. D. McClelland (1961), *The Achieving Society* (Princeton: Van Nostrand).
6. Goffman, op. cit.; W. H. Form and G. P. Stone (1957), "Urbanism, Anonymity and Status Symbolism," *American Journal of Sociology* 62 (5): 504–514.
7. M. Mann (1986), *The Sources of Social Power,* vol. 1 (Cambridge, Eng.: Cambridge University Press).
8. M. Bloch (1961), *Feudal Society,* vols. 1 and 2, trans. L. A. Manyon (Chicago: University of Chicago Press); F. L. Ganshof (1961), *Feudalism,* trans. P. Grierson (New York: Harper and Row).
9. Mann, op. cit., p. 399.
10. Ibid., p. 337.
11. Ibid., p. 409.
12. Ibid., p. 397.
13. Ibid., pp. 381–390; J. M. Vincent (1935), *Costume and Conduct in the Laws of Basel, Bern and Zurich 1370–1800* (Baltimore: Johns Hopkins University Press).
14. S. M. Lyman (1989), *The Seven Deadly Sins: Society and Evil,* rev. ed. (Dix Hills, N.Y.: General Hall), pp. 136–137.
15. Ibid., 141–142.
16. C. Morris (1972), *The Discovery of the Individual: 1050–1200* (New York: Harper Torchbooks), pp. 158–160.
17. Ibid., pp. 139–140.
18. Ibid., pp. 37–49; Mann, op. cit., 383–390.
19. M. Chambers et al. (1974), *The Western Experience* (New York: Knopf), pp. 306–307.
20. Morris, op. cit., p. 74.
21. M. and A. Batterberry (1977), *Fashion: The Mirror of History* (New York: Greenwich House), p. 86.
22. U. Eco (1986), *Art and Beauty in the Middle Ages* (New Haven, Conn.: Yale University Press), p. 7.
23. Ibid., p. 6.
24. Ibid., p. 13.
25. Ibid., p. 15.
26. Mann, op. cit., p. 409.
27. Batterberry, op. cit., p. 71.
28. F. Boucher (1965), *20,000 Years of Fashion* (New York: Harry N. Abrams), p. 164.
29. Ibid., p. 163.

30. Ibid., p. 164.

31. Batterberry, op. cit., p. 71.

32. Ibid., p. 70.

33. *Encyclopedia Britannica* (1911), 11th ed., vol. 27 (Cambridge, Eng.: Cambridge University Press); F. E. Baldwin (1928), *Sumptuous Legislation and Personal Regulation in England* (Baltimore, Md.: Johns Hopkins University Press), p. 45; Vincent, op. cit.; D. Pickering, ed. (1962), *The Statutes at Large from the Magna Carta to the End of the Eleventh Parliament of Great Britain,* vol. 1 (Cambridge, Eng.: Cambridge University Press), p. 466 (originally published in 1701).

34. J. Schneider (1978), "Peacocks and Penguins: The Political Economy of European Cloth and Colors," *American Ethnologist* 5 (3): 413–447.

35. Eco, op. cit., pp. 78, 99, 101.

36. J. Maritain (1924), *Art and Scholasticism,* trans. J. F. Scanlan (New York: Charles Scribner's Sons), pp. 46–55.

37. *Selected Writings of St. Thomas Aquinas* (1965), trans. R. P. Goodwin (New York: Bobbs-Merrill), pp. 111–112.

38. Maritain, op. cit., pp. 19–22.

39. Ibid., pp. 22–25, 40–53.

40. Eco, op. cit., p. 99.

41. Batterberry, op. cit., p. 86.

42. R. Pistolese and R. Horsting (1970), *History of Fashions* (New York: John Wiley and Sons), pp. 154–163.

43. R. S. Weick, ed. (1988), *Time Sanctified: The Book of Hours in Medieval Art and Life* (New York: George Braziller), pp. 27–30.

44. V. Reinburg (1988), "Prayers and the Book of Hours," in Weick, op. cit., p. 39.

45. L. R. Poos (1988), "Social History and the Book of Hours," in Weick, op. cit., p. 34.

46. Ibid., p. 37.

# 10

# Leisure and Political Hierarchy

## Leisure

The dress and adornment of the nobility, according to Veblen, exhibited the following characteristics: It was expensive; it was in the latest fashion; and it signified in style and detail that the wearer could not possibly engage in manual labor and was thus a member of the leisure class.[1] He identified the nobility's preference for expensive materials as conspicuous consumption and its pursuit of fashion as wasteful, calling it conspicuous waste; he regarded the impractical style of the nobility's dress as indicative of conspicuous leisure.[2]

The origins of the clothing of the leisure class, in Veblen's view, go back to the time when "a warlike habit of life" was considered more worthy than the drudgery and toil involved in working the land. To prove that they had successfully ravaged the enemy, warlords returning from military exploits paraded their newly found treasures. Property ownership became associated with the receipt of honor, and one's social worth depended on the amount of property one owned. As ancient society became differentiated, there were those who periodically went on military forays and acquired wealth. There were also those who stayed home, worked hard on the land to eke out a living, and had little property. Those who were free from physical labor and did not have to produce their own food became respected socially. To receive the desired respect, one had to do more than possess wealth and power; they had to be exhibited, because "esteem was accorded only on evidence."[3]

## Political Hierarchy

Shifts in the fortunes of war weakened the power of the autonomous feudal lords and the knightly class and encouraged the growth of monarchical courts and commercial centers. Beginning in the fourteenth century, a time of increasing prosperity in Europe, royal and princely courts attempted to concentrate power under the rule of one man. Exaggerated ceremonial etiquette, lavish banquets, and entertainment were used to persuade the court and noble guests of the power of the ruler. Sumptuous courtly processions and extravagance (in dress

*Francis I, ca. 1525, attributed to Jean Clouet, Louvre, Paris. The king's attire is made of rich satin and is soft and flowing. The black satin stripes provide contrast and restrain the color, which might otherwise seem too pert. The doublet, an outer garment, has a wide-cut neck so that the embroidered shirt can be seen. The sleeves are full but slump off the shoulders, suggesting laxity. The ensemble is sensuous and somewhat seductive. (Reprinted by permission of Alinari/Art Resource.)*

The Field of the Cloth of Gold, *ca. 1520, anonymous, from the collection of Her Majesty the Queen of England. Henry VIII and his entourage of five thousand are winding their way to the Castle of Guiness (left), headquarters of the French. On the right stands the temporary palace and the wine-spouting fountain of the English. At least 820 tents were brought by the*

and other areas) were used to impress the people. In the courts of France, England, and Spain and in the local dukedoms of Italy, cultural ideas, objects, and resources were carefully manipulated to convey the appropriate image. The wealth, physical force, and political and religious authority of the ruler were the intended messages.

Evidence of these spectacles can be found in historical documents and in paintings. At a meeting between Francis I of France and Henry VIII of England in

*English to accommodate the troops. Many of those who came to observe the spectacle, knights and ladies, had to sleep on hay and straw. (Reprinted by permission of Royal Collection Enterprises.)*

June 1520, the rulers relied on such spectacle to conduct "international affairs." The meeting was called "The Field of the Cloth of Gold"; it lasted for twenty days, during which "the kings visited, dined, jousted, and excelled in theatrical acts of courtesy, and friendship," to quote Phyllis Mack (1987).[4] Henry held court in a palace specially built for the meeting. It was ornamented with statues of men in various attitudes of war; its ceilings were covered with white silk, and its roofs were studded with roses on a ground of gold. A great pillar wreathed in gold and

*Henry VIII, 1536, by Hans Holbein, Walker Art Gallery, Liverpool. The king's attire is richly embroidered and perforated, allowing the fabric of his shirt to come through, which makes the garment look as if it is bejeweled. The chain around his chest, padded doublet, puffed sleeves, and fur coat increase his bearing. The hat continues the details of the garments, emphasizing a unified whole. (Reprinted by permission of Alinari/Art Resource.)*

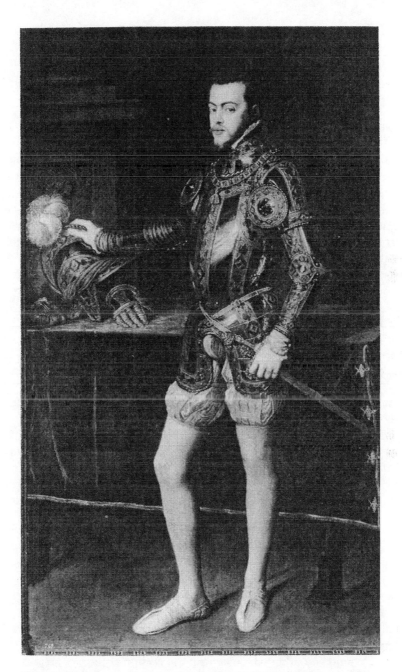

*Philip II of Spain, n.d., by Titian, Prado, Madrid. The king is shown in armor and codpiece. (Reprinted by permission of Lauros-Giraudon/Art Resource.)*

surrounded by four gilt lions supported the whole edifice. Francis rested in a tent "as high as the tallest tower" with thirty-two sides covered in golden cloth that had stripes of blue velvet "powdered" with golden fleurs-de-lis. Nearly four hundred other tents surrounded Francis's, creating an appearance of "an entire town of silver and gold, of silk and velvet, of floating tapestries."[5]

## Court Style, Decorum, and Manners

Dress signified the distinctive style of each court in relation to the population and to its governmental functions, as historian J. H. Elliott (1987) pointed out.[6] The French style was that of public kingship. The monarch lived out his life beneath the public gaze, and the nobles were grouped around the highly visible monarch. Hence, all were sensitive to aesthetics. Competition for patronage was part of the lifestyle of those dependent on the monarchy, including courtiers, artists, and those of the nobility who were financially strapped.[7] The Spanish style, in contrast, was that of private kingship. The tenures of Philip III, Philip IV, and Carlos II were characterized by the kings' social distance. Court ceremonies and rituals were used to isolate the sovereign; his company was limited to a few privileged aristocrats. A somber style of dress prevailed in the Spanish court. The attire included a ruff that imprisoned the neck and made both expression and carriage rigid and dramatic. Pleats were heavy; diamonds, rubies, and emeralds were used lavishly; earrings, diadems, and necklaces oppressed the silhouette.[8]

Veblen argued that "in the last analysis the value of manners lies in the fact that they are a voucher of a life of leisure."[9] Knowledge of good form, he claimed, is prima facie evidence that a portion of a person's life was spent in acquiring accomplishments that were of "no lucrative effect." In *The Civilizing Process* (1978), Norbert Elias argued that political rhetoric underlies the expectation for "civility" and "refinement," terms that describe the conduct and attire required of the leisure class. The demeanor expected of the attendants serving those in authority was also expressed in dress.[10]

Within the households of the great barons of feudal Europe, loyalty was the expected conduct, and the most familiar embodiment of this value was the knight. Knighthood was a privilege. It was not automatically bestowed on members of the nobility; it had to be specifically earned and individually given. To be invested, a novice knight had to pledge to be unflinchingly steadfast in his loyalty to his feudal lord and to be ready to fight and lay down his life. A knight had the right to confer the rank on any man he considered worthy, but he also had the responsibility of giving him guidance.[11]

Knighthood and loyalty declined with the decline of the feudal households.[12] In the fourteenth and fifteenth centuries a new aristocracy came into being that had new patterns of association and interaction. Composed of members of the landed nobility, members of the middle class who had acquired wealth, and gov-

*Philip II of Spain, n.d., by Sanches Coello, Prado, Madrid. The king is shown wearing the characteristic black and white "Spanish habit." It consisted of a padded black parabola. a cone-shaped structure, with a white ruff around the neck. It was starched to rigidity, immobilizing its wearer. The somberness and volume of the attire suggest a desire for distance and self-restraint.*

ernment officials, this aristocracy came to inhabit a new space, the semiurban courts of princes and kings. A nobleman was no longer the master in his own castle. He now lived at the court, serving the sovereign and waiting on him at the table. At the court he had to behave in exact accordance with his own rank and the rank of those who surrounded him. Unlike free lords and knights who were largely unrestrained in their ability to act, be fair, or feel compassion for the downtrodden, the members of the new aristocracy were dependent servants of the king. They were constrained in their behavior and in their freedom to express emotions. Sycophancy, self-restraint, and reserve characterized their behavior. In addition, new expectations for behavior and appearance emerged. Members of the new aristocracy were expected to remain aloof from anything the middle-class or "common" people did or said. In the environment of the absolutist court, etiquette and dress became the crucial means by which the aristocratic courtier asserted his privileged position.[13]

The styles and elements of dress that Veblen described as distinguishing the leisure class also identified the ruling class. The attire signified power and authority, which, in the words of Elias, were required for the formation of a "monopoly of force."[14] As Veblen suggested, court attire indicated a system of domination and was intended to elicit a behavioral response—compliance—and not merely feelings of esteem.[15]

Monarchs' attire may be understood as a strategy and tactic they employed in the ceaseless struggles and confrontations they faced. The representation of power in appearance was not merely to repress, to block, or to reject. Monarchs believed that their attire could transform, strengthen, or weaken their hold.

Power, then, must be understood as something that does not exist by itself, apart from other relations. In reality, power implies a more or less organized, hierarchical, coordinated cluster of relations.

## Notes

1. The root of the word *leisure* is the Latin *lic[re,* which means "to be permitted," suggesting that leisure is about the opportunity to do nothing. It is different from recreation, which is an antidote to work and entails a refreshment of the spirit, body, or both and has always been a culturally legitimate activity. Warren I. Susman suggested that leisure as a cultural value emerged in the beginning of the twentieth century as the belief in abundance permeated public consciousness. See W. I. Susman (1984), *Culture As History: The Transformation of American Society in the Twentieth Century* (New York: Pantheon Books), pp. xxii–xxvii. The notion of abundance has characterized the perception of the United States abroad, at least since the beginning of the twentieth century, suggested Stuart and Elizabeth Ewen (1979) in *Channels of Desire: Mass Images and the Shaping of American Consciousness* (New York: McGraw-Hill), pp. 44–47.

2. T. Veblen (1953), *The Theory of the Leisure Class* (New York: Mentor), p. 42. Originally published 1899.

3. Ibid., p. 42.

4. P. Mack (1987), "Political Rhetoric and Poetic Meaning in Renaissance Culture: Clement Marot and the Field of the Cloth of Gold," in *Politics and Culture in Early Modern Europe*, ed. P. Mack and M. C. Jacobs (Cambridge, Eng.: Cambridge University Press), p. 59.

5. Ibid., pp. 70–71.

6. J. H. Elliott (1987), "The Court of the Spanish Habsburgs: A Peculiar Institution?" in Mack and Jacobs, op. cit., pp. 5–24.

7. Ibid., pp. 19, 21.

8. Ibid., pp. 20, 23–24.

9. Veblen, op. cit., p. 48.

10. N. Elias (1978), *The Civilizing Process: The Development of Manners* (New York: Urizon), pp. 100–101, 216–217.

11. Metropolitan Museum of Art (1982), *The Art of Chivalry: European Arms and Armor* (New York: American Federation of Arts), pp. 11–14; Elias, op. cit., pp. 205–212.

12. The end came about after a series of battles around 1300. Armored mounted knights, surrounded by their retainers, were defeated by armies of infantry pikemen made up of well-to-do farmers and town inhabitants. This sudden shift in the fortunes of war weakened the autonomous lord, hastened the demise of classic feudalism, and eventually led to the death of knighthood and the role behavior and attire of the knight.

13. Elias, op. cit., pp. 102–116.

14. Ibid., p. xv.

15. Veblen, op. cit., pp. 46–49.

# 11

# Commerce and Fashion

## Commerce

As previously discussed, the weakened power of the autonomous feudal lords encouraged the development of commercial centers such as Venice, Florence, and Genoa and the establishment of the great northern ports of Bruges and Antwerp. The government at the time controlled the art and fashion worlds, and periodic changes in desired appearance became sources of wealth and prestige. In a study of the court of the Spanish Habsburgs, J. H. Elliott observed that the lesser rulers were the innovators in matters of display: the fifteenth-century dukes of Burgundy in ceremonial display and the sixteenth-century Medicis in the art of court spectacle. It was only by compensatory effort of this kind that they could hold their own in a world of great powers. But the great powers followed at their own pace and convenience, conferring their own prestige on practices first developed in the lesser courts.[1]

## The Emergence of Fashion

The court of Philip the Good, duke of Burgundy (d. 1467), is considered the "cradle" of fashion.[2] Philip exploited the resources available in the territory he controlled to create new clothing styles. Until this time Paris had been the center of luxurious court dress. As mentioned, the International Gothic Style had been generated in Paris in about 1380, and attire in this style was worn in many of the courts in Europe, which were connected through a complex system of politics and marriage. After the beginning of the fifteenth century, however, Paris was eclipsed as the center of court dress by the court in the southern French duchy of Burgundy. Its scattered possessions extended along the Rhine, the spine of Europe, from Switzerland to modern-day Belgium and Holland, directly within the Mediterranean trade route for goods being transported to the North Sea and England.[3] People, talent, and commodities flowed into its markets. Members of the court took increased interest in their clothes, adorning themselves with elaborate costumes to display wealth and an awareness of style.

*The Duke of Burgundy, Philip the Good, receiving an illuminated manuscript. Attired completely in black, his appearance was in sharp contrast to the colorful dress worn by members of the nobility. His style was adopted by monarchs in Spain, the Netherlands, and elsewhere in Europe. (Portrait of Philip the Good, Dedication Page, Chroniques de Hainault. Bibliothèque Royal Albert I, Brussels, n.d.)*

In the painting *Hunting with Falcons at the Court of Philip the Good* (ca. 1442), discussed in Chapter 8, all participants are dressed in white as part of the theme of the festivities. Some wear attire in the International Gothic Style that came out of Paris. Others wear regional garments, including some from Bruges, Ghent, the Netherlands, and Germany. Some of the mantles, gowns, and hairstyles originated in Italy. The figures of the duke and duchess reveal a new fashion ideal, long and lean. The duke's short gown is belted around the hipline, with carefully arranged pleats in the front; his legs in full-length hose and his pattens, or pointy shoes, are exposed. His sleeves are moderately sized and end with a padded, fur-trimmed cuff. Members of his household, courtiers, retainers, attendants, and musicians wear simpler versions of the same style (nonuniform uniforms). Most of the men wear no hats, and their hair is in a bowl cut; the duke wears "a version of the turban."[4] The duchess Isabella wears an ermine-lined long robe and a very sheer veil. A few of the women wear no headcovering at all.

*Decorated fan and gloves, French, ca. 1885.*

The variety in appearance and the influx of new materials and ideas informed artistic endeavor, helping to develop and support local employment.[5] In addition to its being an international trading center, however, Burgundy also became a fashion center. A sizable Italian community settled in Burgundian territory around Bruges in the Low Countries, formed by Italian merchants who had escaped from Paris along with several Medici bankers during the English occupation. They helped turn the duchy into a cosmopolitan center with exposure to foreign styles and the use of readily available resources (fur and the black cloth manufactured in Flanders). The trade in fashion had begun. By the middle of the fifteenth century, Burgundy had become the center of fashion.[6] Fashion offered a level of prestige to the community that local culture could not. Moreover, aristocrats from the northern countries and other parts of Europe, such as Italy and Spain, copied the Burgundian style and the long, lean, and graceful silhouettes of the court of Philip the Good, thus establishing fashion as a distinct part of elite culture.[7]

## Fashion As an Economic Good

A more recent example of a monarch using fashion to stimulate growth of the economy while increasing national prestige is Louis-Napoléon. He used the Great Exhibitions of 1851 and 1855 in London and Paris to show that the French government was behind its fashion industry, encouraging new technology and the export of dress and ornament. The exhibits included the latest cloaks, gloves, hats, fans, and perfumes, which were displayed alongside the crown jewels and the dresses of Napoléon's wife, Empress Eugénie.

*Lord and Taylor's 1874 copies of Charles Frederick Worth designs.*

The emperor wanted to encourage the well-to-do members of the aristocracy to support the economy by spending money on clothes.[8] There was no doubt that those who frequented the court were expected to dress up and change their costumes often. He also impressed upon Charles Frederick Worth, his court's couturier, that the production of fashion was essential for the well-being of the nation. He encouraged Worth to create a new fashion "each season because everything the Empress wore created a demand first among upper class women and then among the lower classes."[9] He insisted that women who appeared before him be dressed in the latest fashion. Through his efforts, the French fashion industry revived, and it continues to be an important source of revenue for the country.

As Simmel (1957) observed, openness to social mobility is the social condition necessary for fashion to exist.[10] He explained that there is no fashion in a hierarchical society where the boundaries between social classes are tightly shut and there is no possibility for mobility. The clothing of each class acts as a "uniform" that separates the classes and identifies rank. He noted that in Western society the aristocracy often had to compete with the rising middle class for social rewards, wealth, prestige, and power. To do so successfully, the aristocracy had to maintain visual superiority. A new fashion was thus invented by members of the aristocracy as soon as their existing style was adopted by members of the middle class.

Fashion puts a premium on expense. It makes use of novel materials and design innovations, which by their nature are not readily available. Scarcity is the essential element limiting the kinds of fabrics fashionable people are interested in wearing. Fashion often reflects new ideas expressed in art and culture. To determine how to dress, fashionable people monitor what others are wearing so as to "be up to date."

The desire to make what was scarce more readily available encouraged innovation, as John Nef suggested (1958).[11] For example, the demand for calico like that brought to England from India in the eighteenth century stimulated the growth of the cotton industry. The expense and demand for calico, a light, sheer, soft fabric with bright floral patterns, encouraged scientists and practical inventors to concentrate their efforts on finding ways to improve bleaching and dyeing techniques that would facilitate fabric printing and yield washable colors.[12]

## Fashion and the Individual

Fashion, Simmel argued, encourages modification and adoption to individual needs. The wearing of fashionable attire enables individuals to separate themselves from their family, to develop a more distinct identity and a more unique sense of self, and yet to maintain an affiliation with the prestigious aggregate. Individuals can extricate themselves from a setting or a situation, scrutinize the image they present, and tailor it to the social response they desire.

Fashion enables individuals to deal with themselves as persons and as social objects. It makes possible both individuation and social connectedness. As Simmel observed: "There is no institution, no law, no estate of life which can uniformly satisfy the opposing principles of uniformity and individuality better than fashion," because it allows individuals to pursue competing desires for group identity and for individual expression.[13] This separation or objectification allows one to correct the image if necessary to achieve the desired response, explained Simmel. By offering the opportunity for "trial and error," fashion encourages social and personal awareness.

## Notes

1. J. H. Elliott (1987), "The Court of the Spanish Habsburgs: A Peculiar Institution?" in *Politics and Culture in Early Modern Europe*, ed. P. Mack and M. C. Jacobs (Cambridge, Eng.: Cambridge University Press), pp. 5–24.

2. A. Hollander (1978), *Seeing Through Clothes* (New York: Viking), pp. 367–369; M. Scott (1980), *The History of Dress Series, Late Gothic Europe, 1400–1500* (London: Mills

*An urban environment is basic to the wearing of fashion, Simmel suggested. Even in the newly developed urban space in Boston, the Back Bay, and on a rainy day, the woman and her daughter are fashionably dressed. ("Rainy Day," Childe Hassam, 1885. The Toledo Museum of Art.)*

and Boon); M. and A. Batterberry (1977), *Fashion: The Mirror of History* (New York: Greenwich House), p. 89.

3. C. Mukerji (1983), *From Graven Images. Patterns of Modern Materialism* (New York. Columbia University Press), p. 31.

4. F. Boucher (1965), *20,000 Years of Fashion: The History of Costume and Personal Adornment* (New York: Harry N. Abrams), p. 210.

5. Mukerji, op. cit., pp. 166–167, 170–171.

6. Scott, op. cit., pp. 30, 32.

7. Hollander, op. cit., p. 367.

8. E. Saunders (1955), *The Age of Worth: Couturier to Empress Eugénie* (Bloomington: Indiana University Press), pp. 111–113.

9. Ibid., pp. 121–122.

10. G. Simmel (1957), "Fashion," *American Journal of Sociology* 62: 294–323. Originally published in 1904.

11. J. Nef (1958), *Cultural Foundation of Industrial Civilization* (New York: Harper and Row).

12. Mukerji, op. cit., pp. 190–228.

13. Simmel, op. cit., p. 549.

# 12

# Beauty As Perfection of Physical Form

**T**HE FEMININE FASHION IDEAL has often been confused with physical beauty, the harmonious unity of the anatomical form. In *Face Value: The Politics of Beauty* (1984), R. T. Lakoff and R. L. Scherr argued that "beauty is power," but at the same time they contended that the definition of beauty is idiosyncratic: "A choice made by one artist at one time bears no necessary relation to that of another artist. Today's essential ingredient is yesterday's irrelevancy." They concluded that "women have given up much of their potential true power to compete in the beauty game."[1]

Earlier, Simone de Beauvoir in *The Second Sex* (1953) similarly contended that beauty, fashion, and cosmetics have been used to force women into a secondary place in society and into a position of "other."[2] Although the ideal of feminine beauty varies, certain demands remain the same; in particular, to be feminine one must appear to be weak and docile. This appearance gives legitimacy to the belief that women's standing in society should be secondary, since they are not as capable as men. The subjugation of women, suggested de Beauvoir, emanates from the expectation that in sexual intercourse a woman must be possessed by a man and her body must be inert and passive. Costume and style have traditionally been devoted to cutting off the female body from any possible appearance of authority or independence, de Beauvoir argued. Corsets and long, voluminous dresses hampered physical mobility and personal expression. Makeup and jewelry contributed to the passivity in public affairs that was expected of women.[3]

Veblen had made clear the distinction between the novel, the feminine fashion ideal of any period, and the beautiful—perfection of physical form.[4] According to Veblen, the feminine fashion ideal is specific to a period. It is socially constructed and most often emanates from beliefs about what it is in a woman's appearance that will enhance a man's image in the eyes of other men. The "novel" is characterized by the norm of conspicuous waste. The "beautiful," in contrast, maintains its pleasing qualities through time.[5]

## The Novel

In the medieval period the feminine fashion ideal was designed to demonstrate that the man could support his woman, and he did not need her labor to provide for her needs.[6] The feminine fashion ideal demanded delicacy of face, diminutiveness of hands and feet, and a slender figure, all characteristic of idleness.

A plump appearance became the feminine norm during most of the nineteenth century, as L. W. Banner reported in *American Beauty* (1983).[7] For the many immigrants who associated thinness with poverty, the look of prosperity was chubbiness. "A fat bank account tends to make for a fat man," according to an adage of the day. For people in the middle classes, a paunch symbolized economic success. Medical authorities concurred: "No less for a man than for a woman a thin body is unhealthy."[8] It was thought that a woman with plump, rosy cheeks, large breasts, and full hips would have more admirers. As described in *The Laws of Health in Relation to the Human Form:*

> Who can admire hollow eyes, prominent cheek bones, sunken cheeks, angular and shrunken shoulders where the low-necked ball-dress displays at the most inopportune season the sharp collar bones and the edges of the shoulder blades, the flat breast and narrow chest, the skinny arms, the shriveled hands, and thin ankles?[9]

Popular guides to womanly perfection in the nineteenth century included illustrations of buxom women with large derrieres and pudgy forearms.[10] In the *Culture of Beauty* (1877), T. S. Sozinskey commented that to be beautiful a lady should be "of medium stoutness."[11] The *Ladies Home Journal* in 1888 and *Vogue* in 1893 promoted the plump, prosperous ideal. Photographs of society leaders in newspapers and magazines and photos of models in publications devoted to fashion sketches consistently showed women with round faces and ample body proportions.[12]

The 1921 winner of the Miss America contest was the curvaceous Margaret Gorman of Washington, D.C. Samuel Gompers, head of the American Federation of Labor, proclaimed her to be the type of woman America needed—strong, red-blooded, able to take on the responsibilities of "home-making and motherhood."

The following year marked a drastic change in standards of female beauty. The winner of the 1922 Miss America contest, Mary Campbell, lacked the large bosom and hips and the curves that had defined beauty in American women for more than a century. Miss Campbell had a slim athletic build with broad shoulders and straight lines. The 1922 contest had been judged by a panel of illustrators. According to Cole Phillips, one of the judges, the 1922 contest winner represented their view of a new streamlined feminine ideal.[13]

Their selection elicited editorial comment, chiding them for "capriciousness" in deciding on the new ideal of American female beauty. Nevertheless, Miss America reflected the new expectations that modern women should be active

*Miss America 1921,
Margaret Gorman—
full-bodied.*

*Miss America 1922,
Mary Campbell—
streamlined and
action-oriented.*

and healthy; and these expectations, in turn, influenced the female characteristics portrayed in contemporary commercial art. Women were no longer limited to presenting themselves as pale, plump, demure, and retiring, as nineteenth-century conventions dictated.

During the first decades of the twentieth century, literature and art described the slender, active feminine ideal. In his short story "Bernice Bobs Her Hair" and in his novel *The Great Gatsby*, F. Scott Fitzgerald portrayed young people who are spirited and full of energy. In Upton Sinclair's novel *Oil!*, Sinclair derided the superficiality of those in the young leisure class who sought "complicated ways of hitting a little ball" in tennis, golf, and polo matches.

In the summer of 1928 *Vogue* reported that in Paris "narrow hips" were de rigueur and that it was fashionable to be tanned.[14] The boyish look was considered beautiful, for it accommodated the demands of the camera for long legs and a hipless body. Fashion copy described the advantages of the new look, asserting that short skirts allowed a free and swinging walk that showed a graceful length of limb.

Fashion photographers such as Baron Adolph de Meyer, Cecil Beaton, and Edward Steichen helped to establish this new ideal of feminine fashion in accordance with the tastes and values of *Vogue* editors. Their photographs of women were composed to reflect an aura of elegance and refinement, showing women who looked comfortable in their luxurious world. The women's beauty did not necessarily convey perfection of figure and face but emphasized "beauty born of refinement and poise," a beauty that required wealth.[15]

In the 1960s the feminine fashion ideal was represented by Twiggy and Jean Shrimpton, two models who were exceptionally slender and wore short, childlike dresses that left large expanses of the body exposed. At the time, boutiques functioned as laboratories and hangouts. Ideas proliferated as owner-designers sat around chatting with friends. Much of the stock was made in-house with such techniques as rudimentary sewing, tie-dyeing, batik, leathers laced with thongs, and applied studs, macramé, crochet, and appliqué.[16] The styles included "space age abstractions," see-through blouses, and minidresses with peepholes or inset with clear vinyl strips. The styles were playful, like children playing peekaboo. Jelly bean colors—orange, hot pink, lime green, and purple—and dots, stripes, large checks, and other op art patterns in black and white also projected flirtatiousness and fun. Fashion magazines urged their readers to lose their inhibitions, to experiment, and to keep up to date.[17]

The 1960s feminine fashion ideal, like that of the nineteenth and early twentieth centuries, was interpreted as symbolic of wealth, because achieving the look required costly dieting, dressing, and grooming.[18] In earlier eras, however, wealth had been conveyed through luxurious fabrics and styles, accentuating expensive detail. The 1960s clothes conveyed youthfulness and innocence. It is more likely that the new feminine fashion ideal reflected the innocence and vulnerability of the United States, with its emphasis on youth. President John F. Kennedy, inaugurated on January 20, 1961, was the youngest president ever elected in the United States. He personified vigor and campaigned on the theme of "getting the country moving again." Challenging the status quo, he proposed new and daring programs: a multibillion-dollar project to land an American on the moon, "where no one had ever dared to go"; a Peace Corps army of idealistic and mostly youthful volunteers who would bring American skills to underdeveloped countries; and new initiatives in medicine and education.[19]

The vocabulary of the women's liberation movement set the style for the feminine fashion ideal of the 1970s. Revlon hired Lauren Hutton, who personified the natural look and the image of the modern woman: energetic and engaged in purposeful action and able to play many roles. In many ads, Revlon portrayed her as a real woman with a real life. She was shown in different moods, from natural to romantic to glamorous. She looked comfortable and in control in any situation. The implication was that the modern woman was too intelligent to have only one look. She could choose her looks to fit her moods, Lakoff and Scherr pointed out.[20]

When the style, the model, and the photographer stop reflecting the ideals of the period, they are labeled "old-fashioned" and lose their influence. As suggested by Veblen, a fashion is perceived as beautiful only because it conveys the spirit of the time.[21] The feminine fashion ideal is shaped by the events and sentiments of the period.

## The Beautiful

The beautiful is an autonomous attribute, universal in nature and independent of fashion.[22] Its essence lies in the congruence of physical features, in the natural characteristics of the face and form with which one is born. Aristotle observed that beauty depends on an orderly arrangement of parts and a size that is not accidental. One derives pleasure from integrity of design, unity, and order and from symmetry, harmony, and perfection. Those who most closely embody these qualities are considered beautiful.[23]

In *Beauty in History* (1988), historian Arthur Marwick observed that we identify objects as beautiful if they are the focus of admiration and give pleasure to the generality of beholders. The appreciation of beauty has not had a simple, linear development. In preindustrial Europe beauty was perceived as powerful but having a disturbing influence. The beautiful was viewed as the good and was appreciated for the joy it brought. However, as an object of desire and love, it was beheld as superficial, identified with the carnal, and contrasted with the spiritual beauty of the divine. In preindustrial society, the prejudice and confusion about the meaning of beauty, for the most part, resulted in blindness to it.[24]

In twentieth-century American society, physical beauty emerged as a resource, like wealth or talent.[25] Its importance was appreciated in both genders. Champion boxer Muhammad Ali characterized himself as "the greatest" and "the pret-

*Apollo Belvedere, Roman copy of a Greek sculpture from the late fourth century BC. (Vatican Museums, Rome.) The sculpture represents what eighteenth- and nineteenth-century critics considered a supreme example of classical beauty.*

tiest." Beauty is a significant asset in many occupational spheres. Male movie stars and politicians who are handsome are prized for this quality. At the time of his candidacy for the U.S. presidency, John F. Kennedy's youthful good looks were thought by the professionals to be a disadvantage, signifying his inexperience. However, after the first televised debate between Kennedy and Richard Nixon, the political appeal of good looks began to be taken seriously, Arthur Marwick pointed out.[26] Today, the good looks of President Bill Clinton and former vice president Dan Quayle are generally acknowledged as advantages.

Desirable personality characteristics are often ascribed to good-looking people. They are seen as more sensitive, kind, sociable, pleasant, likable, and interesting than those who are plain or unattractive.[27] Similarly, a study by J. Ross and K. R. Ferris (1981) of male employees in two large accounting firms found a positive correlation between employees' physical attractiveness and their performance evaluations and salary increases. The authors concluded that good-looking people tend to be viewed as more intelligent and competent. The harmonious attributes of the physical being lead to positive social evaluation and rewards.[28] In the 1970s sociologists began to report that in the United States beauty had achieved a kind of parity in its social value with wealth and socioeconomic status.[29]

For people working in the service industries in particular, beauty enhances the chances for economic success. Service industries depend upon interpersonal communication and interaction. Good-looking employees are usually pleasing and nonthreatening and can help smooth the way toward successful conclusion of a sale or interaction. The preference for good-looking employees is thus seen as making good business sense.

## The History of Beauty As a Cultural Value

The perfect female body in Greek sculpture was that of a young woman who had reached puberty, unmarked but prepared for childbirth. In contrast, the male nude in Greek art was a physically fit, battle-ready youth.[30] The proud, courageous heroes glorified in Homer's *Iliad* and *Odyssey* reflected societal expectations for appearance and behavior. In early Greece, a male youth with a supple body and well-delineated muscles was deemed beautiful and was entitled to social and sexual rewards.

An important means of upholding the ideal of physical fitness was gossip. Old men, the heads of leading families, sat by the city gate, where they listened to stories about the performance of each young man and evaluated his skill. Slackers suffered ridicule. Greek youths kept in shape for the deities as well as the state. They strove to emulate the physical perfection of the Greek gods, such as Apollo. Displaying athletic prowess was considered a religious activity; competitions honored sacred and secular authorities. Men competed naked during these events because clothing restricted full action and concealed their superior physiques.

The nude as an art form was invented by the Greeks before the sixth century BC.[31] Over the centuries the depiction of the nude in Greek art underwent changes that mirrored changes in desired social conduct. It went "from the physical to the moral sphere," as art historian Kenneth Clark reported. The early sculptures presented youths standing alone, proud and naked. Later, the finely toned muscles of athletes and soldiers in action inspired artists to focus on showing the movement of the body and the idea that the male body should be battle-ready. By the fifth century, when democracy became a political and social goal, a new ideal of beauty was evident in Greek art. The harmonious proportions of the nudes emphasized a balanced whole and communicated grace, strength, and gentleness. Poets, philosophers, mathematicians, and dramatists gave voice to the belief that perfection could be sought even though everyday reality was less than perfect.[32]

In ancient Greece, Plato established the enduring value of beauty when he argued that behind the contemporary embodiment of beauty lay an eternal and absolute form. The beautiful, the true, and the good were different manifestations of one eternal divine perfection. To reach it, one must progress from bodily beauty to beauty of mind, to beauty of institutions, laws, and sciences, and finally to absolute beauty itself. Direct acquaintance with beauty could most easily be achieved through an inner contemplative process. The Greeks, thus, drew no distinction between the aesthetic and ethical spheres; the beautiful and the good were identical. Excesses in one's life were viewed as aesthetically offensive; physical fitness implied exemplary moral behavior. In ancient Greece, the beautiful were believed "blessed" and were less likely than others to be considered as having done wrong.[33]

The moral and intellectual worth attributed to beauty in ancient Greece has been carried into contemporary life. In casting roles in movies and plays, directors have taken literally Plato's view that the beautiful is good and the good, by definition, is beautiful. The "good guy" is portrayed with pleasing and harmonious features; the "bad guy" has jagged and distorted, if not grotesque, features.[34]

Studies examining the effects of the attractiveness of offenders on juridical judgment have found that good-looking defendants usually tend to be treated generously. In contrast to unattractive defendants, they are seen as less dangerous and more virtuous. The tendency to leniency was explained in this manner: We like attractive people more, and those who are better liked are usually punished less than those who are unattractive.

Researchers have found that for crimes unrelated to attractiveness (burglary, for example), more lenient sentences were assigned to the attractive defendant than to the unattractive one. However, for offenses related to attractiveness (swindling, for example), the attractive defendant received the harsher treatment. The researchers concluded that when crimes are attractiveness-related, the advantages held by good-looking defendants are lost.[35] It is as if beauty is a gift, and its malevolent manipulation is condemned.

### Bad Guys and Ugly Shirts

In late 1990s movies, bad guys, crooks, and criminals have been portrayed wearing ugly shirts—shirts in garish prints and clashing colors.[36] In *Rounders*, for example, a poker player who is also an ex-convict is wearing such a shirt. It is sheer, in poly-chiffon brown with orange flowers. Bad guys dressed in loud colors and outdated styles also appeared in the movies *There's Something About Mary* and *Snake Eyes*.[37] Reporter Linda Lee suggests that there is something sexy about a bad guy wearing an ugly shirt. He is so secure that he doesn't care how ugly his shirt is.[38]

Men's fashion shows for spring 1999 showed shirts in garish prints and clashing colors. John Scher offered bright aqua and pink. Sandy Dalal came up with a pistachio-green floral shirt and John Bartlett showed lime-green hibiscus-print jackets.[39] Have "bad guys" and their ugly shirts encouraged a new aesthetic in male dress?

### The Emergence of Beauty As a Modern Value

Eighteenth-century Enlightenment ideas encouraged the development of beauty as a cultural value in keeping with the philosophy, literature, and art of ancient Greece and Rome. The arts were used to show that among educated men the spirit of rational inquiry prevailed. Enlightenment scholars also encouraged the rejection of religion as a theoretical framework for explaining social and natural phenomena, insisting that observation, measurement, and comparison were the rational means of scientific inquiry.[40] In their early studies, some Enlightenment scholars compared animals and people to identify similarities and differences. They next classified people according to race. For example, they compared the face and body measurements of Pygmies in Africa and other hunting and gathering societies with ancient Greek sculpture, which by then was regarded as the standard of perfection.[41]

Physical beauty as a cultural ideal emerged in nineteenth-century England in response to industrialization and urbanization, as strangers were brought together to live and work close to one another. The tension of the new living conditions led to a new search for beauty, which the ancient Greeks had defined as symmetry, harmony, and perfection of the physical form. These qualities were considered to have a calming effect. Beauty as a cultural value was manifested in a preference for better-looking servants and employees, for example, and in beautification of gardens and parks. Pamela Horn (1975) wrote "Personal appearance was very important for any boy aspiring to a position of a footman or page in a large household, for only the tall and well-built were considered. . . . Wages were often related to height, with the tallest men or boys receiving the highest pay."[42] This requirement marked a change from the late eighteenth century, when servants were not intended for display.[43] Similarly, in a history of the English coun-

*Actress Sarah Bernhardt, for whom the purpose of acting was "the creation of that elusive, indefinable quality of beauty." (Quote from E. Salmon, Bernhardt and the Theater of Her Time, 1977; photo by Felix Nadar, 1862.)*

try house, which he wrote in the mid-nineteenth century, Merlin Waterson observed that at the grander country houses the first requirement of a footman, groom, or coachman was a physique to show his livery off "to advantage," that is, to present a physically beautiful appearance.[44]

Courtesans, artists' models, and actresses came from different ethnic backgrounds and had different features, but as Marwick observed, they were similar in that their features were well proportioned and conveyed a harmonious unity. Many of them used their beauty to develop careers. Actress Sarah Bernhardt and fashion designer Coco Chanel, for example, achieved international fame for their beauty as well as their talent. Their fathers and lovers, Marwick pointed out, made them aware of their special impact on men, and they left home searching for their individual destinies.[45]

Neither in body shape nor attire did Sarah Bernhardt conform to the fashion ideal.[46] In an era of voluptuousness, she was thin. "Audiences at first thought she was ridiculous because she was so skinny. When she raised her arms, people would boo because her arms were not fleshy enough," her biographer Robert Fizdale related.[47] Many of her acting roles required her to conceal her looks. Nevertheless, she developed an international reputation as both an actress and a beauty. With dark hair and eyes, she has been described as a "profoundly appealing, unorthodox Jewish beauty [with] the faintest suspicion of [a] too long-nose (though highly enticing)."[48]

The desire to be close to beauty led men to compete with one another. Beautiful women became what Veblen called status symbols, objects that enhanced a man's stature in the eyes of other men.[49]

## Learning to Recognize Beauty

There is little agreement about who is actually beautiful because the emotional response provoked by physical appearance depends on personal experience, which varies. In the United States in the nineteenth century, carnivals and fairs promoted beauty contests as well as sideshows at which human beings with physical anomalies were exhibited.[50] Together, these events helped clarify characteristics of desired and undesired appearance. Dwarfs, microcephalics, armless and limbless people, and non-Western people were exhibited at carnivals, state fairs, and at the Barnum and Bailey Circus. In these sideshows, identified as "freak shows," people with alleged and real anomalies were formally organized to exhibit themselves for amusement and profit. They achieved their greatest popularity between 1840 and 1940, as Robert Bogdan (1988) noted.[51]

Being less than conventionally attractive seems to invite merciless humiliation. Linda Tripp, who taped the confidences of her friend Monica Lewinsky and entertained her bridge group with them, was ruthlessly criticized for her looks in the media. This hostility, she claimed, was the reason she underwent plastic surgery.[52]

Wendy Chapkis, in *Beauty Secrets: Women and the Politics of Appearance* (1986), related how strangers on buses and trains in the United States and Europe went out of their way to make her feel ugly.[53] Because she was a "bearded lady," they touched her face and pulled on her facial hair to see if the mustache and beard were real, all the while laughing and making jokes. They insisted that her hairy face was an aberration that had to be suppressed, and their unwelcome attention in public caused her humiliation and pain. Though she is lonely, she welcomed the safety of her home. To escape feeling ugly, she pointed out, many women go to great lengths to disguise unacceptable features.[54]

*Ella Harper, "the Camel Girl," a pretty thirteen-year-old with severe orthopedic problems. She wrote, "I am called the Camel Girl because my knees turn backward. I can walk best on my hands and knees." (Quoted from R. Bogdan, Freak Show, 1988; Photo by Charles Eisenman 1886. Ron Becker Collection, Syracuse University.)*

## Beauty Through Surgery and Cosmetics

### Restoring Symmetry

Disfigurements caused by war accidents and injuries began to challenge the imagination and creativity of physicians in the period between the two world wars. Plastic surgery focused on reconstruction—for example, replacing a missing jaw or restoring facial contours to recreate a sense of unity. It later became the means to correct birth deformities and malformations caused by cancer.

It also appears that reconstructive surgery was practiced in Renaissance Italy, where knife and sword fights were common. Although at that time this form of surgery was not even taught in European medical schools, a professor of anatomy at the University of Bologna, Gaspare Tagliacozzi (1545–1599), developed procedures to restore mutilated noses, lips, and ears. Few attempts were made after his death, however, to systematize the procedures and make them an integral part of medical care.[55]

Data collected in the 1960s by the National Health Examination Survey involving 14,000 children six to seventeen years old found that tall children scored slightly higher on intelligence tests and performed somewhat better academically than their shorter classmates, perhaps because more was expected of them. The findings were interpreted as suggesting that the shorter students were thought of as younger or less intellectually mature.

To enable children to attain a normal adult height and to correct dwarfism, injections of growth hormone were offered in the 1970s. A *New York Times* editorial warned parents that growth hormone can turn people into giants more than eight feet tall, but it continued: "While no parent would wish giant children, some might seek to add a few inches to the height of children who are below the average stature." According to the editorial, this can be accomplished by a cosmetic use of the growth hormone. Since smallness is not a disease, the editorial commented, parents and pediatricians who elect to make cosmetic use of growth hormone take on a heavy responsibility, but tallness does secure privilege.[56]

### Attaining Physical Harmony

Seeking to realize the fashionable ideal is different from desiring to correct an imperfect body part, most plastic surgeons will point out. In the 1950s people had plastic surgery to change a hook nose to an Irish snub. In the 1990s women have undergone plastic surgery to plump up thin lips and men have surgery to correct cleft chins. Men and women from thirty-five to forty-five have been asking for brow lifts, ear tucks, and chin restructuring. Contemporary plastic surgeons are expected to combine the discipline of surgery with an aesthetic sense, "to put the right nose on the right face."[57]

Patients are also requesting implants to camouflage skinny calves, balance the contours of the face, and increase chest and buttocks size. Patients generally consult with their surgeons before the operation about the size and shape of the body part to be reconstructed. But, as Elizabeth Rosenthal reported, surgeons must often dash unrealistic hopes in order to achieve a natural look and good balance.[58]

### Preserving Ethnic Identity

"Patients do not want to change their ethnicity, they just want something improved," stated a *New York Times* article in 1991. The article went on to say that doctors are making efforts to preserve ethnic features while enhancing beauty.[59] Since the aesthetics of surgery have historically been tailored for Caucasian faces, surgeons now face a "two-pronged challenge": first they need to define beautiful features for African-Americans, Hispanics, and Asian-Americans, and, second, they must determine how to modify standard operations to achieve those goals.

The ideal nose or shape of face is subject to ethnic variation, and the concept of beauty varies among people of different ethnic groups. Asians, for example, strive for "a softer, rounder" look than the sculpted appearance admired by Europeans. Moreover, experts have warned that the different skin qualities of different groups create both advantages and problems in terms of elasticity and scarring. Hence, patients must choose physicians experienced in operating on their specific ethnic group. Improved surgical techniques and a better understanding of

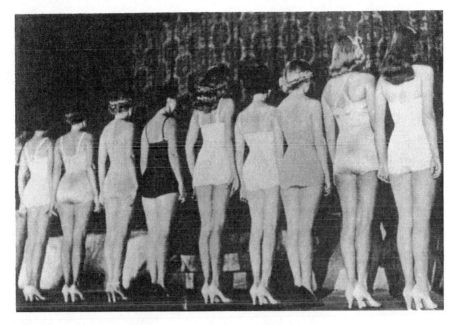

*The swimsuit competition of the Miss America Pageant attests to the importance of self-restraint (through not overeating) and to the principle of universalism (all persons are judged by the same standards). (Photo by Eve Arnold.)*

the anatomical differences among people of different races have greatly aided surgeons' attempts to preserve ethnicity.[60]

### Rejecting the Notion of Vanity

The emphasis on beauty and the use of cosmetics in modern culture has led to much criticism. Harry C. Bredemeier and Jackson Toby (1960) pointed out that a sociocultural standard implies that some people are found wanting.[61] Social standards are internalized even by persons who are "substandard." Self-rejection goes hand in hand with social rejection.[62]

Cosmetics make it possible to hide imperfections and to impart a sense of symmetry and harmony to the face. The use of cosmetics, however, has been condemned as objectifying women and oppressing them. Critics maintain that what matters is not one's surface appearance but rather one's personality and character. Makeup is artifice, a mask, unnatural and immoral.

Some critics also argue that big cosmetic companies manipulate women's insecurities and fears in order to rake in massive profits.[63] In *The Beauty Myth* (1991), Naomi Wolf contends that women in the United States are expected to look pretty, fashionable, thin, and youthful while being enchanting and submissive.

Through these expectations, society controls what women do with their bodies, reducing them to objects. Reducing women to objects enables society to defend the social order, but this alienates women from their bodies, voices, and faces.[64]

Another purpose of controlling female appearance has to do with pay. Wolf also suggests that Western economies are dependent on the continued underpayment of women. For women to accept underpayment, they must be made to feel "worth less." And setting ideal standards of appearance that women cannot meet leads to low self-esteem and a sense of low self-worth.[65]

The importance of being attractive has been promoted by the advertising industry, Diane Barthel suggested in 1988. Advertisements seduce women and men to recognize their less-than-ideal appearance and to take advantage of the advertiser's solution.[66]

Cosmetics encourage people to make the connection between the persons they are and the persons they strive to be. The introduction of new and expensive creams and potions is supported by the use of scientific-sounding terms such as "polymer" and "acetylglucosamine."[67] In this way the beauty industry suggests that the latest advances in science have been marshaled to help women transform their appearance.[68] The second step in selling a product entails a technique that involves physical touch. It is called "Put, Place, Please." Beauty analysts put the product on the back of the consumer's hand and place the bottle in their other hand, while asking, "Would you please hold this for me?"[69] The consumer is thus caught in a unintended interaction, which some may consider an exercise in manipulation.

Opposing the view that the pressure to conform by using cosmetics exploits women, other writers maintain that the use of cosmetics is a basic economic and emotional necessity. To become part of society, to get a job, and to keep a man, a woman must look her best. Cosmetics are also an important tool in the struggle of lower-class women to emancipate themselves from the status of household drudges.[70]

In their study of female college students, Lakoff and Scherr reported the viewpoint of some feminists that it is their prerogative to improve their appearance and that they owed it to themselves and others to use all the means available to do it. Putting one's best face forward in dress and makeup is seen as a boost to one's ego, self-confidence, and productivity in work and social life.[71] Using cosmetics is also seen as a subtle compliment to those with whom one interacts, a way of making them feel better and, as such, a courteous gesture. Unwillingness to take pains to enhance one's appearance is felt to be rude. These young undergraduate women claimed that they relied on the type of cosmetics that bring out "what is hidden . . . enhancing what is already there."[72]

In the early 1990s, Joan Kron wrote an article for *Allure* about shopping for a face-lift. Afraid that she would be accused of vanity, she used a pen name. During the same decade, however, celebrities such as Dolly Parton, Roseanne, Joan

Rivers, Carol Burnett, Mary Tyler Moore, and Geraldo Rivera—all in the public eye and depending for their livelihood on projecting a particular image—had aesthetic surgery and acknowledged it publicly.[73]

The popularity of aesthetic surgery and its ability to vanquish unhappiness has overcome the fear of being seen as vain.[74] More and more, patients appear on television programs and identify the merits of this surgery.

Since the early 1980s it has become more acceptable for older men to marry much younger women, who have come to be known as "trophy wives." Also in the 1980s, many middle-aged men lost their positions in industry and had to compete with younger men for jobs. These trends have increased popular interest in aesthetic surgery.

In her book, *Welcome to Your Facelift* (1997), author Helen Bransford reports on her experience with aesthetic surgery. At the age of forty-seven she was married to a writer seven years her junior, and she suddenly realized that her husband had become aware of the difference in their ages. Looking in the mirror and seeing the ravages of time, she lost her former vivaciousness. Believing that their marriage was in danger, she soon began interviewing surgeons.[75]

Several years after her *Allure* article, Joan Kron dropped her pseudonym to tell about her experience with plastic surgery in her book, *Lift: Wanting, Fearing—and Having a Face Lift* (1998).[76]

Nearly 10 million American adults have had cosmetic surgery and more than 65 percent of these people had household incomes below $60,000.[77] With the procedure demonstrated, discussed, and evaluated on the news, on the Internet, and presented live on web sites, aesthetic surgery has lost much of its stigma.

## The Utility of Beauty

Contemporary beauty contests go well beyond specifying desired female appearance. The Miss America Pageant now celebrates cultural values considered essential for interaction in the public place. The ceremony dramatizes the desirability of winning; it attests to the principle of universalism, that is, that all contestants are treated according to the same standards regardless of their national origin or personal contacts. The basic criterion for winning is achievement. The rituals of the contest delineate behavior that conforms to the rules set by contest promoters.

Contestants are required to put forth energy by performing, dancing, singing, and demonstrating intelligence. The swimsuit competition proclaims the importance of self-restraint (not overeating). It also affirms that beauty today lies in the fitness of the body, its readiness for action, and its agility and flexibility. The evening gown event proclaims the desirability of individual accomplishment and taste; the selection of an elaborate flattering gown requires both attributes. The title goes to the person who most closely meets the desired criteria.

## Notes

1. R. T. Lakoff and R. L. Scherr (1984), *Face Value: The Politics of Beauty* (Boston: Routledge), p. 56.

2. S. de Beauvoir (1953), *The Second Sex*, trans. H. M. Parshly (New York: Knopf), pp. xxx, 336, 408–409, 411–412, 428–429.

3. A. Marwick (1988), *Beauty in History* (London: Thames and Hudson), p. 29.

4. T. Veblen (1953), *The Theory of the Leisure Class* (New York: Mentor Books), p. 108. Originally published in 1899.

5. M. Lerner, ed. (1948), *The Portable Veblen* (New York: Viking), pp. 184–199.

6. Veblen, op. cit., p. 107.

7. L. W. Banner (1983), *American Beauty: A Social History Through Two Centuries of the American Idea, Ideal, and Image of the Beautiful Woman* (New York: Knopf), p. 107.

8. D. H. Jacques (1859), *Hints Toward Physical Perfection*, (New York: Fowler and Wells), pp. 44–49, 223.

9. D. G. Brinton and G. H. Nephys (1870), *The Laws of Health in Relation to Human Form* (Springfield, Mass.: W. J. Holland), p. 48.

10. J. B. Abrams (1983), "The Thinning of America: The Emergence of the Ideal of Slenderness in American Popular Culture 1870–1930," bachelor's thesis, Department of History, Harvard University, pp. 3–6.

11. T. S. Sozinskey (1877), *The Culture of Beauty* (Philadelphia: Alan, Lane and Scott), p. 63.

12. Banner, op. cit., p. 11.

13. Ibid., pp. 266–269.

14. Lakoff and Scherr, op. cit., p. 56.

15. Ibid., pp. 78–79.

16. C. R. Milbank (1989), *New York Fashion: The Evolution of American Style* (New York: Harry N. Abrams), pp. 206, 210, 226.

17. B. Payne, G. Weinakor, and J. Farrell-Beck (1992), *The History of Costume: From Ancient Mesopotamia Through the 20th Century* (New York: HarperCollins), pp. 614–615. See also M. and A. Batterberry (1977), *Fashion: The Mirror of History* (New York: Greenwich House), pp. 383–385.

18. Batterberry, op. cit., pp. 282–283.

19. T. A. Bailey and D. M. Kennedy (1987), *The American Pageant* (Lexington, Mass: D. C. Heath), pp. 589–590.

20. Lakoff and Scherr, op. cit., p. 103.

21. Veblen, op. cit., p. 125.

22. Ibid., pp. 94–97, 109.

23. Marwick, op. cit., pp. 414–415.

24. Ibid., p. 414.

25. M. Webster, Jr., and J. E. Driskell, Jr. (1983), "Beauty As Status," *American Journal of Sociology* 89 (1): 140–165.

26. Marwick, op. cit., p. 393.

27. That physical attractiveness plays an important role in American society is made evident by the old cliché that "What is beautiful is good," observed G. L. Patzer in *The Physical Attractiveness Phenomenon* (New York: Plenum Press), p. 1. See also K. K. Dion (1986), "Stereotyping Based on Physical Attractiveness: Issues and Conceptual Perspectives," in

*Appearance, Stigma and Social Behavior,* ed. C. P. Herman, M. P. Zanna, and E. T. Higgins, The Ontario Symposium on Personality and Social Psychology, vol. 3 (Hillsdale, N.J.: Erlbaum).

28. J. Ross and K. R. Farris (1981), "Interpersonal Attraction and Organizational Outcome: A Field Experiment," *Administrative Science Quarterly* 26: 617–632.

29. D. Bartell (1988), *Gender and Advertising: Putting On Appearances* (Philadelphia: Temple University Press).

30. A. R. Burns (1965), *The Pelican History of Greece* (New York: Penguin Books), pp. 73, 199.

31. K. Clark (1956), *The Nude: A Study of Ideal Art Form* (London: John Murray), p. 25.

32. Ibid., p. 48. See also H. Hoover and J. Fleming (1982), *The Visual Arts: A History,* 3d ed. (Englewood Cliffs, N.J.: Prentice-Hall), pp. 148–149.

33. M. Chambers et al. (1974), *The Western Experience* (New York: Knopf), pp. 76–77.

34. In films bad guys look bad. They are marked by various disfigurements and disabilities, such as missing limbs and eyes, as R. Bogdan found in his study of freak shows. The beautiful queen in *Snow White and the Seven Dwarfs* was transformed into a wart-nosed hunchback before she set out to accomplish her hideous scheme. Another example is the one-legged Captain Hook in *Peter Pan.* In horror films, the association of evil with disability is even more common, Bogdan pointed out. Monsters are deformed, disproportionately built, exceptionally large, exceptionally small, or speech-impaired and in films they are perpetrators of violence. See R. Bogdan (1988), *Freak Shows: Presenting Human Oddities for Amusement and Profit* (Chicago: University of Chicago Press), pp. vii–viii.

35. H. Sigall and N. Ostrove (1975), "Beautiful but Dangerous: Effects of Offender Attractiveness and Nature of the Crime on Juridic Judgement," *Journal of Personality and School Psychology* 31 (3): 410–414.

36. L. Lee (1998), "Really Bad Shirts," *New York Times,* Sept. 13.

37. Ibid.

38. Ibid.

39. Ibid.

40. G. L. Mosse (1978), *The Final Solution: A History of European Racism* (New York: Howard Fertig), p. 94.

41. S. L. Gilman (1985), *Difference and Pathology: Stereotypes of Sexuality, Race and Madness* (Ithaca, N.Y.: Cornell University Press), pp. 15–31, 76–108.

42. P. Horn (1975), *The Rise and Fall of the Victorian Servant* (Dublin, Ire.: ), p. 84.

43. Marwick, op. cit., p. 247.

44. Ibid., p. 247.

45. Ibid., pp. 167–193.

46. J. Richardson (1966), *The Courtesan* (Cleveland: World Publishing); A. Latour (1958), *Kings of Fashion,* trans. M. Savill (London: Weidenfeld & Nicholson).

47. *New York Times,* Sept. 16, 1991.

48. Marwick, op. cit., p. 289.

49. Richardson, op. cit., pp. 220–231.

50. Banner, op. cit., pp. 258–259.

51. Bogdan, op. cit., pp. 3–11.

52. G. Steinem (2000), "Lovely to Look Upon—Or Else," *New York Times,* Jan. 16.

53. W. Chapkis (1986), *Beauty Secrets: Women and the Politics of Appearance* (Boston: South End Press), pp. 1–2.

54. Ibid.

55. M. T. Gnudi and J. P. Webster (1950), *The Life and Times of Gaspare Tagliacozzi: Surgeon of Bologna 1545–1599* (New York: Herbert Reichner).

56. "Children Height Linked to Test Scores," *New York Times*, Oct. 2, 1986; "Two French Doctors Face Charges on Hormone Use," *New York Times*, July 22, 1992.

57. S. Cohen, "Nip and Tuck: To These Six Plastic Surgeons Beauty Is Not Skin Deep. It's a Measure of Creativity," *New York Times*, Aug. 9, 1992.

58. *New York Times*, Sept. 24, 1991.

59. *New York Times*, Sept. 26, 1991.

60. E. Rosenthal (1991), "Revising Plastic Surgery to Preserve Ethnic Identity," *New York Times*, Sept. 25.

61. H. C. Bredemeier and J. Toby (1960), *Social Problems in America* (New York: John Wiley and Son), pp. 17–18.

62. S. L. Gilman (1999), *Making the Body Beautiful: A Cultural History of Aesthetic Surgery* (Princeton, N.J.: Princeton University Press), p. 3.

63. J. Hansen and E. Reed (1986), *Cosmetics, Fashions, and the Exploitation of Women* (New York: Pathfinder Press), pp. 48–50.

64. N. Wolf (1991), *The Beauty Myth: How Images of Beauty Are Used Against Women* (New York: William Morrow), pp. 18, 102–103, 171–172.

65. Ibid.

66. D. Barthell (1988), *Gender and Advertising: Putting On Appearances* (Philadelphia: Temple University Press).

67. P. Underhill (1999), *Why We Buy: The Science of Shopping* (New York: Simon and Schuster).

68. P. Green (2000), "A Miracle a Minute: Skin Cream Heaven," *New York Times*, Apr. 30.

69. Ibid.

70. Hansen and Reed, op. cit., pp. 48–50.

71. Lakoff and Scherr, op. cit., p. 143.

72. Ibid., p. 143.

73. N. Haas (1999), "Now on the Web: Plastic Surgery for Voyeurs," *New York Times*, Sept. 19.

74. Gilman, op. cit., p. 3.

75. H. Bransford (1997), *Welcome to Your Facelift* (New York: Doubleday).

76. J. Kron (1998), *Lift: Wanting, Fearing—and Having a Face Lift* (New York: Viking).

77. Bransford, op. cit., p. 42.

# 13

# The Youth Ideal

IN AN ESSAY on the op-ed page of the *New York Times,* Patricia Bradshaw complained that "today's grannies are likely to look 50"; the reality of age is obscured. Women work hard at being not old and proving it. They jog, diet, stretch, lift weights, and "have some of their parts patched. . . . We have lopped off old age as if it were a double chin," she protested. Women in the United States are free to dress and act as they wish.[1]

Through much of the nineteenth century, however, older women's lives were circumscribed and constrained, observed historian Lois W. Banner (1983). Older women occupied a special sphere. Their clothing, behavior, and physical appearance were designed to set them apart from the young. The feminine fashion ideal was plump, providing the older women with a measure of attractiveness.[2] The marital state conferred an identity upon women; when they married, they were eliminated from the category of youth and entered the "old" category. Beauty did not count. Most people disregarded a married woman's physical appearance.[3] By age thirty-five most women donned caps under which they tucked their hair as a mark of a grandmother status, thus symbolically renouncing their sexuality. Whereas husbands in their forties and fifties were social and professional leaders, honored for their accomplishments, most people considered women dull by the age of forty. Thus, at a point when a man was still considered at the prime of his life, a woman was considered old. Bachelor women were expected to stay home and provide some service to the family. The imperfections that accompany old age were accepted, which discouraged attempts at beautification.

In 1851 novelist Caroline Kirkland published an eloquent attack on negative attitudes toward old age, focusing on society's refusal to allow older women to wear bright colors and youthful fashions. At the time, dress indicated age, as much as any other factor. Behind this constraint, Kirkland suggested, lay the fear that older women might try to attract older men. But the constraint resulted in older women becoming crabbed and censorious, exhibiting just the kind of behavior expected of them.[4]

In the post–Civil War years, the boundary between youth and old age began to break down. The separate forces of feminism and the commercial beauty culture were behind the changes in society's perception of older women.[5] Fashion magazines and beauty advice books recommended that women of all ages should be

*A leading star of the popular musical stage from the late 1870s through the 1890s, Lillian Russell personified the mature, voluptuous ideal. (Reprinted by permission of The Bettmann Archive.)*

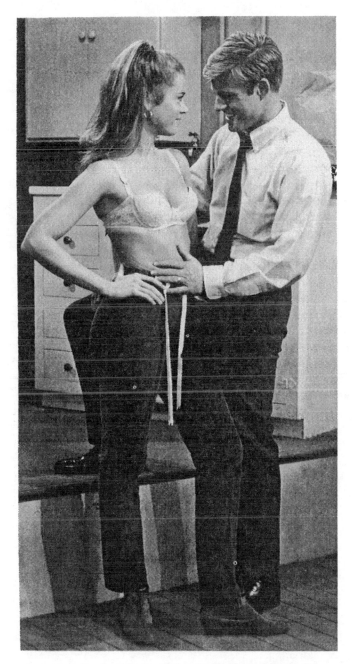

*Actress Jane Fonda with actor Robert Redford in* Barefoot in the
Park, *1967. The photograph shows the youthful, slim ideal of the
1960s. (Reprinted by permission of The Bettmann Archive.)*

permitted and even encouraged to look as young as they wished. Book after book, pamphlet after pamphlet, rammed home the message "that a woman's duty is to be beautiful," observed historian Arthur Marwick (1988). Even scriptural authority was invoked. The harsh corollary was that no woman has the right to be ugly.[6]

By 1870 the popularity of the old-maid legend had declined. Some older women were independent, dressed well, and did not care whether they married, noted Banner. By 1900, stories about the exciting, independent lives of "bachelor women" affected society's perception of women of older age. The career involvement and reform movement of older women in the post–Civil War years established women's right to an age definition similar to that of men. The interests of the commercial beauty industry and those of the women's reform movement intertwined, and their efforts were directed toward a common goal.[7]

Many prominent nineteenth-century actresses not only lived long lives but also remained active on the stage until well into their sixties and seventies. At eighty Sarah Bernhardt became legendary for her ability to play convincingly the part of a young boy. One of the elderly performers in opera, singer Adelina Patti, gave frequent interviews about her ability to retain her youthful beauty. "No tragedy in life is so awful to a woman as the realization that her youth is gone, and in its place are the wrinkles, the dull eyes, and the decrepit figure of age."[8] As the media pointed out, Patti had developed none of these presumed disabilities. She was in her sixties, and her face was unlined, her figure trim, and her step firm.

Discussing in public methods of preserving their looks, older women in the nineteenth century usually stressed diet, exercise, and rest. They also took part in advertising cosmetics. The cultural prohibitions against older women attempting to look youthful declined, and the normal physical attributes of old age— white hair, wrinkles, and sagging muscles—were even more negatively defined than before.

## Creating a Social Identity

The denigration of old age reinforced the value of youthfulness, and old age acquired the status of a stigma.[9] In 1927, Upton Sinclair in his novel *Oil!* wrote "I look at the old women I meet and think which of them do I want to be? And I say, Oh my God! and jump into my car and drive fifty miles an hour to get away."[10] Similarly, in her 1991 book *The Beauty Myth*, Naomi Wolf told of a fifty-four-year-old woman who lost her job without warning because her boss said that he "wanted to look at a younger woman" so his "spirits would be lifted."[11]

Analyzing the attempts of "over-the-hill" sports superstars such as Jim Palmer, Mark Spitz, George Foreman, and Bjorn Borg to return to competitive sports, a *New York Times* editorial pointed to "the dream of youth." Denying age, the superstars attempt to recapture their glorious past.[12] In the article "Senior-Circuited," that he wrote for the Sunday Magazine section of the *New York*

*Times,* Tom Brokaw, the anchor for "NBC Nightly News," suggested that he had accepted the view of the "20-year-old advertising genius who thinks that 50 is just short of death's door." He confessed that at age fifty he was no longer playing the part of the "brash young man, making the daring moves secure in the knowledge that if they don't work out, there will probably be other chances. At this age, mistakes, however daring, are not easily excused. Achievement is not a cause of praise; it is expected."[13]

Growing old in contemporary society is more than experiencing the progressive decline in body functions.[14] People are placed into an undesirable social category, and they have to deal with the problem of lack of acceptance by society, suggested Erving Goffman. These people have to play the social game with the cards stacked against them. They try to separate themselves from what the unfavorable identity implies about them. Some assert independence of the identity; others demonstrate mastery over their lives.[15] The basic problem with a "spoiled identity" is that it can become what sociologist Everett Hughes called a "master status."[16] As such, it obscures all other personal and social attributes. When people withdraw their acceptance from a stigmatized individual, they are distorting the person's identity to fit a negative stereotypical expectation. The stigmatized individual may internalize part or all of the negative views of others, consequently diminishing self-esteem and altering the self-concept.

To avoid making the stigma a master status, stigmatized individuals use what Goffman termed "information control." (For example, they may be reluctant to give their age. Recall Jack Benny's perennial "thirty-nine.") They may manipulate their appearance to minimize the extent to which they will feel hurt or suffer a loss of self-esteem. The stigmatized person is thus prone to victimization and vulnerable to advertising claims, in this case for products that supposedly restore youth.[17]

## Age Stratification

Biological factors and societal beliefs about appropriateness account for a person's ability to perform certain social roles. Few females under the age of twelve or over the age of fifty can have babies. The very young and very old would find it difficult to dig ditches. But most other age limits are culturally and socially defined. Miss America is young because we equate beauty with youth. When airlines first hired flight attendants, there was an upper age limit. The reason was not that the job required talents that were associated with age but that attendants were expected to be decorative.

The negative definition of age can be seen in the behavior of American executives working outside the United States. According to a recent *New York Times* article, K-mart managers in Eastern Europe believe that the need to change attitudes about selling and buying in that part of the world is the basic challenge they face in generating profits. One problem has been changing the relationship be-

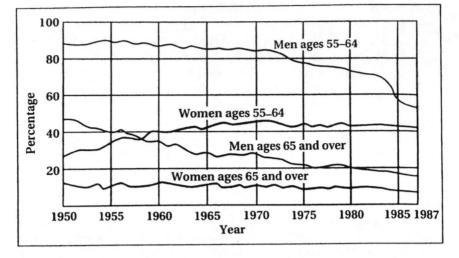

FIGURE 13.1    Labor Force Participation of Older People, 1950-1987, by Sex

*At the turn of the twentieth century the majority of employees remained in the workforce well into their seventies. By 1987 only 16 percent continued to work past the age of sixty-five. (Source: U.S. Bureau of Labor Statistics [1988] Labor Force Statistics Derived from the Current Population Survey, Bulletin 2307 [Washington, D.C.: U.S. Department of Labor, Bureau of Labor Statistics].)*

tween customer and sales clerk. Many Western companies in Eastern Europe, according to the article, refuse to hire Europeans older than forty on the theory that they will not be able to change their habits. Shaping new customs requires changes in personal attitudes and behavior. K-mart managers were surprised, however, "that as many of the 40-plus age group as in the 30-plus age group passed psychological tests that screened candidates for leadership qualities, organizational skills and adaptability."[18] (See Figure 13.1.)

## Sociocultural Background

The preference for youth was encouraged by the new ways of thinking and working that emerged in the post–Civil War era. In *Old Age in the New Land* (1978), Andrew Achenbaum suggested that the following factors contributed to the emergence of a negative attitude toward old age: (1) the rise of professionals who usurped the elderly's reputation for wisdom; (2) a scientific community influenced by the evolutionary theory, which viewed the elderly as afflicted with disorders and not able to keep pace with the evolving world; and (3) a corporate structure that had no use for old people.[19]

In *Captains of Consciousness* Stuart Ewen argued that the economy's production and consumption needs in the post–Civil War years supported the establishment of youthfulness as a cultural value. The requirements of mechanized production, for instance, helped support the preference for youth. Industry and assembly-line production depended heavily on consumption but also on the endurance and reflexes of youth. Once a sign of accumulated productive know-how, age became a detriment; the need for hands and eyes skilled through time and practice was suddenly obsolete, replaced by the need for stamina and swiftness, attributes of the young and required by the "cogs and levers of the increasingly versatile machine."[20]

In explaining their decision to manufacture toilet paper in 1879, the Scott brothers, Edward and Clarence, identified the reasons for their choice. The product is (1) indispensable, (2) disposable, and (3) unreusable.[21] The desirability of the product was determined by the potential for profit. In the developing economy mass production and mass consumption were necessary for economic success.[22]

The belief in the opening decades of the twentieth century that the young were free and unfettered by past conventions also encouraged the establishment of youthfulness as a cultural ideal.[23] Aware that adults are cautious to spend their financial resources, advertisers preferred selling to youth directly. By doing so, they did not have to break old habits. Ads often pictured adults as incompetent and unable to cope with modernity, as Ewen pointed out.[24] Advertising devalued parental authority, deeming it "old fashioned," and conveyed the message that the needs of the child are better understood by industry than by parents. The Pepsodent Company, for example, posed the following question to parents in 1922: "Shall [your children] suffer as you did from film on your teeth?" Parental desire to free children from the limitations suffered by their own generation became a basic theme of advertising.[25]

In his memoirs of American college life at the beginning of the twentieth century, Henry Seidel Canby suggested that the orientation of the American executive at that time was shaped by his experience in college. He wrote "From these campuses came many, if not most, of the two generations of Americans who are now in the executive charge of the country, and the greater part of the codes, ideas, manners, and ideals of living that dominate us."[26]

These were also times when sports solidified their hold in America. The popular sport of football was now played on college campuses, and the most famous football players were college students. By the 1890s Saturday football games assumed major importance as rituals of community cohesion. Sports pages of metropolitan newspapers regularly covered football games, and the articles humanized colleges and made them seem a part of American popular culture with which all Americans could identify. At the same time the frenzy of competitive sports was often duplicated in the intensity of student culture. Students became more involved than ever before in clubs and extracurricular activities, and bouts of drinking and rowdiness were common.[27]

In the prestigious eastern women's colleges, modern dance became a new mode of expressing ideas and feelings. It was introduced by individual students inspired by Isadora Duncan, to whom dance was a means of experiencing one-self, a means of being. These students had something to say, something that was contained within them, and they chose movement as a way to express it. They used the body as a means of creating a new art form, making their audiences think and feel. This new mode of expression grew and became appreciated in and out of academia. In 1926–1927 Wellesley College offered two courses in dance composition, and Smith offered three in rhythmic dancing. In 1928–1929 a student dance group was formed at Smith. The students did their own choreography and performed for fellow students and alumnae groups. Modern dance came to be viewed as a performing art, meant to be presented to spectators. The colleges produced cohorts of performers and audiences reliably following one another. Modern dance and, by extension, the attributes of youthfulness that character-ized the dancers acquired greater visibility in American society, and society gained an art form associated with high culture.[28]

## Mass Marketing

Geared to youth, mass-market production continues to support youthfulness as an ideal by focusing on products that youth feel they need. Clothing is produced that is fitting only for the young. In 1969 an article entitled "The Forgotten Mar-kets" aired the complaint that the fashion industry "is not listening to that vast army of consumers both men and women who aren't going to college, who are over 25, have tremendous quantity of money and taste—and aging wardrobes." It concluded with, "So we wonder whether youth hasn't reigned too long."[29]

Similar sentiments were conveyed in a *New York Times* editorial by James L. Greenfield. He observed that tucked away in the television networks' computers is the fact that half of all spendable income in the United States, $130 billion, is held by people over age fifty. With all that money around, it is logical to suppose that advertisers, particularly those who use television, should be in hot pursuit. Logical but wrong. Most television advertising is still pitched to the eighteen to twenty-five crowd. Not only are the advertisers ignoring the money held by those over fifty, they are also ignoring the fact that those over fifty watch more televi-sion than any other age groups. The reason for the focus on youth is straightfor-ward, according to Greenfield. Most buyers of television time at ad agencies are under thirty, and they buy what they watch. "For them demographics don't count very much"; these are people who essentially think "that at fifty you are brain dead."[30] These young ad executives also seem not to be concerned with the conse-quences, that is, that their negative view of those over thirty may diminish the self-esteem and alter the self-expectations of those over fifty.

*Bifocals are identified with aging; however, Varilux bifocals show no split in the lens—the lens appears to be uniform and continuous. This suggests a more youthful appearance. (Courtesy of Varilux Corp.)*

Youthfulness, moreover, is alluded to even when selling to the mature market. In a May 13, 1991, news story in the *New York Times,* Deirdre Carmody described an ad for sweaters in *New Choices,* a magazine for men and women over fifty. A grandmother, flanked by granddaughter and daughter, is portrayed as having fun wearing a baseball helmet and glove and showing off the ball.[31]

## Demographic Changes

The idealization of youth, that is, the structuring of the perception and feeling that youth and youthfulness are desirable, has become more problematic and poignant with the increase in life expectancy. Since 1900 life expectancy has increased from 47 years for white males and 49 years for white females to 72.6 and 74.5 years, respectively. At the same time, pressures have developed to exclude from the labor force the elderly and children in favor of young and middle-aged adults.[32] Assertiveness, competency, self-control, and power are all qualities associated with holding a job. Aging is associated with the loss of a job, the loss of vigor, and the pain and misery lying ahead. Fearful statisticians see the coming aged society as likely to cause a slide toward inevitable decadence. They fear the implications of "a population of old people ruminating over old ideas."[33]

Baby boomers approaching middle age are courted by marketers who offer them products that enable them to deny their age. In a 1991 news story in the *New York Times,* Peter Kerr reported that as the 78 million Americans of the baby-boom generation begin to bulge, sag and squint their way into mid-40's, companies are striking gold with products that offer a bit of youth to these aging yuppies—a group that demographers are calling grumpies, for grown-up, mature professionals. Retailers are ringing out profits with products like wide-seated jeans, frilly girdles, and bifocals without telltale lines in the lenses.[34]

Consumers seem to be willing to pay extra to maintain the image of youthfulness.

Divorce and the hope for remarriage provoke further anxiety about youthful appearance. The proportion of marriages that end in divorce has risen steadily since the 1970s. Current estimates are that fewer than half of all marriages contracted today will remain intact for thirty years or more.[35] The remarriage rate differs by age and sex, with more women than men remaining unmarried and establishing single-person households.

## Personal Response to Aging

One's personal response to the preference for youth may depend on inner and outer sources of support, sociologist David Riesman (1954) suggested. His research identified three groups of people. Autonomous individuals bear within themselves some psychological sources of self-renewal. For them, aging brings accretions of wisdom with no loss of spontaneity or the ability to enjoy life, and they are relatively independent of the culture's strictures and penalties imposed on the aged.[36] Consider Clint Eastwood in his role as a Secret Service agent in *In the Line of Fire*. As Russell Baker suggested, he provides "an illustrated lecture on the superiority of geezerhood." Eastwood, who is sixty-three, looked it, and was perfectly at ease with it.[37] Adjusted individuals, possibly the majority of older people, bear within themselves no such resources but are the beneficiaries of cultural preservative (derived from work, power, or a long-lasting marriage), which sustains them as long as the cultural conditions remain stable and protective. Barbara Bush, the former U.S. president's wife, is an example. Anomic individuals make up the third group. Protected neither from within nor from without, they lose physiological vitality and decay.[38]

Anomic men and women who read newspapers or magazines or who listen to radio and television talk shows often feel that they can arrest the changes associated with aging. The challenge to look young means escaping feeling old. Jogging, dieting, stretching, lifting weights, and undergoing cosmetic surgery make it possible to discard the age benchmarks. A face-lift reduces loose skin and jowls to produce a younger, less tired look.

Practitioners of the new psychologies, those with a holistic view, suggest that one's effort should go instead into developing the inner self. Making oneself whole should be the focus. For thwarting a stigmatized social identity, personal growth and new sources of fulfillment are superior to cosmetic means. The practitioners suggest that "we must get in touch with what we are, to find out what there is in us to become."[39] Only then, it seems, can people enjoy their age.

## Notes

1. *New York Times*, Nov. 11, 1991.

2. L. W. Banner (1983), *American Beauty: A Social History Through Two Centuries of the American Idea, Ideal, and Image of the Beautiful Woman* (New York: Knopf), p. 219.

3. Ibid., p. 220.

4. Ibid., p. 221.

5. Ibid., pp. 207–208.

6. A. Marwick (1988), *Beauty in History* (London: Thames and Hudson), p. 225.

7. Banner, op. cit., p. 223.

8. Ibid., p. 224.

9. The term *stigma* is of Greek derivation and was originally a mark carved or burnt into the skin to identify undesirables. The ancient Greeks believed strongly that those who violated existing norms (traitors, criminals, slaves) needed to be identified so they could be avoided. Erving Goffman applied the concept to modern society. He argued that those with traits that differ from the normal or normative in society are treated as if they bear a mark of disgrace. The person is stigmatized as others withdraw their acceptance and distort the person's real identity to fit stereotypical expectations. See E. Goffman (1963b), *Stigma: Notes on the Management of Spoiled Identity* (Englewood Cliffs, N.J.: Prentice-Hall)

10. U. Sinclair (1927), *Oil!* (New York: Albert Charles Boni), p. 332.

11. N. Wolf (1991), *The Beauty Myth: How Images of Beauty Are Used Against Women* (New York: William Morrow).

12. *New York Times*, May 28, 1991.

13. T. Brokaw (1991), "Senior-Circuited," *New York Times Magazine*, Jan. 6.

14. B. B. Hess (1976), *Growing Old in America* (New Brunswick, N.J.: Transaction Books), pp. 20–26.

15. Goffman, op. cit.

16. E. C. Hughes (1945), "Dilemmas and Contradictions of Status," *American Journal of Sociology* 50: 353–359.

17. Goffman, op. cit., p. 91.

18. *New York Times*, June 7, 1993.

19. A. Achenbaum (1978), *Old Age in the New Land* (Baltimore, Md.: Johns Hopkins University Press).

20. S. Ewen (1976), *Captains of Consciousness* (New York: McGraw-Hill).

21. C. Perati (1987), *Extraordinary Origins of Everyday Things* (New York: Harper and Row).

22. Ibid., pp. 24–27.

23. P. J. Zingg (1988), "Myth and Metaphor: Baseball in the History and Literature of American Sport," in *The Sporting Image: Readings in American Sport History*, ed. P. J. Zingg (Lanham, Md.: University Press of America), pp. 253–272; also Zingg, "Progress and Flight: An Interpretation of the American Cycle Craze of the 1890s," in *The Sporting Image: Readings in American Sport History*, ed. P. J. Zingg (Lanham, Md.: University Press of

America), pp. 227–246; D. S. Eitzen and G. H. Sage (1988), *Sociology of American Sport* (Dubuque, Iowa: Wm. C. Brown), p. 28.

24. Ewen, op. cit., pp. 41–47.

25. Ibid., pp. 114–116, 162.

26. H. S. Canby (1947), *American Memoire* (Boston: Houghton Mifflin).

27. F. R. Dulles (1940), *America Learns to Play: A History of Popular Recreation 1607–1940* (New York: Appleton-Century); also Zingg, ed., op. cit.

28. L. A. Sussmann (1989), "The Women's Movement, the Women's Colleges and Modern Dance" (paper delivered at the Meetings of the Eastern Sociological Society, Mar. 16–19).

29. M. L. Rosenkrantz (1972), *Clothing Concepts: A Social Psychological Approach* (New York: Macmillan), p. 213.

30. *New York Times*, May 28, 1991.

31. *New York Times*, May 13, 1991.

32. T. Smeeding, B. Boyle Torrey, and M. Rein (1988), "Patterns of Income and Poverty: The Economic Status of Children and the Elderly in Eight Countries," in *The Vulnerable*, ed. J. L. Palmer, T. Smeeding, and B. Boyle Torrey (Washington, D.C.: Urban Institute Press), p. 115.

33. R. Reinhold (1977), "New Population Trends Transforming U.S.," *New York Times*, Jan. 6.

34. P. Kerr (1991), *New York Times*, Aug. 27.

35. J. Weed (1989), "The Life of a Marriage," *American Demographics*, Feb.

36. D. Riesman (1954), *Individualism Reconsidered* (New York: Free Press), pp. 484–491.

37. R. Baker (1993), *New York Times*, July 17.

38. Riesman, op. cit., pp. 486–489.

39. J. B. Kessler (1980), *Getting Even with Getting Old* (Chicago: Nelson-Hall), p. 121.

# 14

# The Health Ideal

**H**EALTH BEGAN TO EMERGE as a cultural ideal in the second half of the nineteenth century as research-oriented hospital medicine was established and germs were discovered to cause illness. The study of cellular pathology, bacteriology, and asepsis led to the further recognition of distinct diseases. The notion of bacterial infection and the rudiments of healing wounds brought about techniques for antiseptic surgery. Analysis and experimentation by Joseph Lister (1827–1912) and Louis Pasteur (1822–1895) revolutionized the practice of medicine. In the United States W. T. Morton (1819–1868) discovered ether in 1846, which made it possible for patients to endure the surgeon's knife.[1]

Once it was found that rats carry the plague and germs cause infections, it was possible to control epidemics through sanitation and vaccination. After a debilitating outbreak of cholera that decimated London in the 1830s, authorities campaigned for sanitation facilities in the home, in the workplace, along public streets, and in public parks. Physician John Snow discovered the correlation between cholera and the water supply in the Soho district of London during the epidemic of 1854. To halt further infection, he advised the parish vestry to remove the handle from the pump from which the afflicted families were drawing their water. The Public Health Act of 1875 encouraged the construction of urban sanitation systems: Fresh water supplies were brought to cities, and sewage plants were established.[2]

The extensive use of vaccinations followed Pasteur's success in using it against anthrax in 1881. Antitoxins against diphtheria and tetanus were discovered in 1891. In 1896 the man considered to have opened up the field of hematology, Paul Ehrlich, began the search for synthetic chemicals effective against infectious diseases. He predicted that specific agents similar to antitoxins would be discovered that would be effective against all bacterial diseases.[3]

All these developments were taking place at a time when it was generally accepted that the restoration of health entailed medical intervention and heroic measures, such as being bled, blistered, or given poisonous laxatives. These practices had emerged centuries earlier and developed from the belief of both medical practitioners and laypersons that the preservation of health required "taking the cure." They assumed that the body possessed a finite amount of "fixed energy," or a "vital force." Physicians believed that health was achieved through an equitable distribution within the body of this fixed quantity of life force. Illness resulted when one area of the body possessed too little or too much of the needed force. Physiological turning points, periods of climacteric change, for both men and women were potentially dangerous because the body at those times was working toward achieving a new balance, and maintenance of balance constituted health. To help the body reach that balance, all practitioners regulated and altered bodily excretions and secretions through various agents.[4]

## Sanitation and Cleanliness

The knowledge that sanitation and cleanliness were means to prevent illness helped upset the fatalism that had characterized medical practice and daily life in Europe since the decline of Rome.[5] Returning Crusaders, however, restored the public bath to Europe, and it became a medieval meeting place where wine and music flowed and the sexes mingled. The bathhouses existed until the fifteenth century, when fear of the bubonic plague caused them to be closed. Bathroom plumbing, which had been refined two thousand years earlier in the courts of Egyptian and Minoan royalty, was negligible or nonexistent even in the grand European palaces. Queen Elizabeth I did "bathe herself once a month whether she required it or not."[6] The Reformation and the Counter-Reformation exacerbated the disregard for hygiene. Protestants and Catholics vying to outdo each other in shunning temptations of the flesh exposed little skin to soap and water. People did not concern themselves with cleanliness. They simply changed their underwear and perfumed themselves with grimy hands. Chamber pots were emptied into the streets. Disease and epidemics overwhelmed villages and towns.[7]

After a long absence of plague, eighteenth-century doctors began to recommend that people wash their hands, face, and neck daily. Washing was done in a basin in the bedroom.[8] The French produced a shoe-shaped tub with running water and a drain in the "toe," which Benjamin Franklin introduced to America in 1790. Most Americans, however, did not take to bathing regularly until a hundred years later. When Boston's Tremont Hotel opened in 1829, it featured the nation's first bathrooms. In the basement of the 170-room building were eight water closets (toilets) and eight bathing rooms. America's first private bathrooms were installed in a row of model houses in Philadelphia in 1832. In 1852, to reduce the threat of disease, New York opened baths for the poor, and by the Civil War most of the city's hotels had bathtubs. Private individuals also became more interested in installing toilets, showers, and tubs in their homes.[9] Sylvester Graham, called the "whirlwind" Presbyterian minister, tirelessly championed bathing up and down the East Coast.[10]

## Diet

Whereas work in the field of bacteriology and in the medical laboratories guided medical practice, individuals who designated themselves as the guardians of health focused on diet. Religious movements in the nineteenth century had a health component; they classified food and recommended temperance, physical education, and dress reform. They thus suggested that the prevention of illness was a "doable goal."

Reducing the threat of disease by proper nutrition was an important component of Sylvester Graham's preaching. He gained many followers as he traveled through the Northeast preaching vegetarianism, bathing, fresh air, sunlight, and sexual hygiene.[11] He recommended that foods should be simple, not concocted from complicated recipes; and he urged the eating of fruits and vegetables and the whole kernel of wheat. Graham developed a wheat cracker that is still eaten today—the graham cracker. Boardinghouses were set up to serve these crackers and other foods recommended by Graham. Oberlin College reserved part of its cafeteria for those following the Graham diet. The Seventh-Day Adventists became followers of Graham's edicts. His dietary reforms included allowing time for the proper digestion of different foods, making the thorough mastication of food a necessity, and abandoning the frying pan.[12] Health behavior, or activity taken for the purpose of preventing illness by persons who believe themselves to be healthy, was thus encouraged throughout the nineteenth century.

## Utopian Writers

Upsetting fatalism and supporting the institution of health as a cultural ideal were goals that were also promoted by utopian writers. Between 1865 and 1917 at least 120 prescriptions for an ideal society, models for solving the problems of the time, appeared in print. The utopian writers speculated about what an ideal society would be like and encouraged dreams and visions that questioned the status quo. The fundamental presupposition of utopianism, the belief that human ills are due to bad institutions, suggested that almost anything imaginable was possible; the utopian writers believed that a universal trend of all things is toward improvement. The utopian commitment to progress was driven primarily by the simple feeling that tomorrow would be better.[13]

## Reducing Risk

A chilly chamber pot in a freezing bedroom, an old heating stove that burned the face while the rest of the body froze, and a general feeling of helplessness against disease were characteristics of life at the beginning of the twentieth century. A new emphasis on therapeutic measures supplanted the emphasis on diagnostic and other medical research that had characterized academic medicine in the United States.[14] Tuberculosis, influenza, and pneumonia were the most common infectious diseases. Antituberculosis associations encouraged the belief that individual behavior can conquer illness and delay death. Reforming personal habits, diet, and hygiene and using drugs less frequently were seen as contributing significantly to averting medical problems. Public-health measures supported the belief that mastery over nature was possible.[15]

## Preventing Tuberculosis

One of the major killing diseases of the nineteenth century, tuberculosis was seen as a disease against which little action was possible.[16] Its impact was likened to that of a plague. Its symptoms—pallor, emaciation, weakness, and persistent cough—were considered fascinating in the early Victorian era. Slow in its course, it did not produce repulsive lesions. Because it affected both rich and poor, some considered it an act of God. Others who realized that the disease tended to run in families thought it was the result of some obscure hereditary defect. The illness was often kept a family secret because telling others decreased one's eligibility for marriage and for certain occupations and decreased the chances that other family members could obtain life insurance.[17] The hope that tuberculosis could be prevented arose around 1900, after Robert Koch, a German bacteriologist, discovered that a germ was responsible for the disease. Bacteriological studies found that the illness could be prevented if the passage of the tubercle bacilli from person to person was blocked.[18]

The antituberculosis forces issued a general appeal to the population to participate in the fight against the disease. Health departments circulated leaflets titled like the one in New York City, "Rules to Be Observed for the Prevention and Spread of Consumption," thus attempting to educate the population. Voluntary organizations, such as the Medico-Legal Society of the City of New York, a group composed principally of lawyers, scientists, and physicians interested in social problems, decided in 1899 to organize an American Congress on Tuberculosis at which "the laws of the several states regarding the disease and its treatment" would be considered.[19] The arrest of the disease and the prevention of its spread were the dominant goals. Education and the personal involvement of members of the community were considered essential.

The all-out attempt by the U.S. Public Health Service to monitor potential sources of infection encouraged awareness. On the front page of the September 4, 1920, *Los Angeles Evening Herald* was the edict of Health Commissioner L. M. Powers to his health deputies—those charged with the duty of inspecting ventilation systems in hotels, restaurants, and apartment houses: "Keep your shoes clean."[20] Public participation in the fight against tuberculosis also took another form. In 1907 the first Christmas Stamp sale took place in Delaware. Its success led to the Red Cross Christmas Seal campaign the following year. The appeal for

*In the early twentieth century women avidly turned to exercise, dieting, and gadgetry to achieve the new slender ideal. The women in this 1929 photograph attempt to shake off excess weight with reducing machines. (Reprinted by permission of the Division of Photographic History, National Museum of American History, Smithsonian Institution.)*

money to support the prevention of illness was now carried out on a national scale.[21]

Bacteriological science made it clear that personal conduct led to the spread of the disease. Individuals who took precautions were less likely to be infected. By the 1920s, tuberculosis yielded to heart attacks its place as the leading cause of death.[22] This new way of thinking about disease was in sharp contrast to the fear of disease and death that shaped seventeenth-century, eighteenth-century, and nineteenth-century attitudes. As the beliefs of the general population and those of medical authorities converged, health as a cultural value became possible.

## Adult Height and Weight Tables

The idea that personal effort could protect a person from illness and subsequent death was made visible through height and weight tables. In 1879 Dr. J. J. Mulheron reported that obesity taxes the body and that the fat person has a much more uncertain tenure of life than people of average weight. He went even further, linking obesity to specific diseases.[23] Other physicians at that time viewed obesity as something that violated the integrity of the human organism. Toward the end of the nineteenth century, physicians and nutritionists began to examine the relationship between weight and health, and by the beginning of the twentieth century plumpness was seen as a danger to health. Further evidence came from the Medico-Actuarial Mortality Investigation of 1889–1912, which concluded that being overweight was clearly disadvantageous for people over thirty-five years of age. Control of weight was now sought by physicians and insurance companies.

Dr. Louis Dublin in 1908 studied the impact of weight on life span and linked obesity with decreased longevity. He then calculated average weights desirable for given heights. With significant statistical evidence in hand, the insurance industry was able to demonstrate the link between fatness and mortality. About 1918, as a statistician for the Metropolitan Life Insurance Company, Dublin replaced his standard table of average weights with a list of desirable weights, which dictated that after early adulthood men and women should weigh somewhat less than the average for their height. These tables were recommended as the standards to be used by physicians and life insurance companies.[24]

In a September 26, 1992, report in the *New York Times,* the Department of Agriculture and the Department of Health and Human Services offered a height and weight table adjusted by age. The report noted that over the years weight charts have varied strikingly, "and there is no significant agreement among health professionals about when a person is overweight or whether it is harmful to gain a little weight as you age." The government's booklet *Nutrition and Your Health: Dietary Guidelines for Americans,* acknowledged that people over thirty-five are likely to weigh more than people between the ages of nineteen and thirty-four. It offered a weight range adjusted by age.

A new genre of books devoted exclusively to weight control and diet appeared on the market after World War I. A book of this genre ranked second on the nonfiction best-seller list of 1924–1925.[25] In her popular beauty guide *Physical Beauty* (1918), Annette Kellerman, the champion swimmer, derided the notion that women were intended by nature to be plump. Women needed to pay attention to their physical appearance, she argued, so they would not grow fat at forty and shrivel up at fifty. "Fat is weakening and in a society where women's weakness was a virtue, fatness in woman may have been desirable. Weakness is no longer a virtue, but a handicap to a woman," she asserted.[26] Eating properly and exercising were seen as the means of maintaining one's ideal weight, and thinness came to reflect the achievement of the new cultural value: health. In *Diet and Health with Key to Calories* (1918), Dr. Lulu Hunt Peters educated her readers about her scientific weight-reduction plan. She explained the role of calories, the composition of a balanced diet, and the hazards of violating the laws of nutrition. She noted that it is impossible with exercise alone to reduce weight.[27] The potbelly and the plump look, which had been fashionable among members of the middle class in the nineteenth century, were now considered evidence of sloth and gluttony.

TABLE 14.1  A Comparison of Major Causes of Death in the United States, 1900 and 1990

| Causes of Death in 1900 | Percent | Causes of Death in 1990 | Percent |
|---|---|---|---|
| Influenza and pneumonia | 11.8 | Heart disease | 33.5 |
| Tuberculosis | 11.3 | Cancer | 23.4 |
| Gastroenteritis | 8.3 | Stroke | 6.7 |
| Heart disease | 8.0 | Accidents | 4.3 |
| Stroke | 6.2 | Pulmonary diseases | 4.1 |
| Kidney disease | 4.7 | Pneumonia and influenza | 3.6 |
| Accidents | 4.2 | Diabetes mellitus | 2.3 |
| Cancer | 3.7 | Suicide | 1.4 |
| Infancy diseases | 3.6 | All others | 20.7 |
| All others | 38.2 | | |

Source: Adapted from the National Center for Health Statistics, U.S. Department of Health and Human Services, Washington, D.C., 1991.

## The Well-Child Clinic

A commitment to children's health and to the optimistic view that medical science could prevent much agony, illness, and death was evident in the establishment of well-child clinics and medical and nursing services in the public school system in the first half of the twentieth century. Vaccinations and the ingestion of vitamins made it possible for children to avoid some illnesses and also made the growing child aware of the importance of maintaining health.[28] In addition to vaccinations, some schools offered nutrition supplements and medical examinations. The examinations included height and weight measurements, which helped the children become aware that there are criteria of appearance that they must meet.

## Prevention of Illness As the Physician's Domain

Since the 1930s medical columns in popular and professional magazines have reflected the fact that the medical profession must broaden its perspective to include preventive health care. Healthy men and women were expected to go to their doctors for routine physical examinations. By the 1980s research had found that degenerative diseases such as heart disease and cancer, rather than infectious diseases, were the leading cause of death (Table 14.1). The medical profession advocated the reform of personal habits, such as smoking, diet, alcohol consumption, and exercise, as means of preventing heart disease and perhaps cancer. Individual responsibility for maintaining health was reaffirmed. Some major medical schools, such as Harvard, Berkeley, and Johns Hopkins, decided to publish "Wellness Letters" to clarify the often conflicting and superficial health information presented in the popular media. The editors claimed that their access to the latest findings regarding threats to health was greater than the mass media's and that

*Today, longevity is a supporting motivation for fitness.*
*(Copyright 1992 by Consumers Union of U.S., Inc., Yonkers, N.Y.*
*10703-1057. Reprinted by permission from* Consumer Reports.
*January 1992.)*

they could offer better guidelines on how to reduce the risk of developing chronic diseases. They made it clear that good health depends on lifestyle choices.[29]

The reform of personal habits—for example, adhering to a diet rich in grains, fruits, and vegetables—is viewed as a nonsurgical and nonpharmaceutical means of reversing, not just retarding or preventing, heart disease. The nation's largest provider of health insurance, Mutual of Omaha, announced in 1993 that it would reimburse patients for participating in programs that offered diet, meditation, exercise, and support groups, thereby acknowledging the value of unconventional forms of therapy.[30] Both individual concerns for staying well and the concerns of the medical establishment reaffirmed the value of health. A trim, fit body with good muscle tone became the symbolic indicator of health.

## The Visual Conjoining of Values

A value may have more than one manifestation, and a visual manifestation may reflect more than one cultural value. A physically fit body, for example, may reflect the values of both self-denial and hard work, which are basic to American culture, as sociologist William Graham Sumner suggested.[31] In a 1989 *New York Times* column, "How to Begin an Exercise Program," sports journalist William Stockton wrote "So you are sedentary and the doctor has scared you with talk of heart disease and a lecture about your weight. Or, a significant other has delivered an ultimatum. Or, you have caught a glimpse of yourself in the bathroom mirror and been unhappy with what you saw."[32] These three statements offer three different motivations for a specific appearance. They demonstrate that the motivation and meaning of the behavior are specific to the individual.

## The Suntan

Upton Sinclair in his novel *Oil!* (1927) interpreted the suntan as an example of Veblen's conspicuous consumption and waste.[33] He claimed that society was divided into two groups: those who worked and remained pale, and those who had leisure time, engaged in sports, and acquired tanned faces. Tanned skin, he argued, indicated that one was not a city or office worker and had the time and money to bask in the sunlight. The suntan thus emerged as a status symbol signifying wealth.

Columbia University professor Paul Nystrom, in his book *The Economics of Fashion* (1928), characterized the suntan differently, calling it a "youthful complexion fad."[34] He saw it as an American phenomenon that indicated modernity, separating younger women from older ones. Older women were brought up with the idea that fairness of skin indicated freedom from manual labor. They continued to take special care against the damaging effects of wind, sun, and saltwater. "White is beautiful" had been the ideal since the Middle Ages and continued to be the ideal even after World War I. White skin made it possible for the veins to be discerned, helping to support the aristocracy's claim to "blue blood," that is, entitlement to special privilege. Younger women, taught the ideas of a new society, including new energy, opportunity, and freedom, were more likely to expose their bodies to the sun, wind, and surf.

In the 1920s women were no longer limited to presenting themselves as pale, demure, shy, and retiring, as dictated by puritanical conventions, and these characteristics were no longer requirements for marriage. Women could look tan and "modern," vigorous in appearance and action. Paleness had also been a characteristic of tuberculosis; suntans suggested youth and health.[35]

The suntan continues to be popular. Tanning parlors have appeared in most major U.S. cities. The correlation between skin cancer and exposure to ultraviolet rays of the sun, discovered by physicians in the 1970s, has not dampened the al-

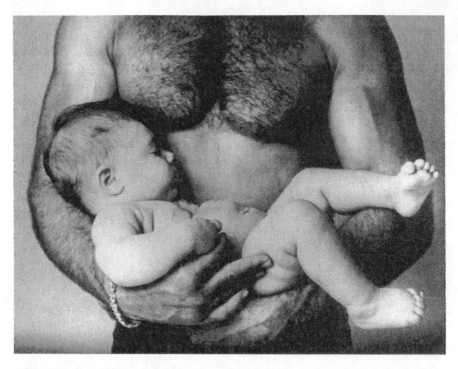

*Edward Vitali and his daughter Alexandra, fall 1993. Vitali, manager of a New York health club, displays this picture in his public office. (Reprinted by permission of Edward Vitali.)*

lure. Lotions that screen out ultraviolet rays and big-brimmed straw hats have been adopted by men and women as means of preventing skin damage but still acquiring a tan. The tanned image continues to project energy, youthfulness, and health.

## The Lean and Muscular Male Body

Few occupations require a body that is lean and well toned. Yet, since the beginning of the 1990s, the beer aesthetic, which had been characterized on MTV by overweight guitar-playing men wearing black T-shirts stretched to the limit, has given way to the ideal of the lean, well-toned male body. Superstars, sports celebrities, male models for Calvin Klein, and young men on city streets are displaying this new standard for male appearance. Shirtless, or wearing shirts open to the waist, or wearing vests with no shirts, they show a somewhat skinny but well-toned musculature.

"Athleticism has taken over and shirts have been taken off; across the cultural board from movies to advertisements men are not wearing too many clothes," reported Peter Watrous in the *New York Times* in 1991. He pointed out that pop personalities such as film celebrities are under pressure to fit current notions of what is desirable. For many male rock and roll stars, the choice is simple: "Nautilus or marginal success."[36]

Enlarged pectorals supported by well-defined intercostal muscles and a well-rounded gluteus have emerged as the new status symbols for men. These have acquired prominence over the conventional emphasis on biceps and bulk. Power and militarism were the traditional reasons for athleticism. Command was signified by broad shoulders, chest, and size. Fitness alluded to readiness to engage in physical aggression or to prevent altercation. Today the totally fit body has different meanings and purposes. It proclaims self-discipline (control over the consumption of food and beverage and an abstention from partying; leisure hours are spent working out). It also indicates control over one's body and the expression of aggression. Breasts in Western culture, however, allude to both nurturing and sensuality, and a tight gluteus intimates superior sexual performance. The ability to contract the muscles in those parts of the body alludes to the ability to give and receive increased sexual pleasure.

The skinny, toned male ideal suggests, in addition to health, a popular desire of men to relate to others beyond the confines of aggression and economics traditionally demanded of them. It may be interpreted as a rebuff to established societal restrictions on the scope of feelings men may experience and express.

## Notes

1. J. R. Head, Sr. (1967), "Medicine from 1800 to 1850," in *The Growth of Modern Medicine,* ed. F. Stenn (Springfield, Ill.: Charles C. Thomas), pp. 107–123.

2. N. Poynter (1971), *Medicine and Man* (London: C. A. Watts), p. 23.

3. M. E. Lichtenstein (1967), "The Origins of Modern Surgery: 1850–1900," in *The Growth of Modern Medicine,* ed. F. Stenn (Springfield, Ill.: Charles C. Thomas), pp. 124–136.

4. S. E. Cayleff (1987), *Wash and Be Healed: The Water-Cure Movement and Women's Health* (Philadelphia: Temple University Press); see also A. C. and M. Fellman (1981), *Making Sense of Self: Medical Advice Literature in Late Nineteenth-Century America* (Philadelphia: University of Pennsylvania Press).

5. Head, op. cit., p. 111.

6. Reader's Digest (1980), *Stories Behind Everyday Things* (Pleasantville, N.Y.: Reader's Digest Association), p. 34.

7. C. Perati (1987), *Extraordinary Origins of Everyday Things* (New York: Harper and Row).

8. Reader's Digest, op. cit.

9. Ibid.

10. Ibid., p. 35.

11. Cayleff, op. cit., pp. 110–112.

12. W. Root and R. de Rochemont (1976), *Eating in America: A History* (New York: Ecco Press); Cayleff, op. cit., p. 118.

13. C. J. Rooney, Jr. (1985), *Dreams and Visions: A Study of American Utopias 1865–1917* (Westport, Conn.: Greenwood Press), p. 159.

14. W. H. Wehrmacher (1967), "Medicine Since 1900," in *The Growth of Modern Medicine*, ed. F. Stenn (Springfield, Ill.: Charles C. Thomas), p. 139.

15. Fellman, op. cit.

16. W. I. Susman (1984), *Culture As History: The Transformation of American Society in the Twentieth Century* (New York: Pantheon Books), p. 112.

17. R. and J. Dubos (1952), *The White Plague: Tuberculosis, Man and Society* (Boston: Little, Brown), pp. 33–43.

18. Ibid., pp. 169–172, 213–219.

19. H. Woods (1910), *The Conquest of Consumption* (New York: Houghton Mifflin).

20. *Los Angeles Evening Herald*, Sept. 4, 1920.

21. F. M. Pottinger (1952), *The Fight Against Tuberculosis* (New York: Henry Schuman).

22. Susman, op. cit., p. 112.

23. J. J. Mulheron (1879), "Obesity—A Few Thoughts on Its Nature and Treatment," *New Preparations* 3 (11): 271.

24. I. L. Dublin (1930), "The Influence of Weight on Certain Causes of Death," *Human Biology* 2 (2): 160–184.

25. L. E. Axtell (1916), "Obesity: Its Related Pathology," *Journal of the Michigan State Medical Society* 15 (5): 226–231.

26. A. Kellerman (1918), *Physical Beauty* (New York: George H. Doran), pp. 15–26.

27. L. H. Peters (1918), *Diet and Health with Key to Calories* (Chicago: Reilly & Lee). This book was ranked sixth on the nonfiction bestseller list in 1923 and first in 1924 and 1925. Reported in A. P. Hackett and J. H. Burke (1977), *Eighty Years of Best Sellers, 1895–1975* (New York: Bowker).

28. E. H. Ackerknecht (1982), *A Short History of Medicine* (Baltimore, Md.: Johns Hopkins University Press), p. 231.

29. The Wellness Letters have also been turned into encyclopedias of health information. See, for example, the University of California, Berkeley (1991), *The Wellness Encyclopedia: The Comprehensive Family Resource for Safeguarding Health and Preventing Illness* (Boston: Houghton Mifflin).

30. *New York Times*, July 28, 1993.

31. W. G. Sumner (1925), *What Social Classes Owe to Each Other* (New Haven, Conn.: Yale University Press), pp. 43–44.

32. *New York Times*, Jan. 23, 1989.

33. U. Sinclair (1927), *Oil!* (New York: Albert Charles Boni), p. 294.

34. P. Nystrom (1928), *The Economics of Fashion* (New York: Roland Press), p. 9.

35. Pottinger, op. cit., pp. 205–208.

36. *New York Times*, Feb. 10, 1991.

# Part Five: Publicspeak

# 15

# Clothing: Tie-Signs

**T**IE-SIGNS IN CLOTHING provide information about a desired social identity. They indicate membership in groups outside the boundaries of dominant institutional discourse and interaction with specific others. They provide information about behavior. Attire that is a tie-sign has only one meaning and can be easily "read." It acts to maintain the individual's bond to the group. The ensemble is carefully conceived by the group's decision makers to convey an image that counteracts the ideas of the dominant culture; wearing such attire encourages a sense of belonging and supports feelings of worth. Individuals and groups who reject society's hierarchical arrangements, those who resist social change, and those who reject a societal designation of inferiority may develop fellowship with similar persons and with it a distinctive mode of appearance and behavior.

The term *tie-sign* was coined by the sociologist Erving Goffman, who observed that in Western society there is no one-to-one fit between the elements and units of public life and the elements and units of social structure. He suggested that visual indicators that designate a "with among a co-present" be called tie-signs. This term can also be used to describe the clothing of groups whose orientation to social life is in a realm separate from mainstream culture.[1] Tie-signs are markers that provide information about such subsets.[2]

When individuals who share the same sentiments about social conditions form groups to achieve a sense of social and personal significance outside mainstream culture, they may use tie-signs as a means of expression and identity. The wearing of tie-signs enables these individuals to place themselves in a sociocultural category and in a system of rights and obligations. The attire sets members apart from nonmembers, which further discourages participation and interaction in the dominant institutional spheres.[3] The decision to wear attire that is a tie-sign is a conscious one. Individuals adopt the attire to announce commitment to the group and are aware that it places them outside the confines of established structural and institutional order. The audience is thus alerted that the social game will be played under different rules. Members of the audience may associate or interact with group members, but only on the group members' terms.

Three categories of groups wear tie-signs. They are differentiated by the forces that led to their evolution and by the extent of communal life.

The first category includes individuals who dissent. They oppose the dominant hierarchical structure and adopt or develop beliefs, values, and lifestyles in opposition to those espoused by the ruling authority. The Hare Krishnas in the United States and the Jains in ancient India are examples. The second category consists of groups that have resisted the social and cultural change that came with the individualism and economic success of the Renaissance, the secularization and industrialization of the nineteenth century, and neocolonialism. Interaction and conduct in these groups continues to be guided by traditional forms of connectedness. The Amish, Hasidic Jews, and the Rastafarians are the most prominent examples. In the third category are individuals who develop a bond because of feelings of isolation, alienation, and lowly social definition. The attire enables the individuals to protest their designation of inferiority. The zoot suit worn by blacks and Mexican-Americans, and the attire of the Hell's Angels, their "colors," are important examples.

## Individuals Who Dissent

### The Hare Krishnas

Imported from India in the 1960s, the Hare Krishna society in the United States recruited middle-class whites in their early twenties, many of whom were college dropouts. The sect's charismatic leader, the Indian monk Swami Bhaktivedanta, sought to save Westerners from what he saw as materialism and atheism by converting them to worship the Hindu god Krishna.[4] In addition, he hoped that Western disciples would inspire Indians to rediscover their own religious heritage.

In the United States, the International Society for Krishna Consciousness offers its members complete personal transformation. Through the adoption of new myths and through rituals, such as dancing and chanting, devotees associate with other devotees and that, in turn, encourages a sense of community and belonging. Their saffron robes and shaved heads bespeak asceticism and celibacy. Through begging on city streets and in airports, they communicate a collective orientation. To achieve Krishna consciousness they reject the Judeo-Christian belief system and American core values (individual achievement, hard work, and goal-directed behavior). The visual manifestation of this religious sect has attracted much public comment and formal negative response.[5]

### The Jains and the Early Buddhists

The imposition of religious beliefs and practices by nomadic Aryan conquerors led to dissent among the indigenous population of ancient India in religious ideas, lifestyles, and attire.[6] The Aryans, who came from central Asia between 2000 and 1500 BC, designated the local people as inferior and therefore destined for subjugation. They assembled them for religious processions and marched

*Members of the Hare Krishna sect in the United States. Their distinct lifestyle, hair, and clothing are apparent. (Reprinted by permission of UPI/Bettmann.)*

them to the sacrificial grounds, sandwiched between rows of Aryan Brahman priests and warriors. Control was achieved through fear—fear of becoming a human offering, a sacrifice deemed most desirable in Vedic texts, the sacred books of the Aryans. For the Aryans, the images of the two most important Aryan deities acted to support the conquest; Agni, the god of fire, and Indira, who symbolized victorious leadership, embodied the power of the Aryans.

Hunters, gatherers, and herders who had been free to roam the countryside were now forced to settle down and till the land to provide food for the Aryan king, his army, and the Brahman priests. The ideas of the local people regarding sexuality and fertility were integrated into Aryan thinking. Religious worship now included bathing, anointing, and applying cosmetics to visual representations of the gods. The sculptures of gods are shown wearing crowns, earrings, pendants, arm-rings, bracelets, jeweled belts, and rings.

Desired appearance required that one look as beautiful and well groomed as one could, regardless of status. Kings and princes appeared in golden robes, warriors in coats of mail, ordinary people in light-textured cloth. Both men and women enhanced their appearance through luxurious adornment—garlands of lush flowers, decorated cloth, and elaborate jewelry.[7]

By 600 BC everyone was assigned a place in a caste system that controlled all aspects of everyday life: whose cooked food one could accept; with whom one could share a meal; whose daughter one could marry; what task one could perform. People were divided into occupationally specialized groups, and no one could shift from one group to another. Everyone was required to request the services and secret rituals of the Brahman priests before proceeding with any endeavor. Taboos were so powerful that a person would rather go hungry and die of starvation than eat food prepared (contaminated) by a person of a lower caste.[8] The stratified social groupings encouraged isolation and narrowed the sphere of possible interaction.

By the sixth century BC the religion of Jainism offered a release from the restrictive social and religious ties. The sage of Jainism, Mahavira (599–527 BC), taught that being reborn as a Jain enabled one to become free of retribution for the rejection of Brahman sacrifice and the violation of caste norms. Sect members rejected the self-indulgent style of the Aryans in favor of abstinence and asceticism. They repudiated gambling, a favorite pastime of the Aryans, and adopted vegetarianism in reaction to the meat-dependent conquerors, who had even brought their own cattle with them. Jains wore face masks to keep from breathing in and harming the souls of all living particles that they believed floated in the air. They regarded jewelry and ornamented cloth as signs of the social arrangement established by the Aryan leaders and were known as the "space-garmented ones." When Alexander the Great invaded India in 326 BC, he recognized that the Jains were distinct from the rest of the population and referred to them as "gymnosophists," naked philosophers.[9]

Like Mahavira, Siddhartha Gautama, later known as Buddha, also provided a set of beliefs that made it possible for Indians to escape the compulsion of prescribed obligations. In 535 BC, at the age of twenty-nine, he renounced his role as a husband and father and his place within the family structure to seek personal salvation and enlightenment. He developed a philosophy and lifestyle based on the idea that suffering would cease if one denied the desire for existing sources of joy and pleasure. Individuals could experience a sense of control by determining what they would allow to affect them.[10]

Buddha advocated cutting one's hair short and giving away one's clothing and other possessions. The monks who followed him were supposed to wear soiled, pieced-together rags. They put on yellow robes and lived like beggars. Through this blatant rejection of conventional clothing, they announced that they no longer subscribed to the dominant system of rights and responsibilities. Their attire was the antithesis of traditional dress, what society considered desirable, and not merely a deviation. It was a powerful visual signifier of the struggle to maintain personal freedom in opposition to the state's domination.[11]

Rejecting the culture of the invaders, these countercultures adopted attire that reflected their contrary sentiments. Through their attire, members of the indigenous population were able to express their discontent, lessening the potential for conflict and social and personal upheaval. Their clothing tie-signs also made it possible for those who spurned the system to become recognized as members of new social groups with their own ideas, beliefs, and values.

## Individuals Who Resist Sociocultural Change

The term "axial period" refers to a major turning point in the history of human development when invasions from without, or inventions and innovations from within, radically alter the course of life. During such a period a type of human being emerges whose structure of existence differs greatly from the previous norm. The Renaissance, the Protestant Reformation, and the secularization and industrialization of the modern world can be considered consequences of axial periods.

Four cultural ideas assumed prominence in Western society in the nineteenth century and led to a new orientation to social life: (1) a propensity for rational thought; (2) the intention to have a hand in shaping one's own destiny; (3) the contention that the human being is what he or she is, not what he or she was; and (4) a belief in a greater degree of personal freedom. These ideas were signified in a change in the basic style of male dress. The young most easily adapted to the new orientation to social life and the new style of dress. However, during any axial period, members of the old aristocracy and those of older generations who refuse to accept the new orientation sometimes form separate groups that continue to be guided by the old beliefs and ideals. They may adopt a style of dress that is rooted in the past yet reflects a new determination to resist change. Such a group forms a subset within an existing group. The Old Order Amish community (a sect of the Mennonite Church), the male Hasidic Jews, and the Rastafarians are examples of this category.

### The Old Order Amish

The Amish who settled in Pennsylvania in the early 1700s formed a hermetically sealed community. They wanted to live without interference from the outside world, which they considered corrupt. They claimed that they were "in the world but not of it."[12] Still today, in their agricultural compounds, continuity of tradition and personal, face-to-face interaction dominate social life. Intense personal relationship encourages dependency on the group. Through praying together, the sharing of food, visiting, and singing every Sunday night, permissible behavior is clarified. In school, intellectual curiosity is discouraged; memorization of facts and differences between right and wrong, good and bad behavior, are emphasized.

*A youth from Lancaster County, Pennsylvania. The Amish wear plain clothes, attire that is not machine-made and is free of color and ornament. (Reprinted by permission of The Bettmann Archive.)*

Clothing is a major mechanism the Amish use to maintain their distinct identity and to ensure conformity to group norms. Amish dress is uniform; any modification that might suggest individuality is rejected. The homemade attire is devoid of jewelry, buttons, belts, collars, lapels, neckties, gloves, pockets, zippers, and other modern trimmings. The style has remained unchanged for 250 years. Except for teenage boys who have not yet been baptized, who may wear color, much of their clothing is black and loose-fitting. Through their attire and lifestyle, the Amish seem to effectively keep outsiders away. In addition, the attire discourages the straying of group members into forbidden places and activities, for it makes them exceptionally visible. Amish women keep their heads covered with a cap or a bonnet at all times; the men wear low-crowned hats with brim widths that vary with their age and rank.[13]

The Amish, for the most part, do not use or buy products that emerged with the secular state and industrialization, including electric lighting, telephones, machinery, movies, television, novels, comic books, and magazines.[14] Because each Amish community is a closely knit unit, gossip, ridicule, and derision are the mechanisms of social control. Excommunication—social isolation—may be imposed on those who buy a car or marry an outsider. As practiced by the Amish today, the ban is an extremely powerful means of eliciting social conformity. When a presiding judge places an errant member under the ban, that person becomes undesirable to all members of the community. No one, including the person's own family, will have anything to do with him or her; even marital relations are forbidden. Informal social-control mechanisms thus serve to maintain the Amish people's rejection of modern industrialization and the modern state.

### The Hasidic Community

The Hasidim also reject the secular dimension of the modern world. In his study of the Hasidic community, Solomon Poll (1962) found that the clothing Hasidic Jews wear is designed to maintain a distinct religious identity.[15] The men consider their attire, including beard and earlocks, to be the traditional Jewish attire—that which was once worn by all Jews. But because most of today's Jews imitate non-Jews, these garments are now exclusively Hasidic. By "looking like a Jew with the image of God upon one's face," the Hasid creates a barrier against assimilation with non-Jews and a protection against sin. As one Hasid expressed it, "With my appearance I cannot attend a theater, or movie or any other places where a religious Jew is not supposed to go. Thus, my beard and my earlocks and my Hasidic clothing serve as a guard and shield from sin and obscenity."[16]

The extent of a Hasidic Jew's affiliation with Hasidism determines the particular kind of garments worn. The attire and prestige of the Hasid are determined by the frequency and intensity of religious observance, observed Poll. The term *frequency* refers to the number of religious services attended in the course of a day; *intensity* refers to the emotional manifestations observed during public ceremonies. The Hasid may sway back and forth during prayers, may pray longer

*The degree of religious commitment of a male Hasidic Jew is indicated by his dedication to traditional attire. (Reprinted by permission of Reuters/Bettmann.)*

than others, or may display during prayer certain mannerisms that are known as religious, symbolic gestures. The greater the number of rituals and the more intensely they are observed, the greater the esteem accorded. The most esteemed Hasid is called a Rebbe, and he is distinguished from the others by his large-rimmed beaver hat, long overcoat worn as a jacket, or long silk coat, and slipper-like shoes with white knee socks into which breeches are folded.[17]

Hasidic garments vary from "extremely Hasidic," worn by the most observant, to "modern," worn by persons whose religious performances are of less frequency and intensity. Although still recognizable as Hasidic, the attire of the latter resembles clothing worn in the secular realm in the Western world. Sometimes outmoded Western clothing is worn: The nineteenth-century double-breasted dark suit that buttons from right to left is a favorite. As Poll reported, the person who wears "extremely Hasidic" clothing would be ridiculed if his behavior were not consistent with his appearance. Religiosity, the major criterion for social stratification, is supported by the Hasidic Jews' attire. The more religious the person, the more traditional is the clothing. The attire supports the group's rejection of secularization in the modern world.

### The Rastafarians

Rastafarianism is a way of life designed to promote spiritual resilience in the face of poverty and oppression. It rejects Jamaica's neocolonial reality and draws

*A Rastafarian with his dreadlocks.*
*(Photo courtesy of Le Roy Woodson.)*

upon a variety of legacies, among them Hebrew theocracy, African traditions, and to a lesser extent Anglo-Hispanic traditions. The Rastafarians seek to achieve freedom for the self, as well as freedom of speech and expression. In the United States Rastafarianism has been related to black liberation forces. Their ultimate goal is emigration and settlement in Africa.[18]

Each aspect of the Rastafarians' appearance is designed to convey their beliefs. In their wild dreadlocks and unkempt beards, they create distance between themselves and the larger society. The dreadlocks hairdo of Rastafarian men simulates the mane of a lion. In its savage appearance it is expected to spur feelings of "dread" in outside communities. Their beards signify their pact with Jah (God) and the fact that the Bible is their major source of knowledge. The Rastafarian elder carries a staff, like Moses, to represent his role as a shepherd leading his flock.

The Rastafarians' clothing is made of plain cloth and is unfitted, simply covering the body. It reflects the belief that in the heart, mind, and spirit of the Rastafarians live wealth and abundance. It is also designed to indicate asceticism, a desire for nothing beyond food and necessities.

Rastafarians are expected to stand fit and feisty, like a lion. The spirit of the lion is also simulated in their emulation of a lion's strut. The image conveys self-reliance and freedom from the rights and obligations imposed by the larger society. The lion is the Rastafarians' most prominent symbol. Its image is found on their houses, flags, and tabernacles, and on objects in their homes. It represents the conquering "Lion of Judah" and Haile Selassie, the former emperor of Ethiopia, their mighty redeemer.[19] It also represents the dominance of men. Male virility, courage, tenacity, energy, and wisdom are denoted by the lion. The female is Rastafarian only through the male, and the male is the physical and spiritual head of the household. The female must seek his guidance.

To show their commitment to Africa, Rastafarians incorporate the colors red, yellow, and green from the Ethiopian flag into their attire. Other important colors are brown, which signifies the earth from which they believe they have emerged, and black, which signifies pride in their skin color. To enable them to withstand evil forces, Rastafarians wear shield-shaped badges, horseshoes for good luck, and a ship motif, which represents their hope of returning to Africa.

## Individuals Who Protest an Inferior Identity

### The Zoot-Suiters

In the late 1930s the term *zoot* was used to describe things worn or performed in an extravagant style. It was in common circulation within the urban jazz culture, as Stuart Cosgrove pointed out in *The Zoot Suit and Style Warfare*.[20] The zoot suit was characterized by extremes. It was made as if it were created for a much larger man than its wearer. It was baggy as if to conceal a bad figure, but it had ample room for a holster under the armpit. The "drape shape," as it was called, was associated with American gangsters, and a version of it was even once worn by Danny Kaye and Frank Sinatra.[21]

The zoot suit evoked and provoked feelings. Notably, it was the attire chosen by the pachucos, Mexican-American youths who often formed gangs. The pachucos were a disinherited generation within a disadvantaged sector of North American society, observed Octavio Paz.[22] They were second-generation working-class immigrants. As such, they had been stripped of their old customs, beliefs, and language. But they did not want to be victims. Rejecting the ideologies of their migrant parents, they rebelled. Rather than disguise their alienation or efface their hostility to the dominant society, the pachucos adopted an arrogant posture.

The pachuco subculture was defined by petty crime, delinquency, drug-taking, and ostentatious fashion. The zoot suit articulated the youths' disdain for establishment definitions and, at the same time, their wish for high social regard. Octavio Paz saw their appropriation of the zoot suit as an admission of the ambivalent place they occupied. "It is the only way [the pachuco] can establish a more vital relationship with the society he is antagonizing which had previously ignored him: as a delinquent, he can become one of its wicked heroes."[23]

The intrusion of the zoot-suiter into the conventions of adult society was met with anger and shock. The zoot-suiter was the antithesis of the World War II serviceman; further, he disrupted the conception of roles assigned to adolescents. Fighting between pachucos and servicemen from military bases broke out on the

*Often worn in protest
of a designation of
inferiority, a 1943 zoot
suit. (Reprinted by
permission of
UPI/Bettmann.)*

first weekend of June 1943, and the Los Angeles police arrested more than sixty zoot-suiters in order to protect them in the event of further fighting.

The symbolic significance of the zoot suit can be identified in the response of the servicemen. Gangs of marines ambushed zoot-suiters, stripped them down to their underwear, and left them helpless in the streets.[24] In one particularly vicious incident a gang of drunken sailors rampaged through a cinema after sighting two zoot-suiters. They dragged the pachucos onto the stage, stripped them in front of the audience, and urinated on their zoot suits. During the ensuing weeks of "rioting," the ritualistic stripping of zoot-suiters became the major means by which the servicemen established their superiority over the pachucos. The repeated acts of stripping indicated the servicemen's desire to terminate the pachucos' attempt at developing self-regard. Cosgrove concluded that the pachuco was both the victim and the assailant; the zoot suit was simultaneously the garb of "the persecutor and the persecuted, the 'sinister clown' and grotesque dandy."[25]

## Hell's Angels

The Hell's Angels occupy a similarly paradoxical position. In everyday life they are victims because they lack what society deems desirable: education and economic success. They are expected to assume the posture of submission. Their contempt for societal definition and expectations is expressed by the menacing attire they wear and by their readiness to pick a fight. Moreover, as Hunter Thompson reported, "Of all their habits and predilections that society finds alarming, the outlaws' disregard for the time-honored concept of an eye for an eye is the one that frightens people most."[26] For example, a man who was marketing Hell's Angels Fan Club T-shirts, on his own, did fairly well until the Angels announced that they would burn all the T-shirts they saw even if they had to rip them off people's backs. Thompson suggested that this belief in total retaliation for any offense or insult is what makes the Angels a problem for police.

Most of the Angels are unskilled and uneducated. In a world increasingly geared to specialists, technicians, and fantastically complicated machinery, the Hell's Angels are obviously losers, and that fact bothers them, Thompson observed. The outlaw motorcyclists see a future with no chance for upward mobility. Their real motivation for joining the club is their certainty that they are out of the ball game. But instead of submitting quietly to their collective fate, they have made it a basis for social vendetta. They do not expect to win anything, but they have nothing to lose. A favorite tattoo among the Angels is "Born to Lose."[27] The occupations they often hold are longshoremen, warehousemen, truck drivers, mechanics, clerks, and casual laborers—any work that pays quick wages and requires no allegiance. Perhaps one in ten has a steady job or a decent income.[28]

Twenty years before the first Hell's Angels chapter was founded, Hollywood created the image of wild men on motorcycles in the movie *Hell's Angels* (1930). That image was later adopted but drastically modified by the real-life Hell's Angels. Hollywood also provided the name for the group. In reality, Hell's Angels originated with ex-GIs, World War II veterans, who rejected the idea of going back to family, job, and school. They wanted privacy, more time to figure things out, and more action. One of the ways to look for action was on a big motorcycle. By late 1947 California was alive with bikes, nearly all of them powerful. Restless veterans founded the first Angel chapter in Fontana, California, in 1950. In 1954 the movie *The Wild Ones* celebrated the motorcycle outlaw.[29]

Politicians, editors, and police, keen on outrage stories of rape, orgies, and senseless destruction, turned the Hell's Angels into a menace in 1965, according to Thompson. Every newspaper in the land denounced the Angels as brutal. The official reports, however, were based on a survey of old police files and the movie *The Wild Ones*. They contained little that was new or startling. In August 1965, *True, The Man's Magazine* reported: "They call themselves Hell's Angels. They ride, rape and raid like marauding cavalry—and they boast that no police force can break up their criminal motorcycle fraternity."[30]

*Members of the Hell's Angels wearing their "colors." (Reprinted by permission of UPI/Bettmann.)*

At the beginning of March 1965, there were eighty-five Hell's Angels in California. After the California attorney general's report on the Angels, "the whole scene changed in a flash. . . . One day they were a gang of bums, scratching for any hard dollar . . . and twenty-four hours later they were dealing with reporters, photographers, free-lance writers, and all kinds of showbiz hustlers talking big money."[31] By the middle of 1965 they were firmly established as "all-American bogeymen." Many of the independent bike riders seeking fellowship and status sought to join. The Angels rejected many membership bids, describing those who wished to join as "a plague of locusts."[32]

The California attorney general described their appearance in this manner: They prefer to ride the large heavy-duty American-made motorcycles (Harley-Davidsons) and have been observed to wear belts made of a length of polished motorcycle drive chain, which can be unhooked and used as a flexible bludgeon.[33]

The Angel's "uniform" consists of grease-caked Levis; a sleeveless denim matching jacket; and tattoos portraying swastikas, daggers, and skulls. Their emblem, termed "colors," is sewn onto the back of the jacket. It must be earned. It consists of an embroidered patch of a winged skull wearing a motorcycle helmet. Just below the wing of the emblem are the letters "MC" for Motorcycle Club. Over the wing is a band bearing the words "Hell's Angels." According to Thompson, "An angel without his 'colors' feels naked and vulnerable—like a knight without his armor."[34] The only consistent difference between the Hell's Angels and the other motorcycle clubs is that members of most of the other clubs wear their insignia only part-time. The Angels "play the role seven days a week." They wear their colors at home, on the street, and sometimes even to work; they ride their bikes to the neighborhood grocery to buy a quart of milk.[35]

The Angels feel that they are outcasts from society and have to defend one another from attack by "the others"—the "mean squares, enemy gangs or armed agents of the Main Cop." When somebody punches a lone Angel, every one of them feels threatened. They are intensely aware of belonging, of being able to depend on each other. Their motto is "All on One and One on All." As Thompson stated, "You mess with an Angel and you've got twenty-five of them on your neck."[36]

In 1966, Hell's Angels clubs existed only in California. Their numbers and clusters increased and spread throughout the country with the widespread publicity about their altercations with the police. The Hell's Angels themselves, however, believe that their brotherhood is based on love of motorcycles; that their negative image was created in Hollywood, and that it persists because it serves the interests of those who are in charge of law and order. In a benefit held in New York and reported in 1991, they sought to raise funds to pay lawyers to get back their clubhouse on East Third Street in Manhattan. In 1985 the federal government had seized their building under the forfeiture act, claiming that the house was used for dealing drugs. The Angels, however, continue to claim that they are regular guys picked on by the police, that they are hard-working people with children.[37]

*      *      *

Groups whose tie-signs developed to show resistance or protest to a social designation of inferiority, like the zoot-suiters and the Hell's Angels, have been loathed by those charged with the maintenance of the social structure. The attire is an attempt to counteract the definition of inferiority. The attire empowers the individual because it affirms the identity he or she desires: for the zoot-suiters, that of mainstream respectability and economic success; for the Hell's Angels, power. The act of wearing the dress was viewed by those in authority as anarchical, the individuals designated dangerous, and the members persecuted.

To conclude, tie-signs in modern society allow for social continuity. They show that people can evaluate their circumstances and the demands made on them by those in authority, and that the shared culture is the source of the image and its meaning. Distress caused by society's moving too fast can be alleviated by holding back and creating communities that preserve more traditional arrangements. Distress caused by social valuation can be lessened by adopting dress and ornament that counteract the imposed identity.

## Notes

1. E. Goffman (1971), *Relations in Public* (New York: Harper and Row), p. 202.

2. Ibid., pp. 195–237. Goffman (1963b) called clothing tie-signs "stigma symbols that are voluntarily employed" in *Stigma: Notes on the Management of Spoiled Identity* (Englewood Cliffs, N.J.: Prentice-Hall), pp. 46, 144–145.

3. The notion of a counterculture, a subculture whose values, norms, and lifestyle challenge the basic assumptions of the surrounding society, has been discussed by M. J. Yinger (1982), *Countercultures: The Promise and Peril of a World Turned Upside Down* (New York: Free Press).

4. C. R. Brooks (1989), *The Hare Krishna in India* (Princeton, N.J.: Princeton University Press).

5. S. J. Judah (1974), *The Hare Krishna and the Counterculture* (New York: John Wiley and Sons); B. E. Rockford (1985), *Hare Krishna in America* (New Brunswick, N.J.: Rutgers University Press).

6. B. Rowland (1981), *The Art and Architecture of India* (New York: Penguin Books), p. 53; D. D. Kosambi (1969), *Ancient India: A History of Its Culture and Civilization* (Cleveland: World Publishing), pp. 108–109.

7. G. S. Ghurye (1958), *Bharatanatya and Its Costume* (Bombay: Bindor), pp. 48–51; M. Stutley (1980), *Ancient Indian Magic and Folklore* (London: Routledge and Kegan Paul), pp. 41–48, 61–64.

8. Kosambi, op. cit., pp. 105, 134.

9. Ibid., pp. 82–102.

10. Ibid., pp. 106–108; R. C. Craven (n.d.), *A Concise History of Indian Art* (New York: Oxford University Press), p. 33.

11. Kosambi, op. cit., pp. 106–111; Craven, op. cit., p. 32; R. F. Willis (1986), *World Civilizations: From Ancient Times Through the Sixteenth Century,* 2d ed. (Lexington, Mass.: D. C. Heath), pp. 70–71.

12. W. M. Kephart (1982), *Extraordinary Groups: The Sociology of Unconventional Life-Styles* (New York: St. Martin's), pp. 48–90.

13. L. M. Gurel (1979), "Four Hundred Years of Custom and Tradition: The Dress of Gentle Folk," in *Dimensions of Dress and Adornment: A Book of Readings,* ed. L. M. Gurel and M. S. Beeson (Dubuque, Iowa: Kendall/Hunt), pp. 40–50.

14. C. Wright (1986), *Mass Communication: A Sociological Perspective,* 3d ed. (New York: Random House).

15. S. Poll (1962), *The Hasidic Community of Williamsburg* (New York: Free Press).

16. Poll, op. cit., p. 60.

17. A. Lurie (1981), *The Language of Clothes* (New York: Random House), pp. 85–86.

18. Juliet Ash considered the Rastafarians' clothing "pure." She noted that the Rastafarians' obsession with appearance reflects their music and social roots. See J. Ash (1988), "The Business of Couture," in *Zoot Suits and Second Hand Dresses,* ed. A. McRobbie (Winchester, Mass.: Unwin Hyman), pp. 208–214.

19. L. E. Barret (1977), *The Rastafarians: Sounds of Cultural Dissonance* (Boston: Beacon Press); R. M. Mulvaney (1990), *Rastafari and Reggae: A Dictionary and Source Book* (Westport, Conn.: Greenwood Press), p. 69.

20. S. Cosgrove (1984), "The Zoot Suit and Style Warfare," in McRobbie, op. cit., pp. 3–22.

21. M. Mazon (1984), *The Zoot Suit Riots: The Psychology of Symbolic Annihilation* (Austin: University of Texas Press), p. 7.

22. O. Paz (1961), *The Labyrinth of Solitude: Life and Thought in Mexico,* trans. L. Kemp (New York: Grove Press). Quoted in Mazon, op. cit., pp. 114–116.

23. Paz, op. cit., quoted in Mazon, op. cit., pp. 109.

24. Mazon, op. cit., pp. 85–89.

25. Cosgrove, op. cit., p. 19.

26. H. B. Thompson (1967), *Hell's Angels: The Strange and Terrible Saga of the Outlaw Motorcycle Gangs* (New York: Ballantine Books), p. 95.

27. Ibid., p. 75.

28. Ibid., p. 73.

29. Ibid., p. 90.

30. Ibid.

31. Ibid., p. 12.

32. Ibid., p. 57.

33. Ibid., p. 102.

34. Ibid., p. 100.

35. Ibid., pp. 100–101.

36. Ibid., p. 96.

37. K. Schoemer, "How Many Angels Danced at the Benefit?" *New York Times,* Oct. 23, 1991.

# 16

# Clothing Tie-Symbols

IN THE NINETEENTH CENTURY Alexis de Tocqueville noted that citizens of the young U.S. republic craved badges of personal identity to distinguish themselves as individuals and to bring order to a society that lacked formal class distinctions.[1] Today, the existence of clothing tie-symbols suggests that social class in the United States is only one of several types of identity that can be overridden by the availability of clothing and various notions of lifestyle and political orientation. Democratic processes and liberal institutions have encouraged the expression in clothing and ornamentation of people's social identities, talents, hopes, and fears.

## Claiming a Divergent Identity

Clothing tie-symbols have been adopted by the young, the disaffected, and those on the cusp of identity change.[2] Social and technical innovations make it easier to break from the past, from "appropriate" identities that have become less relevant. "Extreme shoes" in 1998–1999 were an example. They were based on the technology of athletic shoes, with molded bottoms made of rubberized synthetic materials that conform to the contours of the foot. Combined with features of dress shoes made of leather and fabric, the resulting shoes were stylish enough to wear to the office.[3] Innovations in style and fabric made it possible for members of a group to appear "cool," as if unaffected by passion, agitation, or alarm;[4] and it enabled wearers to acquire confidence, reflecting the new spirit.[5]

Displaying personal preferences for an idea, ideal, or a group, clothing tie-symbols became visual expressions that made it possible for "like to find like." A continuing interest in a particular issue like protecting the environment or finding a cure for breast cancer or AIDS has kept the political T-shirt, the pink ribbon, and the inverted red ribbon alive.[6]

In 1991, support for the Gulf War was demonstrated by wearing a pin or a small cloth depicting the American flag. As memories of the war faded, these tie-symbols lost their relevance and were retired. They remain, however, a part of the

*The inverted "V" red ribbon that symbolizes AIDS awareness.*

*To show support during the Gulf War, people wore clothing adorned with the American flag. (New York Times, Feb. 10, 1991.)*

*American volleyball players shaved their heads in sympathy for a teammate during the Olympics in Barcelona. (New York Times, July 29, 1992.)*

vocabulary of images—the collective memory of American society during that period.[7]

A particular clothing tie-symbol may be used for a variety of purposes. Spike Lee's black baseball cap with the mark "X," for example, reflected his admiration for Malcolm X; but, at the same time, it served to advertise Mr. Lee's movie, *Malcolm X*.[8]

The categories of clothing tie-symbol that acquired new significance in the United States between 1995 and 2000 were those that *claimed a divergent identity*, *supported self-definition*, and *affirmed political values and goals*.

## Trendy Attire

Toward the end of the twentieth century there were about 70 million teenagers and young adults in the American workforce. They had discretionary income and a belief in limitless prosperity and endless economic growth.[9] Within the teenage and young adult subculture, clothing style was used to proclaim a youthful, sexually explicit identity. Affluence made further differentiation and diversification possible, allowing a greater amount of self-expression. Each of the styles differed from what the mainstream culture designated as appropriate.[10]

Members of a clique, a group of friends who hung out together, chose the style of dress that best mirrored their desired identity.[11] Others who liked the style or wanted to associate themselves with the clique adopted the style, creating a visual network of support.

In this context, the word *trendy* is used to describe a style phenomenon that began in the 1990s. It is different from fashion. Fashion is created by designers using good quality, durable fabrics, and customers buy the finished look. "Trendy" styles are put together by young wearers from inexpensive clothing and usually inferior fabrics, and are usually worn for a short time. The fabrics don't have to last long, since they will soon be discarded for the next trendy look.

Some teenage girls do stay with a style for a year or two and then change to another pattern. Or one day they might appear in baggy jeans, a man's sweater, and rugged Timberline boots and the next, a short skirt with over-the-knee, high-heeled boots.[12] Manufacturers pick up on these looks, copying what the young people are wearing and manufacturing the clothing quickly enough to ride the wave of each trend. Designers observe young people in their clubs, neighborhoods, and workplaces to gather ideas for the next trendy look.

Consumption of trendy attire was so strong by the end of the twentieth century that investments, the securities markets, and the careers of executives in the clothing industry were affected.[13] The October 28, 1999, business section of the *New York Times*, for example, reported that disappointing sales led Robert Fisher, president of the Gap, Inc., to resign.[14] Stock analysts criticized Fisher's management for responding slowly to the increasing demand for key trend items, like "cable rib sweaters, paratroopers pants and distressed embroidered denims."[15]

*Trendy fusion. A celebrity couple during the
holiday season in 1999. She wears an armband
tattoo. He wears sneakers with his velvet suit
and an open-necked shirt showing a strand of
beads. A long metal chain hangs from the side
of his trousers and his hair is twisted and
beaded into a style known as "dreads."*
*(Photo: Diane Cohen.)*

Focusing on the "tried-and-true basics,"[16] Gap, Inc., failed to stock enough
trendy items like leather jackets and embroidered jeans.[17]

Like those of Gap, Inc., Levi's jeans were functional and rugged rather than
cool, observed Russell Simmons, maker of Phat Farm jeans.[18] As a result, Levi
Strauss & Company lost market share to new brands and private labels and was
shut out of the youth market.[19]

Some of the young knew the look they wanted. With their peers they searched
the stores to find out what was available and where to find it. Others had an image of what they wanted to achieve. Finding the right style of dress, they claimed,
was "about being yourself."[20] They inquired in stores, clubs, and underground
newspapers about where to find a particular element of dress, a sliplike skirt with
lace, oversized rugby shirts, rave pants, or thick platform shoes that added three
inches to one's height. Others went to specialized stores and watched what their
peers chose as they went through the racks.

Trendy attire consisted of printed leather pants and skirts, modified cargo
pants, glitter bracelets, and stretch shirts with three-quarter-length sleeves; embroidered jeans and capri pants, boots, shrug jackets, puffy vests, and denim jackets.[21] There were plastic sandals, chunky clogs, hiking boots, and knapsacks used
as pocketbooks, which in some cases were in the form of animals such as teddy
bears or kittens. Also popular were Y-shapes modeled on the style worn by the actress Jennifer Aniston in the television series *Friends*, which exemplified youthful
lifestyles.[22] The Y-shaped motif was delicate, like newly branching and budding
trees, suggesting new life.

Casual elements of dress were combined with athletic or dressier components. Fashion models wore white V-neck T-shirt underwear under their suit jackets. Cargo pants were narrowed, with understated zippered pockets; and jean suits came with long jackets.[23] By 1999 trendy attire cut across geographic and economic boundaries, becoming a most profitable category of clothing tie-symbols.

Trendy attire drew upon "high-technology fibers" (used in high-technology firms and produced with high technology) or "super fibers"—fibers that combined high performance with the ability to wick moisture away from the body.[24] It also drew on style. The jeans that were selling had "a personality attached to them," observed Bud Konheim, owner of Nicole Miller fashion firm.[25]

### "Mock Hippie" and Rave Styles

In 1996 a mock hippie style emerged that was reminiscent of the hippie style of American youth rebels in the 1960s and the 1970s. Associated with the rock group the Grateful Dead, the hippie style of thirty to forty years ago had been sloppy and laid back. It included tie-dyed T-shirts. The mock hippie look associated with the band Phish included baggy pants with a big shirt or sweater, woolly socks, and rugged, comfortable Birkenstock sandals that suggested nature and the out-of-doors.[26]

Ravers, those who participate in rave dances, wore jeans made huge by sewing fabric inserts into the pants legs, a T-shirt with a message logo, and running shoes. The rave style of dancing was faster and more energetic than the laid-back hippie style.

Trendy attire through the year 2000 included thigh-length slip dresses, skirts made in delicate, gossamer fabric, fitted shirts, body-hugging T-shirts, midriff and halter tops, and halter tops tied with strings that exposed the back. They were worn with bell-bottoms or capri-length pants, some of which were embroidered or ornamented with fringes, glass mirrors, and beads. The prevailing image was that of immaturity. The embroidery, fringes, and beads were delicate and alluded to the youthfulness of the wearer.

### "Urban Outfitters"

The urban, cutting edge style could be bought in specialized stores called "Urban Outfitters." The style also encourages its wearers to create their own outfits in their own particular way. Many who adopted the style preferred huge or baggy pants, a body-hugging shirt, a long skirt with a short skirt over it, and other skirt/pant combinations. These were sometimes worn in matching colors. The style included also worn-looking vests in distressed leather or suede, hiking or work boots, and one, two, or three bags suspended around the waist by straps and buckled in the front. Hair extensions were transformed into Rastafarian-style dreadlocks.[27] Scarves were worn on the head and dreadlocks might be wrapped in fabric.

A line of nail polish by a company called Urban Decay offered murky colors that contrasted with the traditional cheerful pinks and passionate reds. The range of colors offered was cloudy and included dark brown, muddy green, and murky blue.[28]

### Hip-Hop and Rap Styles

Unlike the hippies, who like their clothes with a well-worn look, hip-hoppers preferred them fresh off the shelf.[29] In the 1990s hip-hop culture, music, and dress became a platform from which African-Americans countered the pain of discrimination and the sense of being under suspicion, ignored, and invisible. A song lyric expressed the mood: you "Don't see us/but we see you."[30] Rap performers initially wore clothes that spoke of an American identity. Hip-hop dress featured large blocks of red, white, and blue and Tommy Hilfiger's logo.[31]

In the early 1990s hip-hop style consisted of a baseball cap sometimes turned backwards, pants five sizes too big, and a swagger that violated the middle class's norm of self-restraint. Teen-age girls and young women wore baggy clothing, chunky gold hoop earrings, and name plates on chains around their necks. The oversize style of dress together with the massive jewelry conveyed the pride and hope of black, urban ghetto teens and young adults. The style was empowering and helped overcome the sense of invisibility.[32]

The term *hip-hop* refers to music used in backing rap. The music is often familiar because it is composed of a collage of excerpts, or samples, of other songs. Rap is a form of rhythmic speaking in rhyme which is repeated again and again. Rap songs deliver a message that is streetwise and reality-oriented. The lyrics encourage listening, evaluating, and reflecting on how one feels or what one thinks. As a listener noted, "You listen and you say, yeah that's right."[33]

Gangsta rap of the early 1990s focused on crime as the means of wealth production. It also emphasized the paranoia, betrayal, revenge, and bloodshed of ghetto life.[34] The gangsta rap style of dress suggested that it could hide guns, knives, and other weapons. Cutting across ethnic and class lines, the hip-hop style was most popular among urban blacks and rich New Canaan, Connecticut, whites, as well as on the dirt-poor Indian reservations of Arizona.[35]

After 1995 player style rap prevailed. It celebrated the player's economic success and reveled in the consumption of luxury goods.[36] Rapper-owned or rapper-associated clothing lines emerged, including FUBU, Mecca, P.N.B. Nation, Sean John,

*Hip-hop jewelry. (Photo: Diane Cohen.)*

*Da Brat and Jermin Dupri at the 1999 Hip Hop award ceremonies. (The Everett Collection.)*

Ecko, and Phat Farm. Their bold colors, oversized jackets and shirts, and baggy pants replaced the styles designed by Tommy Hilfiger. Moreover, they are made in children's sizes and sold in boutiques.[37] The African-American community's reliance on the designer's clothing had declined. Embellishing the hip-hop style was a haircut called "the skin fades," in which a razor and electric clippers were used to trim the hair into intricate designs, creating a rich aesthetic expression.

For an interview before his October 23, 1999, appearance on "Saturday Night Live," Dr. Dre, a rapper and producer who had sold more than 20 million albums, wore an oversized Fubu jersey when he told the reporter, "I'm a winner, man, I'm a leader, an underdog no more."[38]

One of the most popular rappers in the country in 1997 was Wu-Tan-Clan. His music videos and CDs included advertisements for his own line of clothing, which he wore on the show. "Wu Wear" consisted of very baggy black jeans "with the waistline creeping toward the knees," a black baseball cap fitting snugly on the head, and hiking boots, heavy gold chains, crosses, and diamond-encrusted rings. The fans were loyal to the artist, his music, and his clothing.[39]

On April 10, 2000, the *Wall Street Journal* reported that the Tommy Hilfiger Corporation, which had been struggling with disappointing sales of its core men's wear, offered a pessimistic outlook for the current fiscal year.[40]

Brands and logos have been important to American commerce and industry since the early twentieth century. The goal of a brand name or logo is to create an emotional affinity between the product and the consumer. "A brand is a sacred promise of what you (the manufacturer) stand for," observed marketing specialist Douglas Martin.[41] Wu-Wear was more than a brand name. Through his music and clothing, his fans were able to experience the person, and through his dress and ornament, his economic success. His fans' dreams, aspirations, and hopes of achievement seemed "attainable."

Among urban, black, lower-class youth, hip-hop culture had first emerged as a desired identity in the mid-1970s. It implied freedom. The first hip-hop hit, "Rapper's Delight," by the Sugar Hill Gang, came out in 1979. Rap in the early 1980s had been treated like a fad, from which people could bail out if it flopped.[42] Performers like BDP, Eric B. and Rakim, Queen Latifa, and others expanded the genre. They challenged censorship and confronted issues like police brutality, engaging audience emotions.[43]

By the end of the 1990s, a whole generation of young people twenty-five and under—black, white, Latino, and Asian—had grown up with the sound and style of hip-hop. In 1999 more than 70 percent of hip-hop albums were purchased by whites.[44] Strong sales encouraged mainstream department stores—Macy's, for example—to provide space for hip-hop clothes and then increase what it allocated.[45]

### Gothic

The term *Gothic* refers to the style of architecture and art developed in the royal lands of medieval France, including Paris and its surroundings, from about 1150. The early Gothic churches were almost all urban cathedrals characteristically dedicated to the Virgin Mary.

The gothic subculture in the United States had its roots in the music of a splinter of the punk movement, just as punk music was "breathing its last breath."[46] The bands were dressed in black, and their music was gloomy. New-generation gothic bands emerged in the late 1980s and early 1990s and with it an interest in the supernatural and in dark aesthetics. A dark leaning seemed to become prevalent toward the end of the twentieth century, and as the 1990s progressed the aesthetic continued to evolve.[47]

In 1993 books on horror, science fiction, and fantasy were published or repackaged by the Clarkson White Wolf Publishing Company. The company marketed role-playing games in which a player created a character by developing a name for it and choosing its attributes, its mood, its feelings, and its "fashion."[48] "So much stuff is fed to youth these days about how bad things are that people need to have an escape—a little time for their imagination," observed Paul LePree, the company's retail liaison.[49] He added that games that involved dress-up made it possible to escape to the fantasy world.[50] Members of the subculture claimed that the more artistic and more individualistic people of their generation were interested in dressing up and in playing games.[51] Spelling Entertainment produced a television series based on a game, "Vampire: The Masquerade," for the Fox Network. Though it lasted only one season, it amassed a loyal core of followers.[52]

For young adults in 1998 and 1999 the gothic social scene involved going to clubs and living a lifestyle based on gloomy music, black clothes, hair dyed in outrageous colors, black eyeliner, pale skin, and black lipstick and nail polish, as well as literature and art depicting vampires and witches.[53] A "visigoth" was someone, male or female, who merely dressed up in the costume.

The costume usually consisted of an opera cape or a long and flowing dress made of velvet or lace, in black, purple, or another dark color. Bare legs were usually covered by fishnet or nylon stockings worn with boots or high heels. All jewelry was expected to be in silver and included Christian crosses, the Egyptian symbol of everlasting life, the *ankh*, the eye of *Ra*, and the pagan pentagram representing fire, earth, air, water, and the spirit. Chokers where popular, including dog collars with spikes, bondage collars, and velvet ribbons worn around the neck.[54] Most recently the Warner Brothers television network continued the interest in witches and vampires with a prime-time TV series, "Buffy the Vampire Slayer," directed at teenagers and young adults.[55]

### Body Piercing and Tattooing

Body-piercing and tattooing as a social expression emerged early in the 1990s. As the decade progressed, male and female suburban teenagers pierced their tongues, eyebrows, and lips. Professing a desire to return to a time when no rules governed social behavior,[56] they tattooed, pierced, and scarred their bodies and called themselves the "new primitives."[57]

Parents and the public at large were alarmed. The sight of rings along the eyebrows, on the lips, at the tip of the nose, and at the center of the tongue was unnatural and distressing. It was clear that acquiring this type of ornament entails pain. *New York Times* columnist Bob Herbert commented that American essayist Ralph Waldo Emerson was perhaps right when he suggested that there are some people for whom pleasure is not rewarding and who crave pain.[58]

Fashion models in the late 1990s were photographed on the runway with pierced navels and tattoos. By wearing these elements of street fashion, they acted to legitimate the style and to ease parental concerns somewhat. The significance of piercing in American adolescence lessened, however, as jobs were available. Pursuing work opportunities usually required that such ornaments be discarded.

In the course of Western history tattoos have been a means of connecting one-self to a person, idea, or belief.[59] To achieve a feeling of connectedness, images of crosses, anchors, hearts, thorns, eagles, dragons, and swords were etched onto the flesh of convicts, sailors, soldiers, gang members, and members of secret societies.[60] There are tattoos that tell of love and there are tattoos that identify a bond of shared experience.

Goffman noted that the wearing of tattoo tie-symbols can help an individual overcome a sense of alienation by expressing his life experience and solidarity with others.[61] A sailor's tattoo, for example, has marked him as distinct from the "land society," as part of a social base. It showed that he was not alone, that his behavior was not idiosyncratic or deviant, and that he operated within a safety zone of a group of peers.

In some nonliterate societies, at puberty, adolescents choose to go through the body-modification of tattooing, inflicting pain upon themselves. Their purpose, anthropologists suggest, is to experience the pain and suffering they are going to endure as adults.[62]

The association of self-inflicted pain with a personal rite of passage is reflected in comments from a recent student exam paper at the Fashion Institute of Technology: "Some kids, when they graduate from high school, are petrified about going to college. I did two outrageous things the summer after graduation. I shaved my head and pierced my tongue.

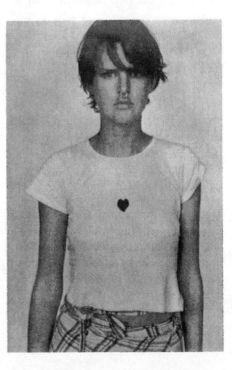

*Stella Tennant, the granddaughter of the Duke and Duchess of Devonshire, in a T-shirt designed by Jean Paul Gaultier, 1994. Photo: Paolo Roversi. From Holly Brubach (1999),* A Dedicated Follower of Fashion *(London: Phaidon Press).*

*A trendy Barbie with a tattooed navel, a knitted halter top, a short denim skirt, and long, flowing, curly hair (1998). (Photo: Diane Cohen.)*

"I had already pierced my ears with 13 holes. The day my father left I got three for the number of people left in the family. I figured, if I could stand the pain of piercing I could definitely survive college."

Pierced belly buttons and tattoos, mostly removable, became a fashion trend among adolescent and young women in the late 1990s. Pants were cut lower on the hips and T-shirts were cropped higher so that adorned navels could be admired. In 1998 Barbie portrayed the style.

Until the beginning of the year 2000, women's tattoos were mostly small and strategically placed to call attention to features of the female body. A study of tattoos worn by women in gyms and health clubs found that the popular designs were small crosses and motifs from nature such as butterflies, hummingbirds, ladybugs, and tiny flowers. Larger designs depicted a dragon, a winged fairy, a mythic horse, Celtic rings, and arm and ankle bracelets. Some women wore the tattoos as good-luck charms and to ward off evil; others in the hope of connecting to a traditional ethnic identity, or of being discovered by a soul mate.[63] Some women have begun wearing male-style tattoos covering the whole upper arm and back.

To escape being classified as "aging," some women of the baby boom generation—born sometime between 1947 and 1964—adopted attire worn by their daughters. Forty-year-old mothers, for example, also adopted a variation on the tattooing and piercing style, decorating the corners of their eyes and noses with real or plastic jewels. In New York City, movie stars have taken town cars to neighborhoods in the borough of Queens that are populated by immigrants from India in order to get their hands covered with inky henna designs suggestive of tattoos.[64]

In India and other places, women who use henna believe that it has the power to influence the events of the future. Women practicing henna paintings offer their design to the spirits, gods, or goddesses in an effort to appease them and win their favor.[65]

Attempts to understand the popularity of body piercing and tattoos in American society in the 1990s fall into two categories. One attributes the phenomenon to tension between public expectation for conformity and a personal desire for individualism. It is an attempt "to fix one's identity permanently as a social being while declaring complete autonomy from social demands."

A second hypothesis suggests that contemporary tattooing is a response to the perception that, in spite of material wealth, American culture has failed to meet basic and fundamental spiritual needs and that people don't feel connected.[66] Moreover, some scholars forecast that the new century will bring novel and more extreme forms of body ornament and that the final result could be an eclectic or ironic mix, perhaps a Pokémon/biker style.[67]

## Seeking Self-Definition

The term *reference group* was advanced by Herbert Hyman in 1942 when he described the phenomenon in which individuals who do not belong to a particular group (the reference group) use that group's ideas, beliefs, and values to guide their behavior.[68]

Since the 1940s adolescents in American society have adopted an appearance that they share in remarkable detail with their peers, one that is strikingly different from those of both adults and younger children.[69] Approval of peers also became paramount in junior and senior high school years, when attire came under close peer scrutiny. The growing child realized that he or she had several choices, and that choice could lead to acceptance or rejection by one's schoolmates. Concern with the questions "Who am I?" and "Who do I want to be?" led to periodic changes of style.

Grade-school children are concerned with fitting in and prefer wearing whatever is worn by other children in school. Dressing "like the herd" is the thrust, Elizabeth Hurlock (1949) pointed out.[70] In the past, children often rejected home-made clothing, usually made by immigrant or rural mothers, in favor of store-bought clothes. Today children resist even new clothing that is different from the clothes worn by their classmates. Convinced that wearing the clothes approved by their peers will win them acceptance, they explain that "Kids don't want to play with you unless you wear the same clothing they do." In the lower grades, attire chosen by the older students seemed to be the preferred style.

In the early 1990s, spiked hair and pierced ears were sources of parental anxiety. Trying to allay such feelings, Lawrence Kutner interviewed psychiatrists and developmental psychologists specializing in adolescence. The child development experts pointed out that "fashion statements" by adolescents were a normal part of the road to adulthood, and that most people adopt the ideals and beliefs of their families when they become adults. The experts recommended that parents allow their children "to make choices and mistakes in this area. Wardrobes can be changed and hair will grow back."[71]

*Spiked hair. (New York Times, Dec. 8, 1991.)*

*Baggy pants. Some high schoolers wear oversized, wide legged jeans that hang below the hips and sag in the back. (New York Times, Dec., 1991.)*

## Anticipatory Socialization

Starting high school marks a critical turning point in the lives of most youth in the United States. It often entails a dislocation from the past and feelings of loss. The sense of belonging and established feelings of familiarity are upset. High school students must step out of the life conditions they had earlier experienced, step away from their playmates and friendships and adjust to new classmates, classrooms, and schedules. Moreover, they must establish an identity. Reference group attire that is associated with a particular type of music often helps to solve the problem of connectedness. A T-shirt with a political message, brightly colored and spiked hair, and metal bracelets and chains are examples of tie-symbols that announce affinity with a particular set of ideas and beliefs. They enable the student to establish a recognizable identity, which facilitates social participation and interaction.

Music and dress offer growing adolescents a means of self-definition. One of the basic motivations of high school students for seeking a job is to buy clothes and music. Through these tie-symbols teenagers become aware of different values and orientations to social life, encouraging self-definition. These representations (clothes and music) may also help to link the young to the adult world, a form of anticipatory socialization. As presented in a 1989 exhibition (see note 74), six reference groups appear to have emerged in American high schools: preppies, jocks, hippies, greasers, freaks, and nerds. Each was identified by a well-defined style of food, level of expected higher education, occupation, leisure activity, and, of course, appearance.[72] Since 1995 two additional groups emerged: in-line skaters and wavers, referring to the high energy style of dance.[73]

## College Groups

The Yale School of Drama is "filled with suffering artists dressed in black," reported Alex Witchel in a 1991 article in the *New York Times Magazine*.[74] Entering college freshmen adopted a particular type of sneaker, jacket, or color in vogue in a particular school, thus affirming and maintaining their new association.

A 1982 study by Margaret Rucker and her colleagues at the University of California–Davis provided information on how the problem of self-definition was worked out in college. The researchers found that students in different majors tended to wear different styles. A long ethnic dress identified female students majoring in art; a suit (blouse, skirt, jacket) characterized textile and clothing students; jeans and plaid shirts were the choice of engineering and psychology majors, and overalls were worn by those studying animal science.[75] Students adopted the appropriate styles to show that they were connected to a particular social aggregate. They thus announced that they had a particular identity and a social base within the larger university population.

## Ethnic Identity

The meaning of dress and what is professional attire for minority women weighs particularly heavily in academia. "There is a special turn of the knife for racial and ethnic women," observes Nell Painter, a black historian at Princeton.[76]

"There are prejudices against people who look too Jewish, too working-class, too Italian, or too much of anything that is different. "[77] "Nothing they do is neutral. If you wear a pair of slacks and no kente cloth that makes a statement, and if you wear kente cloth that makes a statement."[78] Karla F.C. Hollawy, director of African and African American studies at Duke University, found that wearing ethnic prints and wrapping her hair in a braid, like her grandmother did, established boundaries that instituted distance like honorary titles, a distance that "intruders" are less likely to broach.[79]

Many young Afro-American women have used appearance to demonstrate their Afro-American identity: Afro hair styles in the 1960s and 1970s, and in the 1980s, the head wrap and clothing and head coverings made of the African kente cloth.

The head wrap originated in sub-Saharan Africa. When white overlords in colonial America enacted codes that required black women to cover their heads with cloth wrappings, it became an indicator of enslavement.[80] It was part of the slavery stereotype of the "black mommy," a slave nanny or maid. Slave women and their descendants came to regard the head wrap as a "helmet of courage." The head wrap evoked the homeland, and women wore it as a symbolic means of deflecting the experience of slavery.[81]

After the American Civil War, regular attendance at church by urban black women reaffirmed their sense of identity, and for such occasions they chose to wear a fashionable hat. In the rural South, however, many black women continued to wear the head wrap well into the twentieth century.[82]

Traditional African kente cloth, still worn today by Ghanaian chiefs, consists of brightly colored, strip-woven, and patterned fabric. It is worn in America as jackets, dresses, and skirts, and also as a crownlike African hat, the *kofi*.[83]

In his 1964 autobiography, Malcolm X criticized the movement among black youth in the 1950s to straighten and bleach their hair into a European-style hair.[84] In the 1960s and 1970s, politically active Afro-American youth rejected these styles as degrading and saw keeping their hair in its natural form as a sign of self-acceptance.[85]

## Emulating Sports and Entertainment Celebrities

By 1999 it has become increasingly common for marketers to focus on advertising to teenage and young adult consumers, in the hope of developing shopping habits that would become lifelong.[86] ABC joined this trend among advertisers in 2000, hoping to stimulate demand among young consumers for its four daytime soap operas. The programs had suffered a decline in viewership as millions of women went to work outside the home during the hours when daytime dramas were broadcast.

Earlier, "aspirational" ads, that is, ads intended to make consumers emulate the people endorsing the product, were still marketing buzzwords. Consequently, sports figures such as Michael Jordan of the Chicago Bulls basketball team increased their lengthy lists of product endorsements. "It's Official: Michael Jordan Is Now Promoting Gatorade," announced Stuart Elliott on August 9, 1991.[87] "Because he is respected everywhere as a leader in sports and proven performer," William D. Smithburg, chief executive of the manufacturer of the sports drink said in a statement, "Michael is perfect to represent Gatorade." The theme of the commercial was, "Be like Mike. Drink Gatorade."[88] Advertisers had found that teenagers respond to a hero image. It is a wished-for identity bound up with overcoming obstacles.

Becoming popular among men in the summer of 1992 was the bandanna handkerchief tied on the head in an urban gypsy style. It was folded into a triangle, pulled back over the skull, and knotted in back, Woody Hochswender reported in the *New York Times*.[89] He noted that John McEnroe wore a pink paisley bandanna for the U.S. Open and "was savagely chic." Photographer Bruce Weber was well known for the practice and did not use it just for hacking around in the garden: "He went hanky-on-top to Anna Wintour's [the editor of *Vogue*] little soiree at the Paramount Hotel last week," and this gave legitimacy to the look.

For teens of the 1980s the movie *Flashdance* and MTV were important sources of style. Referring to *Flashdance*, one said, "I remember going home and cutting up all my sweatshirts." Another noted, "My mom thought I was crazy, cutting up perfectly good shirts and turning them into rags." And another related, "The movie had a big impact on us kids who watched it. Even guys wore cut shirts and sweatshirts that bared their shoulders and belly buttons."[90] A ripped sweatshirt became the desired style.

With the start of MTV in 1981, music and fashion went hand in hand for teenagers. Madonna's style had a significant effect. Prior to 1983 and Madonna's impact, the oversized man-tailored shirt and tight jeans were part of the most visible trend for this age group. Only a few other trends were seen, such as short dresses, usually in black, worn by teens in the punk movement in the East Village in New York. Madonna's videos, *Borderline*, *Lucky Star*, and *Like a Virgin*, showcased her first "look": a short black dress, big cross-shaped earrings, silver and rubber bracelets, black crosses and many silver chains worn around the neck, and a bare midriff.[91] The short tube skirt, tank tops, cropped leggings, and fingerless glove became "required attire" among those aged 12–16. Fashion forecasters recommended these elements and this style for girls up to age 16.

After the movie *Desperately Seeking Susan* opened in 1985, Macy's New York sponsored a Madonna look-alike contest, "Desperately Seeking Madonna." Hundreds answered the contest call.

As one respondent described it: "I loved the way Madonna dressed—and dressed like her; lace outfits, spandex leggings, tight miniskirts, and tons of rubber bracelets."[92]

## Imitating a President's Wife

Copying the personal preferences of the president's wife in color and style of clothing seems to have a history in American society. It was a means of creating a sense of connectedness to the established social order and the first family.

Karal Ann Marling, a professor of American studies at the University of Minnesota, observed that Mamie Eisenhower's color of choice was pink, and she stubbornly insisted on keeping her "perky forelock."[93] Mrs. Eisenhower was fond of saying, "Ike runs the country, and I turn the pork chops."[94] She also said that "she had a career and his name was Ike."[95] The former first lady may have had an impact on American women in the 1950s that was greater than the color pink.

When President Theodore Roosevelt was in office (1901–1909), his daughter Alice was looked upon as "Princess Alice." Light blue was her favorite color, and it was soon copied throughout the country under the name "Alice Blue." A popular song of the time, "My Sweet Little Alice Blue Gown," reinforced the style.[96]

In 1921, when Mrs. Warren G. Harding came to the White House, the predominant color of her wardrobe was a darker shade of blue, and it became the newly desired color. When Mrs. Calvin Coolidge displayed a preference for red, there were few women around the country who did not possess a red garment of some sort.[97] Jackie Kennedy's fondness for bouffant hair and her adoption of the pillbox hat spread throughout the country.[98] Nancy Reagan's passion for red led to the acceptance of bright colors among the general population. It also caused White House correspondents to start donning red dresses or red ties as a way to catch Ronald Reagan's eye at news conferences.[99] The color took on a regal significance when Reagan staged formal news conferences at the end of a long, red-carpeted hall. Once the vivid emblem of the Russian Revolution, red became "Reagan red," a new and very different tie-symbol.[100]

## Expressing Political Values and Goals

Groups advocating, protesting, or rejecting a political agenda may signify their sentiments in their dress. In the United States such expressions vary. They may involve identifying the side one is on, taking a stand and dressing the part, and sometimes hiding one's identity.

The most familiar, popular, and least radical example of political attire is the slogan T-shirt, which appeared in the 1960s. Many artists were involved in producing such shirts, the best known being British designer Katharine Hamnett. She received so many orders for her T-shirts that she had to stop making them in 1987.[101]

Beginning about 1991, T-shirts were used as a means of environmental education and as a form of fund-raising for environmental and other causes. James Brooks reported in the *New York Times* that T-shirts are being sold to adults to raise funds for research on how to protect the sea turtles and were being given free to schoolchildren as a means of educating them about the endangered species.[102]

Benetton, an Italian-based company that produces and distributes colorful sportswear for men, women, and children, has been portraying itself as antiracist. The company's trademark, "The United Colors of Benetton," depicts people of all ages and different races holding hands to symbolize racial and multicultural harmony. Since its initial advertising campaign in 1983, racial equality and civil rights have been among the themes used, rather than pictures of clothing, to appeal to the consumer. Its ads, the company claims, are intended as a hymn to global understanding. They often carry more than one message. To promote AIDS awareness, for example, condoms in pastel colors and out of their wrappers are placed horizontally next to one another on a white background. In one sense, the multicolor emphasis suggests global unity; at the same time it champions social and sexual responsibility.[103]

### Revolutionary Tie-Symbols

Protestant reformers in the sixteenth and seventeenth centuries rejected the morality of the official Church and searched for a new connectedness to God. They refused to accept the Church's contention that to commune with God, elaborate ritual and sumptuous vestments were necessary. The name "Puritan" was first used in 1566 because this group of reformers sought to purify the English Church. Puritans campaigned against clerical attire, religious statues, stained-glass windows, and sacred music. These were seen as impediments to spirituality because, in the Puritans' view, a spiritual experience emanated only from a direct relationship with God. Self-direction and conscience, not unquestioning submission to those in authority, became the new determinant of behavior. Adopting dark and plain clothing made of wool or cotton was in keeping with their ideal of religious simplicity and directness.[104]

In eighteenth-century Paris, the term *sans culottes* referred to the attire worn by urban workers at the time of the French Revolution. Instead of the fitted breeches (culottes) worn by the aristocracy, the workers wore long trousers striped in red and blue. In addition, they wore white shirts, open at the neck; short, loose jackets; wooden shoes; and the red Phrygian cap, a symbol of revolution. The anti-aristocratic attire indicated their desire for complete social equality.[105]

Rejecting the Vietnam War and the draft, hippie appearance and clothing reflected their "revolution" against the traditional values of rationality, self-restraint, and goal-directed behavior. In contrast to the conformity of the "gray flannel suit" and the impeccable, modest mien required by the establishment, they looked disheveled and unkempt. Their hair was long, and jeans and work shirts became their "uniform." Young men often went shirtless and wore Indian headbands, amulets, shell necklaces, beads, and embroidered vests. See-through outfits flaunted sexuality.[106]

The hippies of the 1960s and 1970s demanded the right to full self-expression. In a study of hippie communities, "Generational Experience and the Development of Freak Culture"(1974), Weider and Zimmerman found that immediacy, spontaneity, and hedonism were favored, rather than sobriety and industry. Ownership of property was rejected by the hippies because it identified privilege; but they had no qualms about panhandling or receiving welfare.[107]

As a cohort (a group of people born during the same time period), this generational unit was critically aware of inequality and the mindless pursuit of affluence. Rejecting traditional concepts of career, education, and morality, they produced a culture in opposition to technocracy. They searched for alternatives to the received traditions of lifestyle and occupationally linked identity. Their disaffiliation took different forms. For some it was militant and political; for others it was mystical and religious.[108]

### Reactionary Tie-Symbols

The Ku Klux Klan is a white supremacist group whose members hide behind a white pointed hood, mask, and gown. This special costume is worn only at group gatherings. On such occasions it acts more as a tie-sign than as a symbol, since it is required attire with only one meaning. The Klan first appeared after the Civil War and sought a return to the racial caste system. White people in the South, particularly the middle class, were impoverished as a result of the war. Many of them were deprived of the right to vote because of their participation in the war against the Union. The Ku Klux Klan, with its strange rituals and ghostly costumes, provided a means of frightening the local black population into remaining servile. The activity of the Klan continued until it had accomplished its racist goal of empowering white people while reducing the black vote. By 1877 the original Klan had been officially disbanded.[109]

The twentieth-century Klan was formed in 1915 by William Joseph Simmons at Stone Mountain, near Atlanta, Georgia. Klan activities were now directed also against Roman Catholics, Jews, and the foreign-born as well as blacks. This Klan claimed to protect the racial "purity" and moral values of the native-born, white, Anglo-Saxon Americans and claimed a superior morality and dedication to religious fundamentalism. The Klan was not strictly regional in its appeal, and its influence spread to other parts of the country such as Colorado, Indiana, New Jersey, Oklahoma, and Oregon. Its tactics for inculcating fear and intimidation included whipping, tarring and feathering, branding, mutilation, and lynching.

The Klan reached the height of its power in the early 1920s when it probably had between 4 million and 6 million members. As a political force the Klan was effective and prompted the election of many officials on the local level. In 1924 the Klan was powerful enough to help split the Democratic presidential convention; but after that its influence began to wane.

*Worn to frighten blacks and avoid personal responsibility, Ku Klux Klan attire is a reactionary clothing tie-symbol.*

*In 1998 members of the Ku Klux Klan were allowed to march in New York City only if their faces were uncovered. The turnout was very small.*
*(Photo: Diane Cohen.)*

The Klan was revived again in Georgia after World War II. Similar white supremacist organizations arose in the South to counteract the spreading movement for greater civil rights for African-Americans. As an aftermath of the Supreme Court decision on school desegregation in 1954 and the Civil Rights Act of 1964, many bombings and murders were attributed to the Klan in the 1960s and 1970s.[110]

Similar angry feelings fuel the hatred that the Skinheads of today feel toward African-Americans and other minorities. Beatings, stabbing, and killings in defense of "white power" have occurred in cities as diverse as Portland, Oregon; Denver, Colorado; and New York City. Skinhead attire is their everyday dress and not limited to special occasions. There is also more variety than in the Klan costume. Their heads are almost completely shaved and they wear caricatures of working-class attire: old-fashioned shirts, braces with shrunken trousers, and heavy oversized shoes or military jackboots.

To summarize, when an individual *chooses* to dress like a person or a group that reflects his or her own sentiments, such attire is a tie-symbol, and wearing it reflects a temporary identity. When, however, the tie-symbol reflects a set of ideas, involves a lifestyle, and is worn by an age cohort, it acquires a more permanent identity. The tie-dyed T-shirt of the Grateful Dead is an example of such a tie-symbol.

## Notes

1. A. de Tocqueville (1945), *Democracy in America* (New York: Knopf). Originally published in 1832.

2. S. C. Ryan (2000), "Like Daughter like Mother," *San Francisco Chronicle*, Jan. 4. The article initially appeared in the *Boston Globe*.

3. A. Schiro (1999), "By Design," *New York Times*, Jan. 19.

4. The expression "cool" came out the jazz club scene of the 1930s. Coolness implies a deliberately slow and lackadaisical form of bodily locomotion. M. Danesi (1994), *Cool: The Signs and Meanings of Adolescence* (Toronto: University of Toronto Press).

5. Interviews with students at the Fashion Institute of Technology in New York City.

6. *New York Times*, Mar. 1, 1993.

7. *New York Times*, Feb. 10, 1991.

8. *New York Times*, Dec. 8, 1991.

9. T. H. Watkins (1999), "The Boom Generation," *New York Times*, Oct. 8.

10. The mother of the bride is an example of such an attitude. The mother of the bride traditionally wore a pale tunic and skirt or a decorous dress in beige and sequins. Women in their sixties are choosing dresses that are "body-skimming"—tasteful but sexy. Most modern mothers want to feel young. Ruth La Ferla (2000), "Here Comes the Bride," *New York Times*, May 2.

11. N. Black (1999), "Yes, I'm in a Clique," *New York Times*, Apr. 29.

12. Reported by F.I.T. students.

13. L. Kaufman (1999), "President of Gap Resigns, but Stays on the Board," *New York Times*, Oct. 28.

14. Ibid.

15. Statement by stock analyst J. D. Morris, in Kaufman, op. cit., p. 19.

16. Ibid.

17. Ibid.

18. Ibid.

19. Ibid.

20. A. Goodnough (1997), "Guess Who? Preppies, Jocks, Hippies, Skaters, Freaks. You're a Teenager. Your Clothes Tell a Story," *New York Times*, New Jersey ed., Sept. 7.

21. Ryan (2000), op. cit.

22. *Wall Street Journal*, July 17, 1998.

23. S. Mitchell (1999), *Generation X: The Young Adult Market* (Ithaca, N.Y.: New Strategist Publications), p. 4.

24. T. Hongu and G. O. Philips (1990), *New Fibers* (New York: Ellis Horwood), pp. 3–6.

25. "The View from Outside: Levi's Needs More Than a Patch," *New York Times*, Feb. 28, 1999.

26. W. Hochswender (1996), "About Rich-Hippie Look," *Bazaar*, Mar.

27. Ibid.

28. W. Hochswender (1998), "Nail Polish Is Another Subject I Find Myself Returning to Again and Again," *Bazaar*, Mar.

29. Goodnough, op. cit.

30. C. J. Farley (1999), "Hip-Hop Nation," *Time*, Feb. 8, pp. 55–58.

31. L. Goldstein (1999), "First: The Fashion Industrial Complex: Tommy Sings America," *Fortune*, Sept. 6.

32. Farley, op. cit., pp. 56–57.

33. Farley, op. cit., p. 56.

34. S. Reynolds (1999), "It Isn't Easy Being Superman," *New York Times*, Oct. 5.

35. P. Zollo (1999), *Wise Up to Teens* (Ithaca, N.Y.: New Strategist Publications), p. 71.

36. Reynolds, op. cit.

37. R. Pallazolo (2000), "L.A. Story Fred Segal Has His Pulse on What Kids Want. Step into This High-Fashion Trendsetting Department Store," *Earnshaw's*, Mar., pp. 73–74.

38. J. Pereles (1999), "The Street Talk, He Says, Is a Bum Rap," *New York Times*, Nov. 14.

39. Ibid.

40. T. Agins (2000), "Not So Haute: Hilfiger Shares Plunge on Lackluster Forecast for Fiscal Year," *Wall Street Journal*, p. B21.

41. D. Martin (2000), "What's in the Name: The Allure of Labels," *New York Times*, Jan. 9.

42. Chuck D., Public Enemy (1999), "The Sound of Our Young World," *Time*, Feb. 8, p. 66.

43. Ibid.

44. Farley, op. cit., pp. 55–58.

45. S. R. King (1999), "Where Does Generation Y Go to Shop? 70 Million Young Buyers Without a Thing to Wear," *New York Times*, Aug. 28.

46. A. Porter (1994), "Origins of Gothic," *Alternative Press*, Nov.

47. Ibid.

48. N. W. Cook (1996), *Atlanta Journal and Constitution*, Nov. 14.

49. D. Plummer (1996), *Atlanta Journal and Constitution*, Dec. 4.

50. The games, called "chronicles" of vampire life, were played in many U.S. and European cities.

51. Student interviews collected and written in 1999 by Fashion Institute of Technology graduate Barbara Cannon.

52. Ibid.

53. Interviews by the author and term papers written by students at the Fashion Institute of Technology.

54. Porter, op. cit.

55. S. Elliott (2000), "ABC Goes in Search of Younger Audience for Its Soap Operas," *New York Times*, May 19.

56. Vale, V., and A. Juno, eds. (1989), *Modern Primitives: An Investigation of Contemporary Adornment and Ritual* (San Francisco: Re/Search Publications).

57. D. Johanson (1995), "Problems of Piercing," *New York Times Magazine*, Apr. 23.

58. B. Herbert (1997), "Maybe This Time," *New York Times*, Aug. 31.

59. D. Terry (1996), "Getting Rid of Badges That Seem like Targets," *New York Times*, Feb. 26.

60. J. Caplan, ed. (1999), *Written on the Body: The Tattoo in American and European History* (Princeton, N.J.: Princeton University Press).

61. E. Goffman (1963b), *Stigma: Notes on the Management of Spoiled Identity* (Englewood Cliffs, N.J.: Prentice-Hall).

62. B. Bettleheim (1954), *Symbolic Wounds* (New York: Free Press).

63. The author conducted a three-year study of female members of a health club in mid-town Manhattan. Women wearing tattoos were identified in the locker room and were later interviewed.

64. J. Steinhauer (2000), *New York Times*, Jan. 1.

65. L. Roome (1998), "What Is Mehndi?" In *Designs for the Hands: The Timeless Art of Henna Painting* (New York: St. Martins).

66. D. Wojicik, quoted in Steinhauer, op. cit.

67. D. Wojicik, quoted in Steinhauer, op. cit.

68. H. H. Hyman (1942), "The Psychology of Status," *Archives of Psychology* 269. See also T. Sibutani, "Reference Groups As Perspectives," *American Journal of Sociology* 60 (May 1955): 562.

69. M. L. Rosencranz (1972), *Clothing Concept: A Social-Psychological Approach* (New York: Macmillan), pp. 104–105.

70. E. Hurlock (1949), *Adolescent Development* (New York: McGraw-Hill), p. 15.

71. *New York Times*, July 30, 1992.

72. R. Martin and H. Koda (1989), *Jocks and Nerds: Men Styles in the Twentieth Century* (New York: Rizzoli).

73. Goodnough, op. cit.

74. *New York Times Magazine*, Nov. 10, 1991.

75. See S. B. Kaiser (1985), *The Social Psychology of Clothing* (New York: Macmillan), pp. 239–240.

76. A. Schneider (1998), "Frumpy or Chic? Tweed or Kente? Sometimes Clothes Make the Professor," in M. L. Damhorst, K. A. Miller, and S. O. Michelman (1999), *The Meanings of Dress* (New York: Fairchild Publications), pp. 251–254.

77. Ibid., p. 254.

78. Ibid.

79. Ibid., p. 254.

80. H. B. Griebel (1995), "The African American Woman's Headwrap: Unwinding the Symbols," in *Dress and Identity,* ed. M. E. Roach-Higgins, J. B. Eicher, and K. K. P. Johnson (New York: Fairchild Publications), pp. 448–449.

81. Griebel, op. cit., p. 222.

82. Griebel, op. cit., p. 224.

83. H. B. Griebel (1994), "New Raiments of Self: African American Clothing in the Antebellum South," Ph.D. diss., University of Pennsylvania.

84. Malcolm X (1965), *Autobiography* (New York: Ballantine).

85. The 1973 *Ebony Pictorial History of Black America* (Chicago: Johnson Publishing) depicts the following singers and actors wearing an Afro: Melba Moore, Clarence Williams III, Judy Pace, Don Mitchel, Roberta Flack, Michael Jackson, and the Staple Singers.

86. Elliott, op. cit.

87. "It's Official: Michael Jordan Is Now Promoting Gatorade," *New York Times,* Aug. 9, 1991.

88. Ibid.

89. *New York Times,* Sept. 11, 1990.

90. Student papers, 1993–1994, Fashion Institute of Technology, New York.

91. *Toby Reports,* Spring 1985, p. 88; G. Dullea, "Madonna's New Beat Is a Hit, But Song's Message Rankles," *New York Times,* Sept. 18, 1986.

92. The Madonna look-alike contest took place in May 1985 (store communication).

93. A *New York Times* report of a seminar in Gettysburg, Pa. on Nov. 8–9 sponsored by Gettysburg College and timed to coincide with the 100th anniversary of Mrs. Eisenhower's birth on Nov. 14. The article that followed was called "Mamie As More Than a 1950s Woman," *New York Times,* Nov. 17, 1996.

94. Ibid.

95. Ibid.

96. E. B. Hurlock (1965), "The Arbiters of Fashion," in *Dress Adornment and the Social Order,* ed. M. E. Roach and J. B. Eicher (New York: John Wiley and Sons), p. 354.

97. Ibid., p. 355.

98. *Women's Wear Daily,* 1969, pp. 4–5; Rosencranz, op. cit. p. 224.

99. *Newsweek,* Feb. 1, 1982, p. 59; "Nancy Reagan's Preference for Red," *Harper's Bazaar,* Feb., 1984, p. 164.

100. *New York Times,* Dec. 8, 1991.

101. P. Mathur, "Katharine Hamnett, An Interview," *Blitz* (London).

102. *New York Times,* Dec. 17, 1991.

103. "Benetton's True Colors," *Ad Week,* Aug. 24, 1992, pp. 27–30; "Corporate Profile: Benetton Colorful and Color Blind," *PR,* Sept. 1991, pp. 35–36; G. Schafer, "Benetton's United Front for Casual, Colorful Fashion," *California Apparel News,* June 14, 1985, pp. 30–31.

104. R. H. Bainton (1952), *The Reformation of the Sixteenth Century* (Boston: Beacon Press); M. Mann (1986), *The Social Sources of Power,* vol. 1 (Cambridge, Eng.: Cambridge University Press), pp. 463–472.

105. B. Payne, G. Weinakor, and J. Farrell-Beck (1992), *The History of Costume: From Ancient Mesopotamia Through the Twentieth Century* (New York: HarperCollins), p. 438; see also M. and A. Batterberry (1977), *Fashion: The Mirror of History* (New York: Greenwich House), pp. 194–197.

106. M. J. Horn and L. M. Gurel (1981), *The Second Skin: An Interdisciplinary Study of Clothing*, 3d ed. (Boston: Houghton Mifflin), p. 196.

107. D. L. Weider and D. H. Zimmerman (1974), "Generational Experience and the Development of Freak Culture," *Journal of Social Issues* 30 (2): 137–161.

108. M. Brake (1985), *Comparative Youth Culture* (New York: Routledge), p. 91.

109. D. M. Chalmers (1985), *Hooded Americanism: The First Century of the Ku Klux Klan 1865–1965* (Garden City, N.Y.: Doubleday).

110. Ibid., p. 194.

# 17

# The Presidency and Contemporary Fashion

THE DEVELOPMENT OF the fashion process, the periodic change in desired appearance, emerged in Western society whenever economic and political forces made social mobility possible, observed sociologist Georg Simmel (1957).[1] Where there was no opportunity for social mobility, styles of dress were fixed, and the sumptuousness of one's appearance identified one's place in the social hierarchy.

Beginning in the court of Burgundy in the 1400s, the ideas and preferences of royalty and others in authority were conveyed in the fashionable image.[2] Fashionable attire is a cultural construct, a story that emerges from the interplay between political and economic forces. Fashionable attire provides "a sub-rational but instant and very brilliant illumination" of a particular period, observed author Tom Wolfe.[3] Fashion is the expression of what in German is called the Zeitgeist, the spirit of the period.[4]

Prior to the nineteenth century, the desired style of appearance, the fashion, was determined by those in authority and was often designed with a particular *political* message. Francis I of France used his jewels not merely to demonstrate his wealth but to create a beautiful image. He was the first to realize that coordinating the color and texture of the attire of the members of the court would create a mass that was overwhelming in its magnificence and would assert preeminence.[5] He insisted that the style of dress adopted by his wife and the other women of the court complement that of the men.

In his quest for supremacy, Louis XIV dressed in gold. The goal of Jean-Baptiste Colbert, one of the most important of Louis XIV's ministers, was that France would dominate the luxury textile and ornament trade and that fashion should be for France what the gold mines of Peru were to Spain. For this goal to be achieved, France had to establish itself as the arbiter of European fashion.[6]

The Baroque style was characterized by exuberant decorative richness and was first introduced by the Counter-Reformation movement in the sixteenth century. It was reintroduced nearly a century later into Louis XIV's court, creating what fashion historians consider the most magnificent court in the history of the West-

The New York Times *included this photograph in an early article on the grunge look. (New York Times, Nov. 15, 1992; reprinted by permission of Kim Garnick/NYT Pictures.)*

*Interpreting the grunge look into fashion: white shirt hanging below a cropped black vest, loosely knotted tie, and unbuttoned shirt sleeves. Designed by Joan & David. (Women's Wear Daily, Aug. 18, 1993; photo by George Chinsee; reprinted by permission of Fairchild Syndication.)*

ern world. To demonstrate his dominance, Louis XIV's attire was emblazoned with gold fleurs-de-lis and completely lined in ermine. France began to export costly and prestigious items that included tapestries, silk brocades, lace, ribbons, wigs, and feather accessories to the rest of Europe.[7] It is reputed that Louis XIV had his subjects melt down furniture that was made of precious metals "in order to keep his ladies adorned." He insisted upon appropriately sumptuous dress for all who participated in the ritual of court life. François de La Rochefoucauld, a seventeenth-century French writer, observed that during that period clothes became a "national fixation." In his writings he commented: "In all professions one affects a particular look and exterior in order to appear what he wishes to be thought . . . so it may be said that the world is made out of appearances."[8] Physical imperfection was unacceptable to a ruler whose reign was based on divine right, and fashions often developed as a result of a monarch's effort to conceal physical flaws. When Louis XIII of France became bald at the age of twenty-three, for example, he adopted a curly wig to hide the imperfection and mitigate his

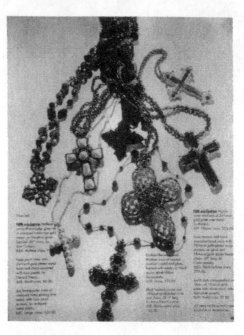

*Crosses become a fashion accessory.*
*(Advertisement by Neiman Marcus,*
*Sept. 5, 1993; reprinted by permission*
*of NYT pictures.)*

feelings of inferiority.[9] As a result, wigs became an important element of male fashion in France, England, and even the Puritan colony of Massachusetts.[10]

In twentieth-century America, the dictates of Paris were not always obeyed.[11] For a style of dress to become fashionable, it had to appeal in some way to a large number of people. Fashion in the United States had become a cultural expression that required popular support. The theme, character, and meaning of fashion could also reflect the feelings of different groups in society.

In the early 1990s, for example, the "grunge" fashion had its roots in the despondent music of the band Nirvana, as well as in the attire worn by the band's teenage audience on the streets of Seattle. Tattered garments, flimsy floral print dresses in a 1930s style, ripped jeans, and untucked flannel shirts were worn with heavy boots. The style was thrift-shop-inspired and spoke of dressing in what was on hand, suggesting poverty.[12] Youth who were pessimistic about the future were responsible for the style, according to Tom Julian, fashion director of the Men's Fashion Association.[13] The perception that no significant economic recovery was at hand in the early 1990s may explain why the teenagers' style became fashion. The high-priced version of the grunge style consisted of a layered, unkempt look. It included shirts with unbuttoned sleeves, transparent or see-through flimsy fabrics, and clunky shoes or boots. Designer Marc Jacobs sent beautiful models down the runway in grunge attire appearing as if they had not slept or washed their hair for a week.

The fashion also included jewelry and accessories that called forth the intervention and protection of supernatural powers. These included Christian crosses, Judaic Stars of David, pendants of mystical, spiritual origin, such as Egyptian ankhs, New Age angels, traditional beads, Ethiopian tribal talismans, and Chinese good-luck shields.[14] The crochet-and-lace sleeveless coats, vests, sweaters, and skirts went back to the Edwardian era. It was as if the sense of malaise that grunge fashion reflected was ameliorated through the use of superhuman and human sources of support that were both popular and traditional.

Besides power, wealth, and mood, fashions vary by the period of life being idealized. Empire fashion popular after the French Revolution and in the first decades of the nineteenth century idealized youthfulness. It consisted of a short-sleeved white muslin dress with a high waistline. The belt separated the breasts from the rest of the torso, accentuating the lines of the body as a whole.[15] As the middle class acquired wealth after the mid–nineteenth century, maturity was idealized, and the fuller figure became fashionable. The total bulk of the female body was increased by a fashion that depended on crinoline.[16]

Since the beginning of the twentieth century, simplicity of line, little ornament, and short skirts characterized the appearance of children, and these characteristics came to represent youthfulness.[17]

## The U.S. Presidency and Male Fashion

The U.S. presidency is an office of great power. The successful operation of the American constitutional system requires that this power be used. Presidents who did not use their power vigorously were condemned as weak, as Warren G. Harding (1921–1923) and Calvin Coolidge (1923–1929) were judged.[18] Probably more than the monarchs of the past, the president of the United States is a figure who draws together the people's hopes and fears for their future. A president is the human symbol of national unity, the only official who can speak for the United States and who has ready access to the media.[19]

A president's personal preferences in dress, like those of the monarchs of the past, were often emulated. In his memoirs, Russell Baker, a senior columnist for the *New York Times*, reported that Herbert Hoover's preference for a detachable collar made that style popular among men in the early 1930s.[20] In 1937, during Franklin D. Roosevelt's presidency (1933–1945), *Esquire* championed the "command look" for men. It consisted of a padded, fitted jacket with broad shoulders. Until then a loose-fitting jacket with natural shoulders was the preferred style. Roosevelt himself is described as "magisterial," having the look of a leader.[21]

John F. Kennedy's (1961–1963) preference for a two-button suit (because it better accommodated his back brace) became popular in the 1960s. His rejection of the hats—some say because he had a full head of hair and was proud of it—led to the demise of hats even for formal occasions.[22]

## The U.S. Presidency and Female Fashion

The impact of the American president on the female fashion ideal is more difficult to discern. Prior to World War II, most fashions for U.S. women originated in
Paris, the city usually viewed as the capital of fashion. The fashion industry in
Paris had behind it tradition, resources, and governmental support. In fact, to become known, to acquire an international reputation, a designer had to show his
or her collection there.

Paris fashion is an entrepreneurial enterprise designed to generate profit. Since
the 1970s, many of the top Paris designers have turned to clothing that is mass-
produced for the ready-to-wear market. The styles presented on runways were
conceived to demonstrate the talent and ability of the designer and to show that
he or she understands, moreover, what is going on in art and society. The *couture
shows* present what designers think is happening here and now; however, since
many of the consumers of the French ready-to-wear industry live in the United
States, Parisian designers have to be sensitive to American society, its culture, and
its changing values and moods.[23]

Another reason it is difficult to accept the notion that a U.S. president can have
an impact on female appearance is that female fashion is viewed as a frivolous
phenomenon. It seems preposterous that a male president could have an impact
on such an insignificant manifestation, especially one that affects the female gender. In addition, presidents vary in their effect on culture and society.

But the vision or agenda a president brings to the office, his desire and ability
to pursue it, and the degree of energy he expends in the office are the variables
that some political scientists believe are related to a president's impact on the nation. Thus, success at making policy and the degree of energy expended in office
may also be significant in appraising the impact of a presidency on fashion.[24] The
questions that emerge are, Is contemporary fashion related to the president's
*agenda*? And how does the president's level of *activity* affect fashion trends?

## The Reagan Presidency

Ronald Reagan's presidency (1981–1989) is considered strong but passive. He had
a definite agenda and was able to get it through. Hence, he has been judged as a
strong president. His political discourse centered on the state of the domestic
economy. His goal, he claimed, was to restrain the power of an increasingly intru-
sive government. Reagan established the priorities for his presidency and gave
substance to the ideas of the conservative branch of the Republican party. He set
the national priorities that conferred power and respectability on the modern
conservative movement.[25] At the same time, Ronald Reagan was less than active.[26] As virtually every report illustrates, he was the most inattentive and indifferent of presidents, largely following scripts that led him through his eight years

in the White House, as noted by Lou Cannon, a *Washington Post* reporter who covered Mr. Reagan's entire political career.[27]

The decade of the 1980s was characterized by a glorification of capitalism, free markets, and finance and by an ostentatious celebration of wealth. Political analyst Kevin P. Phillips observed that as the decade ended, there were too many stretch limousines in Manhattan, too many yachts off Newport Beach, and too many fur coats in Aspen.[28] He commented that it was the very wealthy, more than anyone else, who flourished under Reagan, and that greed and ostentation pervaded the culture.

Throughout her tenancy in the White House, Nancy Reagan's delight in clothes, balanced for color and ornament, extravagant and luxurious, was consistently reported in the news. It is thus suggested that through her use of clothing she offered visual support to her husband's political and personal agenda, helping to make up for his passivity in office.

In an interview before the Reagans left the White House, Mrs. Reagan remarked that, despite the "terrible press" she received over her fondness for designer gowns throughout her tenure in the White House, she hoped that history would remember her for her efforts to solve the drug problem.[29]

### The Public Wife

On November 17, 1987, the headline of a *New York Times* article by fashion reporter Bernadine Morris asked, "The Sexy Look: Why Now?" Fashion in the 1980s had become increasingly form-fitting, slinky, and slithering, accentuating female curves. It focused on what Flugel described as "the interplay of concealment and half transparencies." Exposed backs, low necklines, side and front slits, and the pouf were designed to create sexual allure. The attire was colorful and often made use of fabrics that shimmered or glittered. The display of wealth and sexiness characterized the fashion of the 1980s. It reflected President Reagan's vision of burgeoning economic success and women in traditional female roles. The notion of the "public wife" explains how the ideals of a passive president became visible, and the term *nouveau riche* helps to explain why pride in economic success was expressed in a sexually alluring and showy fashion.

The notion that a wife's attire supports her husband's policies and rank is rooted in the history and experience of Western society. Martin Luther had carried the idea further when he suggested that the wife of a minister of the church is a public figure who must in dress and action be exemplary in dress and in action, since she represents her husband's ideas and values. To affirm his position, the conduct and attire of the public wife must convey his ideas and values.[30] Veblen called such attire *vicarious consumption*.[31] Today in the corporate world, the wife of a candidate for an executive position is often scrutinized before he is offered the job. She is an additional source of information about him.

A president's wife has a choice about whether she will become a public figure

*Nancy Reagan in a red dress that hugged her body and
delineated its contours, characteristics that ancient
Church authorities defined as seductive. The dress was
designed by Bill Blass.*

and how she will participate in public life. Whereas Nancy Reagan did play an active public role, Pat Nixon refused to do so. In 1972 the fashion industry sought Pat Nixon's support in introducing the midiskirt, a below-the-calf-length skirt. The industry hoped that the miniskirt fashion trend had run its course and that it was time for a change. When Pat Nixon publicly announced that neither she nor her daughters would adopt the new length, the midi died on the vine.

Because of her social distance, the passage of time, and the momentous events that took place during the Nixon presidency, it is difficult to determine exactly why Pat Nixon rejected the longer skirt. But not only did the midi lack political support; it also lacked popular support. For the consumer, the early 1970s was still a time of rebellion and youthful exuberance, which the miniskirt signified.

In 1987 a similar attempt by Seventh Avenue designers to introduce a different length skirt (short this time) was supported by Nancy Reagan, who appeared in public wearing an above-the-knee hemline. But the style was rejected by working women. In a report on the style page of the *New York Times* on July 17, 1987, Michael Gross stated that the short skirt called attention to the body and was therefore provocative and inappropriate for work. Women seeking to build a ca-

*Expressing the need for comfort and nurturing, pacifiers
made in bright colors in hard plastic became a fashion
accessory among teenagers during the Bush years.* (New
York Times, *Dec. 2, 1992;* Newsweek, *Dec. 28, 1992.*)

reer rejected the style, which led to weakness in sales. Two months later, in another *New York Times* story titled "Knees and Even More: Hems Are Up, Sort of," Georgia Dullea reported that women were holding fast to their hemlines, waiting to see whether the storm on Seventh Avenue would blow over. "It is nothing like the 60s, when the mini blew in on the hips of the young in a glut of sex and rebellion. For today's women it was one more calculation, as they sized up the 21-inch length versus the 19-inch." Their attitude, the reporter observed, was affecting the consumption of this fashion trend: "For the city's retailers, the reservations have translated into uneven sales." The failure of the short skirt, signifying youthfulness, to become fashion after being endorsed by Nancy Reagan suggests that a wife can only support her husband's vision; she cannot introduce her own.

### The Notion of Nouveau Riche

The term *nouveau riche* describes people of modest means who have acquired new wealth and use dress, ornament, and other material objects to show off their newly found success. In the United States between 1830 and 1860 and again after 1865, there were periods marked by a rapid urban and industrial growth. During those times, a person of "humble means was brought into contact with those of vast wealth, and a temptation to imitate the customs and to strive for the enjoyments of those who possess larger means rose," wrote Catherine Beecher. L. W. Banner reports that after the Civil War, at least 10 percent of New York's financial elite were individuals who had risen from poverty to riches. Members of the upper class, such as Charles Astor Bristed, Nathaniel Parker Willis, and Anna Cora Mowat, unmercifully criticized the newly rich for their coarse faces, loud voices,

and vulgar display of wealth.[32] Recent observations on the consumption of fashion among "old blood and old money" also support the contention that the
newly rich are more likely to engage in what Veblen called conspicuous consumption. Proud of their personal success, they are more likely to flaunt it.[33]

The Reagans were born to families of modest means. Hollywood was a place of
wealth and glamour. While they lived in Hollywood, Nancy Reagan sought to
capture the spotlight on formal occasions and wore glittering evening dresses
that she had borrowed. The female fashion ideal of the 1980s stemmed from a
newly rich family proud of its achievement and success, its *stardom.*

## The Bush Presidency

In his inaugural address, George Bush set himself apart from the Reagan presidency and its concern for display. His intention was "to celebrate the quieter
deeper successes that are not made of gold and silk."[34] Moreover, Bush came from
a social class characterized by sociologists as "old blood and old money," a class
that underplays the possession of wealth. These two personal factors alone suggested that a change in fashion would occur.

During his presidency (1989–1993) George Bush's principal sphere of interest
was foreign policy. He was described as having approached politics with a view of
the world that was more pragmatic than ideological. His domestic policy was described as being on a holding pattern. A cartoon by Jeff Danziger of the *Christian
Science Monitor* portrayed a planning session to reelect Bush in 1992. His ten ad-
visers are seated around a table searching for an appropriate slogan. They agree on
one: The nothing president,[35] in keeping with the observation that rather than
make law, the president used his veto power. "Two years into his first term, and
having vetoed 20 public bills, President Bush is emerging as a Veto President," observed Ruti Teitel, an associate professor of constitutional law. By contrast, in the
entire eight years of his office, Ronald Reagan vetoed sixty-five bills, twenty-nine in
his first term of office and thirty-six in his second.[36] In an editorial entitled "The
Energetic Naysayer," the *New York Times* editors supported her conclusions.[37]

Conservative Republicans have considered George Bush an inadequate heir to
Ronald Reagan. Only at times did he cater to their politics on issues like abortion
and, for a time, taxes, as *New York Times* reporter Andrew Rosenthal pointed out.
Rather than propelling their ideology, conservative leaders claim that Bush went
his own way.[38] Bush was thus perceived as having had no agenda, and his activities as having been unrelated to domestic economic needs. His presidency can be
considered weak and passive. Popular sentiments were, therefore, more likely
than political sentiments to determine fashion themes during his administration.

Although the glittery, body-hugging, sexy attire that characterized the Reagan
era continued into the Bush era, in 1989–1990 a new feminine fashion ideal came
into being: the short skirt. It was worn with a form-following jacket that covered
the hips. Also new were the loose-fitting lingerie dress and tights showing the legs

and worn with an oversized shirt. All three outfits exposed different parts of the body, but the breasts, waistline, and hips, the traditional means of anchoring women in society, were deemphasized.[39]

### The Meaning of the Image

If Halbwachs's notion of public memory is valid, fashion's meaning and significance must be found in the vocabulary of images available to a society. Power and powerlessness, authority and lack of authority, are some of the earliest constructs that inhabit public memory. In the *Palette of Narmer*, commemorating the unification of Egypt in 3300 BC, and in stelae celebrating victory in ancient Mesopotamia, those holding power and authority are more completely clothed and protected than those who are poor or vanquished. The female fashion during the Bush presidency, with its flattening of the breast, long stretches of revealed body, and easy access to the torso, conveyed *vulnerability*.

The validity of this interpretation can be supported by examining the accessories worn. They spoke of the desire for self-empowerment and self-protection. Jewelry consisted of crystals and richly colored stones; they were used on hair, belts, and pocketbooks. Earrings were long and jackets had fringes. Gloves and coats were full and in bold, natural colors—pigments that are a part of nature. In tribal societies an extra measure of energy is acquired by tapping into forces that power the universe. The accessories worn in the Bush years, together with their style and color, were those believed to capture the power of the universe, making the wearer feel less vulnerable.[40] The 1989–1990 fashion thus alluded to anxieties and fears and attempts to conquer them.

Behind the 1989–1990 styles lay a crisis in leadership. The national deficit and the savings and loan banking scandal were threatening the economy; the problems of homelessness, AIDS, and environmental pollution continued; and there was a growing feeling that the president might be unable to solve these problems.

### The Evolving Fashion Trend

If the interpretation given in the previous section is accurate, then a change in the perception of the president, as well as changes in political and economic conditions, should be reflected in the further evolution of the trend. With the Gulf War, the sense of powerlessness receded. By the end of January 1991 consumer confidence in the president's leadership was manifested in a surge of stock prices as well as in a newly desired style of dress. Raincoats that gleamed like sunshine in the rain suddenly appeared. Baby-doll dresses in floral prints and in pink, the color of innocence, graced the advertising pages. Rather than the empowerment offered by crystals and colored stones dug from the earth, jewelry consisted of flower buds, blossoms, and petals. It suggested the fragility of bloom, rebirth, and hope.

More important, perhaps, was the new fashion style: The waist was now cinched, the hips accentuated, and the breasts emphasized. Examples included a flaring skirt, a fitted jacket over a bell-shaped skirt, and the sleek, tight-fitting

*Chanel's rendition of the Doc Martens work shoe supports the idea that American street style influences high fashion. The boots reflect a desire for empowerment. (New York Times, Feb. 28, 1993.)*

rubberized scuba dress. The new femininity may have come as a counterpoint to the military uniforms traditionally worn by men.[41]

In the March 1991 fashion shows, themes of vulnerability, protection, and empowerment merged. Leggings were in color. The cat suit—a one-piece, body-hugging garment made of stretch fabric—delineated the body, making the person wearing it more susceptible to harm. In all ways imaginable the attire was further elaborated by adding fake jewels and swirled metal stitching. Body jewelry, heavy bracelets, macramé dresses and vests, jackets over rubberized leggings, and blasts of color all signified the emphasis on empowerment and protection.[42] In addition, ethnic group culture and the traditional home were important sources of style. In Paris, Oscar de la Renta showed plaids. In New York, Christian Francis Roth reproduced Amish quilt patterns, and Isaac Mizrahi evoked the American Indian culture with beaded leathers and fringe. The language of the Aztecs was represented in a multicolor patchwork coat by Christian Lacroix.

Baseball-style caps, bringing to mind a game associated with childhood and fatherhood, acquired new popularity. They also offered a degree of physical and emotional shelter.

The origins of the 1991 image also lay in the streets of New York City and in the notion of *role strain*. Role strain occurs when the roles one occupies demand more than one can fulfill. Women in 1991 had to deftly juggle marriage, career, family, school, home, and an exercise program. Overextended and with tight schedules, they often left the health club wearing tights or bicycle shorts and a jacket. The look was sexy and symbolic of "being with it." It was imitated by the young and became prominent on the streets of New York, inspiring Seventh Avenue and later Paris fashion houses.

## Historical Perspective

The fact that two distinct visual images were seen in the presidencies of Reagan and Bush—the former presidency characterized by personal convictions and political agenda and the latter by the population's fears, anxieties, and attempts at self-empowerment—raises questions about earlier presidencies and their relative influences on fashion. Do the ideas of the strong and active president help determine desired female appearance? And what are the stylistic sources of fashion during presidencies that are considered weak and passive? Presidents Woodrow Wilson and Harry Truman are viewed by some political scientists as strong and active. Presidents Warren Harding, Calvin Coolidge, and Dwight Eisenhower have been described as weak and passive.[43] If there is a pattern of impact, it is likely to appear in a comparison of fashion in these two groups.

### The Wilson, Harding, and Coolidge Presidencies

Woodrow Wilson, a president described as strong and active, initiated policies that empowered women. During World War I women were asked to abandon the steel corset for the war effort. They were admitted to the army, the navy, and the marine corps and could also join the workforce and acquire independent economic means. When World War I was officially declared in 1917, the fashionable ideal was a matronly figure. The skirt was long and flared, and bosom and hips were emphasized. By 1919, however, the flared skirt was replaced by a tunic-style dress that hung from the shoulders. Loose-fitting, the clothing denied the traditional elements that anchor the female identity to the womanly role—that is, the breasts and the hips. Requiring no fastenings, the dress was simply pulled over the head.[44]

The highest possible compliment during the 1920s was "My dear, you have got absolutely nothing," where "nothing" meant that the woman was flat "behind and before," as fashion historian Doris Langley Moore (1949) reported.[45] "Audacious decorations in contrasting lines and colors" completed the look. Hairstyles and hemlines became short, and the vogue was considered "boyish." By 1924 the naked neck appeared longer, and women played nervously with their necklaces, flourishing long cigarette holders. The fashion was popular enough to evoke both admiration and rebuke.[46]

*With flapper fashion, women were freed from the constraints of the corset. This 1924 Chanel dress was designed to be hipless and bosomless.*

The presidents of the era, Warren G. Harding (1921–1923) and Calvin Coolidge (1923–1929), who assumed the office upon Harding's death, had no particular agenda. Both were considered weak and passive presidents.[47] These characteristics made it possible for the other, more diffuse cultural forces to take over and visually define the period. The flapper fashion of the Roaring Twenties was an American invention made possible by these weak and passive presidents.

The origin and popularity of flapper fashion have been attributed variously to the seeking of mindless fun and the despair in response to the consequences of World War I; to the fact that young women were now employed and could "call the tune"; and to the fact that the fashion embodied the dynamism and energy of the new technology.

Frederick Lewis Allan's *Only Yesterday* (1931) described a revolution in manners and morals that took place in the 1920s. The 1920 census found that the great majority of Americans were living in urban areas where there was greater freedom from traditional "gatekeepers" and increased possibilities for wearing "outrageous" fashion.[48] Another influence that supported the consumption of the flapper fashion was the shift of the economy from a base of capital goods to one of consumer goods. In fashion as in the other artistic expressions, such as jazz and literature, the fashionable ideal reflected the activism, dynamism, and speed of new technology—trains, planes, telephones, and the telegraph. When a president is weak and passive, has *no* domestic agenda, and has a low level of activity, he has little direct impact on fashion. Sentiments existing within the popu-

*The 1950s were seen as
a time for families,
babies, and the home.
(Photo by Eve Arnold.)*

lation at large—the dreams, fears, and hopes of the people—can be expressed,
and are reflected in, fashion.

### The Truman and Eisenhower Presidencies

In April 1945, with the death of President Roosevelt, the mantle of the presidency
of the United States fell on Harry Truman. World War II continued, but victory
over Hitler was in sight. Truman's most pressing task was to follow through and
win both the war and the peace. He was active in all three aspects of his presidential role: chief executive (domestic policy), head of state (foreign policy), and
commander in chief (the military arena).[49]

On the home front millions of men who had been in the armed forces, men
trained to use force, had to be demobilized and rapidly transformed into civil-
ians. Providing them with educational benefits and housing loans became a pri-
ority. A "new look" for women, a tight waistline that emphasized the size of the
bust and the hips, traditional maternal attributes, was introduced into fashion by
Christian Dior in 1947.[50] The president's domestic agenda gave the style legitimacy, and the new look was established as a full-scale fashion.

The Truman presidency was characterized by executive assertiveness as defined
by the famous remark, "The buck stops here." Political scientists have evaluated
his performance in the office as strong and active. He had a definite agenda, setting the presidency as central to national debate, and was for the most part successful. He expended much personal energy in office.[51]

The Eisenhower presidency (1953–1961) has been evaluated as weak and passive. Fashion during the Eisenhower years continued the theme of the female in the maternal social role. Styles varied, but the emphasis on hips and bust remained.[52] The increase in the birthrate that began in the early 1940s continued until the beginning of the Kennedy era, producing the "baby boom generation."

Fashion is a visual image that tells a story about the important ideas, events, developments, and core tensions of a given period. The ideas and values of a strong and active president seem to be reflected in female fashion and behavior. In the case of President Wilson, this impact led to clothing that allowed greater physical and social freedom. In the case of President Truman, it led to a new emphasis on family and on women in maternal and nurturing roles.

President Eisenhower, in contrast, cultivated a leadership style that projected an image of sincerity, fairness, and optimism. He enjoyed harmonizing the efforts of potentially quarrelsome allies. In the White House he struck the pose of an "unpolitical" president and is considered to have "soothed the anxieties of his troubled countrymen much as a distinguished and well-loved grandfather brings stability to his family."[53] These characteristics made it possible for the style trend initiated in the Truman era to continue through the end of the Eisenhower presidency.

## The Clinton Presidency

The economic recession that began under President Bush, a president considered weak and inactive, continued into the presidency of Bill Clinton. The fabrics and styles of fall 1993 continued to exhibit a sense of pessimism about the future and a pervasive sense of vulnerability. The accessories seemed to act as a means of protection.

Through his personal behavior and his political agenda, the Clinton administration had an important impact on American and European clothing and fashion. During his first year in office, a major issue was the passage of the North American Free Trade Agreement. The treaty encouraged further the move to offshore production of stylish, moderate-priced clothing, a phenomenon that came to be known as commoditization of fashion.[54] Globalization and free trade, the president believed, would lead to a higher standard of living that could become a reality for much of the world's population.[55]

Clothing figured prominently in the public's furor over the president's relationship with Monica Lewinsky. The telltale navy dress she wore to the White House was "a simple little number, an off-the-rack staple," bought at the Gap,[56] one of the companies that contributed to the commoditization of fashion. Despite the fact that it was mass-produced, the dress's fit must have been attractive.

The modern silhouette President Clinton has worn since 1993 may have had a greater impact. Mr. Clinton preferred "drape shape Donna Karan suits with ventless jackets, low riding buttons and double-pleated pants meant to make the Pres-

*By 1993 the vulnerable look had replaced the opulent image of the 1980s. Waiflike Kate Moss (left) sports the vulnerable look; supermodel Christy Turlington (right) sports the opulent look. (Women's Wear Daily, Feb. 5, 1993.)*

ident's thickset frame look longer and leaner."[57] The suits were made to measure by Martin Greenfield, a master tailor based in Brooklyn, who creates suits from soft, stretchy crepe-wool fabric. They had a roomy cut, held shape during hard travel, and gave the president a trimmer look.[58] The president's new style may be prophetic. The March 2000 issue of *Earnshaw's* showcasing "the industry's most innovative manufacturing depicted a green-blue denim shirt worn over . . . pants that looked longer and leaner."

The wearing of uniforms in public schools became a part of the president's political agenda, with the goal of preventing violence and promoting academic achievement. In 1994 school violence, a perceived breakdown of discipline, and poor academic performance led the Long Beach school district, the largest public school district in California, to request the president's support for school uniforms. Parents overwhelmingly supported the idea.[59] President Clinton endorsed the idea with the observation that earlier dress code cases asserted that public school students "shed their constitutional rights to freedom of speech and expression at the school's gate."[60]

Much public discussion ensued.[61] Schools in large American urban centers nevertheless proceeded to encourage uniforms as desired attire. School authorities contended that gang colors and gang-related clothing sometimes intimidated nonmembers of gangs; that uniforms were a visible sign of structure, coherence, and seriousness; and that uniforms would reduce potentially dangerous situations and minimize violence. Another factor in favor of uniforms was that they would limit competition for costly fashionable attire.[62]

## 1990s Fashion Process

The process by which a new fashion emerges and grows to become popularly accepted by consumers is different in the United States from that in European countries. In Europe, the traditional elite decides on the fashion, and the same mode is found in most stores. In the United States, a new fashion is the result of "collective selection," as Herbert Blumer observed (1969).[63] A designer offers about thirty styles on the runway. About six to eight designs are chosen by the buyers—"a highly competitive and secretive lot," Blumer observed. Their choices are made independently, without knowledge of the other buyers' selections. Yet their choices converge because the buyers are immersed in the common world of what is happening to women. Through avid reading of fashion publications and close observation of one another's lines of products, buyers develop common sensitivities and similar appreciations.

Designers also develop an "intimate familiarity" with the most recent expressions of the modern spirit as they appear in the fine arts, current literature, political debates, and general "discourse in the sophisticated world," observed Blumer. They translate themes from these areas and from the media into dress designs. It is not surprising that designers working apart from one another in a large number of fashion houses independently create remarkably similar designs. They "pick up ideas of the past but always through the filter of the present," explained Blumer.[64]

The fashion is thus set through a process of free selection from a large number of competing but similar models. The creators of the models seek to catch and give expression to what Blumer called "the direction of modernity."[65]

The decade of the 1970s was an era of the designer boom and nationally advertised fashion brands.[66] The department stores used to be the vehicle that introduced merchandise concepts to the customer. By the 1970s the brand became important. Through advertising, editorials, and fashion shows, designers communicated directly with the consumers. In many instances the public became aware of the new fashions as soon as the retailers did. Designers became household names in apparel, accessories, perfumes, and bedding. Consumers' choices from among the styles offered by designers, store buyers, and boutique owners were the ones that were reordered and became the fashion.

As designer brands moved to center stage, department stores organized their sales floors into brand name boutiques such as Liz Claiborne, Ellen Tracy, or Jones New York. As brands began to dominate, store buyers became less inclined to try out new and unfamiliar labels. They believed that consumers were insecure about fashion and needed the brand label as the voice of authority.[67]

Through market research since the 1980s, the industry has become even more geared to producing styles that are emotionally relevant. The new thrust in production is to anticipate a demand and be able to furnish the "right" product. "The consumer-is-king" approach became the practice among manufacturers and retailers. The profitable way of doing business, they insisted, is to study the customers, find out what they wanted, and make and market it.[68]

The impetus for the production of fashion thus shifted away from the artist, manufacturer, and specialist to the consumer. The perception of a new social dynamic led to a joint selection of a particular fashion theme. Because of different traditions and climatic conditions, however, fashionable attire in New York may have a slightly different manifestation from attire in Paris, London, or Milan. But the image and its meaning are likely to be the same. Designers claim that the similarity in fashion themes occurs because, as people with artistic perception, the designers "put their ear to the ground and hear the rumble long before the train appears." They read the same newspapers and magazine articles, visit art exhibits, go to plays and watch movies, and visit clubs and other night spots, watching for changing social sensibilities.

In the 1970s career women of the baby-boom generation needed clothes to wear to work. What developed were women's brands like Liz Claiborne, Jones New York, Chaus, and J. H. Collectibles. These brands dominated the women's floors in department stores. Dozens of specialty chains also appeared with their own private-label lines, including the Limited, Casual Corner, and Ann Taylor.[69] Other marketing strategies included the discounting of women's fashions in factory outlet malls and in stores like Marshall's and Loehmann's.

Growth in women's fashions came to a halt in the fall of 1987 when designers sought to bring back the short skirt, while women who had been seeking to convey an image of authority had stocked their closets with calf-length hemlines.[70] This was a setback, for designers like Liz Claiborne spent hundreds of thousands of dollars to shorten skirts already in production for their fall deliveries.

Encouraged by editorials, millions of women did not buy the short skirt, just as they refused in 1999 to buy clothes whose dominant colors switched from black to gray just because the industry had decreed it.

Beginning in the nineteenth century, the principles underlying the marketing of clothing in America have been mass production at prices affordable to middle-class and working-class consumers. Discounting and bargain hunting continued to increase through the early 1990s. Department stores were unable to decide what to mark down, and their uncertainty about pricing levels led to an upheaval in the industry. In 1994, for example, only 20 percent of Liz Claiborne's output sold at full price; 80 percent of that company's production was discounted.[71]

Designer-initiated fashions—like the "waif" look of frilly velvet and droopy ruffled blouses, the unkempt grunge look, and the "fishtail" dress with its asymmetrical hemlines—were "commercial flops."[72] In 1994 the apparel industry had entered a third year of slumping sales, and retailers and designers alike were baffled. Nothing that they had done seemed to work.[73]

In the early 1990s, marketing analysts coined the term "commoditization of fashion," which described the new era in which production moved to low-cost and offshore factories. The trend, which began many years ago with the production of cheap lines of clothing, expanded vastly in the 1990s. This time the aim was to manufacture clothes in "classic" (nontrendy) "simple chic" and minimalist styles that were good-looking and moderately priced.[74] At the same time, large-scale production of attractive, reasonably priced clothes emerged as mega-brands, made by companies such as the Gap, the Limited, J. Crew, and Banana Republic.[75]

Also at this time, to make sure that they were carrying the latest trend, major retailers such as Sears, Macy's, and Bloomingdale's formed a new strategy by centralizing the buying of apparel. Instead of allowing individual store managers to decide what to buy for their stores, the decision was left to the more informed.[76]

Traditionally, apparel manufacturers had produced a few lines, and retailers could reorder the successful styles. Increasing the trend toward economy of production, mega-brand manufacturers produced an initial output that included more styles than before, to be retailed at moderate prices. Once this stock was sold, however, it could not be reordered.

The quality of the mega brands was not as good or as durable as the clothes made by, or copied from, French designers, but they were good-looking as long as they lasted and could be economically replaced. With each cleaning, however, the garments' looks and fit suffered and consumers visited the malls and searched the catalogs for the latest desired styles.

To acquire wider appeal, some design houses hired stylists to help designers focus their ideas and create lines that had a lifestyle orientation. Stylists were persons who had been on the fringes of art and fashion, had traveled extensively, and knew what was going on in the various design rooms. Stylists were thought to know the pulse of the moment and to be able to help designers capture the emerging look.[77]

With discounting and bargain hunting there was a decrease in the sharp delineation between fashion that emanated from London, Paris, and Milan and styles offered by companies such as the Limited, the Gap, Banana Republic, and J. Crew.[78] These mass-marketers offered good-looking clothes that were functional. Moreover, they used style consultants to advise the consumer on everything from fit to how to accessorize the outfits. Along with style consultants came other luxury services such as alterations.[79] The notion that stylish clothes "belonged exclusively to the elite was thus deflated."[80]

Mega-brand marketing led to what *New York Times* reporter Constance White called "the failure virus."[81] Sales of high fashion in the United States became stagnant, and many designers and boutiques went out of business. As fashion declined in profitability in the 1990s, so did fashion advertising and the fashion magazines that depended on it. Seeking new ways to attract the attention of consumers, these publications replaced supermodels on their covers with film and TV actresses.[82] The fashion magazine *Elle* redefined itself as a lifestyle magazine to include travel, furnishings, and food.[83]

New strategies were also sought by retailers. One approach was to develop a bridge collection—clothes that carried a designer label but were priced at 30 percent less than the top designer line.[84] Designer Norma Kamali, for example, could not sell her clothes through the department stores because her prices couldn't compete favorably with those of offshore production. In addition to selling clothes in her own boutique in 1993, she created a lower-price label and offered a toll-free number for ordering the clothes. However, she retained her OMO Norma Kamali label for her expensive line.[85]

Another way of surviving in the fashion business was through the practice of licensing, in which a brand-name company allows another to use its name and reputation. For example, there were frequent comments about the J. Peterman clothing catalog company in "Seinfeld," the 1990s TV situation comedy series about young adult urban lifestyles. This was a real company, a Polo's women's wear licensee.[86] Its owner, John Peterman, was the founder of the upscale image mail-order business. It is interesting to note that actor Jerry Seinfeld and the actress Julia Louis-Dreyfus, who played Elaine, had both been J. Peterman catalog customers before references to it were written into the script.[87]

Discussion of licensing is a regular feature of *Earnshaw's* magazine, a trade publication for children's wear. The March 1998 issue, for example, announced that the New Hampshire-based Timberland Company, known for its hiking boots, had authorized the apparel company Albert S.A. of Les Herbiers, France, to make clothes using the Timberland label[88] because of its ability to convey the spirit of the outdoors. Albert S.A. is the second-largest children's wear company in Europe and also serves as a licensee for DKNY Kids.

A designer's name is important to the consumer; it suggests integrity in design and materials. Designers, however, sometimes realize too late that mass merchandising tends to have a negative impact on their reputations. Calvin Klein's attempt to terminate a licensing agreement with Warnaco is an example.

In fall 2000 Calvin Klein Inc.'s signature line consisted of spare leather and woolen frocks and pale-blue python skirts. The high-fashion segment of Calvin Klein wins awards but loses money. The total Calvin Klein Inc. empire, however, is built on mundane goods that bear the CK brand, such as $14 cotton briefs and $40 perfumes.[89] Mr. Klein had followed in the footsteps of Pierre Cardin, Yves St. Laurent, and others who licensed manufacturers to use their names on their products for a cut of the profits. The Calvin Klein design team was responsible for carrying out his design instructions and philosophy, while the licensee handled the complicated logistics of manufacturing the merchandise and negotiating with department stores. The CK name was licensed to Warnaco, from whom Calvin Klein earned millions of dollars in royalties in 1999.[90]

In 1999 Mr. Klein sought to sell his design house but failed; potential buyers remained aloof. Costume historian and entrepreneur Didier Grumbach explained that in Europe, "It is better to be known for an embroidered gown than underwear."[91]

Mr. Klein then sought to cancel his contract with Warnaco, but Warnaco refused. He sued to regain control over the CK brand, claiming that the quality of merchandise, consisting of both jeanswear and underwear lines, did not meet his standards and that his name had been cheapened.[92]

## European Fashions

For most of the twentieth century, the "trickle-down theory of fashion" prevailed. First stated by Georg Simmel (1957), the theory holds that the phenomenon of fashion depends on the efforts of the lower classes to establish new status claims by adopting the clothing of those higher in rank. Members of the higher classes seek to maintain their positions of distinction and adopt a new style, leading to a fashion change.[93] In this way new fashions have emanated from designers who satisfied the need of the upper classes for beautiful, elegant clothing.

Fashion shows were staged twice a year in Paris, Milan, and New York. They were posh events where couture originals were shown on beautiful models. Paris designers have traditionally set the standards, and Seventh Avenue manufacturers have copied and adapted the styles for the mass market. This mode of production led to the full-skirted "new look" after World War II, the "sack" in the 1950s, the space-age sleek look of the 1960s, and the "pouf" party dress in the 1980s.[94]

In the early 1990s there were 1,500 major showings in Paris alone. TV cameras joined in capturing runway footage for fashion news programs. The shows tried to outdo each other with "seminude costumes, strange hair and makeup, and gimmicky staging."[95] Fashion had become entertainment rather than art.

This strategy, however, did not arouse the interest of the public. European designers had failed to realize that sales of high fashion were stagnating. In the United States, retailers had developed a new way to mass-market designer clothes through bridge collections carrying designer labels at lower prices.

Many of the European designers who were born after World War II, even when trained in the classical tradition of couture, also designed for the ready-to-wear market. In their designs they challenged stereotypes of class and gender. British designer John Galliano (b. 1960) used less exclusive fabrics to create clothes for the younger, funkier sisters of his mainline buyers. He tapped into the trend for drag in the London clubs and introduced the notion of "underwear as outer wear." Satin knickers were shown with feathered bras and leather caps.[96]

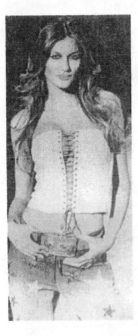

*Representing guilt-free sexuality is the new popular model, Gissele. Her hair falls low below the shoulders and her peekaboo bustier, which laces in front, exposes her midriff and navel. (Photo: Gregory Kitchen.) Calvin Klein too has replaced the pale, gaunt, hollow-eyed, vulnerable ideal with a sensual look that is "softer, prettier, fresh and clean kind of sexy." He attributes the change to a change in the Zeitgeist. (New York Times, Feb. 8, 1998.)*

In France, Jean-Paul Gaultier (b. 1952) in his ready-to-wear dismantled the notion of masculine styling by producing skirts as an option for heterosexual men. He also injected kitsch onto the runway, glamorizing street style. In 1990, when designing the costumes for Madonna's Blond Ambition tour, he ignored the principle of modesty. A corset was traditionally a hidden garment whose function was to provide structure from which to hang the outer garment. Gaultier used the corset to erect a barrier, to shield the body from the outer world. Moreover, breasts were shaped like cones and given a hard structure by stitching. Rather than soft, malleable objects, they were turned into weapons.[97]

Two Italian-born designers, Dolce and Cabana (b. 1958 and 1962), violated the Church's norm of modesty and designed sexually alluring clothing for the women's ready-to-wear market. They revived the southern Italian sex-bomb look and mixed supermodels with screen stars to present images that oozed earthy sexuality.

The company created sexy clothes for women who "wanted to revel in their voluptuous femininity." They took items such as satin corsets, bodices, black stockings, and fishnet and put them together in a way that enabled women to escape from the unisex, sporty style.[98] Their men's wear collection featured muted shades of earthy brown, black, and touches of scarlet. In designing clothes for women and men who wanted to portray their sexuality, they had created bestsellers.

Designers in London, Paris, and New York
have been dressing their models in the basic
silhouettes and fabrics that young rebels are
wearing on the street. Street style is
presented in a savvy form.

TOP LEFT: *Cargo pants on a runway.*
*(NYT Pictures.)*

TOP RIGHT: *The conservative Burberry*
*plaid was used to create a skirt that is cut*
*low, exposing the midriff and navel.*
(New York Times, *Jan. 5, 1999.)*

LEFT: *A celebrity in a leather outfit with a*
*short skirt. (Photo: Diane Cohen.)*

In the 1990s two approaches to fashion were dominant. One created styles that made headlines and proclaimed the wearer's desired identity. In Veblen's terms, these styles were "the novel."

On the other hand, there were clothes that existed outside a particular time period. They were characterized by tasteful opulence, refinement, and grace[99] and constituted "the beautiful."

At the beginning of the twenty-first century, fashion design is entering an exploratory period. A new, forward-looking approach to fashion is evolving to meet the needs of a highly complex society in which consumers have more freedom of choice than ever before.

## Notes

1. G. Simmel (1957), "Fashion," *American Journal of Sociology* 62: 294–323. Originally published in 1904.

2. Empress Eugénie in the nineteenth century is considered to have been the last of the long dynasty of royal fashion leaders. See J. C. Flugel (1966), *The Psychology of Clothes* (London: Hogarth Press), p. 146. (Originally published in 1930.) Other theorists, however, suggest a set pattern and speak of historical continuity. Some provide illustrative data for long-term and cyclical fashion trends. See E. Sapir (1931), "Fashion," *Encyclopedia of the Social Sciences*, vol. 6 (New York: Macmillan).

3. T. Wolfe in his introduction to René König (1973), *A la Mode on the Social Psychology of Fashion*, trans. F. Bradley (New York: Seabury Press), p. 19.

4. Flugel, op. cit., pp. 149, 160.

5. M. and A. Batterberry (1977), *Fashion: The Mirror of History* (New York: Greenwich House), pp. 107–109.

6. V. Steele (1988), *Paris Fashion* (New York: Oxford University Press), p. 23.

7. Batterberry, op. cit., p. 144; Steele, op. cit., p. 22; B. Payne, G. Weinakor, and J. Farrell-Beck (1992), *The History of Costume* (New York: HarperCollins), pp. 364, 398–399.

8. Batterberry, op. cit., p. 143.

9. Ibid., pp. 140–142.

10. A. M. Earle (1903), *Two Centuries of Costume in America 1620–1820* (Rutland, Vt.: Charles E. Tuttle), pp.323–348; W. E. Wyckopf and H. Pitz (1935), *Early American Dress* (New York: B. Blom), p. 165.

11. Flugel, op. cit., p. 147.

12. R. Marin (1992), "Grunge: A Success Story," *New York Times*, Nov. 15.

13. J. Jeaninne, "Fashion's Young and Downwardly Mobile Set," Newark (N.J.) *Sunday Record*, Feb. 7, 1993.

14. "Faith and Fashion Cross Paths in New Talisman Jewelry, Soul Chains," *Mademoiselle* (June 1993), p. 14.

15. A. Hollander (1978), *Seeing Through Clothes* (New York: Viking), pp. 117–118.

16. Payne et al., op. cit., pp. 501–503.

17. Flugel, op. cit., p. 159.

18. A. M. Schlesinger, Jr. (1996), "The Ultimate Approval Rating," *New York Times Magazine*, Dec. 16, pp. 46–51; See also S. Neal (1995), "Putting Presidents in Their Place," *Chicago Sun-Times*, Nov. 19, pp. 30–31.

19. R. E. Neustadt (1960), *Presidential Power* (New York: John Wiley and Sons); see also P. Woll and S. E. Zimmerman (1992), *American Government: The Core* (New York: Mc-Graw Hill), pp. 197–200.

20. R. Baker (1982), *Growing Up* (New York: New American Library), pp. 88–89.

21. R. J. Sickels (1980), *The Presidency: An Introduction* (Englewood Cliffs, N. J.: Prentice-Hall), p. 6.

22. M. J. Horn and L. M. Gurel (1981), *The Second Skin: An Interdisciplinary Study of Clothing*, 3d ed.(Boston: Houghton Mifflin), p. 59.

23. The French, Italian, and Japanese designer boutiques that line Madison Avenue in New York City also have displays in major department stores throughout the United States. *New York Times.* Sept. 25, 1990.

24. J. D. Barber (1977), *The Presidential Character: Predicting Performance in the White House*, 2d ed. (Englewood Cliffs, N.J.: Prentice-Hall); see also J. D. Barber (1980), "The Presidential Character," in *Classics of the American Presidency,* ed. H. A. Bailey, Jr. (Oak Park, Ill.: More Publishing), pp. 41–49. Barber suggested that the level of activity of a president and his enjoyment of life may be used to predict the quality of a presidency.

25. S. R. Weisman (1984), "Ronald Reagan's Magical Style," in *American Government Personalities and Politics*, ed. P. Woll (Boston: Little, Brown), pp. 175–190.

26. Ibid.

27. L. Cannon (1990), *President Reagan: The Role of a Lifetime* (New York: Simon and Schuster), p. 20.

28. K. P. Phillips (1990), *The Politics of Rich and Poor: Wealth and the American Electorate in the Reagan Aftermath* (New York: Random House).

29. *New York Times*, Jan. 14, 1989.

30. S. M. Lyman (1989), *The Seven Deadly Sins: Society and Evil*, rev. ed. (Dix Hills, N.Y.: General Hall), pp. 72–74.

31. T. Veblen (1953), *The Theory of the Leisure Class* (New York: Mentor Books). Originally published in 1899.

32. L. W. Banner (1983), *American Beauty: A Social History Through Two Centuries of the American Idea, Ideal, and Image of the Beautiful Woman* (New York: Knopf), p. 13.

33. B. Barber and L. S. Lobel (1952), "Fashion in Women's Clothes and the American Social System," *Social Forces* 31: 124–131.

34. G. M. Boyd, "Bush Inaugural Will Signal Open, Accessible President," *New York Times,* Jan. 21, 1989, p. 7.

35. *Christian Science Monitor*, Nov. 11, 1990.

36. *New York Times*, Dec. 9, 1990.

37. Ibid.

38. *New York Times*, Sept. 7, 1991.

39. See *Fashion* magazine's offerings for fall 1990.

40. W.E.A. Budge and W. Thompson (1961), *Amulets and Talismans* (New Hyde Park, N.Y.: University Books).

41. There are other examples in history of fashion becoming more feminine during wartime. The most obvious was a 1991 exhibit of World War II fashion at the Metropolitan Museum of Art in New York.

42. "Faith and Fashion Cross Paths," op. cit.

43. A. M. Schlesinger, Sr. (1980), "Our Presidents: A Rating by 74 Historians," in Bailey, op. cit., pp. 380–386; D. B. James (1988) "Values, Structure and Presidential Power," *Presi-*

*dential Studies Quarterly* 18 (4): 761–784; R. G. Hoxie (1980), "The Power to Command," in Bailey, op. cit., pp. 91–98.

44. R. Pistolese and R. Horsting (1970), *History of Fashion* (New York: John Wiley and Sons), pp. 287–288; Batterberry, op. cit., pp. 294–303.

45. D. L. Moore (1949), *The Woman in Fashion* (London: B.T. Batsford), p. 174.

46. Pistolese and Horsting, op. cit., p. 287.

47. A. T. Bailey and D. M. Kennedy (1987), *The American Pageant* (Lexington, Mass.: D.C. Heath), pp. 722–732.

48. F. L. Allan (1931), *Only Yesterday* (New York: Harper Brothers).

49. B. J. Bernstein, ed. (1970), *Politics and Policies of the Truman Administration* (Chicago: Quadrangle Books).

50. C. R. Milbank (1989), *New York Fashion: The Evolution of American Style* (New York: Harry N. Abrams), p. 143; also Payne et al., op. cit., pp. 604–607.

51. R. J. Donovan (1977), *Conflict and Crisis: The Presidency of Harry S. Truman* (New York: Norton), p. 163; see also G. W. Cobliner (1950), "Feminine Fashion As an Aspect of Group Psychology: Analysis of Written Replies Received by Means of Questionnaire," *Journal of Social Psychology* 31: 283–289.

52. Payne et al., op. cit., pp. 614–615; Batterberry, op. cit., p. 383.

53. Bailey and Kennedy, op. cit., p. 842.

54. Born in 1946, Bill Clinton was the first of the baby boom generation to be elected president. S. White (1994), "Top Dog," *New York Times*, Jan. 10.

55. In 1999, with Prime Minister Tony Blair of Britain, Mr. Clinton founded the "Third Way," an organization of left-of-center presidents and prime ministers who stood for globalization and free trade and also insisted on strong government support for social justice, education, and public health that dislocations may bring about. E. L. Andrews (2000), *New York Times*, June 4.

56. J. Barron (1998), "The Future Will Know Them for What They Wore," *New York Times*, Aug. 23.

57. T. S. Purdum (1997), "Yankee Doodle Dandy?" *New York Times*, Jan. 19.

58. Ibid.

59. K. L. Paliokas (1996), "Trying Uniforms On for Size," *American School Board Journal*, May.

60. Supreme Court decision in *Tinker* v. *Des Moines Independent Community School District* (1969).

61. See *New York Times*, Feb. 11, 1998; Feb. 12, 1998; Feb. 26, 1998; Sept. 4, 1999.

62. Ibid. See also "Dressed to Drill: School Uniforms Are Hot and Merchants Are Cashing In," *Business Week*, Sept. 1997.

63. H. Blumer (1969), "Fashion: From Class Differentiation to Collective Selection," *Sociological Quarterly* 10: 275–291.

64. Ibid.

65. Ibid.

66. T. Agins (1999), *The End of Fashion: The Mass Marketing of the Clothing Business* (New York: William Morrow), p. 179.

67. Ibid.

68. In a news story reporting that Wal-Mart outdistanced Sears as top U. S. retailer, the reporter attributed Wal-Mart's success to its use of new technology and new distribution

methods. These innovations made it possible for Wal-Mart to keep better track of what sold and what did not sell and reorder what did. (Associated Press, Apr. 12, 1991).

69. Agins, op. cit., p. 182.

70. Ibid.

71. Ibid. p. 184.

72. Ibid., p. 183.

73. Ibid.

74. Ibid., p. 13.

75. "Chains have definitely taken over Gotham," reports CheckOut, a buyer's guide to shops, sales, and services. New York City houses "a staggering 66 Gaps, 24 Banana Republics, and 17 Nine Wests to name just a few of the biggies." Public reaction to new items is tested in the flagship store—i.e., the one with the largest space and best location. A. Onecare (2000), "Strongest Links in the Chains," *CheckOut*, Mar. 23–30.

76. L. Kaufman (1999), "Can J.C. Penny Evolve?" *New York Times*, June 26.

77. C.C.R. White (1998), "The Rise of the Stylist: A Double Edged Sword," *New York Times*, Sept. 1.

78. Agins, op. cit., p. 11.

79. C.C.R. White (1998), "Banana Republic Catalogue," *New York Times*, Sept. 15.

80. Ibid.

81. C.C.R. White (1988), "Patterns," *New York Times*, October, 27.

82. A. Kuczynski (1999), "Trading on Hollywood Magic: Celebrities Push Models Off Women's Magazine Covers," *New York Times*, Jan. 30.

83. A. Kuczynski (1999), "Old Formula for a Magazine on Fashion Is Out of Style," *New York Times*, June 21.

84. Agins, op. cit., p. 37.

85. Ibid.

86. Ibid., p. 105.

87. D. Edwards (1999), "Seinfeld and the Real John Peterman," in *The Meanings of Dress*, ed. M. L. Damhorst, K. A. Miller, and S. O. Michelman (New York: Fairchild Publications), p. 444.

88. *Earnshaw's*, Mar. 1999.

89. T. Agins and R. Quick (2000), *Wall Street Journal*, June 1, p. 1.

90. Ibid.

91. Ibid., p. 8.

92. Ibid.

93. Simmel (1957), op. cit.

94. Agins, op. cit., p. 9.

95. Agins, op. cit., p. 37.

96. R. Arnold (1997), "Dolce and Cabana," in *The St. James Fashion Encyclopedia: A Survey of Style from 1945 to the Present,* ed. R. Martin (Detroit: Invisible Ink Press), pp. 141–142.

97. C. Cox (1997), "Gaultier, Jean-Paul," in Martin, op. cit., pp. 142–144.

98. R. Martin (1997), *The St. James Fashion Encyclopedia: A Survey of Style from 1945 to the Present* (Detroit: Invisible Ink Press), pp. 106–107.

99. H. Brubach (1999), *A Dedicated Follower of Fashion* (New York: Phaidon), p. 221.

# The Personal Self

**T**HE TERM *personal self* refers to the "I" component that invariably influences individuals when dressing the public self.[1] Elements of dress and styles of appearance that individuals choose to represent the personal self are part of a dialogue between self and society. The clothing allows the individual to integrate personal self with the public one. The personal self is both the author and the audience of one's appearance.

English anthropologist E. R. Leach suggested that there is a difference between public-sociological symbols (which identify social persona, are a part of the "collective representations," and are readily available to interpretation) and private-psychological symbols, whose meanings may lie in the individual's unconscious. Private-psychological symbols are, however, expressed as public behavior. They affect the emotional state of the performer.[2]

## Legitimacy of an Individuated Self

Courts in recent years have supported the distinction between the public and the personal self. Judges have ruled in favor of school boards trying to implement dress codes for teachers, but they have distinguished between work attire and an individual's choice of personal appearance. They have maintained that long hair, a beard, or a mustache is an aspect of a teacher's personal self. To try to regulate these elements of appearance represents a violation of individual rights.[3]

On November 11, 1986, New York State's highest court ruled that a Rastafarian inmate who had not cut his hair for twenty years "cannot be compelled to shed his four foot long dreadlocks." The court struck down a state prison regulation that required inmates entering state prisons to get haircuts and a shave for purposes of security and identification, ruling that the regulation "needlessly infringes" on the prisoner's beliefs.[4]

In Boston, the court ruled otherwise on June 30, 1992. Six "mustachioed" members of the police force claimed that they had a constitutional right to maintain their appearance. The Commonwealth of Massachusetts insisted that they "bare their upper lips" because a clean-shaven face is part of the state police identity.[5] Not only for police but for all men, facial hair alters the individual's appearance and how he is perceived by others. Such alteration can be cosmetic, such as

*Two of the six mustachioed members of the Massachusetts Metropolitan, Capitol, and Registry Police who sued the police department rather than shave. (New York Times, July 1, 1992; reprinted by permission of by Evan Richmond/NYT Pictures.)*

growing a beard to cover up a weak chin or jowl or growing a mustache to provide a horizontal element in a long, angular face, as noted in *Man at His Best: Esquire's Guide to Style*. A beard can also be a political statement, as it was for many activists of the late 1960s.[6]

Analogous to male facial hair is the use of cosmetics by women. They are free to wear makeup or not, as they see fit; however, much pressure does exist. A ticket-counter agent at Logan International Airport was dismissed by Continental Airlines in 1991 because she refused to wear makeup on the job.[7] The agent had spoken to the Civil Liberties Union of Massachusetts and was ready to sue. A spokesman for the airline claimed that cosmetics were in keeping with the company's attempt to improve its image in terms of its aircraft, its facilities, and its service to its customers. In line with the new image, the airline adopted a personal appearance code that required female ground workers to wear makeup. Within a week, after much public outcry, Continental had retracted its mandate and the agent was back at her job.[8]

## Continuant Identity

The particular emphasis, nuance, or innuendo of the "I" component can emanate from individual history, memory, and experience. It may be a continuant mode of dress, lasting throughout life—a personal hallmark. Or it may be temporary, in response to a particular situation, a mood or event. In the latter case the particular emphasis reflects the present rather than the past.

A story in the *New York Times* about the author Norman Mailer provides an example of how the personal self, or the "I," is reflected in the attire worn for a front-stage performance. Describing the author's choice of dress, the reporter noted that "Mr. Mailer himself is still appearing in public in his usual ensemble of a slightly rumpled blue blazer, with tan pants." The image, according to our vocabulary of images, conveys approachability and defiance.[9] Norman Mailer's attire was continuant and reflected his personal self. It was informal in a formal situation and somewhat unkempt when neatness was the norm. Power and the limits of coerciveness are issues that inform much of Mailer's writing. They are most evident in his novel about World War II, *The Naked and the Dead.*

Patterns of socialization, family interaction, communication with significant others, and biological characteristics help to form the distinct way in which each individual interprets the world and relates to it. The diversity and individualism of American society, as well as lack of knowledge about expected attire, make it possible for adults to modify the dress they wear for front-stage performance, reflecting the "I," and incur minimal disapproval for such modification.

## Temporary Identity

Attire that reflects the "I" may also be worn in response to a special place, situation, or event. In the early 1970s, before disco became popular, whatever one wore during the day would be just as good at night, noted fashion designer Bob Mackie.[10] With disco, however, young women and men discovered that there were places for dancing where reality was suspended, where "fantasy had a chance to thrive," where rules of everyday dressing were thrown out. People could indulge in wearing any clothes they wished to the disco.[11] However, gatekeepers ensured that those dressed in attire that would ruin the fantasy, attire that was associated with the workplace, were kept out.

The attire chosen for disco was determined by personal imagination and dreams. The disco was a highly visual environment, and clothing became an integral part of the milieu. In a disco environment, soft lighting mixed with shadows away from the dance floor and bright flashing lights created a stage-show atmosphere around the dancers. Special clothes were essential to a charged environment that brought together personal fantasy, music, lights, and dancing.

Seven general disco "looks" developed: the Basic Disco Look, Bodywear, Futuristic, Thrift-Shop, Jock/Roller, Rock and Roll, and Prep-Collegiate. They could be put together any which way, but the attire had to have glitter and shine. Men got down on the dance floor wearing silk shirts or shiny imitations, gold chains, and decorative rings or wrist jewelry. For women, entire makeup lines with sparkle and glitter were available, along with books on how to use them. Things that

*The rock 'n' roll disco look.*
*(Photo by Mike Kuentz.)*

shine are nice to look at; they provide pleasure and a release from the day, explained Terry Melville of Macy's.[12] He related that in the past only in the period before Christmas did retail stores feature "dressed up" clothes that people could wear for the holidays. But with disco such merchandise was available year round. The new category of night life led to using fabrics like Lurex and velvet and anything that had trimmings on it, such as rhinestones or beads. A whole segment of the fashion industry was geared to outfitting discoers.[13]

## Motives for Personal Dress

News stories and observations by psychologists suggest that in the dialogue with society, dress is used for four personal motives: (1) to validate personal identity, (2) to protect the personal self, (3) to portray a wished-for identity, and (4) to proclaim one's personal values.

### Validation of Personal Identity

Attire used to validate personal identity reflects the self-image. Public memory, the vocabulary of images that exists in American society, is the core source for self-image. Images from the past are often updated. The nineteenth-century ideal of ruggedness and masculine self-reliance, for example, was updated in 1991 and 1992 ads that portrayed Ralph Lauren in a well-worn work shirt, jeans, a jean jacket, a belt with a large buckle, and boots. The mass media are the vehicle through which ideas and images materialize. Stereotypes are often used because they are familiar, easily understood, and likely to be unquestioned; for example, nearly everyone associates eyeglasses with learning and a large body with brawn. Public memory and the media offer options, possibilities, and parameters for the personal self. The following sections describe different aspects of self-identity that are validated through attire.

*Meeting the Challenges of Nature.*    At the beginning of the twentieth century, social critics argued that the new emphasis on clothing symbolized the vice and immorality of the city, the corruption that had increased with the advent of industrialization and urbanization. Urban newspapers advertised that "the goodness of America lies in the small town where life and nature meet to make for genuine living."[14] Durable overalls, blue denim pants, and cotton work shirts signified the high "moral fiber" and productivity of rural life. These attributes were personified by the farmer, the hunter, and the woodsman: strong, self-reliant, and capable of meeting the challenges of nature. In the 1990s television show "Northern Exposure," for example, the ensemble of a pair of jeans or overalls, work boots, a flannel shirt or a work shirt, a leather belt with an ornamented metal buckle, and a sleeveless jacket or vest, worn by men and women, was seen as an image of independence and self-reliance.[15]

*Practicality.*    Attire that requires little upkeep and is durable and roomy is considered practical. Clothes in dark colors often do not show dirt; housedresses do not restrict the body; and clothes developed for backpacking, hunting, and fishing typically have both these characteristics. A down vest, for example, keeps the body warm and accommodates additional layers of clothing both under and over itself; and it can be shoved into a backpack or shoulder bag when the noonday sun is shining. Equally practical are oversized heavy wool shirts that can be worn as jackets and shirts of wool flannel and chamois cloth. Worn for activities outside the realm for which they were designed, they suggest that pragmatism and efficiency may be essential elements of self-definition.[16]

*Encouraging Approach.*    The word *casual* signifies both a category of dress and an attitude of openness to interaction, as the editors of *Esquire* noted. T-shirts and parkas, open-neck shirts, $6.00 gray sweatshirts with the sleeves cut off, and $50.00 white dress shirts with sleeves rolled up are components of dress that encourage approach.[17] The wearing of soft collars and bright colors also facilitates communication. Flugel observed that such attire signifies a freer play of emotions. He noted, moreover, that the readiness with which a woman removes her cloak or coat when she enters a public place such as the theater or a party suggests her degree of friendliness and willingness to invite sexual admiration.[18]

*Corporate Self-Importance.*   Within the corporate world, personal taste is judged by the attention given to the proportion and fit of clothing. For men, the goal is to create a sense of solidity and a unified whole. The shirt collar, in combination with a knot in the necktie and the lapels of a suit, serves to frame a man's face, directing attention toward his face and providing support. The suit, the rock upon which the professional man's wardrobe is founded, constructs the public persona. It asserts status, establishes identity, and announces intentions. Choosing the right suit is of paramount importance. Personal preferences are secondary. Basic features such as cut, color, and fabric must be pertinent to the profession, office culture, and body type.[19]

Despite such prescriptions, or maybe because of them, many older, more mature men come to view the "correct" suit, shirt, and tie as reflecting a "personal" self. Paradoxically, the corporate prescription becomes a personal self.

*Female Personality Types.*   In their research, S. Sweat and M. Zentner examined the notion that women actively choose among appearance alternatives and attempt to select styles that will communicate desired impressions. They identified four female personality types associated with clothing styles and with a distinct orientation to interaction:[20] dramatic, characterized by clothing with bold or severe lines; natural, characterized by informal clothing with minimal ornamentation; romantic, characterized by clothing incorporating gently curved lines to convey a feminine air; and classic, characterized by clothing employing simple, tailored lines.

Sweat and Zentner also found that observers distinguished among the four but construed the images differently from what the researchers expected. Dramatic attire was read as very unconventional, approachable, somewhat sophisticated, and somewhat dominant; natural, as very conventional, somewhat approachable, somewhat unsophisticated, and slightly dominant; romantic, as unconventional, very approachable, sophisticated, and somewhat submissive; and classic, as conventional, somewhat approachable, very sophisticated, and very dominant. The researchers concluded that although sender and receiver do not necessarily share in the meaning of the image, four distinct styles of appearance with relatively consistent characteristics do exist.

*Immunity from Frivolous Distraction.*   Inconspicuous appearance, as Flugel observed, may be a standard internalized by the self and designed to demonstrate seriousness of mood and devotion to duty.[21] He explained that a preference for clothing that is unprovocative in color, ample in size, thick, and stiff indicates immunity from frivolous distraction. Referring to nineteenth-century attire, he pointed out that preference for physical stiffness has been symbolically associated with moral probity and firmness; the real protective value of thick clothing

*Sunglasses created by Mercura New York, Fine Art to Wear. (Reprinted by permission.)*

is to guard against moral dangers because the body is perceived as a source of evil passions.[22]

The norm of modesty is so powerful that the people adhering to this norm consider certain styles of dress to be, in themselves, immodest. A décolleté dress is censured by those holding the norm of modesty. A puritanically minded person, Flugel noted, often does not change out of formal modest attire even in the privacy of the home. Although husbands may appreciate the bold appearance of other women, they often prefer their wives not to attract attention. As a result, married women tend to wear more conventional clothes, more layers of clothing, and darker colors than unmarried women.[23] A beautiful woman is more likely to focus on her appearance because it is easy for her to derive pleasure from adorning physical beauty. By contrast, Flugel observed, "the impulse of modesty has an easier task when a woman possesses an aesthetically inferior body." She is less likely to beautify and display herself because the pleasure derived from doing so is inherently more limited.[24]

*Artwear.*    Some artistically minded people prefer to dress themselves in original works of art. Since the 1970s this style of dress has become more available. A number of American artists have decided that rather than create art that hangs on the wall they will make "wearable" art. The fact that it is worn is secondary to its being art. They transform static two-dimensional surfaces into one-of-a-kind works of art in motion. This clothing and jewelry is sold in special galleries.[25]

American popular culture has inspired the work of French artist Jean Charles de Castelbajac. His dresses are shapeless canvases with sleeves. They bear images of Coke bottles, Campbell's soup cans, the dial faces of telephones, and cartoon characters, such as Woody Woodpecker. His unisex jackets and coats are cut from blankets to evoke the comfort and warmth of the security blanket immortalized by the *Peanuts* character Linus. Castelbajac translated the Jack Kerouac classic *On the Road* into a practical design to be worn or mounted like a sculpture. The modern nomad is depicted in a one-piece hooded coverall with many deep pockets. The coverall is made of tent cloth, creating the image of a kind of movable house; the pockets are the rooms and the hood is the roof.[26]

*Energy and Physical Prowess.*    Vigor and athletic prowess are suggested when one wears the attire adopted by "jocks," young athletes in their prime. With the widespread promotion of health and exercise centers, physical conditioning became possible for people of all ages, not just the young. Clothes once worn exclusively by athletes such as running shoes, sweat suits, "muscle shirts," tank tops, and side-vented shorts are now worn outside the gym. Bicycle messengers in New York adopted the sweatband and the knee-length spandex shorts worn by competitors in the Tour de France.[27] Athletic gear was appropriated for street use by such diverse figures as Elvis Presley, Andy Warhol, and New York's working women before and after the April 1980 subway strike.[28]

LEFT: *Rain poncho created by Jean Charles de Castelbajac. Blown up, it can be used as a buoy. It is a protective and playful garment. (Reprinted by permission of Jean-Charles Castelbajac.)*

RIGHT: *Latticework woman's evening wear kimono by Darlene Kay Riggins. (Wearable Art: Art in Motion. 1985. Indianapolis Museum of Art: reprinted by permission of Darlene Riggins.)*

Richard K. Donahue, president and chief operating officer of Nike Inc., commented that to grow, the sporting goods industry must go "beyond the sock and jocks image: It must appeal to women by offering them what they would like. Only about 10 percent of the women's market consists of committed athletes who buy solely for function. The other 90 percent consider both function and style." He noted that women do not respond to the same sales messages as men. Women will not buy a product just because a superstar, Michael Jordan, for example, wears it. Nike, Reeboks, and L.A. Gear Inc. all scheduled new advertising campaigns in the early 1990s that focused on women acquiring greater "command" over their lives and their emotions.[29]

*"Nerds."*    Although women may be "nerds," the term is used mostly to describe men. In contrast to the muscular grace of a star athlete, the nerd is bookish and physically underdeveloped and often wears glasses. In focusing on intellectual development and research (particularly engineering), he seems to ignore matters of appearance and style. In the media he is often depicted as ineffectual, unsophisticated, and oblivious to physical comfort. His shirt is buttoned to the collar, but he wears no tie. The "nerdpack," a plastic pocket protector, is the distinctive element of his dress. It allows a pocket to be stuffed with pens, pencils, rulers, and calculators. His pants are often too short. Working long hours and into the night encouraged employees in the computer industry to acquire a sloppy look.

The nerd is also described as compassionate and vulnerable. In the comic strips, Clark Kent, wearing dark-rimmed glasses, can step into a telephone booth and emerge as Superman. In the film *Revenge of the Nerds* (1984), a young woman commends one of the characters for his sexual performance. He reminds her that nerds don't spend their spare time in self-centered exercising to keep themselves muscular; they think about sex. The character of the nerd emerges as a sexual creature, vulnerable and feeling, a perfect partner because he is not concerned only with himself.

The preeminent nerd exemplar is filmmaker and actor Woody Allen. The traditional garments Allen has appropriated, among them the oxford cloth shirt with button-down collar, are sought after. As art historian Richard Martin suggested, they have come to characterize the nerd image, making it a more desirable social category.[30]

### Protecting the Personal Self

When people find themselves among others who are unsympathetic or among people they feel superior to, have nothing in common with, or fear, they adopt mechanisms to protect the self, Flugel observed.[31] They manipulate style and color to become invisible, to create distance, or to turn their clothing into shelter, thus shielding the self.

*Becoming Invisible.*    "Fade into the woodwork" to elude the street thief, advised Enid Remy in a *New York Times* article.[32] Robbers and muggers are unable to dis-

*Covering the eyes makes one inscrutable. Wearing sunglasses has the added effect of keeping other people at bay. (Advertisement entitled "Wire Rims for the '90s," Esquire Gentleman, Spring 1993; reprinted by permission of Alexis Rodriguez-Duarte.)*

tinguish between the real and the fake, be it jewelry, handbag, or fur. Defensive dressing is the smart choice. There are some women who no longer carry handbags. Lipstick and keys go in one pocket, money and a credit card in another; they carry nothing else. Afraid to draw unwanted attention, a young career woman with long blond hair will tuck every last strand under a beret before leaving home in the morning. She takes the beret off only when she reaches her office building.

Fear of sexual harassment is often a reason for choosing attire that enables the individual to be "invisible." Some female graduate students seeking to escape undesired attention wear shabby jeans and oversized work shirts, and their faces are half covered by unkempt stringy hair.

*Creating Distance.*     Creating distance is another method of protecting the personal self. Sunglasses may be used to create distance. Like a mask, they keep the person's eyes concealed and intruders remain uninformed. Mirrored lenses, the kind that make the wearer look like a state trooper, are most effective in turning back the intruding looks of others.[33]

A man in a dress suit will often wear an overcoat while walking in the street, even in warm weather, observed Flugel. He feels he needs to wear the overcoat because most of the other people in the street are not in formal dress and are likely to regard his dress suit with a degree of suspicion and hostility.[34]

Flugel also noted that women sometimes keep their outer wrap on at the theater or other public functions to preserve distance. They may be bashful, or they may feel out of harmony with their surroundings and not wish to invite intimacy from those around them.[35]

When in an unfriendly environment, whether human or natural, people tend to button up and to draw their garments closely around their bodies. On a chilly day, when people leave their warm houses and enter into an inhospitable street, they turn up their collars and settle as snugly as possible into their coats. General unfriendliness prompts people to withdraw their inner selves into the protection of their clothes, much as the tortoise withdraws its head into its shell, Flugel pointed out. Sensitivity to cold is heightened under conditions of unfriendliness. A student from the United States studying in London wrote: "It may be that homesickness calls for more clothes."[36]

Coldness is a universal metaphor for lack of love. Individuals who feel unloved are more likely to feel cold. They use clothing to protect themselves from both the cold and the unfriendliness of the environment. They are less ready to make the body visible and may keep a coat on indoors for warmth and to preserve a certain aloofness.[37]

### Portraying Wished-For Identities

Images that enable a person to feel as if he or she personifies a desired social ideal fall into the category of images that portray a wished-for identity. Societal prescriptions for gender appearance and behavior are often represented in idealized images by the media. Individuals appropriate goods and services to claim a desired identity. When failure to achieve the ideal ensues and rationality prevails, vicarious consumption may result. The pursuit of full-breastedness by women and the longing of men to look and feel like a "he-man" (or its opposite, to "feel like a woman"—cross-dressing) are prime examples of wished-for identities.

*Cross-Dressing.*   Trying out female attributes is the dream of cross-dressers, males who periodically dress in female attire. Self-gratification, rather than social deception, underlies their behavior, as John Talamini pointed out in his book *And Boys Will Be Girls.* He found that cross-dressers come from all socioeconomic backgrounds and hold conventional jobs. Many have children and have served in the military.[38]

Because cross-dressing violates social norms, confusion and guilt may accompany such behavior. Since the liberation movements of the 1970s, at least two societies, The Society for the Second Self and the International Alliance for Male Feminism, have been formed to offer men a means of meeting other cross-dressers and forming a subculture and support system. Through attending their weekly meetings, one researcher found that members referred to one another as sisters when they cross-dressed. Their meetings included discussions on buying wigs, clothes, and makeup. Members frequently joked in a good-natured way about their bizarre outfits. They were careful to avoid "dirty" or erotic language.[39] Their ability to acquire clothes at retail stores is hampered by fear of exposure. They worry that salespeople will know that the desired item is actually for them, so they often use the excuse that they are preparing for a masquerade party or purchasing for a woman who is "about their size."

Unaccustomed to the feminine world of dress and makeup, cross-dressers have a tendency to overdo "femininity." Those who feel they can pass as a woman often venture forth in public. They shop, go to the movies or restaurants, ride buses and trains; however, they usually avoid bars because of the possibility of being approached by another man who is fooled by the feminine disguise.

### Proclaiming Personal Values

Personal values consist of ideas and goals that are reflected in personal conduct as well as ideas and goals that underlie societal behavior. Two alignments seem to exist. The first consists of an orientation that justifies social class hierarchy, that is, the "rightness" and desirability of the unequal distribution of resources as well as pride in personal success. Accumulating and demonstrating one's wealth is expected social conduct. The second is an orientation toward egalitarianism and equality. Emotional growth and the actualization of personal talents underlie social conduct.

*Conspicuous Consumption and the "Good Life"*  Economic success at the turn of the twentieth century was often accompanied by a lavish display of the ability to consume. As economist and social critic Thorstein Veblen pointed out in 1899, the goal of such consumption was simply to impress others, to show off one's success by engaging in wasteful behavior. Veblen argued that this conduct violated the tradition of Puritanism and the ideal of democracy.[40] Public discussion of conspicuous consumption reemerged with Nancy Reagan's reported $46,000 inaugural wardrobe and her $200,000 china for the White House dinner table. Her pattern of consumption contributed to the depiction of the 1980s as the "greed decade."

The yuppies, the young urban professionals of the affluent 1980s, provide another example. They were groomed by their parents in all manners of taste and tact and indoctrinated into a prescribed style of life that included college. Once graduated, they sought to enjoy the "good life." They rejected the homogeneity of the suburbs, where many of them grew up, and sought the excitement of city life. Their "swinging singles and mingles" lifestyle stimulated the development of urban condominiums, small luxury apartments, two-bedroom townhouses, and converted lofts. Long-forgotten neighborhoods were rediscovered and revitalized with "upscale" services. The yuppies were devoted to consuming the best that money could buy. Bespoke tailoring, which was popular among movie stars in

*Cross-dressing. "Empress Razor Sharp," a man dressed in female
attire for Night of a Thousand Gowns, a benefit for New York City
Gay and Lesbian Community Services. (Members of the Imperial
Court of New York, Program Notes, Mar. 16, 1991.)*

the 1930s and 1940s, was again being sought after by those that could afford it.
Yuppies were obtaining shirts and suits custom-made in London.[41]

*Egalitarianism.*    Among the youth of the 1960s, debate about inequality, injustice, and the Vietnam War led to the view that one's personal vision for society
may be expressed in dress. In contrast to those for whom economic success and
expensive attire were major goals, there were others who sought deeper meanings
in life and rejected symbols of economic achievement. Jeans, painter's coveralls,
and work shirts indicated egalitarianism. The attire symbolized the rejection of
hierarchy, injustice, and privilege.[42]

This symbolic embodiment of ideology underlies the consumer typology developed in 1978 by the Stanford Research Institute in Menlo Park, California. The
typology was created to provide American producers of clothing with a better
understanding of the market and a means for projecting trends. Different categories of consumers were defined according to their wealth, education, emotional
needs, values, and lifestyle: Need-directed consumers have low education and are

*The sack suit worn by the man on the right obliterates a barrier to interaction. Without the padded "shield," the suit suggests a greater ability to respond to specific situations and needs. (Reprinted by permission of Garry Rosso/NYT Pictures and Steve Dworin.)*

caught up in the struggle for survival. Outer-directed consumers are driven by the psychological need for approval. They buy with an eye toward appearances; what other people think is more important to them than their own inner satisfaction. Inner-directed consumers feel that self-approval is more important than the approval of others. Well-educated, their lifestyle and buying habits are diverse. The researchers concluded that the higher the individual is in the social class hierarchy (education, occupation, and income), and the greater his or her psychological maturity, the more his or her clothing is likely to reflect personal values.[43] This typology led to the lifestyle orientation in marketing and advertising.

## Alternatives and Ambiguity

In the beginning of the 1990s the sack suit became a viable alternative for young men whose occupations were associated with media and the arts, where creative imagination is desired. Two styles of male suits have since come to reflect the two distinct orientations to structure—discipline and self-expression. A news report on the field of advertising had the following headline: "By Design, Deutch Chooses a Non-Madcap President."[44] To clarify, the reporter, Stuart Elliot, asked a rhetorical question: Can an account executive who works for "straightlaced packaged-goods clients like Unilever and dresses like an investment banker" find happiness in the "most aggressively creative and controversial advertising agency?" The photograph that accompanied the story showed Steve Dworin, the new president of the Madcap agency, in a traditional-style jacket, pants, and a tie. The creative director of the agency, Donny Deutch, was wearing a sack suit—a loose-fitting jacket and pants with the shirt buttoned up and no tie. Management, the exercise of authority, is signified by structure and constraint, and awareness of the latest intellectual and artistic trends is intimated by the informally structured attire.

## Notes

1. Sociologists generally agree that socialization is the process by which one internalizes culture and develops a sense of self. The notion of the self as an individuated being apart from family and community has its roots in the medieval period. It was in the late nineteenth century that the *idea* of private, personal identity became common. With the work of Henry James, Charles Horton Cooley, and George Herbert Mead, the study of the self came to be established as an important scientific pursuit. These theorists regarded the self as a distinct "universe" that could advance knowledge on the human condition. They saw the self and society as mutually intertwined. Critical theory, in contrast, views the self as a hostage of social arrangements. Responding to the question of why capitalism survived despite Karl Marx's expectation of its demise, critical theorists have suggested that capitalism encouraged the deepening and redoubling of false consciousness. Through experiences in the early years, the self had been further "co-opted." It had become accustomed to processes of domination and reification, developing false needs.

2. E. R. Leach (1957), "Magical Hair," *Journal of Royal Anthropological Institute* 88 (2): 147–164.

3. T. J. Flygare (1977), "Teachers' Private Lives and Legal Rights," *Educational Digest* 42 (6): 26–28.

4. J. Rangel (1986), "Top State Court Allows Inmate to Shun Haircut," *New York Times*, Nov. 12.

5. "Mustaches Are Issue for Police," *New York Times*, July 1, 1992.

6. W. Wilson and the editors of *Esquire* Magazine (1985), *Man at His Best: Esquire Guide to Style* (Reading, Mass.: Addison-Wesley).

7. "Airline Removes Agent for Not Using Makeup," *New York Times*, May 11, 1991.

8. "Continental Retracts Its Makeup Mandate for Female Workers," *New York Times*, May 16, 1991.

9. "Judging a Book's Sales by the Cover's Color," *New York Times*, Nov. 26, 1991.

10. L. McGill (1980), *Disco Dressing* (Englewood Cliffs, N.J.: Prentice-Hall), p. 5.

11. Ibid., p. 1.

12. Ibid., p. 4.

13. Ibid., p. 5.

14. K. Anspach (1967), *The Why of Fashion* (Ames: Iowa State University Press), p. 314.

15. T. Egan (1991), "Northwest Noir: An Art of Seriously Goofy," *New York Times*, July 14.

16. Wilson et al., op. cit., p. 188.

17. Ibid., p. 147.

18. J. C. Flugel (1966), *The Psychology of Clothes* (London: Hogarth Press), pp. 76–77. Originally published in 1930.

19. Wilson et al., op. cit., pp. 20–32, 67.

20. S. J. Sweat and M. A. Zentner (1985), "Attributions Toward Female Appearance Styles," in *The Psychology of Fashion*, ed. M. R. Solomon (Lexington, Mass.: Lexington Books), pp. 321–333.

21. Flugel, op. cit., p. 75.

22. Ibid., pp. 74–76.

23. Ibid., pp. 61–62.

24. Ibid., p. 64.

25. R. A. Yassin (1985), "Art in Motion: Wearable Art," Indianapolis Museum of Art Exhibit, Mar. 2–31. In a story in *Women's Wear Daily* (Apr. 3, 1992), a distinction was made between wearable art and fashion. The story reported that Robert Lee Morris, who had designed fashion jewelry for Donna Karan, was opening a new show in his Soho gallery, Artwear. The collection would consist of fantasy pieces that could be worn.

26. On exhibit at the galleries of the Fashion Institute of Technology, Feb. 11 to Apr. 19, 1986.

27. Reporting from Paris (*New York Times*, July 24, 1989), Carrie Donovan noted that although fashion trends used to start in Paris and in due time show up in New York, now trends go both ways. Since 1988 New Yorkers have been sporting biker shorts as street fashion; now (in 1989) Parisians have taken them up in a big way. The snug shorts are worn with well-cut jackets, flat pumps, and chic Chanel-type bags.

28. Wilson et al., op. cit., pp. 22–23.

29. Reported by Jerry Schwartz in the *New York Times*, Feb. 8, 1992.

30. R. Martin and H. Koda (1989), *Jocks and Nerds: Men's Style in the Twentieth Century* (New York: Rizzoli).

31. Flugel, op. cit., pp. 79–84.

32. *New York Times*, July 11, 1991.

33. S. Inoue (1980), "Interactions and Interpretations in Everyday Life," in *Studies in Symbolic Interaction*, ed. N. K. Denzin (Greenwich, Conn.: JAI Press), p. 1; also, William Grimes reports on a new type of sunglasses, E–54, that are popular because they are flirty. Glasses are designed to cover up, and a woman who pushes this pair of glasses down her nose, ostensibly to get a better look, "throws out a provocative gesture." See W. Grimes, *New York Times*, May 31, 1992.

34. Flugel, op. cit., p. 79.

35. Ibid., p. 80.

36. Ibid., p. 81.

37. Ibid., p. 83.

38. J. Talamini (1982), *And Boys Will Be Girls* (Washington, D.C.: University Press of America); also A. Levin (1978), "Dressing Up in Limbo," *New Times*, Aug., p. 7.

39. D. H. Feinbloom (1976), *Transvestites and Transsexuals* (New York: Delacorte Press).

40. T. Veblen (1953), *The Theory of the Leisure Class* (New York: Mentor Books), pp. 111–140. (originally published 1899); also J. Books (1979), *Showing Off in America* (Boston: Little, Brown).

41. See B. B. Hess, E. W. Markson, and P. J. Stein (1991), *Sociology,* 4th ed. (New York: Macmillan), pp. 350, 543. In trying to predict what the 1990s would be like for executives, Deirdra Fanning observed, "Executive stress is in vogue for 1991, but only because the country has slipped into recession." Executives will have to work longer and harder just to keep pace economically. See D. Fanning, *New York Times,* Aug. 31, 1992.

42. N. and E. Calas (1971), *Icons and Images of the Sixties* (New York: Dutton).

43. A. Mitchell (1978), *Values and Life Styles* (Menlo Park, Calif.: Stanford Research Institute [SRI]).

44. *New York Times,* July 18, 1991.

# Conclusion

THERE HAS ALWAYS BEEN some awareness that clothing plays an important role in social life. But it has never been clear the extent to which clothes, in the form of visual images that transmit meaning, act to integrate organizations and structures with their functions. Familiarity with these images makes society's patterns of interaction visible.

When seeking to understand the meaning of a cultural expression, knowing something about the author's purpose and social situation is at the center of valid interpretation, suggested literary critic E. D. Hirsch, Jr. (1967), art historian Michael Baxandall (1985), and sociologist Wendy Griswold (1989).[1]

Designers respond to the period's ideas and tensions with styles they believe are relevant. Like other artists and authors, they seize upon a prevailing perception and build a line around it.

Sexiness characterized the fashion in the year 2000. There were skirts that looked like flimsy silk half-slips, shoes styled like bedroom slippers, and body-hugging pants made of snakeskins and with wild animal prints. Harking back to the Garden of Eden and the jungle, snakes and wild animals suggested sexual temptation and danger. The fashion reflected a specific type of sexiness that came to characterize the end of the 1990s.

## Notes

1. M. Baxandall (1985), *Patterns of Intention: On Historical Interpretation of Pictures* (New Haven, Conn.: Yale University Press), 41–42; E. D. Hirsch, Jr. (1967), *Validity in Interpretation* (New Haven, Conn.: Yale University Press); W. Griswold (1989) "A Methodological Framework for the Sociology of Culture," *Sociological Methodology* (Vol. 17) Clifford C. Clogg (ed.).

*Wild animals declare the free expression of sexuality.*
LEFT: *A celebrity attending a theater performance in New York in a leopard print dress, Dec. 1999. (Photo: Diane Cohen.)*
ABOVE: *Actress Farah Fawcett carrying a shoulder bag simulating leopard skin, Dec. 1999. (Photo: Diane Cohen.)*

# Bibliography

Achenbaum, A. 1978. *Old Age in the New Land*. Baltimore: Johns Hopkins University Press.

Ackerknecht, E. H. 1982. *A Short History of Medicine*. Baltimore: Johns Hopkins University Press.

Agins, T. 1999. *The End of Fashion: The Mass Marketing of the Clothing Business*. New York: William Morrow.

Aguilar, L. E. 1984. *Latin America*. Washington, D.C.: Stryker-Post Publications.

Alexander, F. 1990. *The Venus Hottentot*. Charlottesville: University Press of Virginia.

Allan, F. L. 1931. *Only Yesterday* New York: Harper Brothers.

Ames, F. 1986. *The Kashmir Shawl*. Woodbridge, Suffolk, England: Antique Collector's Club.

Apollonaire, U., ed. 1973. *Futurist Manifestos: Documents of Twentieth Century Series*. New York: Viking Press.

Arnold, E. 1978. *Flashback! The 50's*. New York: Alfred A. Knopf.

Bade, P. 1979. *Femme Fatale: Images of Evil and Fascinating Women*. New York: Mayflower Books.

Bailey, H. A., Jr., ed. 1980. *Classics of the American Presidency*. Oak Park, Ill.: More Publishing.

Baker, R. 1982. *Growing Up*. New York: New American Library.

Banner, L. W. 1983. *American Beauty: A Social History Through Two Centuries of the American Idea, Ideal, and Image of the Beautiful Woman*. New York: Alfred A. Knopf.

Barber, B., and L. S. Lobel. 1952. "Fashion in Women's Clothes and the American Social System," *Social Forces* 31:124–131.

Barber, J. D. 1977. *The Presidential Character: Predicting Performance in the White House*, 2d ed. Englewood Cliffs, N.J.: Prentice-Hall.

Barewald, M., and T. Mahoney. 1960. *The Story of Jewelry*. New York: Abelard-Schumer.

Barret, L. E. 1977. *The Rastafarians: Sounds of Cultural Dissonance*. Boston: Beacon Press.

Barthes, R. 1967. *Elements of Semiology*. Trans. A. Lavers and C. Smith. London: Jonathan Cape.

———. 1972. *Mythologies*. Trans. A. Lavers. New York: Hill and Wang.

———. 1977. *Image-Music-Text*. Trans. S. Heath. New York: Noonday Press.

———. 1983. *The Fashion System*. Trans. M. Ward and R. Howard. New York: Hill and Wang.

Batterberry, M. and A. 1977. *Fashion: The Mirror of History*. New York: Greenwich House.

Baudrillard, J. 1979. *Seduction*. Trans. B. Singer. New York: St. Martin's Press.

———. 1981. *Simulacres et Simulation*. Paris: Éditions Galilée.

Bell, Q. 1976. *On Human Finery*. New York: Schocken Books.

Benton, M. 1992. *The Illustrated History of Superhero Comics.* Dallas: Taylor Publishing.

Berman, M. 1982. *All That Is Solid Melts into Air: The Experience of Modernity.* New York: Simon and Schuster.

Bernstein, B. J., ed. 1970. *Politics and Policies of the Truman Administration.* Chicago: Quadrangle Books.

Bird, P. 1974. "Images of Women in the Old Testament." Pp. 41–87 in *Religion and Sexism: Images of Women in Jewish and Christian Traditions,* ed. R. R. Reuther. New York: Simon and Schuster.

Bishop, K. 1992. "Schools Order Students to Dress for Safety Sake," *New York Times,* Jan. 22.

Bloch, M. 1963. *Feudal Society.* Trans. L. A. Manyon. Chicago: University of Chicago Press.

Blumer, H. 1968. "Fashion." *International Encyclopedia of the Social Sciences.* New York: Macmillan.

_____. 1969. "Fashion: From Class Differentiation to Collective Selection." *Sociological Quarterly* 10: 275–291.

Boehn, M. von. 1927. *Modes and Manners of the Nineteenth Century.* Vol. 3, 1843–1878. Trans. M. Edwards. London: Dent.

_____. 1932. *Modes and Manners.* Vol. 1, *From the Decline of the Ancient World to the Renaissance.* Trans. J. Joshua. New York: Benjamin Blom.

Bogdan, R. 1988. *Freak Shows: Presenting Human Oddities for Amusement and Profit.* Chicago: University of Chicago Press.

Boucher, F. (1965) *20,000 Years of Fashion: The History of Costume and Personal Adornment.* New York: Harry N. Abrams.

Brain, R. 1979. *The Decorated Body.* New York: Harper and Row.

Bredemeier, H. C., and J. Toby. 1960. *Social Problems in America.* New York: John Wiley and Sons.

Brenninkenmeyer, I. 1963. *The Sociology of Fashion.* Librairie du Recueil Sirey. Köln-Opladen, Germany: Westdeutscher-Verlag.

Brooks, C. R. 1989. *The Hare Krishna in India.* Princeton, N.J.: Princeton University Press.

Brown, P. 1988. *The Body and Society: Men, Women and Sexual Renunciation in Early Christianity.* New York: Columbia University Press.

Brubach, H. 1999. *A Dedicated Follower of Fashion.* New York: Phaidon.

Budge, W.E.A., and W. Thompson. 1961. *Amulets and Talismans.* New Hyde Park, N.Y.: University Books.

Bullough, V. and B. 1978. *Prostitution: An Illustrated Social History.* New York: Crown.

Bureau of Labor Statistics. 1988. Bulletin 2307, Washington D.C.: U.S. Government Printing Office.

Carlyle, T. 1967. *Sartor Resartus.* New York: Dutton. Originally published in 1838.

Carman, W. Y. 1957. *British Military Uniforms from Contemporary Pictures: Henry VII to the Present Day.* London: Leonard Hill.

Cassirer, E. 1961. "Ideational Content of the Sign." Pp. 1004–1008 in *Theories of Society: Foundations of Modern Sociology,* ed. T. Parsons et al., vol. 2. New York: Free Press.

Caygill, S. 1980. *Color the Essence of You.* Millbrae, Calif.: Celestial Arts.

Chalmers, D. M. 1985. *Hooded Americanism: The First Century of the Ku Klux Klan, 1865–1965.* Garden City, N.Y.: Doubleday.

Chambers, M., R. Grew, T. Herlihy, T. Rabb, and I. Woloch. 1974. *The Western Experience.* New York: Alfred A. Knopf.

Chauncey, G. 1994. *Gay New York: Gender, Urban Culture, and the Making of the Gay Male World 1890–1940.* New York: Basic Books.

Child, H., and Colles, D. 1971. *Magic and Superstition: Ancient and Modern.* New York: Charles Scribner's Sons.

Clark, K. 1956. *The Nude: A Study of Ideal Art Form.* London: John Murray.

Clegg, R., and W. A. Thompson. 1979. *Modern Sports Officiating: A Practical Guide,* 2d ed. Dubuque, Iowa: William C. Brown.

Cobliner, G. W. 1950. "Feminine Fashion As an Aspect of Group Psychology: Analysis of Written Replies Received by Means of a Questionnaire." *Journal of Social Psychology* 31: 283–89.

Cohan, S. 1997. *Masked Men.* Bloomington: Indiana University Press.

*Comics, Comix and Graphic Novels.* London: Phaidon Press, 1996.

Coser, L. A. 1992. *Maurice Halbwachs on Collective Memory.* Chicago: University of Chicago Press.

Cosgrove, S. 1984. "The Zoot Suit and Style Warfare." In *Zoot Suits and Second Hand Dresses,* ed. A. McRobbie. Winchester, Mass.: Unwin Hyman.

*Costumes of Religious Orders of the Middle Ages.* 1983. West Orange, N.J.: Albert Saifer. Originally published in 1718.

Craven, R. C. (n.d.) *A Concise History of Indian Art.* New York: Oxford University Press.

Creelan, P., and Granfield, R. 1989. "The Polish Peasant and Pilgrim's Progress Morality and Mythology in W. I. Thomas' Social Theory." Paper delivered at the Meetings of the American Sociological Association.

Cunnington, P., C. Lucas, and A. Mansfield. 1967. *Occupational Costume in England from the Eleventh Century to 1914.* London: Adam and Charles Black.

Damhorst, M. L., K. A. Miller, and S. O. Michelman. 1999. *The Meanings of Dress.* New York: Fairchild Publications.

Danesi, M. 1994. *Cool: The Signs and Meanings of Adolescence.* Toronto: University of Toronto Press.

Davenport, M. 1972. *The Book of Costume.* New York: Crown.

Davis, F. 1986. "Gender, Fashion and the Dialectic of Identity." Paper prepared for the Society for the Study of Symbolic Interaction Symposium on Information, Communication and Social Structure, University of Iowa, May 1–3.

————. 1992. *Fashion, Culture, and Identity.* Chicago: University of Chicago Press.

de Certeau, M. 1985. *Heterologies: Discourse on the Other.* Trans. B. Massumi. Minneapolis: University of Minnesota Press.

de Lauretis, T. 1987. *Technologies of Gender: Essays on Theory, Film and Fiction.* Bloomington: Indiana University Press.

Deruisseau, L. G. 1939. "Dress Fashions of the Italian Renaissance." *CIBA Review,* Jan.

Donovan, R. J. 1977. *Conflict and Crisis: The Politics of Harry S. Truman.* New York: W. W. Norton.

Douglas, M. 1970. *Natural Symbols.* New York: Pantheon Books.

Dulles, F. R. 1940. *America Learns to Play: A History of Popular Recreation, 1607–1940.* New York: Appleton-Century.

Dutton, K. R. 1995. *The Perfectible Body: The Western Ideal.* New York: Continuum.

Ebin, V. 1979. *The Body Decorated.* London: Thames and Hudson.

Eco, U. 1985. "How Culture Conditions the Colors We See." In *On Signs,* ed. M. Blonsky. Baltimore: Johns Hopkins University Press.

Ehrenreich, B. 1983. *The Hearts of Man and the Flights from Commitment.* Garden City, N.Y.: Doubleday.

Eicher, J. B., S. L. Evenson, and H. A. Lutz. 2000. *The Visible Self,* 2d ed. New York: Fairchild.

Elley, D. 1984. *The Epic Film: Myth and History.* London: Routledge.

Eder, D., and S. Parker. 1985. "Cultural Reproduction of Gender Relations and Values: The Effect of Extracurricular Activities on Peer Group Culture." Paper delivered at the Meetings of the American Sociological Association.

Elliott, J. H. 1987. "The Court of the Spanish Habsburgs: A Peculiar Institution?" Pp. 5–54 in *Politics and Culture in Early Modern Europe,* ed. P. Mack and M. C. Jacobs. Cambridge, Eng.: Cambridge University Press.

Erman, A. 1971. *Life in Ancient Egypt.* New York: Dover Publications. Originally published in 1894.

Fairlie, H. 1973. *The Kennedy Promise.* New York: Doubleday.

Faludi, S. 1991. *Backlash.* New York: Doubleday.

Faris, J. C. 1972. *Nuba Personal Art.* London: Duckworth.

Farren, M. 1985. *The Black Leather Jacket.* New York: Abbeville Press.

Ferguson, G. 1977. *Signs and Symbols in Christian Art.* New York: Oxford University Press.

Fisk, J. 1989. *Understanding Popular Culture.* Boston: Unwin.

Flugel, J. C. 1966. *The Psychology of Clothes.* London: Hogarth Press. Originally published in 1930.

Forbes, W. H. 1968. "Laboratory Field Studies: General Principles." Pp. 320–329 in *The Physiology of Heat Regulation and the Science of Clothing,* ed. L.H. Newburgh. New York: Stretchet Haffner.

Form, W. H., and G. P. Stone. 1957. "Urbanism, Anonymity and Status Symbolism," *American Journal of Sociology* 62 (5): 504-514.

Foucault, M. 1972. *The Archeology of Knowledge.* New York: Harper and Row.

Fraser-Lu, S. 1989. *Handwoven Textiles of South-East Asia.* Oxford, Eng.: Oxford University Press.

Gains, J., and C. Herzog. 1990. *Fabrications: Costume and the Female Body.* New York: Routledge.

Galbraith, J. K. 1969. *The Affluent Society.* Boston: Houghton Mifflin.

Gallagher, C., and T. Lacquer, eds. 1987. *The Making of the Modern Body: Sexuality and Society in the Nineteenth Century.* Berkeley: University of California Press.

Gans, H. J. 1974. *Popular Culture and High Culture.* New York: Basic Books.

Gaster, T. H., ed. 1959. *The New Golden Bough: A New Abridgment of Sir James George Frazer's Classic Work.* New York: Criterion Books.

Gelb, I. J., P. Steinkeller, and R. M. Whiting, Jr. 1991. *Earliest Land Tenure Systems in the Near East: Ancient Kudurrus.* The Oriental Institute: University of Chicago Publications, vol. 104.

Ghurye, G. S. 1958. *Bharatanatya and Its Costume.* Bombay, India: Bindor.

Gilman, S. L. 1999. *Making the Body Beautiful: A Cultural History of Aesthetic Surgery.* Princeton, N.J.: Princeton University Press.

Gnudi, M. T., and J. P. Webster. 1950. *The Life and Times of Gaspare Tagliacozzi: Surgeon of Bologna 1545–1599.* New York: Herbert Reichner.

Godson, S. H. 1984. "Women Power in World War I." *Proceedings of the U.S. Naval Institute.* Annapolis, Md.: U.S. Naval Institute.

Goffman, E. 1951. "Symbols of Class Status," *British Journal of Sociology* A (4): 294–303.

_____. 1959. *The Presentation of Self in Everyday Life.* Garden City, N.Y.: Doubleday.

_____. 1963a. *Behavior in Public Places.* New York: Free Press.

_____. 1963b. *Stigma: Notes on the Management of Spoiled Identity.* Englewood Cliffs, N.J.: Prentice-Hall.

_____. 1967. *Interaction Ritual.* New York: Doubleday/Anchor Books.

_____. 1971. *Relations in Public.* New York: Harper and Row.

Gombrich, E. 1979. *The Sense of Order: A Study in the Psychology of Decorative Arts.* Ithaca, N.Y.: Cornell University Press.

Gorman, T. 1979. *Three and Two.* As told to Jerome Holtzman. New York: Charles Scribner's Sons.

Gottdiener, M. 1977. "Unisex Fashions and Gender-Role Change." *Semiotic Scene* 1 (3): 13–37.

Griebel, H. B. 1994. "New Raiments of Self: African American Clothing in the Antebellum South." Ph.D. diss., University of Pennsylvania.

Gross, E., and G. P. Stone. 1964. "Embarrassment and the Analysis of Role Requirements." *American Journal of Sociology* 57: 1–15.

Guthrie, L. M. 1984. "I Was a Yeomanette." *Proceedings of the U.S. Naval Institute.* Annapolis, Md.: U.S. Naval Institute.

Hacker, H. M. 1957. "The New Burdens of Masculinity." *Marriage and Family Living* 19: 227–33.

Haiken, E. 1997. *Venus Envy: A History of Plastic Surgery.* Baltimore, Md.: Johns Hopkins University Press.

Halbwachs, M. 1980. *The Collective Memory.* Trans. F. J. Ditter, Jr., and V. Y. Ditter. New York: Harper and Row.

Hamilton, R. W. 1998. "Textile Style Regions of Mindanao and Sulu," In *From the Rainbow's Varied Hue: Textiles of the Southern Philippines.* Los Angeles: UCLA–Fowler Museum of Cultural History.

Hamlin P. 1979. *Magic and Superstition.* New York: Hill and Wang.

Hansen, J., and E. Reed. 1986. *Cosmetics, Fashions, and the Exploitation of Women.* New York: Pathfinder Press.

Hargreaves-Mawdsley, W. N. 1963. *A History of Academic Dress in Europe Until the End of the Eighteenth Century.* Oxford, Eng.: Clarendon Press.

_____. 1963. *A History of Legal Dress in Europe Until the End of the Eighteenth Century.* Oxford, Eng.: Clarendon Press.

Hargrove, E. C. 1980. "Presidential Pesonality and Revisionist Views of the Presidency." In *Classics of the American Presidency,* ed. H. A. Bailey, Jr. Oak Park, Ill.: Moore Publishing.

Harris, M. 1985. *Bikers: Birth of a Modern-Day Outlaw.* London: Faber and Faber.

Hartmann, S. M. 1982. *The Home Front and Beyond: American Women in the 1940s.* Boston: Twayne Publishers.

Harvey, J. 1995. *Men in Black.* Chicago: University of Chicago Press.

Head, J. R., Sr. 1967. "Medicine from 1800 to 1850." In *The Growth of Modern Medicine,* ed. F. Stenn, Springfield, Ill.: Charles C. Thomas.

Hebdige, D. 1979. *Subculture: The Meaning of Style.* New York: Methuen.

Hemenway, D. 1993. *Prices and Choices: Microeconomic Vignettes,* 2d ed. Cambridge, Mass.: Ballinger.

Hess, B. B. 1976. *Growing Old in America.* New Brunswick, N.J.: Transaction Books.

Hill, D. A. 1968. *Magic and Superstition*. London: Feltham Hamlin.

Hollander, A. 1978. *Seeing Through Clothes*. New York: Viking.

Hooper, W. 1915. "The Tudor Sumptuary Laws." *English Historical Review* 30: 444–449.

Hoxie, R. G. 1980. "The Power to Command." In *Classics of the American Presidency*, ed. H. A. Bailey, Jr. Oak Park, Ill.: Moore Publishing.

Hyman, H. H. 1942. "The Psychology of Status." *Archives of Psychology* 269.

Inglis, B. 1965. *A History of Medicine*. New York: World Publishing.

Jacques, D. H. 1859. *Hints Toward Physical Perfection*. New York: Fowlers and Wells.

James, D. B. 1988. "Values, Structure and Presidential Power." *Presidential Studies Quarterly* 18 (4): 761–784.

Johnson, H. 1990. *Sleepwalking Through History: America in the Reagan Years*. New York: W.W. Norton.

Johnson, J. D., and P. J. Xanthos. 1981. *Tennis*, 4th ed. Dubuque, Iowa: Wm C Brown.

Joseph, N. 1986. *Uniforms and Nonuniforms: Communication Through Clothing*. Westport, Conn.: Greenwood Press.

Kahlenberg, M. H., and A. Berlant. 1972. *The Navajo Blanket*. New York: Praeger.

Kaiser, S. B. 1985. *The Social Psychology of Clothing*. New York: Macmillan.

Kantrowicz, E. H. 1966. "Kingship under the Impact of Scientific Jurisprudence." In *Twelfth-Century Europe and the Foundations of Modern Society*, ed. M. Claget, G. Post, and R. Reynolds. Greenwich, Conn.: Greenwood Press.

Kearns, D. 1977. "Lyndon Johnson's Political Personality." Pp. 104–131 in *The Presidency Reappraised*, 2d ed., ed. E. T. Cronin and R. G. Tugwell. New York: Praeger.

Kellerman, A. 1918. *Physical Beauty*. New York: George H. Doran.

Kessler, J. B. 1980. *Getting Even with Getting Old*. Chicago: Nelson-Hall.

Kimmel, M. 1996. *Manhood in America: A Cultural History*. New York: Free Press.

Kinsey, A. C., W. B. Pomeroy, and C. E. Martin. 1948. *Sexual Behavior in the Human Animal*. Philadelphia: W. B. Saunders.

Kirsch, J. 1997. *The Harlot by the Side of the Road: Forbidden Tales from the Bible*. New York: Ballantine.

Kitzinger, S. 1983. *Woman's Experience with Sex*. New York: G. P. Putnam's Sons.

König, R. 1973 *A La Mode: On the Social Psychology of Fashion*, trans. F. Bradley. New York: Seabury Press.

Kosambi, D. D. 1969. *Ancient India: A History of Its Culture and Civilization*. Cleveland: World Publishing.

Kunz, G. F. 1915. *The Magic of Jewels and Charms*. Philadelphia: J.B. Lippincott.

Lamy, P., and Levin J. 1984. "Punk and Middle-Class Values: A Content Analysis," Paper delivered at the Annual Meetings of the American Sociological Association.

Lane, J. F. 1960. "The Money in Muscles." *Films and Filming*, July 9, p. 33.

Langner, L. 1959. *The Importance of Wearing Clothes*. New York: Hastings House.

Laver, J. 1937. *Taste and Fashion: From the French Revolution to Today*. London: George C. Harrap.

_____. 1963. *Costume*. New York: Hawthorne Books.

_____. 1969. *Modesty in Dress*. Boston: Houghton Mifflin.

Lawner, L. 1987. *Lives of the Courtesans*. New York: Rizzoli.

Lawrence, C. F. 1981. "The German 'Bauernkrieg' of 1525: Organization and Action in Peasant Revolt." Ph.D. diss., New School for Social Research. (On file at Ann Arbor, Mich.: University of Michigan Microfilm International.)

Leach, E. R. 1957. "Magical Hair." *Journal of Royal Anthropological Institute* 88 (2): 147–164.

Leach, M., ed. 1971. *Dictionary of Folklore, Mythology, and Legend*. New York: Funk and Wagnals.

Levin, A. 1978. "Dressing Up in Limbo," *New Times*, Aug., p. 7.

Levin, D. B., with W. Hoffer. 1992. *Inside Out: A True Story of Greed, Scandal and Redemption*. New York: Berkley Books.

Lewis, P. 1978. *The Fifties*. Philadelphia: J.B. Lippincott.

Lichtenstein, M. E. 1967. "The Origins of Modern Surgery: 1850–1900." In *The Growth of Modern Medicine*, ed. F. Stenn. Springfield, Ill.: Charles C. Thomas.

Lobelle-Caluwe, H. (n.d.) *The Memling Museum in St. John Hospital*. Bruges, Belgium: Die Keure.

Lofland, L. H. 1973. *A World of Strangers—Order and Action in Urban Public Space*. New York: Basic Books.

Lurie, A. 1981. *The Language of Clothes*. New York: Random House.

Lurker, M. 1980. *The Gods and Symbols of Ancient Egypt*. London: Thames and Hudson.

Lyman, S. M. 1978. *The Seven Deadly Sins: Society and Evil*. New York: St. Martin's Press.

McClelland, D. 1961. *The Achieving Society*. Princeton, N.J.: Van Nostrand.

McGill, L. 1980. *Disco Dressing*, Englewood Cliffs, N.J.: Prentice-Hall.

Mack, P., and M. C. Jacob, eds. 1987. *Politics and Culture in Early Modern Europe*. Cambridge, Eng.: Cambridge University Press.

Mahood, L. 1990. *The Magdalenes: Prostitution in the Nineteenth Century*. New York: Routledge, Chapman and Hall.

Majors, R. G., and J. U. Gordon, eds. 1994. *The American Black Male*. Chicago: Nelson-Hall.

Malinowski, B. 1948. *Magic, Science and Religion and Other Essays*. Garden City, N.Y.: Doubleday/Anchor. Originally published in 1925.

Malvano, L. 1988. *Fascismo e Politica dell'Immagine*. Torino, Italy: Bollati Boringhieri.

*Manifesto of the Futurist Painters*. Published in two parts in Lacerba, Florence, Mar. 15, 1914, and Apr. 1, 1914, with two different titles, and as a leaflet by Direzione del Movimento Futurista, Mar. 18, 1914.

Mannheim, K. 1952. *Essays on the Sociology of Knowledge*, ed. Kecskemeti. London: Routledge and Kegan Paul.

Maritain, J. 1924. *Art and Scholasticism*. Trans. J. F. Scanlan, N.Y.: Charles Scribner's Sons.

Martin, R. 1997. *The St. James Fashion Encyclopedia: A Survey of Style from 1945 to the Present*. Detroit, Mich.: Visible Ink Press.

Martin, R., and H. Koda. 1989. *Jocks and Nerds: Men's Style in the Twentieth Century*. New York: Rizzoli.

Marwick, A. 1988. *Beauty in History*. London: Thames and Hudson.

May, E. T. 1988. *Homeward Bound: American Families in the Cold War Era*. New York: Basic Books.

Mayer-Thurman, C. C. 1975. *Raiment for the Lord's Service: A Thousand Years of Western Vestments*. Chicago: Art Institute of Chicago.

Mayo, J. 1984. *A History of Ecclesiastical Dress*. New York: Holmes and Meier.

Mazon, M. 1984. *The Zoot Suit Riots: The Psychology of Symbolic Annihilation*. Austin, Tex.: University of Texas Press.

Mellen, J. 1977. *Big Bad Wolves: Masculinity in American Films*. New York: Pantheon.

"Message of Importance for the Serious Reader, A." *Esquire*, Dec. 1968, pp. 186–189.

Miles, M. R. 1985. "The Virgin's One Bare Breast: Female Nudity and Religious Meaning in Tuscan Early Renaissance Art." In *The Female Body in Western Culture*, ed. S. R. Suleiman. Cambridge, Mass.: Harvard University Press.

Miller, R. 1984. *Bunny: The Real Story of Playboy*. New York: New American Library.

Millman, M. 1980. *Such a Pretty Face: Being Fat in America*. New York: W.W. Norton.

Mitchell, S. 1999. *Generation X: The Young Adult Market*. Ithaca, N.Y.: New American Library.

*Modern Europe*. Cambridge, Eng.: Cambridge University Press.

Molloy, J. T. 1978. *Dress for Success*. New York: Warner Books.

_____. 1977. *The Women Dress for Success Book*. Chicago: Follett.

Montrose, L. A. 1983. "Shaping Fantasies Figurative of Gender and Power in Elizabethan Culture." *Representations* 1:2.

Moore, D. L. 1949. *The Woman in Fashion*. London: B.T. Batsford.

Morgan, T. E., ed. 1990. *Victorian Sages and Cultural Discourse*. New Brunswick, N.J.: Rutgers University Press.

Morris, C. 1972. *The Discovery of the Individual: 1050–1200*. New York: Harper Torchbooks.

Mosse, G. L. 1978. *The Final Solution: A History of European Racism*. New York: Howard Fertig.

Mukerji, C. 1983. *From Graven Images: Patterns of Modern Materialism*. New York: Columbia University Press.

Mulvaney, R. M. 1990. *Rastafari and Reggae: A Dictionary and Source Book*. New York: Greenwood Press.

Murray, H. A., ed. 1960. *Myth and Mythmaking*. Boston: Beacon.

Myers, R. J. 1972. *Celebrations: The Complete Book of American Holidays*. Garden City, N.Y.: Doubleday.

Nef, J. 1958. *Cultural Foundation of Industrial Civilization*. New York: Harper and Row.

Neustadt, R. E. 1960. *Presidential Power*. New York: Wiley.

Newburgh, L. H., ed. 1968. *The Physiology of Heat Regulation and the Science of Clothing*. New York: Stretchet Haffner.

Nickel, H., H. W. Pyhrr, and L. Tarassuk. 1982. *The Art of Chivalry*. New York: Metropolitan Museum of Art.

Oates, W. E. 1971. *Confessions of a Workaholic: The Facts About Work Addiction*. New York: World Publishing.

Oliver, W. 1994. "The Symbolic Display of Compulsive Masculinity in the Lower Class Black Bar." In *The American Black Male*, ed. R. G. Majors and J. U. Gordon. Chicago: Nelson-Hall.

Olsen, M. E., and M. N. Martin, eds. 1993. *Power in Modern Societies*. Boulder, Colo.: Westview Press.

Ortíz, A. 1969. *The Tewa World Book: Space, Time, Being, and Becoming in a Pueblo Society*. Chicago: University of Chicago Press.

Ostrander S. A. 1984. *Women of the Upper Class*. Philadelphia: Temple University Press.

Payne, B., G. Weinakor, and J. Farrell-Beck. 1992. *The History of Costume: From Ancient Mesopotamia Through the Twentieth Century*. New York: HarperCollins.

Perati, C. 1987. *Extraordinary Origins of Everyday Things*. New York: Harper and Row.

Perinbanayagam, R. S. 1987. "Drama in Everyday Life." In *Studies in Symbolic Interactionism*, vol. 8, ed. N. Denzin. Greenwich, Conn.: JAI Press.

Petras, J. W. 1975. *Sex Male Gender Masculine*. Port Washington, N.Y.: Alfred Publishing.

Pickering, D., ed. 1962. *The Statutes at Large from the Magna Carta to the End of the Eleventh Parliament of Great Britain*. Cambridge, Eng.: Cambridge University Press. Originally published in 1701.

Poll, S. 1962. *The Hasidic Community of Williamsburg*. New York: Free Press.

Powell, P., and L. Peel. 1988. *'50s & '60's Style*. New York: Chartwell Books.

Poynter, N. 1971. *Medicine and Man*. London: C. A. Watts.

Pritchet, H. C. 1977. "The President's Constitutional Position." In *The Presidency Reappraised*, ed. T. E. Cronin and R.G. Tugwell. New York: Praeger.

Rabinow, P. 1975. *Symbolic Domination: Cultural Form and Historical Change*. Chicago: University of Chicago Press.

Reagan, R. 1990. *An American Life: The Autobiography*. New York: Simon and Schuster.

Rechy, J. 1977. *The Sexual Outlaw: A Documentary*. New York: Grove Press.

Reuther, R. R., ed. 1974. *Religion and Sexism: Images of Women in Jewish and Christian Traditions*. New York: Simon and Schuster.

Richardson, J. 1967. *The Courtesan*. Cleveland: World Publishing.

Riesman, D. 1954. *Individualism Reconsidered*. New York: Free Press.

Roach, M. E., and J. B. Eicher, eds. 1985. *Dress, Adornment and the Social Order*. New York: John Wiley and Sons.

Robinson, D. 1961. "Economics of Fashion Demand." *Quarterly Journal of Economics* 75 (Aug.).

Rockford, A., and E. Burke 1985. *Hare Krishna in America*. New Brunswick, N.J.: Rutgers University Press.

Root, W., and R. de Rochemont. 1976. *Eating in America: A History*. New York: Ecco Press.

Rose, P. I. 1972. *Seeing Ourselves: Readings in Sociology and Society*. New York: Alfred A. Knopf.

Rowland, B. 1981. *The Art and Architecture of India*. New York: Penguin Books.

Rucker, M., D. Taber, and A. Harrison. 1981. "The Effect of Clothing Variation on First Impressions of Female Job Applicants: What to Wear When?" *Social Behavior and Personality* 9 (1): 53–64.

Rudofsky, B. 1971. *The Unfashionable Human Body*. Garden City, N.Y.: Doubleday.

Safire, W. 1990. "Keep Your Shirt On." *New York Times Magazine*, May 13.

Salmon, E., ed. 1977. *Bernhardt and the Theater of Her Time*. Westport, Conn.: Greenwood Press.

Sapir, E. 1931. "Fashion." *Encyclopedia of the Social Sciences*, vol. 6. New York: Macmillan.

Saunders, E. 1955. *The Age of Worth: Couturier to Empress Eugénie*. Bloomington: Indiana University Press.

Schlenker, B. 1980. *Impression Management: The Self-Concept, Social Identity, and Interpersonal Relations*. Monterey, Calif.: Brooks-Cole.

Schlesinger, A. M., Sr. 1980. "Our Presidents: A Rating by 74 Historians." In *Classics of the American Presidency*, ed. H. A. Bailey, Jr. Oak Park, Ill.: Moore Publishing.

Schneider, J. 1978. "Peacocks and Penguins: The Political Economy of European Cloth and Colors." *American Ethnologist* 5 (3): 413–447.

Scott, M. 1980. *The History of Dress Series, Late Gothic Europe, 1400–1500*. London: Mills and Boon.

*Selected Writings of St. Thomas Aquinas* 1965. R. P. Goodwin, trans. New York: Bobbs Merrill.

Sennett, R. 1974. *The Fall of Public Man.* New York: Alfred A. Knopf.

Severin, T. 1973. *Vanishing Primitive Man.* New York: American Heritage Publishing.

Shapiro, P. 1995. "Somewhere over the Rainbow Dorothy Got Totaled: Postmodernity and Modern Film." Pp. 197–215 in *Postmodern Representations,* ed. Richard Harvey Brown. Champaign, Ill.: University of Illinois Press.

Sickels, R. J. 1980. *The Presidency: An Introduction.* Englewood Cliffs, N.J.: Prentice-Hall.

Sigall, H., and N. Ostrove. 1975. "Beautiful but Dangerous: Effects of Offender Attractiveness and Nature of the Crime on Juridic Judgement." *Journal of Personality and Social Psychology* 31 (3): 410–414.

Simmel, G. 1957. "Fashion," *American Journal of Sociology* 62: 294–323. Originally published in 1904.

Sinclair, U. 1927. *Oil!.* New York: Albert Charles Boni.

Smeeding, T., B. Boyle Torrey, and M. Rein. 1988. "Patterns of Income and Poverty: The Economic Status of Children and the Elderly in Eight Countries." In *The Vulnerable,* ed. J. L. Palmer, T. Smeeding, and B. Boyle Torrey. Washington, D.C.: Urban Institute Press.

Smith, G., and B. J. Smith, eds. 1972. *The Police Gazette.* New York: Simon and Schuster.

Sorensen, T. C. 1965. *Kennedy.* New York: Harper and Row.

Sozinskey, T. S. 1877. *The Culture of Beauty.* Philadelphia: Allen, Lane and Scott.

Spencer, H. 1969. *The Principles of Sociology,* ed. S. Andreseki. Hamden, Conn.: Archon Books.

Steel, V. 1996. *Fetish Fashion, Sex and Power.* New York: Oxford University Press.

Steele, V. 1985. *Fashion and Eroticism.* New York: Oxford University Press.

_____. 1988. *Paris Fashion.* New York: Oxford University Press.

_____. 1991. *Women of Fashion: Twentieth-Century Designers.* New York: Rizzoli.

Stern, J. 1986. "Literary Images of Women in Work Force: Colonial Times to Present," *F.I.T. Review* 3(1).

Stone, G. P. 1962. "Appearance and the Self." In *Human Behavior and Social Processes,* ed. A. M. Rose. Boston: Houghton Mifflin.

Stone, L. 1965. *The Crisis of the Aristocracy.* London: Oxford University Press.

_____. 1968. "Literacy and Education in England 1640–1900." *Past and Present* 42: 00–00.

Strommenger, E. n.d. *500 Years of the Art of Mesopotamia.* New York: Harry N. Abrams.

Stutley, M. 1980. *Ancient Indian Magic and Folklore.* London: Routledge and Kegan Paul.

Suleiman, S. R. ed. 1985. *The Female Body in Western Culture.* Cambridge, Mass.: Harvard University Press.

Sumner, W. G. 1925. *What Social Classes Owe to Each Other.* New Haven, Conn.: Yale University Press.

Susman, W. I. 1984. *Culture As History: The Transformation of American Society in the Twentieth Century.* New York: Pantheon Books.

Taylor, F. 1911. *The Principles of Scientific Management.* New York: Harper Brothers.

Thompson, H. B. 1967. *Hell's Angels: The Strange and Terrible Saga of the Outlaw Motorcycle Gangs.* New York: Ballantine Books.

Thompson, J., ed. 1983. *Image Impact for Men.* New York: A&W Publishers.

Thompson, J. B. 1990. *Ideology and Modern Culture.* Stanford, Calif.: Stanford University Press.

Tolmach, R. L., and L. R. Scherr. 1984. *Face Value: The Politics of Beauty.* Boston: Routledge and Kegan Paul.

Turner, V. W. 1969. *The Ritual Process.* New York: Aldine.

U.S. Bureau of Labor Statistics. 1988. *Labor Force Statistics Derived from the Current Population Survey.* Bulletin 2307. Washington D.C.: U. S. Department of Labor, Bureau of Labor Statistics.

Uzane, L. O. 1898. *Fashions in Paris: The Various Phases of Feminine Taste and Esthetics from 1797 to 1897.* London: William Heinemann.

Van Dalen, D. B., E. D. Mitchell, and B. L. Bennett. 1953. *A World History of Physical Education.* Englewood Cliffs, N.J.: Prentice-Hall.

Veblen, T. l953. *The Theory of the Leisure Class.* New York: Mentor Books. Originally published in 1899.

Vicary, G. Q. 1989. "Visual Art As Social Data: The Renaissance Codpiece." *Cultural Anthropology* 4 (1): 3–25.

Wagner, R. 1986. *Symbols That Stand for Themselves.* Chicago: University of Chicago Press.

Walch, M. 1985. "American Sportswear Colors." *American Fabrics and Fashion* 133: 4–5.

Walkowitz, J. R. 1980. *Prostitution and Victorian Society: Women, Class and the State.* Cambridge, Eng.: Cambridge University Press.

Wax, M. 1957. "Themes in Cosmetics and Grooming." *American Journal of Sociology* 62: 588–593.

Weed, J. 1989. "The Life of a Marriage." *American Demographics,* Feb.

Weyr, T. 1978. *Reaching for Paradise: The Playboy Vision of America.* New York: New York Times Books.

Williams, R. H. 1982. *Dream Worlds: Mass Consumption in Late Nineteenth-Century France.* Berkeley: University of California Press.

Williams, R. M., Jr. 1970. *American Society: A Sociological Interpretation,* 3d ed. New York: Alfred A. Knopf.

Willoughby, B., and R. Schickel. 1974. *The Platinum Years.* New York. Random House.

Wilson, M. 1967. *Gems.* New York: Viking Press.

Wilson, W., and the editors of *Esquire Magazine.* 1985. *Man at His Best: The Esquire Guide to Style.* Reading, Mass.: Addison-Wesley.

Witherspoon, G. 1977. *Language and Art in the Navajo Universe.* Ann Arbor: University of Michigan Press.

Wolf, N. 1991. *The Beauty Myth: How Images of Beauty Are Used Against Women.* New York: William Morrow.

Wolf, R. 1991. *Goya and the Satirical Print in England and on the Continent.* Boston: Boston College Museum of Art.

Woll, P., and S. E. Zimmerman. 1992. *American Government: The Core.* New York: McGraw-Hill.

Wood, M. 1990. "Consumer Behavior: Impression Management by Professional Servers." Paper prepared for presentation at the 85th Annual Meeting of the American Sociological Association, Washington, D.C., Aug. 11–15.

Wulsin, F. R. 1968. "Adaptations to Climate Among Non-European Peoples." In *Physiology of Heat Regulation and the Science of Clothing,* ed. L. H. Newburgh. New York: Stretchet Haffner.

Yellis, K. A. 1969. "Prosperity's Child: Some Thoughts on the Flapper," *American Quarterly* 21 (1): 44–64.

Zanker, P. 1990. *The Power of Images in the Age of Augustus.* Trans. P. Shapiro. Ann Arbor: University of Michigan Press.

Zollo, P. 1999. *Wise Up to Teens.* Ithaca, N.Y.: New Strategist Publications.

# Index